THE SCIENCE OF
OVERABUNDANCE

THE SCIENCE OF OVERABUNDANCE

DEER ECOLOGY AND POPULATION MANAGEMENT

EDITED BY WILLIAM J. McSHEA, H. BRIAN UNDERWOOD, AND JOHN H. RAPPOLE

SMITHSONIAN INSTITUTION PRESS
Washington and London

To Graeme Caughley,
whose critical insight
into the ecology of wildlife
will be sorely missed

COPY EDITOR: Eva Silverfine
PRODUCTION EDITOR: Deborah L. Sanders
DESIGNER: Janice Wheeler

Library of Congress Cataloging-in-Publication Data

The science of overabundance : deer ecology and population management / edited by
William J. McShea, H. Brian Underwood, and John H. Rappole.
    p. cm.
Includes bibliographical references (p.   ) and index
ISBN 1-56098-681-6 (cloth : alk. paper)
1. White-tailed deer—Ecology—North America. 2. Mule deer—Ecology—North
America. 3. White-tailed deer—Control—North America. 4. Mule deer—Control—
North America. 5. Ecosystem management—North America. 6. Wildlife management—
North America. 7. Wildlife conservation—North America. I. McShea, William J.
II. Rappole, John H. III. Underwood, H. Brian.
QL737.U55S362 1997
333.95'9652'0973—dc21   97-3327

British Library Cataloguing-in-Publication Data available

Manufactured in the United States of America
04 03 02 01 00 99 98 97 5 4 3 2 1

The paper used in this publication meets the minimum requirements of the American
National Standard for Permanence of Paper for Printed Library Materials Z39.48-1984.

For permission to reproduce illustrations appearing in this book, please correspond
directly with the owners of the works (the authors of the chapter, unless otherwise indicated in the caption). The Smithsonian Institution Press does not retain reproduction
rights for these illustrations individually or maintain a file of addresses for photo sources.

Printed on recycled paper

Contents

Contributors

William S. Alverson
Harvard University Herbaria
22 Divinity Avenue
Cambridge, MA 02138

Richard M. Bartmann
Research Section
Colorado Division of Wildlife
317 West Prospect
Fort Collins, CO 80526

Jeff Beringer
Missouri Department of Conservation
Fish and Wildlife Research Center
1110 South College Avenue
Columbia, MO 65201

Michael A. Bowers
Department of Environmental Sciences and
   Blandy Experimental Farm
University of Virginia
Post Office Box 175
Boyce, VA 22620

James E. Childs
Viral and Rickettsial Zoonoses Branch
Centers for Disease Control and Prevention
1600 Clifton Road
Atlanta, GA 30333

Jerry L. Cooke
Department of Wildlife and Fisheries
   Sciences
Texas A&M University
College Station, TX 77843

William R. Davidson
D. B. Warnell School of Forest Resources
   and Southeastern Cooperative Wildlife
   Disease Study
College of Veterinary Medicine
The University of Georgia
Athens, GA 30602

David S. deCalesta
U.S. Department of Agriculture Forest
   Service
Northeastern Forest Experiment Station
Post Office Box 928
Warren, PA 16365

J. Andrew DeWoody
Department of Biological Sciences
Texas Tech University
Lubbock, TX 79409

Gary L. Doster
Southeastern Cooperative Wildlife Disease
    Study
College of Veterinary Medicine
The University of Georgia
Athens, GA 30602

Lonnie P. Hansen
Missouri Department of Conservation
Fish and Wildlife Research Center
1110 South College Avenue
Columbia, MO 65201

William M. Healy
U.S. Department of Agriculture Forest
    Service
Holdsworth Hall
University of Massachusetts
Amherst, MA 01003

Rodney L. Honeycutt
Department of Wildlife and Fisheries
    Sciences
Texas A&M University
College Station, TX 77843

W. Matt Knox
Virginia Department of Game and Inland
    Fisheries
Route 6, Box 410
Forest, VA 24551

Suh-Yuen Liang
Appalachian Environmental Laboratory
Center for Environmental and Estuarine
    Studies
University of Maryland
Frostburg, MD 21532

Matthew J. Lovallo
School of Forest Resources
The Pennsylvania State University
University Park, PA 16802

Nancy E. Mathews
University of Wisconsin-Madison
216 Russel Lab
1630 Linden Drive
Madison, WI 53706

Richard E. McCabe
Wildlife Management Institute
1101 14th Street, NW, Suite 801
Washington, DC 20005

Thomas R. McCabe
U.S.G.S. Biological Resources Division
1011 East Tudor Road
Anchorage, AK 99503

Dale R. McCullough
Department of Environmental Science,
    Policy and Management and Museum of
    Vertebrate Zoology
University of California-Berkeley
Berkeley, CA 94720

William J. McShea
Conservation and Research Center
Smithsonian Institution
1500 Remount Road
Front Royal, VA 22630

Karl V. Miller
D. B. Warnell School of Forest Resources
The University of Georgia
Athens, GA 30602

Charles M. Nixon
Illinois Natural History Survey
Natural Resources Building
607 East Peabody Drive
Champaign, IL 61820

John J. Ozoga
Route 1, Box 991
Munising, MI 49862

William L. Palmer
Pennsylvania Game Commission
Harrisburg, PA 17110

William F. Porter
Department of Environmental and Forest
    Biology
State University of New York, College of
    Environmental Science and Forestry
1 Forestry Drive
Syracuse, NY 13210

Randall Quinn
Letterkenny Army Depot
Chambersburg, PA 17201

John H. Rappole
Conservation and Research Center
Smithsonian Institution
1500 Remount Road
Front Royal, VA 22630

Ken L. Risenhoover
Department of Wildlife and Fisheries
    Sciences
Texas A&M University
College Station, TX 77843

Allen T. Rutberg
Humane Society of United States
2100 L Street, NW
Washington, DC 20037

Oswald J. Schmitz
School of Forestry and Environmental
    Studies
Yale University
New Haven, CT 06511

Steve W. Seagle
Appalachian Environmental Laboratory
Center for Environmental and Estuarine
    Studies
University of Maryland
Frostburg, MD 21532

A. R. E. Sinclair
Centre for Biodiversity Research
Department of Zoology
University of British Columbia
Vancouver, V6T 1Z4, Canada

Loren C. Skow
Department of Veterinary Anatomy and
    Public Health
Texas A&M University
College Station, TX 77843

Gerald L. Storm
U.S.G.S. Biological Resources Division
Pennsylvania Cooperative Fish and Wildlife
    Research Unit
The Pennsylvania State University
University Park, PA 16802

Walter M. Tzilkowski
School of Forest Resources
The Pennsylvania State University
University Park, PA 16802

H. Brian Underwood
U.S.G.S. Biological Resources Division
State University of New York, College of
    Environmental Science and Forestry
1 Forestry Drive
Syracuse, NY 13210

Donald M. Waller
Department of Botany
University of Wisconsin
430 Lincoln Drive
Madison, WI 53706

Chris Wemmer
Conservation and Research Center
Smithsonian Institution
1500 Remount Road
Front Royal, VA 22630

Gary C. White
Department of Fisheries and Wildlife
   Biology
Colorado State University
Fort Collins, CO 80523

Mark L. Wilson
Department of Biology and Epidemiology
University of Michigan
Ann Arbor, MI 48109

Wen Yan
Department of Wildlife and Fisheries
   Sciences
Texas A&M University
College Station, TX 77843

Acknowledgments

We thank the many participants—presenters and spectators alike—of the symposium, the contents of which have now become the substance of this book. The level of discussion generated as a result of each presentation exceeded our greatest expectations and was the fuel to kindle the fires under our feet when the mundane tasks associated with the production of this book became tiring. To you all, we owe a great debt of gratitude. The symposium and the production of this volume were supported by the Smithsonian Institution's National Zoological Park, the National Biological Service, the National Park Service, and the Virginia Chapter of the Wildlife Society. Critical technical review of papers is key to a successful book. We thank the following professionals for unselfishly acting as chapter reviewers: H. R. Akçakaya, T. Bowyer, M. S. Boyce, D. E. Capen, D. deCalesta, D. Edge, D. L. Ellsworth, J. H. Eve, D. Fish, D. J. Forester, D. L. Garner, R. L. Kirkpatrick, S. G. Kohlmann, R. A. Lancia, J. A. Litvaitis, T. R. McCabe, L. Morgantini, G. Parker, B. C. Patten, J. Rieger, J. Roseberry, A. Speilman, D. Steffen, R. Stoll, D. W. Sugg, O. Torgerson, V. Van Ballenberghe, L. J. Verme, R. J. Warren, K. Winker, and A. Whitten. Any errors or omissions that remain are most assuredly our own. A special thanks goes to A. R. E. Sinclair for gracefully listening to all the papers and then summing the symposium up in a presentation of his own. He pulled yeoman's duty, and the symposium was better for it. Eva Silverfine took our rough manuscripts and made them smooth, and Deborah

Sanders kept the whole project on schedule. Finally, we would like to thank the following people for assisting in the day-to-day management of this project: R. Scholl, K. Needham, K. Korth, and H. Waters. Without their help, especially in the final hours of preparing the manuscripts, this book would not have made it to press.

1

INTRODUCTION
Deer Management and the Concept of Overabundance

WILLIAM J. MCSHEA, H. BRIAN
UNDERWOOD, AND JOHN H. RAPPOLE

Common knowledge too often serves as the bible of management decisions. Enhanced by anecdotes and accumulated lore, speculative ideas or hypotheses become transformed into a dogma that is extremely resistant to change. There is, perhaps, no research endeavor that contains more common knowledge than the study of deer. All who have hunted deer, observed one in their yard, or seen an animated film on the subject consider themselves experts. There is something about the species that allows everyone a clear insight into the mysteries of deer biology. In many cases, the ideas expressed reflect the perspective of the individual. When foresters, wildlife biologists, hunters, and animal welfare activists discuss deer, one might be hard pressed to acknowledge that they are all talking about the same animal.

One tenet of common knowledge today is that deer in North America are overabundant. The concern that deer populations have burgeoned and currently exist at densities exceeding historical levels has been expressed not only in the scientific literature (Alverson et al. 1988; Warren 1991) but in radio, television, newspaper, and popular-magazine reports. Deer populations *are* above densities that existed over large portions of the continent at the turn of the century (deCalesta, Chapter 16; Healy, Chapter 15; Knox, Chapter 3), when deer had been extirpated from many parts of their historical range. However, the hypothesis that deer are more abundant now than they were prior to European colonization is equivocal at best. It is extraordinarily difficult to obtain an accurate estimate of precolonial population sizes (McCabe and McCabe, Chapter 2). There is intensive debate over how to obtain accurate counts of existing populations (Buckland et al. 1993), let alone how to determine numbers of deer from periods before the counting of deer had even begun.

Even if accurate assessments of precolonial deer populations were available, the data likely would be of limited value. All of our large forest tracts are secondary forests, different in both appearance and species composition from those forests that existed even 200 years ago (Braun 1974; Duffy and Meier 1992; Rappole 1996). Extinctions and extirpations from these precolonial ecosystems have removed critical plant and animal components, and without these components, it is difficult to place the current effects of deer on their environment into a realistic historical perspective. For example, the historical role of deer in tree-seed consumption and seedling establishment in eastern forests is moot when a major seed predator, the passenger pigeon *(Ectopistes migratorius)*, and a major seed producer, the American chestnut *(Castanea dentata)*, have both been removed from the system.

The term "density" itself is problematic. If deer exhibit a functional response to forage availability (Schmitz and Sinclair, Chapter 13) or distribute themselves nonrandomly across the landscape (Risenhoover et al., Chapter 22), no static number of deer per square kilometer can provide an accurate reflection of the dynamics of the system. For instance, while the deer population in Virginia has increased from an estimated 20,000 individuals in 1950 to over 900,000 individuals at present, populations in the southwestern portion of the state have remained relatively sparse throughout this period and populations on some federal lands have maintained high densities for 30 years or more (Knox, Chapter 3). Changes in deer abundance over a broad scale do not necessarily reflect what is happening within specific refuges.

A more relevant question for managers might be to inquire how deer presently affect specific aspects of ecosystem function, such as seedling establishment. Clearly, deer browsing affects some species, but is this effect sufficient to affect ecosystem functioning? Does a forest composed of browse-resistant species have any less biological worth than one with a significant complement of browse-sensitive species? At present, we do not know enough about forest function to answer such questions; the easier, but not necessarily correct, approach is to say if deer are abundant in comparison with historical densities, then their numbers should be reduced.

As alluded to by several authors in this volume (McCabe and McCabe, Chapter 2; McCullough, Chapter 6; Rutberg, Chapter 4; Sinclair,

Chapter 23), overabundance is a value judgement that has a clear meaning only when placed in a specific context. Caughley (1981) defined four contexts in which the term "overabundance" can be understood when referring to an animal population: (1) when the animals threaten human life or livelihood, (2) when the animals depress the densities of favored species, (3) when the animals are too numerous for their own good, and (4) when their numbers cause ecosystem dysfunction. Each of these contexts for overabundance has been put forward by one or more constituencies as an argument for reducing deer densities. For instance, the idea that a high deer density is harmful to the population is a common-knowledge argument often advanced to justify hunting. Often cited is Leopold's (1943) example of the mule deer *(Odocoileus hemionus)* population on the Kaibab Plateau, which exploded and then crashed after the removal of predators. This story has long since passed from the realm of anecdote into accepted dogma (McCullough, Chapter 6; Underwood and Porter, Chapter 12). Regardless of the accuracy of the Kaibab Plateau example, the argument is a form of species-based management in which deer populations are monitored and managed to assure that densities do not become so high as to harm the health and vigor of the herd (Davidson and Doster, Chapter 11). From this perspective, elevated levels of disease or decreased mean body size are considered to be evidence of overabundance, though disease outbreaks and mean body size can fluctuate independently of density (Davidson and Doster, Chapter 11; Palmer et al., Chapter 10).

Caughley's (1981) overabundance categories 1, 2, and 4 are similar in that they focus on the effect of deer populations on other species. This approach has been used by the U.S. Forest Service when arguing that high deer populations can have negative effects on forest resources (deCalesta, Chapter 16). Conservation biologists have expanded this argument recently to include noncommercial species such as rare plants (Warren 1991; Balgooyen and Waller 1995), conifers (Alverson et al. 1988; Alverson and Waller, Chapter 17), and migratory birds (McShea and Rappole, Chapter 18). However, care must be taken to assure that subjective criteria about what the natural world should look like are not confused with objective management goals (Sinclair, Chapter 23). Caughley (1981) felt only when high-density populations disrupt ecosystem function (category 4) should they be considered truly overabundant.

The purpose of this book is to provide a sound, factual basis for sifting through the various perspectives on the meaning of the term "overabundance" for populations of the two most common and widespread deer of North America, the white-tailed deer and the mule deer. Throughout this volume, "deer" refers either to cervids generally or to white-tailed deer *(Odocoileus virginianus)* unless otherwise specified. The volume is divided into three parts, though chapters in one part often have relevance to those in others. The parts are as follows: Part One: Philosophical Perspectives, Part Two: Population Effects, and Part Three: Ecosystem Effects.

The first part provides background on the issue of overabundance from profoundly divergent constituent viewpoints: wildlife biology (McCabe and McCabe, Chapter 2), international conservation (Wemmer, Chapter 5), state game management (Knox, Chapter 3), and animal welfare (Rutberg, Chapter 4). These chapters highlight the issues involved in attempting to manage high-density deer populations, and each author draws from different sources to arrive at strikingly different conclusions.

The second part includes chapters that address the demographic consequences of high densities on deer populations. These chapters pose such questions as the following. (1) Do high densities necessarily cause reduced carrying capacity (McCullough, Chapter 6)? (2) Are disease outbreaks a direct consequence of high density (Davidson and Doster, Chapter 11)? (3) Are there demographic (Palmer et al., Chapter 10), behavioral (Miller and Ozoga, Chapter 9), or genetic (Mathews et al., Chapter 7) consequences to high deer population levels? (4) Is it possible to determine if populations are self-regulating (White and Bartmann, Chapter 8)? (5) Do the classic paradigms fit the data from real populations (Underwood and Porter, Chapter 12)?

Chapters in the third part examine the influence deer have on their environment, including the following questions. (1) Does deer browsing determine the succession patterns of old field (Bowers, Chapter 19) or forest (Seagle and Liang, Chapter 21) systems? (2) Is the abundance of specific woody species (Alverson and Waller, Chapter 17; Healy, Chapter 15) or bird species (McShea and Rappole, Chapter 18) influenced by deer abundance? (3) Can deer populations serve as a reservoir for transmission of diseases to other species (Wilson and Childs, Chapter 14)? (4) Does vegetation biomass regulate the abundance of herbivores (Schmitz and Sinclair, Chapter 13)? (5) Can the impact of deer on forest resources be predicted by density or must forage availability also be considered (deCalesta, Chapter 16)? (6) How do landscape features influence the dispersion of deer (Hansen et al., Chapter 20; Risenhoover et al., Chapter 22)?

The last chapter is a synthesis by A. R. E. Sinclair on how the concept of carrying capacity may be used to tie together the many contrasting views presented in this volume.

A key point made by authors in all parts is that even if agreement could be reached on a correct density of deer, maintaining such a level would be both difficult and of questionable value. Stability in either a deer population or an ecosystem is an elusive state. Flux and change are the natural condition of most forest ecosystems (Schmitz and Sinclair, Chapter 13; Seagle and Liang, Chapter 21). For deer populations, annual fluctuations in the weather or periodic changes in forage populations can swamp any density-dependent effects on population size (Healy, Chapter 15; McCullough, Chapter 6; White and Bartmann, Chapter 8). There is no evidence of prolonged stability for deer populations at either a regional (deCalesta, Chapter 16; Knox, Chapter 3; Rutberg, Chapter 4) or continental (McCabe and McCabe, Chapter 2) level. In addition, the idea that predators can serve to maintain prey populations at stable levels may be incorrect (Houston 1982; Skogland 1991). Therefore, attempts to recreate a mythical stable population density through hunting pressure may not be a sound strategy, if the goal is to maintain ecosystem health (Caughley 1981; Schmitz and Sinclair, Chapter 13; Sinclair, Chapter 23).

An additional problem for determining appropriate deer densities is that we often lack sufficient data. Landscape-scale experiments are required to determine the long-term effects of different deer densities on populations and ecosystems. Without these data, it is not possible to design appropriate management strategies for given pieces of land. The call for adaptive management has been made in the past (MacNab 1983; Sinclair 1991) and is made by several authors in this volume (e.g., Schmitz and Sinclair, Chapter 13; White and Bartmann, Chapter 8). Managers too frequently are forced by a dearth of information to pick one management option and apply it across the entire landscape. As is made clear by chapters in this volume, we don't know enough about how deer are dispersed across the landscape (Risenhoover et al., Chapter 22) or how protected lands can affect that distribution (Hansen et al., Chapter 20) to make the proper decisions necessary to achieve management goals. What is needed is an acceptance of our ignorance and a willingness to test different management options at the landscape level.

It is popular to view public lands as multiple use, with a myriad of activities being conducted at the same time and at the same location. This scenario, however, is difficult to produce in reality. At the forest-stand level, deer densities sufficient to satisfy hunter demands may be too high to permit sapling recruitment for a preferred browse species (deCalesta, Chapter 16; Healy, Chapter 15). Unfortunately, the old adage that good forestry management is good wildlife management may be appropriate for encouraging species such as white-tailed deer or ruffed grouse *(Bonasa umbellus)* that thrive under early successional conditions but may not hold for other organisms, such as forest interior birds, salamanders, and wildflowers. In order to manage all species effectively, forest management must move beyond the forest-stand level into the landscape or regional level (deCalesta, Chapter 16; Schmitz and Sinclair, Chapter 13) and deer management must move beyond a population-based approach into an approach that considers ecosystem effects (McShea and Rappole, Chapter 18) and the nonrandom dispersion of individuals (Risenhoover et al., Chapter 22).

These broader views may result in incompatible management objectives at the stand or refuge level. At these finer scales there will be disagreement on what to do about high deer densities (Rutberg, Chapter 4). This disagreement is not unlike that confronting conservation biologists trying to preserve species that are globally endangered but locally overabundant (Wemmer, Chapter 5). The solution for conservation biologists abroad, and maybe within our own refuges, is not to try to make each patch a naturally balanced ecosystem but rather to designate management priorities for each patch (Sinclair, Chapter 23).

We hope that careful consideration of the material gathered in this volume will cause constituent groups trying to manage high-density deer populations to reexamine their stock of common knowledge. Beyond the realm of common knowledge, there are valid reasons for both creating areas of low deer densities and allowing deer densities in other areas to fluctuate in an "unmanaged" fashion. The conservation of some species may be dependent on periodic or consistently low deer densities (Alverson and Waller, Chapter 17). These conditions do not necessarily reflect the natural world (McCullough, Chapter 6) but rather the management objectives of the refuge. Specific management goals may be met by reducing deer densities, but reducing deer densities to achieve more "natural" conditions is based more on common knowledge than on science.

REFERENCES CITED

Alverson, W. S., D. M. Waller, and S. L. Solheim. 1988. Forests too deer: Edge effects in northern Wisconsin. Conservation Biology 2:248–258.

Balgooyen, C. P., and D. M. Waller 1995. The use of *Clintonia borealis* and other indicators to gauge impacts of white- tailed deer on plant communities in northern Wisconsin. Natural Areas Journal 15:308–318.

Braun, E. L. 1974. Deciduous Forests of Eastern North America. The Free Press, New York.

Buckland, S. T., D. R. Anderson, K. P. Burnham, and J. L. Laake. 1993. Distance Sampling: Estimating Abundance of Biological Populations. Chapman and Hall, New York.

Caughley, G. 1981. Overpopulation. Pages 7–20 in Problems in Management of Locally Abundant Wild Mammals. (P. A. Jewell and S. Holt, eds.) Academic Press, New York.

Duffy, D. C., and A. J. Meier. 1992. Do Appalachian herbaceous understories ever recover from clearcutting? Conservation Biology 6:196–201.

Houston, D. B. 1982. The Northern Yellowstone Elk: Ecology and Management. Macmillan Publishing Co., New York.

Leopold, A. 1943. Deer irruptions. Wisconsin Conservation Bulletin 8:3–11.

MacNab, J. 1983. Wildlife management as scientific experiment. Wildlife Society Bulletin 11:397–401.

Rappole, J. H. 1996. The importance of forest for the world's migratory bird species. Pages 389–406 in The Conservation of Faunal Diversity in Forested Landscapes. (R. DeGraaf and R. Miller, eds.) Chapman and Hall, London.

Sinclair, A. R. E. 1991. Science and the practice of wildlife management. Journal of Wildlife Management 55:767–772.

Skogland, T. 1991. What are the effects of predators on large ungulate populations? Oikos 61:401–411.

Warren, R. J. 1991. Ecological justification for controlling deer populations in eastern national parks. Transactions of the North American Wildlife Natural Resources Conference 56:56–66.

PART ONE

Philosophical Perspectives on Managing Deer

2 Recounting Whitetails Past

THOMAS R. MCCABE AND
RICHARD E. MCCABE

It has been more than a decade since we examined white-tailed deer historic abundance, cultural values, and comeuppance with the advance of modern civilization (McCabe and McCabe 1984). Although neither of us has done extended research on white-tailed deer—its history or otherwise—for the past 10 years, nothing we have read in the interim casts doubt on the data we compiled, our conclusions, or perspectives about the species' historic numbers and circumstance.

We began our investigations by attempting to verify the widespread notion that white-tailed deer were more abundant in the 1980s than at the time of Columbus' purported discovery of the North American continent. There was very little in the wildlife literature that supported such a view and certainly nothing very scientific to validate the claim one way or another. The best guesstimate of whitetail numbers in pristine America was that of Ernest Thompson Seton, who initially supposed an average "primitive times" density of 4 whitetails/km^2 for the species' range of 5 million km^2, or 20 million animals (Seton 1909:78). Twenty years later, Seton (1929) revised his estimate by doubling it—to 40 million whitetails in the Americas before European explorers arrived.

Seton was a remarkable naturalist, perhaps one of the best and most prolific that North America has produced. His writings are benchmark and the foremost points of departure for ethnozoological inquiry. His information was gathered through vast accumulation of anecdotal and second-hand recounts of animal numbers witnessed by explorers, fur traders, hunters, settlers, and others. Seton also identified species' ranges in this manner and by correlating them to habitat types, quite in accord with Bailey's (1978) ecoregion delineations that are the current basis for recognizing habitat associations.

Nevertheless, we were surprised to find that no one had ever seriously challenged Seton's numbers. Such inquiry was the cornerstone of our work (McCabe and McCabe 1984). Accordingly,

- we analyzed dozens of archaeological reports on late prehistoric–early historic period village sites and middens;
- we studied historic regional Native American hunting and utilization of whitetails to ascertain when, where, how, and how many animals were taken;
- we immersed ourselves in the continuing, annoying debate on pre-Columbian Native American population demographics;
- we scrutinized literally hundreds of books, journals, diaries, and compendia of correspondence from the earliest exploration and settlement periods, including all traceable Seton references and a great many more to which Seton did not have access; and
- we looked at frontier habitats by reviewing biotic information from cadastral and geological surveys.

Perhaps our biggest challenge in these and other, less-successful sidetracks was determining the credibility of historic literature. There are fantastic accounts of deer numbers, many of which we had to ignore for want of verifiability. We discounted all third-person reports. But most importantly, we relied extensively on the wisdom of professional historians to warn us away from fanciful reporters. In this manner, we discarded some of the most interesting and unusual recorded observations.

Especially frustrating was the dearth of reliable information from Mexico. Furthermore, the earliest accounts of whitetails from Mexico were in the form of pictographs, codices, and liberal translations from Spanish missionaries and opportunistic Portuguese merchants. More often than not, even by going back through the Library of Congress to find the original published records and then enlisting linguists knowledgeable of sixteenth- and seventeenth-century prose, we were unable to verify with certainty what ungulate species were reported. And the archaeological data from Latin America's late prehistoric period is all but silent on zoological detail.

HISTORIC NORTH AMERICAN WHITETAIL ABUNDANCE

The following is a synopsis of some of what we found, particularly information that relates to Seton's (1909, 1929) assertions and the prevailing notion that North America currently supports more deer now than in the time of Columbus.

First, in scrutinizing the historic range of whitetails, at least subsequent to the last period of extensive glaciation, we found that it was roughly 7.8 million km², not 5 million as Seton assumed (Figure 2.1). We had the luxury of the National Geographic Society cartographers to refine our maps; Seton did not.

Second, based on hard data from midden excavation, hide and fur trade manifests, firsthand documentation of Native American consumption rates and harvest and hide use, and numerous other records, we were able to estimate the precolonial whitetail population size and density for the United States and Canada. To do so, however, we had to account for a number of deer population characteristics—most significantly, the influence of Native American harvest relative to sustainability. Except for poorly documented hide-trade acquisitions records, we had little to go on concerning actual Native American take of whitetails, so we speculated about deer population ramifications at various harvest levels. We recognized, for example, that Native Americans took deer year round, so their effect on populations was *at least* analogous to that of other major predators. We learned, however, that among certain Native American tribes, nations, or other social units that relied heavily on whitetails for food and other products, such as the Cheraw in the Southeast, Prairie Potowatomie in the Midwest, and Huron of the Northeast, the equivalent of at least 3.5 adult whitetail hides per person per year were needed (or at least used) just for clothing. Where, from midden records and early accounts, information was available on whitetails as a significant part of the Native Americans' subsistence economy—nearly 90% in a few cases (Salwen 1970; Williams 1972)—we determined that, on average, about 9.5 average-size whitetails were consumed per person per year (see McCabe 1982). Calculating then the hunting territory of certain whitetail-dependent Native Americans and factoring in Gramly's (1977) estimate of carrying capacity necessary to provide for sustained yield, we came up with an annual harvest rate by whitetail-dependent Native Americans of approximately 34%. Obviously, for Native Americans less dependent on whitetails the rate was lower and, for some Native American groups within the species' historic range, considerably lower.

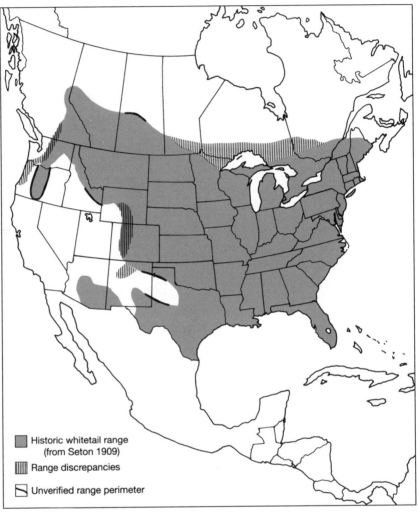

FIGURE 2.1. Possible late prehistoric–early historic range of white-tailed deer in the United States and Canada (from McCabe and McCabe 1984). The unverified and discrepant range perimeters are those for which the authors found no supporting or convincing data.

Third, as closely as we could determine for the year 1500, there were 2.34 million Native Americans within the range of whitetails (see Spinden 1928; Oswalt 1966; Driver 1968). If, on average, each Native American ate 0.9 kg of animal food per day and 25% of that food was deer (both conservative assumptions), Native Americans in Canada and the United States harvested 4.6 to 6.4 million whitetails annually, given reliable food value measurements for whitetails.

We also assumed that the whitetail population, when considered over the species' entire range, was fairly stable. We had no proof or reason to consider otherwise. It was assumed as well that the deer population sex ratio approximated 50:50. At most times of the year, Native Americans did not select for age, sex, or even size of deer. We assumed, too, that habitat resources, particularly food, available to whitetails allowed for a mean level of whitetail reproductive potential. Therefore, based on an average annual whitetail reproductive rate of 1.3 fawns per doe, a minimum population of 7.1 to 9.9 million deer would have been necessary to allow for annual food consumption of 4.6 to 6.4 million deer by Native Americans within the species' range.

We then assumed that Native American harvest probably was equivalent to the predation by bears, lions, wolves, bobcats, coyotes, eagles, and other nonhunting mortality influences; the whitetail population would need to have been 14.2 to 19.4 million to sustain this total annual mortality. These estimates are roughly equivalent to today's population figures. Since assigning 50% of total whitetail mortality to Native American hunting undoubtedly was too liberal, we calculated that Native Americans were responsible for no more than 30% of the annual mortality, which is much closer to an optimal sustainability level and only somewhat more than modern harvest (see Stransky 1984). At this level, whitetails would have numbered between 23.6 and 32.8 million.

That is the short version of our deductive process, and we ultimately were most confident in the 24 to 33 million range. Interestingly, our numbers fell between Seton's (1909, 1929) 20 million and 40 million estimates. But because we were able to expand the known historic range of whitetails, our estimate of average whitetail density of 3.1 to 4.2 deer/km^2 closely approximated Seton's earliest figures. We had the fortune to have Gary C. White (Colorado State University) to verify our computations; Seton did not.

Despite our reasonable confidence that there were about 24 to 33 million whitetails in the United States and Canada around 1500, we acknowledge that the prehistoric population likely fluctuated locally from year to year and certainly exhibited oscillations over longer periods of time in response to weather conditions and habitat changes. We have no evidence to suggest that disease played much of a factor and feel it unlikely that the population experienced irruptions of the degree that twentieth-century whitetails have encountered periodically. The species' foremost limiting factor in prehistoric time was habitat and, in pristine circumstance, local events probably did not significantly affect total population size.

From 1500 to 1900, in our opinion, white-tailed deer underwent three distinct population phases (Figure 2.2).

The first, from 1500 to the early 1800s . . . was characterized by massive harvest, primarily at the hands of Indians smitten with trader geegaws, metalwares, guns, alcohol, textiles, and promises. The period began with the population of perhaps 23 to 34 million whitetails. It ended with a whitetail population of perhaps 35 to 50% of its pre-1500 size—but by no means devastated. Habitat modifications of this era probably did not significantly affect deer, inasmuch as destructive influences seem to have been countered generally by practices that opened the primeval forest. And for the most part, settlement was clustered around colonial hubs along the eastern seaboard.

The second stage, from about 1800 to 1865, saw a regrowth of whitetail numbers. Settlement invaded the continental interior, and nearly all Indian influence on the landscape within whitetail range was terminated. The increase was modest (in comparison to the probable pre-Columbian whitetail population), but it was an increase nevertheless. However it must be recognized that the apparent "boom" of whitetails was observed in new habitats, not necessarily the old, and by persons a generation or more removed from those who had witnessed whitetails in the pristine East. Also, as in the earlier period, land-use practices that altered deer habitat for better or worse on the whole probably offset one another, with the exception that much of the land abandoned in the East and South by westward-bound emigrants was allowed to revert to natural condition and, for a time, was favorable for deer. Therefore, it is this population—some of which was on the biological rebound, some of which was seen for the first time in pristine environs, and some of which was beginning to reestablish in reverting former habitat—that most frequently is regarded as the starting point for historical estimates of the species' abundance.

It is this population that became the target for market and subsistence hunters in the third stage, or exploitation era (1850–1900).

Although more deer were killed in the 300-plus years that constitute the first stage than were killed in the 50-year exploitation era, the latter timeframe represents the period of greatest hunting pressure on wildlife *ever*. With respect to whitetails, the intensity of harvest was magnified because (1) at the era's outset the deer population was only a fraction of its pre-Columbian size, (2) there were no more wilderness sanctuaries in which whitetails could thrive beyond the reach of hunters, and (3) positive land-use impacts on habitat were prevented or negated by continual influx of people. (McCabe and McCabe 1984)

Our investigations indicated that white-tailed deer historically occupied, at some time, all of the habitat that was available to them and probably were less vulnerable to marked population fluctuations than is the case and potential in modern times. Like bison, elk, waterfowl, songbirds, wolves, coyotes, badgers, eagles, and virtually all wildlife, whitetails thrived in the cornucopia that is any temperate area not dominated by persistent human influence.

There is little proof, except for exotics, that any fish or wildlife populations in North America are much more numerous now than in 1492. There is certainty that many species are less abundant, less widespread, and less stable than prior to European discovery of the New World and before encroachment by human imperialism, Manifest Destiny, and sprawl. Whereas the continent may not have been everywhere the Eden that inspired grandiloquent chroniclers of yesteryear, it was a land of great plenty and diversity. Colonization and settlement of the Americas were quests of exploitation. New World nationalism was predicated on utilizing, subjugating, or eliminating those things that were barriers to more and better. The literature of yore is replete with glorified references to taming wild America. If the practice of conservation was anywhere in the New World psyche, it was well hidden and did not appear in print until barely a century ago. So different was early America from civilized Europe in its natural bounty and space that the new wilderness was over awing and daunting. Even today, immigrants, visitors, and vacationers are astounded by the amount, diversity, and novelty of wild things and places in North America. Yet those things and places are but isolated remnants of the continent's historic and prehistoric circumstance.

Our look at historical whitetail abundance was not a statistical assessment. We arrived at our population figures and an overview based on as much credible data as we could gather, compare, and apply to some fairly standard principles of deer biology. Those figures have been scrutinized and apparently accepted. So we find it curious and a bit paradoxical, in this era of "modern" wildlife management, high science, and computer technology, that there is no consensus on the size of the present whitetail population. During the last several years, we have heard tell that white-

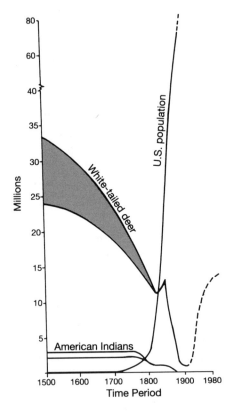

FIGURE 2.2. Conceptual diagram of white-tailed deer population status in the United States and Canada, 1500–1980 (from McCabe and McCabe 1984).

tails in the United States now number 15 million, 17.5 million, 19 million, 21 million, or 25 million. At least these are the figures that have appeared in the popular media; only one qualified its source. In that instance, the story cited a study by the Southeastern Cooperative Wildlife Disease Study (SCWDS; College of Veterinary Medicine, University of Georgia, Athens). If such a count was made by the SCWDS, we are unaware of it. Until we can examine a concerted scientific census, we will remain skeptical of any assertion that U.S. whitetails exceed 16 or 17 million.

In any case, we still seriously doubt that the current whitetail population exceeds, equals, or approaches that of Columbus' time. What is important here is not whether or not there are more deer now than any time since Columbus. The real significance is that, by making such public statements without benefit of scientific evidence, a false and misleading message is perpetuated. At a time of whitetail abundance such that some herds are close to or actually unmanageable, for whatever reason, the suggestion that there are more deer now than ever imparts a public perception of mismanagement.

CURRENT TRENDS AFFECTING WHITETAIL ABUNDANCE

From historical research, we found that history is the evidence of trends and both profit and bane of progress. On the positive side, history reveals capacity and capability. It gives careful students insight into past motivations and mistakes so that misactions or inactions are not repeated. On the negative side, history, incomplete or muddled, aborts circumspection and misdirects the energies of progress. For us, the real beauty of historical inventory and reporting is that once the data are laid out, the reporters can use that information to launch off in any interpretive direction they choose. And that is what we will do here.

We choose to discuss a number of trends, or our impression of trends, that relate to the status of white-tailed deer and have implication for the species' management. The first trend involves wildlife management itself. In the past decade or two, it appears that the profession has gradually moved away from the umbrella of game management. Since the 1970s, managers have been charged with accountability for protection and conservation of a much broader range of resources and resource values. The increase of mandated responsibility for the full gamut of wildlife species, populations, habitats, and uses has stretched the profession's work force, workload, and operational resources. The public and political embrace of things environmental has not been paralleled by a commitment of wherewithal to accommodate the national flush of conscience, however faddish, about natural resources.

Perhaps most telling is the national embarrassment of the Fish and Wildlife Conservation Act of 1980 (16 U.S.C. 2901–2911). This was the law passed—and passed convincingly—to give priority and dollars to nongame resources. But its funding and appropriation mechanisms were gutted, and repeated efforts to authorize funding from the general treasury have failed.

Nevertheless, the wildlife profession has seen in that Act a mandate to consider all creatures, which is good. However, about 75% of research and management dollars for all wildlife come almost exclusively from expenditures by hunters in recreational pursuit of game species via the Pittman–Robertson Act (Federal Aid in Wildlife Restoration Act of 1937, 16 U.S.C. 669–669i) (Sparrowe 1993). Even though the research and management funds used to benefit game populations are not selective exclusively for game species, there have been concerted attempts to raid or revise the Pittman–Robertson program. None, to date, has succeeded in diverting those earmarked funds—a subterfuge that likely would devastate the practice, if not the science, of wildlife management. The defense of Pittman–Robertson dollars has been viewed by some, even within the profession, as stonewalling against nongame programs or catering to hunters. That simply is not the case. Pittman–Robertson funds continue to be guarded because they represent the minimal dollars available for game species. Should we jeopardize those species and populations by subdividing the investment? We think that would prove disastrous. What's more, it would forestall any incentive to expand the funding base needed for all wildlife. We are certain about one thing—without game management and Pittman–Robertson investments since the 1930s, a lot of nongame would be nonentities.

What is occurring in our profession is a shift in interest and inclination toward nongame, but that shift, for one reason or another, unfortunately has not been attended by the material support to subsidize research and management. The shortage of funds for all wildlife programs seems to have spurred another trend, namely, the reinvention of conservation per se. This, plainly, has stretched the profession's imagination.

At the outset, the reinvention has been semantic infighting—posturing and positioning for equity. In some measure, the terms "biological diversity," "conservation biology," and "ecosystem management" are conceptualizations of revised professional agenda. In some measure, they are "crisis disciplines" (Primack 1993:7) and byproducts of profession frustrations with political reluctance to ante up for legislative mandates and impositions, with public reneging on a call for heightened environmental awareness, and with a general, even global, apathy to respond proactively to time lines for maintaining genetic, species, and community-level diversity. In some measure, unfortunately, these new disciplines are triggers of professional divisiveness, splitting resource agencies, departments, organizations, and individuals into distinct philosophical camps—game versus nongame, applied management versus research, traditionalism versus holism, and species management versus ecosystem management.

There always have been separate emphases and interests within the professional community, and it seems to us that such variance has been healthy in that it has given better focus and broader scope to ecological outlook. But where separate camps emerge piously self-righteous, zealously self-protective, and shamelessly self-promoting, there is reduced cooperation among essential disciplines and an undermining of public confidence in resource professionals to explain problems much less address them effectively.

Each camp, it appears, wants a bigger piece of a hunter-baked pie. It appears, too, that what becomes an issue is not the size, source, or ownership of the pie, but the mere fact that it comes from a special, minority, recreational interest. It seems untenable, from a professional standpoint, that game species in the United States, which represent less than 5% of all wildlife species, should receive nearly 97% of the available dollars for management; that the 238 endangered species, or 11% of all wildlife species, receives approximately 2.8% of the available management dollars; and that the majority, 85% nongame and nonendangered species, receives less than 0.2% of the management funds (Wildlife Management Institute 1994). But professionals—learned people—ought not to approach the disparity in a territorial fashion.

Perhaps as a consequence there is a more onerous trend among some in the profession. Whether to justify budgets or lobby for unrelated program credibility, some wildlifers are inclined to ignore, deny, or denigrate the role of hunting historically or currently as a management tool and option. Some, furthermore, are apologists for recreational hunting. It is not required or even expected that wildlife professionals be hunters, but surely they should understand the role of recreational hunting economically, biologically, and culturally in the management history of designated wildlife populations. They should understand, too, the costs and other consequences of removing hunting as a factor of wildlife population control. It is no less irresponsible for wildlifers to dismiss hunting as a practical and practicable management method in most cases, particularly those of adjudged overabundance, any more than it is to suppose that all regulated hunting is biologically defensible.

The second trend area that we choose to discuss is public perception of deer. Historically, whitetails represented a primary source of subsistence. Venison and other parts provided nutritional sustenance, footwear and other apparel, currency, and commerce. For the most part—until the 1880s in most areas—whitetails were a providential crop harvested opportunistically. Thereafter, with a concomitant rise in technology and the drop of whitetail numbers at least until the early 1900s, there was widespread regulation of harvest season and limit. Throughout much of the species' range for the next 30 to 50 years, whitetails were rarities. In part through the subliminalizing genius of Walt Disney, whitetails came to symbolize benign forest creatures and Nature itself. With population recovery well underway by the 1960s, whitetails were again a resource—aesthetic and recreational. With continued growth, the whitetail population appears now to be viewed narrowly as a recreation resource and also as a menace in some areas. Its novelty has been somewhat diminished or tempered and so, too, its aesthetic appeal.

If this rather blithe capsulization of the whitetail's public persona is reasonably characterized, we can further capsulize the trend of perception as one of economic factor to oddity to anthropomorph to target to obtuse amenity. People now seem to appreciate whitetails, but not splayed out on the top of hunters' pickups or imprinted in the grills of other vehicles, or doing the midnight Lindy through rows of beefsteak tomatoes or dining alfresco on nasturtiums. It is unlikely, however, that the public knows or cares of the whitetail's ecological niche. This may be explained in part by the American tradition of taking our landscape and renewable resources for granted and, in part, by prevailing economic theories of supply and demand and individual utility, which indicate that we tend to devalue desirable commodities in converse proportion to their availability.

The science of wildlife ecology deals with the biological nature of things, for the most part independent of sociological parameters, including human economics. Wildlife management is the practice of applying biological principles to wildlife systems and in balance with societal conditions and expectations. Wildlife managers attempt to create opportunities to optimize wildlife recruitment in relation to available habitat and to maintain wildlife numbers in relation to habitat viability by regulating mortality. To do less would be a violation of legal mandates and public trust of stewardship. The problem of wildlife overabundance, or of underabundance in suitable habitat, occurs when societal conditions and expectations change, especially locally, at a rate or in a manner that is separate from biological rhythms. There is no science that can correlate natural circumstance to the happenstance of prevailing economics and the constant flux of human attitudes or values. Wildlife management is, at best, a win–lose profession. Even when management results in wildlife populations that are healthy and in balance with available habitat, there are segments of society that will object to the animals' numbers, distribution, composition, or behavior, to the cost or methodologies of the management, or to the ostensible motivations for the wild populations' condition.

The public must be fairly confused by such breast-beating proclamations that we have more deer now than ever before and that whitetails are wildlife management's foremost success, while simultaneously hearing from farmers, suburbanites, transportation officials, and journalists that deer are verging on pest status in a growing number of places. As professionals, we are obligated to set the record straight, or at the very least, not mislead. And that applies in this instance to the concept of "overabundance"—a highly value-laden and contentious term in the context of wildlife populations.

Whitetail abundance is relative. Where the species exists and poses a threat to human priority, those deer—at whatever density—will be considered overabundant and a problem. The problem becomes conflict not so much by adjustment of the deer numbers but by changing or competing human priorities. We know of few places, except for artificial enclosures—physical or political—where whitetails are overabundant in a biological, carrying capacity sense. On the other hand, we are well aware that deer numbers approach or exceed human tolerance levels in many areas. And just as humans define overabundance, so too do humans proscribe biodiversity: it is what suits us most conveniently and conventionally at the time. *Homo sapiens* may or may not be the most intelligent life form on this planet, but it is certainly the most sanctimonious and doubtlessly the most environmentally disruptive.

Which brings us to the next trend we would like to illuminate. In the 10 years following completion of our study into historic whitetail abundance, the U.S. human population has increased 10% to nearly 260 million (U.S. Bureau of the Census 1993). We have added nearly 322,000 km of roads (Federal Highway Administration, unpublished data, 1992), driven on by 17% more vehicles, which equates to an additional 20 million vehicles (U.S. Department of Transportation, unpublished data, 1992). We have built more than 27,000 new shopping centers, 10,000 new office buildings, 2,000 new airports, and 12 million new homes (U.S. Bureau of the Census 1993). Urban–suburban sprawl has claimed more than 5.7 million of 7.3 million ha of rural lands lost between 1982 and 1992, including 2.4 million ha of prime farmland—representing a surface area equivalent to the states of Connecticut, Vermont, and New Hampshire combined (U.S. Soil Conservation Service 1994). During that same time span, 56,700 ha of wetlands were lost—20,250 to agriculture and 36,450 to nonagricultural uses (U.S. Soil Conservation Service 1994). We now use 4,927 liters of water per person per day, three times that of any other industrialized nation (National Energy Information Center, unpublished data, 1994), and we consume 51% more lumber (46.3 billion board feet) than 10 years past (U.S. Forest Service, unpublished data, 1992). Since 1984, we have released more than 10,000 new chemicals into the environment (Environmental Protection

Agency, unpublished data, 1994). Between 1982 and 1992, our per capita energy consumption has increased 16% to 82.1 quadrillion British thermal units, and we have produced nearly twice the nuclear energy of any other country. Americans currently spend more on ski equipment and clothing than on management of whitetails, than on management of all deer, than on management of all big game species combined.

In 1982, 24,667 deer–vehicle collisions were reported in Pennsylvania. In 1992, that number was 42,539—an increase of 72% (Pennsylvania Game Commission, unpublished data, 1992). Whitetail numbers had increased in Pennsylvania in that interval, but so too did the number of roadway kilometers through deer habitat, the number of vehicles using those roads, and the per capita number of kilometers driven. In 1982, 1,476 whitetails were killed in Pennsylvania in response to damage complaints. In 1992, 3,534 deer were dispatched for the same reason—an increase of 139%. We aren't picking on Pennsylvania. To the contrary, Pennsylvania is quite typical for the whitetail states, yet it does a better job than most of tracking and reporting on wildlife–human interactions.

The final trend that we want to speak to may come closest to the heart of the problem of overabundance in unmanaged deer populations. It is the matter of privatization (Griffith 1987). Wildlife population management cannot be imposed or effectively enforced on private lands. Ownership, however enlightened about wildlife science, defines and dictates access. Public or private ownership of land refers to both space and legal authorities. For the most part, wildlife that resides on or moves through private space is, by law, publicly owned. But, inasmuch as access to wildlife or wildlife habitat on private land is privately controlled, the wildlife there is owned de facto by private interests (Benson 1992), who may neither know nor care about wildlife population dynamics or who may choose to exercise rights of exclusion to the mechanisms or mechanics of habitat management or animal population regulation. Also, wherever business, industry, or residential development expand—either wholesale or piecemeal—within deer habitat, the prospects and utility of management for the species are precluded by or subordinated to other ownership objectives, prerogatives, or perverse incentives. The last—perverse incentives—is economic jargon that refers to financial rewards associated with resource exploitation that leads to damaging results to wildlife (see Rasker and Freese, in press). The rate of wildlife habitat alteration—in this case, reduction of habitat—appears to be greatly outpaced by the rate of land lockup and consequent privatization.

The point we are trying to make is that when we are confronted with conflicts with otherwise desirable wildlife that is productive, healthy, and below both habitat carrying capacity and known population thresholds, use of the term overabundance probably better references the accuser than the accused both in fact and in context. Second, we suspect that wildlife science—under whatever set of philosophical terms and dimensions—will not gain adequate public attention, priority, and support until our society is willing first to see and remedy its own browse lines.

History in North America shows that we are reactive to wildlife problems mainly and usually at the level of dilemma, but also that most reactions have been favorably remedial. Given our social conundrums and loggerheads, not the least of which correlate directly to human population size and growth, there surely will be, before long, a point of diminishing return in our ability to react quickly enough and with enough concerted effort to stem biological imbalances. Every such circumstance has and will continue to require society to make a choice. Either we attempt to salvage biological integrity or we let it be compromised and use our creative energies instead to excuse or justify the consequent less wild, less diverse, less organic environment. That *seems* to be our nature; it *is* our history.

We don't want to finish without qualifying our own sanctimony. We didn't accept the invitation to produce this chapter because of any personal or professional need to reappraise our conclusions of a decade ago or desire to expand the audience for that work. We accepted mainly because we have been distant from the sometimes isolating pragmatics of whitetail research and management, and it is healthy to revisit that science and learn where it has been and where it is going.

REFERENCES CITED

Bailey, R. G. 1978. Description of the ecoregions of the United States. U.S. Forest Service Miscellaneous Publication 1391, Ogden, UT.

Benson, D. E. 1992. Commercialization of wildlife: A value-added incentive for conservation. Pages 539–553 *in* The Biology of Deer. (R. D. Brown, ed.) Springer-Verlag, New York.

Driver, H. E. 1968. On the population nadir of Indians in the United States. Current Anthropology 9:330.

Gramly, R. M. 1977. Deerskins and hunting territories: Competition for a scarce resource of the northeastern woodlands. American Antiquity 42:601–605.

Griffith, C. 1987. Turning wildlife private. Oregon Bowhunter, July:4–5.

McCabe, R. E. 1982. Elk and Indians: Historical values and perspectives. Pages 61–164 *in* Elk of North America: Ecology and Management. (J. W. Thomas and D. E. Toweill, eds.) Stackpole Books, Harrisburg, PA.

McCabe, R. E., and T. R. McCabe. 1984. Of slings and arrows: An historical retrospection. Pages 19–72 *in* White-Tailed Deer: Ecology and Management. (L. K. Halls, ed.) Stackpole Books, Harrisburg, PA.

Oswalt, W. H. 1966. This Land Was Theirs: A Study of the North American Indians. John Wiley and Sons, New York.

Primack, R. B. 1993. Essentials of Conservation Biology. Sinauer Associates, Sunderland, MA.

Rasker, R., and C. Freese. In press. Wildlife and the marketplace: Opportunities and problems. *In* Our Fundamental Policies in Wildlife Conservation. (V. Geist and I. Mctaggart-Cowan, eds.) Detselig Publishers, Calgary, Alberta.

Salwen, B. 1970. Cultural reference from faunal remains: Examples from three Northeast coastal rites. Pennsylvania Archeology 40 (1–2): 1–8.

Seton, E. T. 1909. Life Histories of Northern Mammals. Vol. I. Charles Scribner's Sons, New York.

Seton, E. T. 1929. Lives of Game Animals. Vol. III, part 1. Doubleday, Doran and Co., Garden City, NY.

Sparrowe, R. D. 1993. What is wise use of waterfowl populations? Pages 85–86 *in* Waterfowl and Wetland Conservation in the 1990s—A Global Perspective. (M. Moser, R. C. Prentice, and J. Van Vessom, eds.) International Waterfowl Research Bureau Special Publication 26, Slimbridge, United Kingdom.

Spinden, H. J. 1928. The population of ancient America. Geographic Review 18: 641–660.

Stransky, J. J. 1984. Hunting the whitetail. Pages 739–780 *in* White-Tailed Deer: Ecology and Management. (L. K. Halls, eds.) Stackpole Books, Harrisburg, PA.

U.S. Bureau of the Census. 1993. Statistical Abstract of the United States. 113th edition. U.S. Government Printing Office, Washington.

U.S. Soil Conservation Service. 1994. Summary Report: 1992 National Resources Inventory. U.S. Department of Agriculture, Washington.

Wildlife Management Institute. 1994. For the unhunted: A reprieve? Outdoor News Bulletin 48 (6): 3–4.

Williams, L. E. 1972. From Shantok and Fort Corchang: A comparative study of seventeenth century culture contact in the Long Island Sound area. Doctoral dissertation, New York University, New York.

3 Historical Changes in the Abundance and Distribution of Deer in Virginia

W. MATT KNOX

Historical changes in white-tailed deer distribution patterns and population trends in Virginia are similar to those of most southeastern states. When the first European settlers arrived in North America at Jamestown Island, Virginia, in 1607, they described an abundance of the animal that would become commonly known as the Virginia white-tailed deer *(Odocoileus virginianus)*. Early accounts demonstrate that white-tailed deer were found statewide, and the highest population densities apparently were located in the coastal Tidewater physiographic region.

The number of deer that inhabited the Commonwealth of Virginia at the outset of European settlement is unknown. There are no established estimates of Virginia's precolonial deer herd. However, Seton (1909) estimated the deer herd in the eastern United States at the time of European colonization to be 4 deer/km². Seton's 1909 estimate extrapolated to the land area of Virginia produces a precolonial population of approximately 400,000 deer. McCabe and McCabe (1984) developed a mathematical model based on North America's estimated Native American population and several other factors to arrive at a precolonial white-tailed deer population estimate of 3.1 to 4.2 deer/km². For Virginia, the McCabe and McCabe model produces an estimated population of between 313,000 and 433,000 deer ($\bar{x} = 373,000$).

Following colonization, Virginia's deer population declined. In 1699, to address this decline, Virginia was one of the first colonies to set a closed season for hunting deer (Mann 1952). Frequently cited as standard factors precipitating the colonial decline of deer in Virginia are habitat loss due to deforestation and agriculture, overharvest, and lack of effective law enforcement. Of these three, an extensive overharvest compounded by ineffective law enforcement would appear to have been the most damaging. Theoretically, initial clearing of forests and land-use changes from forest to agriculture should have benefitted Virginia's early colonial deer herd. History indicates that this was not the case. Any improvement in deer habitat conditions was apparently negated by continued overharvest.

The overharvest of Virginia's deer resource assumed several stages. During the early decades of European settlement, venison and deer hides were an essential staple of everyday colonial life. Colonial laws that were passed to protect deer in Virginia frequently contained an exemption for those settlers living on the western frontier (Reeves 1960). Subsistence hunting was followed by a commercial trade in deer hides that peaked around 1700. For the years 1698–1715, historical records indicate that 14,000 hides were exported to Europe from Virginia annually (Crane 1928). Market hunting for meat succeeded the trade in deer hides. One market hunter in northwestern Virginia was reported to have killed over 2,700 deer prior to 1860 for an average price of 22 cents per kilogram (Thornton 1955).

Like most southeastern states, Virginia's deer herd reached its lowest population level during the early 1900s. By 1900, the deer herd in nearly all of Virginia's western Mountain and Piedmont physiographic regions had been extirpated (Reeves 1960). Quinn (1953) estimated the deer population in the 31 counties west of the Blue Ridge to have been around 500 animals at the turn of the century.

There is sufficient evidence, however, to confirm that a few counties in northwestern Virginia contained sizeable remnant herds of native deer. At a time in the 1920s when native deer were considered extirpated from nearly all of western Virginia, Bath and Highland counties reportedly had a population of between 500 and 2,500 deer (Bailey 1929). In the Tidewater region, remnant herds remained in areas (such as river swamps and refuges) that were inaccessible to humans. Robertson (1931) estimated the statewide deer population to be approximately 25,000 in 1931. The exact time deer numbers began to increase significantly in Virginia is open to speculation. Downing (1987) suggested that deer abundance did not increase significantly in North America until the 1930s.

THE DEER RESTORATION PROGRAM

In 1916, the Virginia Department of Game and Inland Fisheries (VDGIF) was formed. A considerable amount of the new agency's time and effort was spent on a deer restoration program initiated by VDGIF in 1926. In the program's early stages, 1926–51, 1,305 deer were imported from out-of-state sources into Virginia. The average cost of deer purchased from out of state was $50 per deer, with costs ranging from $25 to $125 (Peery and Coggin 1978). In total, deer restoration efforts resulted in the restoration, or stocking, of more than 4,200 deer over 67 years, 1926–92 (McDonald and Miller 1993). With the exception of just a few eastern counties, nearly all restocking in Virginia was done west of the Blue Ridge Mountains.

DEER DISTRIBUTION PATTERNS
AND POPULATION TRENDS

One of the first maps of deer distribution in Virginia was developed by Patton (1938), who described three distinct patterns of deer distribution but gave no indication of relative abundance (Figure 3.1A). First, there were 22 areas, mostly in western Virginia, with deer attributed to restoration efforts. Second, three areas of native deer herds were identified; the largest contiguous area of native deer populations was in the coastal Tidewater region and extended into the central and southern Piedmont. Third, deer were reportedly absent in over half of the state in 1938, including most of the Mountain region west of the Blue Ridge as well as the northern and southwestern Piedmont.

Following Patton's map, a series of maps produced by the Southeastern Cooperative Wildlife Disease Study (SCWDS) at the College of Veterinary Medicine at the University of Georgia updated changes in deer distribution and relative abundance for the southeastern United States, including Virginia, in 1950, 1970, and 1980 and for the entire United States in 1988 (Figure 3.1B–E). These maps were prepared from data compiled by the respective state game and fish biologists.

By 1950, Virginia had one of the more extensive southeastern deer herds. It should be remembered that by 1950 Virginia had had an ongoing restoration program for over 25 years and had relocated approximately 2,000 animals (McDonald and Miller 1993). The 1950 SCWDS map of

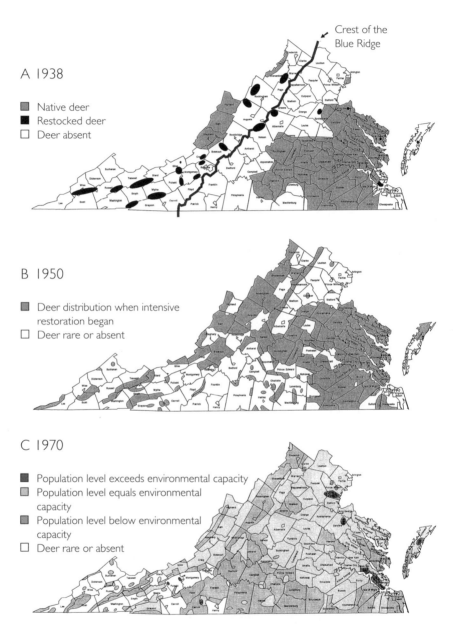

FIGURE 3.1. Distribution and relative abundance of deer in Virginia at five periods. Note that no relative abundance estimates are provided for 1933 and 1950. The 1938 map was developed by Paton (1938); the remaining maps were produced by the Southeastern Cooperative Wildlife Disease Study from data compiled by state wildlife biologists of the Southeastern Association of Fish and Wildlife Agencies.

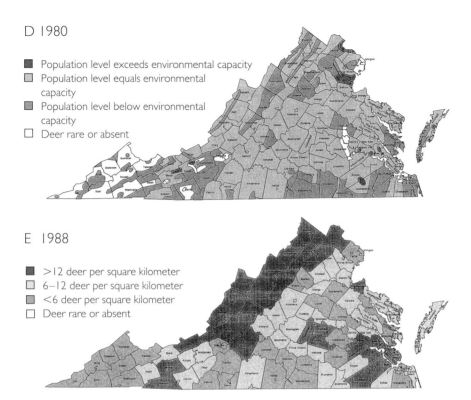

D 1980

- ■ Population level exceeds environmental capacity
- ▢ Population level equals environmental capacity
- ▨ Population level below environmental capacity
- ▢ Deer rare or absent

E 1988

- ■ >12 deer per square kilometer
- ▢ 6–12 deer per square kilometer
- ▨ <6 deer per square kilometer
- ▢ Deer rare or absent

FIGURE 3.1. *Continued.*

Virginia designated locations of deer where intensive restoration occurred but gave no indication of relative abundance. By the early 1950s, however, Virginia's statewide deer population was estimated to have expanded to 150,000 animals (Reeves 1960).

Like the Patton map of 1938, the 1950 SCWDS map depicted that deer occupied a majority of the coastal Tidewater region and Tidewater herds had started to repopulate the central Piedmont. In 1950, the south-western and northern Piedmont remained unoccupied. Most of the south-central Piedmont was described as absent of deer except for isolated pop-ulations scattered throughout the area. West of the Blue Ridge, the 1950 SCWDS map indicated that the native and restocked deer herds of the northwest mountains had repopulated approximately 75% of the avail-able range. Deer herds in the southern mountains were described as iso-lated populations, and vast areas of range remained unoccupied. Most of the isolated deer herds delineated in southwestern Virginia in 1950 were closely correlated in distribution to the U.S. Forest Service's Jefferson National Forest.

The 1970 SCWDS map demonstrated a significant increase in the distribution of deer (Figure 3.1C). The northern and southern Piedmont, which lacked deer in 1950, were repopulated by deer by 1970. Virtually all available range east of the Blue Ridge and the northern mountains was occupied by deer by 1970.

In addition to significant range expansion, Virginia's deer population was continuing to grow. By 1970, Virginia's statewide deer population was estimated to be approximately 215,000 animals (VDGIF, unpublished data). On the 1970 SCWDS map, relative indexes of deer population abundance were provided for the first time. Four categories of population abundance were provided: population levels exceeding the environmental capacity, population levels equal to the environmental capacity, population levels below the environmental capacity, and deer rare or absent.

Environmental carrying capacity for deer, as it was used in Virginia at that time, represented optimum population levels based on sustained yield management (Gwynn 1965) or population levels held at or below the carrying capacity, as described by McCullough (1984). As described by Dasmann (1964), optimum density is equivalent to the term "carrying capacity" in range management and is representative of wildlife populations levels where habitat is not limiting and condition and reproductive indexes approach the maximum. As noted by Gwynn (1965), deer management based on managing for optimum population levels reflects a compromise between conflicting points of view, such as those of recreational deer hunters and farmers. Today, these management goals and carrying capacity evaluations are defined as cultural carrying capacities (Ellingwood and Caturano 1988).

Data taken from mostly unpublished deer distribution maps (see VDGIF 1970 for published maps) of Virginia during the same period (around 1970) support a generalization that areas identified as below the environmental capacity had deer densities of less than 1.9 deer/km², areas described as equal to the environmental capacity contained 1.9 to 9.7 deer/km², and areas identified as exceeding carrying capacity contained more than 9.7 deer/km².

In several areas, the effects of habitat type and land ownership on deer distribution and abundance are clearly visible in the 1970 SCWDS map. In most of the Shenandoah Valley in northwestern Virginia, distinct habitat differences were associated with low deer densities in the valley floor and higher deer densities in the mountains on either side, east and west. In 1970, federal property, such as the Jefferson National Forest, still had clear effects on deer distribution patterns in southwestern Virginia, which still remained characterized by isolated populations that had demonstrated little expansion since 1950. Even more striking are the effects of federal and state properties on areas designated as above environmental capacity. In 1970, 10 small, isolated populations of deer described as above environmental capacity were identified within the state. Most of these were associated with distinct federal and state properties (e.g., military bases, national parks, state parks, and refuges).

The 1980 map of the SCWDS series (Figure 3.1D) suggested significant increases in the relative abundance of deer in Virginia between 1970 and 1980. By 1980, a majority of the Tidewater, Piedmont, and northern Mountain physiographic regions were described as fully occupied at environmental carrying capacity. The statewide deer population had expanded to an estimated 422,000 animals (VDGIF, unpublished data). Southwestern mountain populations had expanded slightly but were still designated below environmental capacity, and there were still significant areas where deer were described as being rare or absent. As in 1970, a few very small, isolated populations were described as above environmental capacity by 1980; a majority of these areas were attributed to federal and state properties.

In 1988, SCWDS updated its white-tailed deer distribution map for the entire United States. In contrast to the earlier maps, this map presented specific density estimates on a county basis (Figure 3.1E). Population estimates for each of Virginia's counties' deer herds were obtained from models extrapolating average estimated antlered buck harvest rates per unit forested area from big game check station data and Virginia Department of Forestry data. In 1987, on the basis of these models, the statewide deer population was estimated to have grown to 575,000 animals (VDGIF, unpublished data).

SUMMARY

Changes in deer distribution and abundance documented by the Patton and SCWDS maps over the past five decades are substantiated by trends in hunter harvests (Figure 3.2). From an estimated 793 deer in 1923 to approximately 200,000–210,000 deer in each of the past three seasons (1992–94), Virginia's annual deer harvest has, with the exception of a

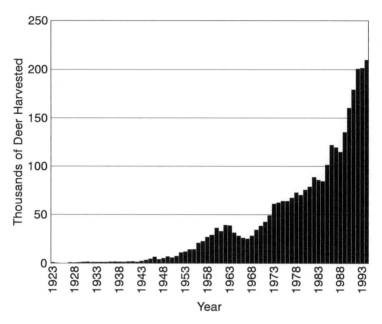

FIGURE 3.2. Virginia deer harvest, 1923–1994 (VDGIF 1995).

short period during the early to mid-1960s, demonstrated a consistent increase (VDGIF 1995). Current population estimates, based on computer reconstruction models (Downing 1980), indicate that the statewide Virginia deer herd is stable at a conservative population estimate of approximately 900,000 animals (VDGIF, unpublished data).

The recovery of Virginia's deer herd is a testament to the professional stewardship of earlier generations of wildlife biologists, administrators, and politicians who had the foresight to establish resource management programs and laws. The growth of Virginia's deer herd from an estimated 25,000 to 900,000 over the past 65 years is also a striking testament to the adaptability and reproductive potential of white-tailed deer. Lastly, it demonstrates just how recent a phenomenon is the widespread abundance of the Virginia deer herd.

Like other southeastern states, growth in Virginia's deer herd has been accompanied by change in management direction and the development of new management challenges. Change in deer management direction from establishing and allowing deer herd expansion to controlling deer population growth has been based primarily on the cultural carrying capacity. Although deer herds are frequently cited as overpopulated, Virginia does not currently have many significant widespread deer herds at biological carrying capacity. Most of Virginia's deer herds are managed at moderate to low population densities, in fair to good physical condition, and below the biological carrying capacity.

REFERENCES CITED

Bailey, V. 1929. Report on itinerary, physiography, and life zones. Virginia: Bath and Highland counties April 6–8, 1929. Game and Fish Conservation 9 (1): 3–6.

Crane, V. W. 1928. The Southern Frontier, 1670–1732. Duke University Press, Durham, NC.

Dasmann, R. F. 1964. Wildlife Biology. John Wiley and Sons, New York.

Downing, R. L. 1980. Vital statistics of animal populations. Pages 257–262 in Wildlife Management Techniques Manual. 4th edition. (S. D. Schemnitz, ed.) The Wildlife Society, Washington.

Downing, R. L. 1987. Success story: White-tailed deer. Pages 45–57 in Restoring America's Wildlife, 1937–1987. U.S. Fish and Wildlife Service, Washington.

Ellingwood, M. R., and S. L. Caturano. 1988. An evaluation of deer management options. Connecticut Department of Environmental Protection Publication DR-11, Hartford.

Gwynn, J. V. 1965. Sustained yield deer herd management. Virginia Wildlife 26 (11): 4–6, 22.

Mann, H. 1952. The first hundred years of conservation in Virginia. Virginia Wildlife 13 (4): 10–12.

McCabe, R. E., and T. R. McCabe. 1984. Of slings and arrows: An historical perspective. Pages 19–72 in White-Tailed Deer: Ecology and Management. (L. K. Halls, ed.) Stackpole Books, Harrisburg, PA.

McCullough, D. R. 1984. Lessons from the George Reserve, Michigan. Pages 211–242 in White-Tailed Deer: Ecology and Management. (L. K. Halls, ed.) Stackpole Books, Harrisburg, PA.

McDonald, J. S., and K. V. Miller. 1993. A history of white-tailed deer stocking in the United States. Quality Deer Management Association, Research Publication 93-1, Greenwood, SC.

Patton, C. P. 1938. A preliminary distributional list of the mammals of Virginia. Master's thesis, Virginia Polytechnic and State University, Blacksburg.

Peery, C., and J. Coggin. 1978. Virginia's White-Tailed Deer. Virginia Department of Game and Inland Fisheries, Richmond.

Quinn, I. T. 1953. Annual Report of the Commission of Game and Inland Fisheries for the Fiscal Year Ending June 30, 1952. Virginia Department of Game and Inland Fisheries, Richmond.

Reeves, J. H., Jr. 1960. The history and development of wildlife conservation in Virginia: A critical review. Doctoral dissertation, Virginia Polytechnic and State University, Blacksburg.

Robertson, J. T. 1931. Building up the Virginia deer herd. Game and Fish Conservation 11 (4): 75–77, 82.

Seton, E. T. 1909. Life Histories of Northern Animals. Vol. I. Charles Scribner's Sons, New York.

Thornton, J. E. 1955. An old man remembers. Virginia Wildlife 16 (11): 8–9, 17, 22.

VDGIF (Virginia Department of Game and Inland Fisheries). 1970. Deer harvest and population trend studies. Pages D1–D54 *in* Virginia Game Investigations, Annual Progress Report, July 1, 1969–June 30, 1970. Virginia Game Commission, Federal Aid in Wildlife Restoration, Report W-40, Richmond.

VDGIF (Virginia Department of Game and Inland Fisheries). 1995. 1994 Virginia deer harvest summary. Virginia Department of Game and Inland Fisheries, Wildlife Research Bulletin 95-4, Richmond.

4 The Science of Deer Management

An Animal Welfare Perspective

ALLEN T. RUTBERG

The success of the white-tailed deer in colonizing and multiplying in the late-twentieth-century landscape of croplands, woodlots, parks, and suburbs has brought the issue of deer "overpopulation" before the public in many different contexts. In suburbs, high deer densities raise concerns about traffic safety, damage to ornamental plantings, alteration of so-called natural areas, and other issues. In agricultural communities, deer depredation of crops and orchards is the fundamental issue. In state and national forests and parks high deer densities may raise concerns about the achievement of management objectives, whether they be oriented towards timber production, recreation, historical interpretation, or the preservation of biodiversity and natural ecosystem dynamics.

As other chapters in this volume instruct us, deer population and community ecology are complex and highly interesting. Unfortunately, this picture of deer ecology does not resemble the "science" applied to deer management in the field, especially in the context of suburban deer conflicts. The scientific arguments in favor of deer management are commonly founded more on dogma than on data and more on intuition than on logic. Slide shows substitute for studies. The weakness of these arguments is not lost on large segments of the public and does much to fuel controversy and suspicion.

In this chapter, I argue that the scientific justification for using specific management actions to reduce deer populations, especially public hunts, commonly is weak, especially in suburban and park settings. I further argue that those deficiencies remain in large measure because it is in the interest of the public hunting advocates, who dominate wildlife management agencies, not to correct them. Pure sport hunting is far less acceptable to the public than is management or subsistence hunting, and by discouraging rigorous scientific inquiry into the management effectiveness and biological impacts of hunting, the agencies blur the line between sport and management hunting and shield the public from awareness of the impacts of hunting. I also discuss how these scientific weaknesses become amplified and distorted in public discussion and outline the course by which I believe deer overpopulation controversies must be resolved.

First, I describe the ethical perspective from which I write.

AN ANIMAL PROTECTION PERSPECTIVE

Like all large social movements, the animal protection movement incorporates a broad range of views on hunting and wildlife management. One view, which for simplicity I will label the "animal rights" view, is truly antimanagement. In this view, animals have a right to exist without human interference of any kind. Killing, injuring, or otherwise meddling in the lives of wild animals is morally wrong, and killing wildlife for sport is especially obnoxious because of the human presumptuousness it implies.

In a second simplified view, which I will label the "animal welfare" view, human interference in the lives of animals is acceptable, but suffering must be minimized; deliberate cruelty is immoral. "Suffering" is defined broadly to include psychological as well as physical pain, such as may be caused by close confinement, neglect, lack of appropriate stimulation, or other failures to provide for normal behavioral responses. In the animal welfare perspective, wildlife management may be accepted to prevent or end suffering of the animals themselves; to reduce risks to public health or safety; to prevent harm to other wildlife, especially endangered wildlife, to habitat, or to rare or otherwise desirable wild plants; and—sometimes—to prevent wildlife from interfering excessively with the ability of people to support themselves economically. Lethal management is acceptable only as a last resort, and higher standards of justification are required if lethal management is being considered. Human recreation is no justification for killing; consequently, sport hunting is considered to be morally wrong.

Among practitioners, of course, animal rights and animal welfare perspectives often blend. For example, animal rights supporters will frequently endorse euthanasia to end animal suffering and may tolerate benign, nonlethal wildlife management; animal welfare supporters frequently endorse "let nature take its course" policies even though animal suffering may result. In this chapter, I write as a behavioral ecologist who has an animal welfare perspective.

HUNTING: MANAGEMENT, SUSTENANCE, AND SPORT

Most species currently hunted in the United States do not require management and provide only minimal sustenance. Ducks and geese; pheasants, mourning doves, and other upland birds; squirrels, rabbits, raccoons, and other small- to medium-sized mammals may be consumed, but very few American hunters effectively feed their families with such small game. As a rule, these species are not associated with ecological or social problems that would justify population management, and where they might be (i.e., where medium-sized mammals are disease vectors), hunting is usually not an appropriate management tool. Thus, hunting of most species in the United States is primarily, if not entirely, recreational.

Consequently, the hunting community has focused the hunting debate on large mammals such as deer, where plausible arguments for subsistence and management hunting may be presented to the public. A deer in the freezer makes a significant contribution to a family's annual protein budget, and charitable programs where hunters donate deer meat to needy families drive home that point. When an estimated one million deer are hit by cars in the United States each year (Conover et al. 1995), it is easy to justify sport hunting as a necessary management tool for controlling deer populations.

Although these arguments are plausible, they are not necessarily supported by data. There are certainly rural areas in the United States where deer hunting provides an important, even vital, contribution to the family food budget. But estimates of cost per pound of venison calculated from total expenditures on deer hunting, number of deer taken, and estimates of dressed weights show that hunting is not, for most Americans, a cost-effective way to secure meat. As early as 1975, Williamson and Doster (1981) estimated that deer hunters spent $1.1 billion on food, transportation, lodging, licenses, equipment, and supplies to harvest 44.3 million kg of venison. Even excluding the costs of processing and freezing, as well as the time costs of hunting, this comes out to $24.85/kg ($11.27/pound)—in 1975 dollars. More recently, the Maryland Department of Natural Resources (unpublished data) estimated that hunters spent $51 million to harvest 46,317 deer in 1990, or $1,101/deer. Assuming a dressed carcass weight of 40.9 kg and that meat makes up 48% of dressed weight (McCabe and McCabe 1984; Sauer 1984), the average Maryland hunter spends $56.20/kg ($25.49/pound) for venison, not including processing. Clearly, the nourishment provided by deer hunting can be provided much more cheaply from other sources, and deer hunting is motivated by something other than basic food needs.

In my view, managers currently rely on two fundamental dogmas to justify most deer management actions. The first fundamental dogma is that deer management is always necessary to prevent deer overpopulation. That dogma is implicit in the title of this volume and is routinely encountered in state game agency pronouncements about deer management in parks, refuges, and suburbs.

The second fundamental dogma is that hunting is essential for deer management. In wildlife management conferences, "hunting" is often used synonymously with "management," and "antimanagement" is used as a misleading codeword for "antihunting." This dogma lies at the heart of the problem; it is used to justify hunting that is primarily recreational, especially hunting with bows, muzzleloaders, and other exotic weaponry that is too ineffectual to provide time- and cost-effective population control.

Purely recreational hunting is not popular with the public. A nationwide poll of 1,612 adults published by the *Los Angeles Times,* 25 December 1993, found that 54% "generally oppose the hunting of animals for sport." A similar poll conducted for the Associated Press by ICR Survey Research Group (Media, Pennsylvania) found that 51% of Americans surveyed believed that "it's always wrong to hunt an animal for sport." Opposition to sport hunting may be even higher in suburban areas, where deer controversies are becoming common. In one Long Island, New York, community confronting a deer controversy, nearly 70% of residents "strongly disagreed" with recreational hunting of deer (Decker and Gavin 1987).

In a 1987 survey of California residents, however, 55.5% of respondents agreed that hunting was a useful tool for balancing wildlife populations with habitat (Schmidt 1989).

The differences in public perception of hunting as recreation versus management is explicitly recognized in the management community. In advising hunters how to debate antihunters, the official periodical of a western state natural resource agency (Gasson and Kruckenberg 1993) urges readers, "Don't defend hunting as sport. Remember that, despite what we might think, most of the American public opposes 'sport' hunting. Instead emphasize the personal . . . [and] utilitarian values of hunting."

Thus, state game agencies, which continue to associate closely with the hunting community, have a strong interest in convincing the public that hunting is necessary for management. And, consequently, careful scientific scrutiny of the fundamental dogmas is not encouraged by the traditional wildlife community.

HOLES IN THE FUNDAMENTAL DOGMAS

In spite of repeated assertions of the fundamental dogmas and their corollary—sport hunting is necessary to prevent deer overpopulation—scientific tests are rare enough and counterexamples are common enough to raise doubts in the minds of both scientists and thoughtful laypersons. The exponential rise in white-tailed deer populations in the United States during the last two decades makes a strong case that sport hunting has not controlled deer populations.

Rigorous Testing Is Not Applied

Tests of deer population control efforts rarely include even the most basic elements of scientific methodology. Controls, or baseline data, against which to evaluate treatment effects are rarely presented. Without a baseline for comparison, there is no clear measure of success. One commonly cited study (Wolgast and Kuser 1993) purports to show that bow hunting stabilized a deer population in Princeton Township, New Jersey. The study presents data from Princeton that (1) deer mortality caused by vehicle collisions (used as an index of deer population) rose from 1972 to 1983 and then stabilized from 1983 to 1992 and (2) deer mortality due to archery hunting rose steadily from 1972 to 1986 and then stabilized from 1986 to 1992. The article further describes a progressive liberalization in archery regulations from 1972 to 1986. No data are presented from areas experiencing different management over that period, thus precluding comparison. The result is a loose time correlation between archery regulations, archery mortality, and vehicle mortality.

Without baselines for comparison, the hypothesis that hunting controls deer populations cannot be rejected. In my experience with wildlife managers, a hunt that is followed by a reduction in deer population size is considered effective; a hunt that is followed by a stabilization in deer population size is considered effective; and a hunt that is followed by a rise in the deer population size is considered effective because, the rationalization continues, without the hunt the population would have grown even more. Under these rules, failure is impossible.

Replicate studies, with multiple treatment and control sites, are rare. In practice, success is often claimed when animals are removed from the population without criminal violations, damage to property, or injuries to hunters or bystanders. One paper, for example, concludes that "deer kills in urban and suburban areas during archery hunting seasons . . . have contributed significantly to controlling deer at levels tolerated by residents" (McAninch 1993). However, the paper presents only data on harvest numbers in different suburban areas, along with a description of hunt methodology. No direct data on deer populations or impacts are offered.

The science surrounding deer management may be weak in part because much of it escapes peer review. Most data relevant to day-to-day management are presented in agency reports, compilations of meeting proceedings, master's theses, and other unrefereed formats. Articles reproduced in *Transactions of the North American Wildlife and Natural Resources Conference* are routinely cited as if these were refereed, which they are not. Hadidian (1993) evaluated 61 reports of studies on white-tailed deer biology in the national parks; only 28% had undergone journal-quality peer review. A glimpse of this phenomenon may even be seen in the *Journal of Wildlife Management*, which itself subjects submissions to a rigorous peer review process. The 1995 volume, for example, includes one article on deer population dynamics (McNay and Voller 1995); approximately 40% of the references in this article are theses, unpublished reports, proceedings, symposium volumes, and state agency publications. By contrast, two articles on other aspects of deer biology (nutrition, Gray and Servello 1995; molecular biology, Travis and Keim 1995) each contain only one reference (of 19 and 39, respectively) to sources other than refereed journals and standard reference works. Thus, I believe, much of the deer management literature may lack strict scrutiny that would screen out flawed methodology and unwarranted conclusions.

Data on Unhunted Deer Populations Are Scarce

Several authors in this volume (McCullough, Chapter 6; Palmer et al., Chapter 10; Underwood and Porter, Chapter 12) review the handful of long-term studies on deer populations that were neither hunted nor systematically culled. They describe population dynamics that vary in different environments and at different times: irruption and crash cycles, stable high-density populations, stable low-density populations, populations whose dynamics change through time, and populations that show density dependence and populations that do not. Other volume authors (Bowers, Chapter 19; Schmitz and Sinclair, Chapter 13; Seagle and Liang, Chapter 21) note that the impacts of deer populations on plant communities and on the ability of vegetation to recover from heavy browse vary with history, latitude, plant type, and other variables. The unpredictability of deer population dynamics and community impacts, which is entirely typical of complex ecological systems, does not prevent most game managers and public advocates of hunting and culling from repeating the predictions of catastrophe should deer be left "unmanaged."

Hunting Often Fails to Control Deer Populations

The most visible weakness in the assertion that hunting is necessary to control deer populations is that it has largely failed to do so over the last two decades. In the absence of better measures, harvest trends are often used as a population index (Hayne 1984). An analysis of white-tailed deer harvest trends in states east of the Rockies (Table 4.1; Anonymous 1995) shows that harvests more than doubled in the 20 years between 1973 and 1993 in 26 of 29 states surveyed; harvests increased by a factor of five or more in 12 of those states. In the 10 years between 1983 and 1993, harvests more than doubled in 21 of 36 states. The only states among the 36 showing relatively stable harvests were Maine, New Hampshire, Vermont, and South Dakota. These trends are supported by population estimates for nine northeastern states (Storm and Palmer 1995). These data suggest that sport hunting, as it has been administered and practiced over the last two decades, controls white-tailed deer populations either not at all, only in isolated areas, or in habitats near the boundaries of the species' range.

Failures exist at the particular as well as the general level. Since 1974, managers of the Great Swamp National Wildlife Refuge, New Jersey, have been holding a "management hunt" to control the refuge's white-tailed deer population. Total harvests have risen erratically but consistently since 1974, and the 1995 harvest was almost exactly twice the 1974 harvest (U.S. Fish and Wildlife Service, unpublished data; Figure 4.1). Again, to a skeptical citizen, this does not look like effective population control.

If there are enough hunters in the woods, and they are shooting a high

TABLE 4.1

White-tailed deer harvest by state

State	1973	1983	1993
Alabama	121,953	192,231	350,500
Arkansas	33,794	60,248	110,401[a]
Connecticut	—	3,791	10,360
Delaware	—	2,231	7,465
Florida	57,122	77,146	104,178
Georgia	—	164,000	306,253[a]
Illinois	13,862	28,666	115,491
Indiana	8,244	25,232	101,214
Iowa	14,030	35,619	76,430
Kansas	4,112	17,558	30,900[a]
Kentucky	—	18,732	73,278
Louisiana	74,500	137,000	213,100
Maine	24,720	23,799	27,402
Maryland	—	18,420	51,234
Massachusetts	—	—	8,345
Michigan	70,990	158,410	330,980
Minnesota	69,035	138,390[b]	202,928
Mississippi	976	196,147	262,409
Missouri	34,723	64,427	172,120
Nebraska	7,955	18,761	26,683
New Hampshire	5,462	3,280	9,889
New Jersey	11,318	23,305	49,942
New York	75,193	167,106	220,288
North Carolina	47,469[c]	96,236	217,743[a]
North Dakota	27,780	35,709	62,252
Ohio	7,594	59,812	138,752
Oklahoma	7,567	21,920	57,831
Pennsylvania	126,891	136,293	408,557
Rhode Island	102	222	1,462
South Carolina	23,703	57,927	142,795
South Dakota	—	46,727[d]	48,394
Tennessee	11,411	48,875	138,542
Texas	—	318,344	452,509
Vermont	9,600	6,630	13,333
Virginia	60,789	85,739	201,122
West Virginia	25,863	89,840	169,014
Wisconsin	90,561	230,476	270,592

Source: Anonymous 1995. (Reprinted with permission from the *1996 Deer Hunters' Almanac,* © 1995, Krause Publications.)

[a] 1992 deer harvest; 1993 data not available.

[b] 1984 deer harvest; 1983 data not available.

[c] 1972 deer harvest; 1973 data not available.

[d] 1985 deer harvest; 1983 and 1984 data not available.

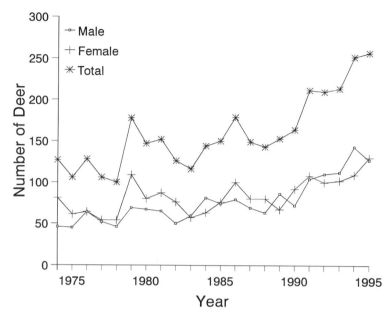

FIGURE 4.1. Deer harvests at the Great Swamp National Wildlife Refuge, New Jersey, 1974–1995 (U.S. Fish and Wildlife Service, unpublished data).

enough proportion of females, deer populations will be significantly reduced (e.g., Hesselton et al. 1965; McCullough 1984). However, there is often a large gap between what is possible and what is real, and an honest science of wildlife management must methodically examine which strategies lead to success and which strategies lead to failure. Just because deer are being killed doesn't mean that deer populations are being controlled.

OTHER SHORTCOMINGS OF THE SCIENCE OF DEER MANAGEMENT

The Complexities of Ecological Systems Are Not Recognized

Both data (discussed above) and models (Risenhoover et al., Chapter 22) of deer ecology demonstrate that the population dynamics and community effects of deer are difficult to predict, as is true of any complex ecological system. In practice, however, game managers rely on a few specious ecological arguments to justify hunts and other lethal reductions.

Probably the most widely used of these myths is that presettlement populations of deer were controlled by predators, removal of predators ended natural control, and, consequently, hunters are needed to control deer populations. Aside from the obvious fact that there are no contemporary data to indicate that predators controlled presettlement deer populations, this argument ignores the modern literature, which so far indicates that large ungulate prey populations are controlled by mammalian predators only under fairly restricted circumstances (Skogland 1991; Boutin 1992). Rather, experimental and circumstantial evidence suggest that mammalian herbivore populations are regulated through a complex interaction of food availability, predators, and other variables (Krebs et al. 1995).

Also common is the argument that deer population densities now exceed those found in presettlement North America and are therefore too high and must be controlled. Empirical estimates of presettlement deer densities do exist (McCabe and McCabe 1984, Chapter 2). However, the presettlement argument rests on the assumption that modern climates and habitats are comparable to those of the seventeenth and eighteenth centuries. The mosaic of disturbed woodlands, modern farms, and low-density suburbs in which deer now thrive differs dramatically from the late-Pleistocene woodland complex occupied by deer prior to European settlement. Additionally, the period of European settlement of North America coincided with the Little Ice Age, which extended from 1350 to 1870. Continental and alpine glaciers expanded in the west and north and bitterly cold winters, cooler summers, and increased precipitation prevailed in other areas, including those occupied by white-tailed deer (Pielou 1991). Managing deer populations to presettlement levels has little biological justification.

The Biological Effects of Hunting Are Rarely Studied

In responding to recent research in wildlife contraception, the wildlife management community has, appropriately, asked a series of tough questions about the potential risks of these technologies to deer and deer populations. Managers have asked about effects of contraception on deer behavior and social organization, energetics, population health and genetics, and other issues.

Such advocacy of scientific rigor would be admirable were it not so hypocritical. Almost no one in the wildlife management community has asked these questions about sport hunting, even though the answers are likely to prove harsh. In his summary of white-tailed deer research needs, Halls (1984) does not mention any of the possibly harmful effects of hunting, except indirectly, when he examines whether a female-skewed sex ratio might allow some does to go unfertilized. Rigorous scientific evaluations of the effects of sport hunting on deer behavior, population structure, and population genetics are astonishingly rare, whereas the number of master's theses on the food habits of deer would probably fill a small library.

Hunting, as commonly practiced, may have profound effects on the age and sex structure of deer populations. Sport hunter preferences for shooting bucks skew sex ratios toward females, sometimes dramatically. This problem has been widely recognized in the management community, though principally as a concern for population productivity and hunter satisfaction, and some state wildlife agencies are acting to reduce the more extreme biases. However, less concern is shown about the population, behavioral, and genetic effects of heavy, early adult mortality.

Data from the Great Swamp National Wildlife Refuge are again instructive. In the 1995 hunt, 98% of the males and 93% of females killed were 2.5 years old or younger (U.S. Fish and Wildlife Service, unpublished data). The oldest (three) males taken were 3.5 years old; the oldest (two) females taken were 4.5 years old. The implications for deer biology are potentially staggering. I mention two below.

First, hunting may select for early reproduction. In most large terrestrial mammals, including deer, mortality in natural populations tends to be concentrated very early and very late in the potential life span (Deevey 1947; Sinclair 1977; Clutton-Brock 1988). Females that survive to maturity commonly experience a number of years of low mortality before the onset of senescence (Hayne 1984; Clutton-Brock et al. 1988). Heavy hunting pressure changes that pattern of mortality, imposing heavy mortality on young adults that would normally show high survivorship and fecundity.

A well-established body of life history theory suggests that reproductive strategies are profoundly affected by the relative magnitude of juvenile and adult mortality (Stearns 1976; Horn and Rubenstein 1984). Under this theory, heavy adult mortality should select females for early reproduction and reduced body size, as energy for growth is diverted to reproduction. Application of this theory to deer suggests that heavy hunting pressure should select for more frequent reproduction by fawns, production of larger litters by yearlings and young adults, and reduced body size in females; these changes should be genetically based. I know of no data to support or refute this hypothesis.

Second, although mammalian social structure varies widely between and within species, matrilineal societies are extremely commonplace

(Greenwood 1980; Wrangham 1980; Clutton-Brock et al. 1982; Armitage 1986). In such societies, close spatial associations between mothers, daughters, and other matrilineal relatives are maintained into adulthood. Presumptively, knowledge about the location of food, water, cover, and potential dangers are actively or passively transmitted along generations of female relatives. At least some populations of white-tailed deer in which females are not hunted show this social structure (Nelson and Mech 1987; Porter et al. 1991). In heavily hunted populations, where adult does rarely live long enough to see their granddaughters' first winter, it is unlikely that such a social structure can be maintained. With the disintegration of such a structure may come a loss in knowledge of resources, especially resources used during special circumstances, such as severe snow cover or drought. I know of no comparative studies of social structure in hunted and unhunted populations or of the diversity of resource use in hunted and unhunted populations.

State Agencies Avoid Sponsoring Controversial Research

This critique of the science of deer management is not entirely novel. Wildlife scientists have already discussed many of the concerns raised and amplified here (Romesburg 1981; Wagner 1989). It is not uncommon for applied science to lag behind "pure science"; dogmas entrenched in professional thinking and popular culture persist for decades before the public becomes aware that these ideas have been seriously questioned or even discarded by scientists. I do not believe, however, that the gap between deer ecology and deer management can be completely explained by a simple "trickle-down" delay. Instead, I believe that the state wildlife agencies will not fund, and the cooperative research facilities will not sponsor, studies that may embarrass hunters or damage hunting interests.

CONCLUSIONS: THE PUBLIC VIEW OF
DEER MANAGEMENT

Resolving deer overpopulation controversies is extraordinarily difficult. As discussed above, deer ecology is complex, and these complexities are routinely ignored by game managers who rely instead on fundamental dogmas and instinct. One problem is that the term "deer overpopulation" conceals an unrecognized mix of biology and values. In my own experience with deer conflicts, "deer overpopulation" encodes not a problem but a solution, which is usually lethal population reduction. When pressed for a rationale for deer population reduction, advocates may mention a specific ecological or social problem (e.g., failure of oak regeneration, damage to ornamental plantings, or Lyme disease), but when alternative solutions to that specific problem are suggested, other problems are raised. Methodical identification of problems associated with high deer numbers is rare, and comprehensive, solution-oriented responses are even rarer. Commonly, "deer overpopulation" is nothing more than the intuitive, experience-based response of a game manager that "there are just too many deer," or, "the system is out of balance."

Inadequate science and confusion over the meaning of deer overpopulation is just the beginning of the problem, however. The print and broadcast media have not played a constructive role in resolving deer controversies. Newspaper, radio, and television reporters encourage polarization by structuring their stories around simple, clearly contrasting viewpoints. More often than not, "reporting" consists of predesigning a story and then identifying appropriate spokespersons who can fill in the quotes that the story assigns them. Someone in the hunting community will be found to call the local animal advocates "Bambi-lovers," and someone in the local animal advocate community will be found to call the hunters "murderers." The story is followed by published exchanges of angry letters between members of the identified factions, exchanges that sometimes degenerate into personal threats.

Science that is already weak and data that are usually inadequate are further simplified and distorted once they reach the public domain. Advocates on both sides grab hold of half-truths and shout them in each others' faces. I have heard population reduction advocates argue without evidence that a deer population is starving en masse yet is doubling every 2 years—an assertion that is biologically dubious. I have also heard population reduction advocates argue that a deer population of over a thousand individuals is both increasing and inbred, although inbreeding is more likely a problem for small and shrinking populations (Futuyma 1986). On the other hand, animal welfare advocates routinely argue that hunting increases deer populations, a misleading interpretation of the data.

It is the responsibility of wildlife managers to discourage the use of plausible myths and half-truths by both sides. Unfortunately, wildlife managers are not in a very good position to do this. To begin with, the inadequacy of the science that is often presented to the public by wildlife managers invites criticism from thoughtful laypersons and undermines the managers' position as arbiters of good science. In my experience, public skepticism may become so severe that it is difficult for wildlife managers who are collecting good data to convince critics of the integrity of their efforts.

Public skepticism is also aggravated by the identification of state wildlife managers with hunting interests. Regardless of the integrity and intentions of any specific wildlife manager, the conflict of interest, or at least the appearance of a conflict of interest, is real and inescapable. As long as state wildlife commissions and departments are dominated by hunters and other consumptive users, and as long as wildlife departments are principally funded through the sale of hunting and fishing licenses and other income from consumptive uses (Hagood, in press), there will be significant public skepticism about the impartiality of state wildlife managers in resolving deer controversies. State representatives advocating public hunting to solve urban wildlife problems instantly raises suspicions.

The greatest difficulty in resolving deer overpopulation controversies is that they revolve not around questions of biology but questions of fundamental values (Decker et al. 1991; Underwood and Porter 1991). In virtually every deer controversy that I've encountered (probably close to 50), concerned citizens on all sides ask officials, "How many deer should there be?" Most officials answer the question with a number or range, for example, "5–15 per square kilometer of deer habitat." These numbers have emerged from a history of balancing agricultural and silvicultural interests against hunting interests, but in most present-day deer controversies these numbers are both irrelevant and indefensible. The best answer a deer manager can give to the question of "How many deer should there be?" is another question, "How many do you want?"

It is, of course, up to wildlife scientists and managers to provide to the public quantitative information on the relationship between deer density and deer impacts. As deer have become the source of important public policy questions, data have begun to accumulate on their impacts on forest regeneration, wildlife species diversity, vehicle accidents, economic losses, and other factors (Alverson et al. 1988; Tilghman 1989; DeCalesta 1994; Conover et al. 1995; McShea and Rappole, Chapter 18). These are enormously important studies and must be multiplied.

Ultimately, however, it is up to the public to decide what kind of deer impacts will be tolerated (see also Decker et al. 1991). It is up to the public to decide whether it is willing to accept 100 deer–vehicle collisions a year to be able to view deer regularly in an urban park or whether it is willing to reduce deer populations to promote oak regeneration, preserve wild *Trillium,* or eliminate damage to hybrid azaleas. Wildlife managers trying to facilitate the resolution of deer controversies must resist the tendency to prescribe arbitrary densities to the public and should instead focus public attention on finding specific solutions to specific problems.

Unfortunately for the resolution of deer controversies, the public is not a single constituency. Although concern for public safety is relatively consistent, people vary widely in the value they place on oak seedlings, *Trillium,* azaleas, and the lives of deer. One constituency (e.g., The Nature Conservancy) may find itself opposed to policies put forth by another (e.g., The Fund for Animals), even if these groups are in substantial agreement on related issues, such as endangered species protection. Finding common ground between bow hunter associations and animal rights groups is even harder. In the end, a solution that satisfies 51% of the public, and doesn't offend most of the rest, may be the best that can be achieved. Finding that solution is the task of the deer manager and the land manager; it is up to the wildlife biologist to give the manager and the public the information needed to make that solution an effective one.

ACKNOWLEDGMENTS

The author thanks J. Grandy, J. Hadidian, S. Hagood, J. Kirkpatrick, and the Humane Society of the United States Mid-Atlantic Regional Office for their help with the manuscript. P. McElroy assisted in final manuscript preparation.

REFERENCES CITED

Alverson, W. S., D. M. Waller, and S. I. Solheim. 1988. Forests too deer: Edge effects in northern Wisconsin. Conservation Biology 2:348–358.

Anonymous. 1995. Deer Hunters' 1996 Almanac. Krause Publications, Iola, WI.

Armitage, K. B. 1986. Marmot polygyny revisited: Determinants of male and female reproductive strategies. Pages 303–311 *in* Ecological Aspects of Social Evolution. (D. I. Rubenstein and R. W. Wrangham, eds.) Princeton University Press, Princeton, NJ.

Boutin, S. 1992. Predation and moose population dynamics: A critique. Journal of Wildlife Management 56:116–127.

Clutton-Brock, T. H. 1988. Reproductive Success. University of Chicago Press, Chicago.

Clutton-Brock, T. H., S. D. Albon, and F. E. Guiness. 1988. Reproductive success in male and female red deer. Pages 325–343 *in* Reproductive Success. (T. H. Clutton-Brock, ed.) University of Chicago Press, Chicago.

Clutton-Brock, T. H., F. E. Guiness, and S. D. Albon. 1982. Red Deer, Behavior and Ecology of Two Sexes. University of Chicago Press, Chicago.

Conover, M. R., W. C. Pitt, K. K. Kessler, T. J. DuBow, and W. A. Sanborn. 1995. Review of human injuries, illnesses, and economic loses caused by wildlife in the United States. Wildlife Society Bulletin 23:407–414.

DeCalesta, D. S. 1994. Effect of white-tailed deer on songbirds within managed forests in Pennsylvania. Journal of Wildlife Management 58:711–718.

Decker, D. J., and T. A. Gavin. 1987. Public attitudes toward a suburban deer herd. Wildlife Society Bulletin 15:173–180.

Decker, D. J., R. E. Shanks, L. A. Nielsen, and G. R. Parsons. 1991. Ethical and scientific judgements in management: Beware of blurred distinctions. Wildlife Society Bulletin 19:523–527.

Deevey, E. S., Jr. 1947. Life tables for natural populations of animals. Quarterly Review of Biology 22:283–314.

Futuyma, D. J. 1986. Evolutionary Biology. 2nd edition. Sinauer Associates, Sunderland, MA.

Gasson, W., and L. L. Kruckenberg. 1993. Hunting, with or without a future? Wyoming Wildlife, September: 36–41.

Gray, P. G., and F. A. Servello. 1995. Energy relationships for white-tailed deer on winter browse diets. Journal of Wildlife Management 59:147–152.

Greenwood, P. J. 1980. Mating systems, philopatry and dispersal in birds and mammals. Animal Behaviour 28:1140–1162.

Hadidian, J. 1993. Science and the management of white-tailed deer in the U.S. national parks. Pages 77–85 in Proceedings of the Seventh Conference on Research and Resource Management in Parks and Public Lands, George Wright Society, Hancock, MI.

Hagood, S. In press. State Wildlife Management: The Pervasive Influence of Hunters, Hunting Culture, and Money. The Humane Society of the United States, Washington.

Halls, L. K. 1984. Research problems and needs. Pages 783–790 in White-Tailed Deer: Ecology and Management. (L. K. Halls, ed.) Stackpole Books, Harrisburg, PA.

Hayne, D. W. 1984. Population dynamics and analysis. Pages 203–210 in White-Tailed Deer: Ecology and Management. (L. K. Halls, ed.) Stackpole Books, Harrisburg, PA.

Hesselton, W. T., C. W. Severinghaus, and J. E. Tanck. 1965. Population dynamics of deer at the Seneca Army Depot. New York Fish and Game Journal 12:17–30.

Horn, H. S., and D. I. Rubenstein. 1984. Behavioural adaptations and life history. 2nd edition. Pages 279–298 in Behavioural Ecology. (J. R. Krebs and N. B. Davies, eds.) Sinauer Associates, Sunderland, MA.

Krebs, C. S., S. Boutin, R. Boonstra, A. R. E. Sinclair, J. N. M. Smith, M. R. T. Dale, K. Martin, and R. Turkington. 1995. Impact of food and predation on the snowshoe hare cycle. Science 269:1112–1115.

McAninch, J. B. 1993. Bowhunting as an urban deer population management tool. Pages 33–36 *in* Proceedings of the Western Bowhunting Conference, Bozeman, MT.

McCabe, R. E., and T. R. McCabe. 1984. Of slings and arrows: An historical retrospection. Pages 19–72 *in* White-Tailed Deer: Ecology and Management. (L. K. Halls, ed.) Stackpole Books, Harrisburg, PA.

McCullough, D. E. 1984. Lessons from the George Reserve, Michigan. Pages 211–242 *in* White-Tailed Deer: Ecology and Management. (L. K. Halls, ed.) Stackpole Books, Harrisburg, PA.

McNay, R. S., and J. M. Voller. 1995. Mortality census and survival estimates for adult female Columbian black-tailed deer. Journal of Wildlife Management 59:138–146.

Nelson, M. E., and L. D. Mech. 1987. Demes within a northeastern Minnesota deer population. Pages 27–40 *in* Mammalian Dispersal Patterns. (B. D. Chepko-Sade and Z. T. Halpin, eds.) University of Chicago Press, Chicago.

Pielou, E. C. 1991. After the Ice Age. University of Chicago Press, Chicago.

Porter, W. R., N. E. Matthews, H. B. Underwood, R. W. Sage, and D. F. Behrend. 1991. Social organization in deer: Implications for localized management. Environmental Management 15:809–814.

Romesburg, H. C. 1981. Wildlife science: Gaining reliable knowledge. Journal of Wildlife Management 45:293–313.

Sauer, P. R. 1984. Physical characteristics. Pages 73–90 *in* White-Tailed Deer: Ecology and Management. (L. K. Halls, ed.) Stackpole Books, Harrisburg, PA.

Schmidt, R. H. 1989. Animal welfare and wildlife management. Pages 468–475 *in* Transactions of the 54th North American Wildlife and Natural Resources Conference, Wildlife Management Institute, Washington.

Sinclair, A. R. E. 1977. The African Buffalo. University of Chicago Press, Chicago.

Skogland, T. 1991. What are the effects of predators on large ungulate populations? Oikos 61:401–411.

Stearns, S. C. 1976. Life history tactics: A review of the ideas. Quarterly Review of Biology 51:3–47.

Storm, G. L., and W. L. Palmer. 1995. White-tailed deer in the northeast. Pages 112–115 *in* Our Living Resources. (E. T. LaRoe, G. S. Farris, C. E. Puckett, P. D. Doran, and M. J. Mac, eds.) U.S. National Biological Service, Washington.

Tilghman, N. G. 1989. Impacts of white-tailed deer on forest regeneration in northwest Pennsylvania. Journal of Wildlife Management 53:524–532.

Travis, S. E., and P. Keim. 1995. Differentiating individuals and populations of mule deer using DNA. Journal of Wildlife Management 59:824–831.

Underwood, H. B., and W. F. Porter. 1991. Values and science: White-tailed deer management in eastern national parks. Pages 67–73 *in* Transactions of the 56th North American Wildlife and Natural Resources Conference, Wildlife Management Institute, Washington.

Wagner, F. H. 1989. American wildlife management at the crossroads. Wildlife Society Bulletin 16:354–360.

Wolgast, L. J., and J. E. Kuser. 1993. Bowhunting stabilizes a New Jersey white-tailed deer population. Bulletin of the New Jersey Academy of Sciences 38: 5–6.

Wrangham, R. W. 1980. An ecological model of female-bonded primate groups. Behaviour 75:262–300.

Williamson, L. L., and G. L. Doster. 1981. Socio-economic aspects of white-tailed deer disease. Pages 434–439 in Diseases and Parasites of White-Tailed Deer. (W. R. Davidson, ed.) Tall Timbers Research Station, Tallahassee, FL.

5 The Challenge of Conserving Large Mammals, with an Emphasis on Deer

CHRIS WEMMER

Large vertebrates are highly visible, charismatic, and usually tangible elements of ecological communities. As such, they are valued but perishable commodities. Among the 43,000 vertebrate species, this small group enjoys a disproportionate share of attention from wildlife agencies, nongovernment conservation organizations, the media, and the public. Mammals figure prominently among the charismatic large vertebrates, but in spite of their appeal, utility, and potential economic value, large mammals present as many challenges to conservation as more elusive and less-known species.

The significance of large mammals to ecology and conservation is linked to several of their characteristics.

1. As Gould (1974) noted in his study of allometry in the Irish elk *(Megaloceros giganteus),* "Size has a fascination of its own." The living large mammals of several mammalian orders represent the culmination of the evolutionary trend to larger body size (Simpson 1953) and as such have inherent scientific interest. As scientists, we try to observe scrupulous objectivity, but we also recognize that every organism has its own fascination (though it may be largely intellectual). As humans, however, we are more often awed by subjective effects, and here large body size is a powerful factor. The perceptual impact of many adaptations is all the more apparent when born of large bodies. An elephant may not be swift for its size, but its effect on the human psyche is unforgettable if it crashes through the undergrowth in your direction.

2. Large mammals evoke strong sentiments. In affluent nations, where heated debate rages over the ethics of recreational hunting, large mammals are admired for their aesthetic qualities and stir the imagination of an audience that is sympathetic to nature. In the developing nations of Latin America and Asia, they are seen as meat for the table, sources of medicine capable of curing a wide range of ailments, and competitors for food, and therefore a threat to family and community well-being. By virtue of their size, danger, and effects on crop fields, their presence is intolerable even to the most forbearing Hindus and Buddhists. Karma and fate offer little consolation to a family whose kin was killed by a tiger or rhinoceros.

3. Many large mammals are keystone species, and their removal can have major consequences on ecological communities. Large mammals that do not qualify as keystone species often have equally impressive ecological effects and, when released from predation, may wreak disastrous havoc. Many ungulates fall into this dubious category.

4. Large mammals often encompass the ideal features of "flagship species." Being charismatic, they lend themselves well to conservation organizations that emblazon the organization's logos with pandas, tigers, elephants, and whales. Considering their special attributes and aesthetic appeal, the capacity of deer to elicit public concern and support is not surprising. Even the pudu *(Pudu mephistopheles)* from the cordilleras of northern South America (which some say looks more like a degenerate bush dog than a deer) has adequate visual appeal to muster support for its own conservation.

5. Large mammals are demographically enigmatic. Although there are few *r*-selected ungulates or prolific large mammals, almost every species of ungulate exhibits at least some characteristics of *K*-selected species, such as delayed sexual maturity, long interbirth intervals, and almost universal small litter size (Eisenberg 1980). Yet, under favorable conditions, they have a robust capacity to expand into "swarms." When released into foreign environments, they often proliferate with such vigor that the term irruption (an invasion or violent entry) has been used to describe the phenomenon (Caughley 1970). Ironically, recovery efforts for endangered species rarely have the success of alien introductions.

GENERAL CONSERVATION ISSUES

Few species resist extinction with more flourish than do large mammals. In their fragmented refuges, steadily eroding to an unremitting human population, they are a clear and present danger to their human neighbors. Confrontation is inevitable. In the heat of conflict between man and beast, the lethal consequences of the beast's behavior are often unintentional, but the message is inescapable: large creatures have large effects. The challenges to conserving large mammals fall into three interrelated categories.

Containment and Protected Areas

Large mammals usually have large home ranges and often undergo seasonal movements (Harper 1955; McNab 1963; Wing and Buss 1970; Leuthold 1977; Desai 1991). The most spectacular movements—the wildebeest migrations of East Africa—have been celebrated in film, but many other ungulates, including the white-tailed deer, undergo seasonal migrations between winter and summer ranges or dry and wet season ranges (Talbot and Talbot 1963; Craighead et al. 1972; Sukumar 1992). When people convert the habitat of migratory corridors to agroscape, large mammals usually do not adjust their movement patterns to compensate for the change. They just keep coming and going the way they always have. Memories of lost habitat fade but slowly; physical barriers such as electrified high-tension wire, fences, and ditches, for example, usually have finite effects (Seidensticker 1984; Khan, n.d.). Similarly, when the home ranges of large mammals are modified by cultivation, the affected animals do not necessarily cease from using the former area (Desai 1991).

For these reasons, wildland conversion and land modifications surrounding protected areas often have serious consequences for human settlers. The Accelerated Mahaweli Development Program in Sri Lanka, funded by the World Bank, is a stunning example of the chronic tragedy that plays out as a consequence of ecologically short-sighted planning. The plan to dam the Mahaweli River and irrigate over 0.25 million ha overlooked the welfare and economic consequences of the populations of resident elephants and settlers (Jayawardene 1984, 1986, 1989, 1990). Expert consultation and costly remedial actions, including the creation of protected areas, were mandated to quell a crisis of disturbance, destruction, and death to people and elephants. The drama is still playing out, over 20 years after its inception.

Most protected areas are too small to support large populations of large mammals in the long run. Armbruster and Lande (1993) showed that only 35% of 20 parks and game reserves in East and Central Africa were larger than 2,590 km² (1,000 mi²) and that on the basis of population viability analysis, smaller areas "may need to be artificially repopulated (unless management can mitigate risk factors including droughts)" (page 607). Two thousand five hundred and ninety square kilometers was identified as the minimum habitat size for elephants.

A debate simmered for several years over the merits of various reserve designs (Meffe and Carroll 1994). To have a "single large or several small" reserves—SLOSS—was the question. Because individual species differ in range requirements, philopatry, and dispersal, there is no correct answer to the debate; what's more, in the developing world, reserve size and shape is more often determined by political and geographic factors than by design. However, the so-called rescue effect (Brown and Kodric-Brown 1977) has different consequences in affluent versus underdeveloped countries. In the suburban United States, where white-tailed deer are abundant, for example, new and uninhabited areas are repeatedly colonized by transients. Great numbers meet with misadventure and perish, especially on roads and highways, but the supply often seems almost unlimited.

The situation is much different in Latin America and Asia, where few cervids become so abundant. An exception is Madras, India, where a large population of axis deer *(Axis axis)* invades the back streets of the city to feed on garbage. Most deer biologists accept that some species, particularly browsers, live in diffuse populations, but there are many more species (mixed forage feeders) that resemble the white-tailed deer in ecology and yet are threatened with extinction. These situations beg the question of whether these species are inherently different in their biology or the context is different.

The Park–People Conflict

The attraction of wildlife to cultivated land adjacent to their sanctuaries is great, but even greater is the attraction of uncultivated land to people who live next to sanctuaries. The chemistry of this reciprocal attraction is often deadly to both sides. Large carnivores provide the most scintillating examples of conflict. Eighty-two percent of the human attacks by Asian lions take place outside India's Gir Forest, the protected area set aside for the conservation of the species. The nocturnal forays of Asian lions—some as far as 40 km beyond the park and sanctuary boundaries, compel villagers to pen their livestock nightly or even take their livestock into their homes. While penning livestock reduces overgrazing in the countryside, doing so greatly frustrates the people (Saberwal et al. 1994).

Ironically, threatened ungulate species can become local nuisances to farmers living near protected areas. The greener pastures phenomenon also applies to livestock and wildlife that mutually encroach each other's habitat. Villagers graze livestock inside the park boundaries, and in due course the boundary habitat becomes degraded, a wasteland with greatly reduced carrying capacity. Because croplands are not as easily denied to wild ungulates as they are to livestock, wild ungulate incursions increase, and the foragers are shot. Active hunting, of course, reduces the wild ungulate population to a nonthreatening size. This situation often prevails where there are populations of threatened deer.

Multiple-use buffer zones, environmental education, and regulated development of rural communities evince hope for the immediate future as a holding action, but curtailing human population growth is the only way of insuring the persistence of the ecosystems that large mammals and people depend upon for survival. Sustainable development is an oxymoron, because it is based on the premise of continuous growth. As noted by Edward Abbey, "Growth for the sake of growth is the ideology of the cancer cell."

Minimum Viable Populations

The consequences of small reserve and population size have commanded considerable attention by conservation biologists in North America (Soulé 1987). The problem is essentially how many animals can be supported in a given reserve during the leanest of times and what are the genetic and demographic consequences of different size populations. The basic demographic and genetic data do not exist for most species, let alone large mammals, and a great deal of basic ecological research remains to be done in limited time. It is not likely, however, that the needed data will be in hand before management decisions will be necessary to stave off extinction. The future of many small and isolated reserves harboring large-mammal populations is doubtful, and the persistence of many threatened species is questionable unless systems of management can be put into place that integrate discontinuous populations as metapopulations (Meffe and Carroll 1994). The administrative and logistical challenge is daunting even for zoos, which have tackled a similar problem but have the advantage of knowing what they have and where it is.

A FOCUS ON DEER

The family Cervidae (true deer) has approximately 45 species (depending on who is counting); its sister families, the musk deer (Moschidae) and the mouse deer (Tragulidae), have 4 species each. As a group, deer constitute about 26% of the 175 ungulate species and eight families.

The Geography of Conservation Knowledge

Most knowledge of deer derives from north temperate species. If one graphed scientific publication frequency by species, one would probably find that our effective knowledge of deer biology is highly skewed, with about seven to eight northern species, or 13–15%, contributing most of our information. Of the 53 deer species, the geographical distribution of 55% (i.e., 29 species) falls within 23 degrees of the equator. Of the 33 countries within this tropical range (11 Asian and 22 Latin American), only 3 (Costa Rica, Thailand, and Malaysia) would be classified as affluent or so-called developed countries. Baseline knowledge to address conservation issues is lacking in most of the tropical-range countries. One hundred and twenty-four subspecies of deer from all regions are considered not secure or free of significant threats: 58% are of uncertain status, meaning information on status is lacking, and the remaining 42% are classified as endangered, critical, or vulnerable. It is only fair to state that the status of most of the taxa are based on opinions rather than data. Thus we encounter disparities; there is an imbalance of information on the status of temperate versus tropical cervids and their relatives. We have a predominance of populations of threatened or unknown status in the tropics and well-studied temperate populations of such local abundance that they are practically considered pests.

The Geography of Status Determinations

To the deer biologist the world can be divided into those countries in which the natural legacy of species is secure or those countries in which the species are threatened with extinction. Countries with predominantly secure populations share certain features, such as regulated harvests and strong management authorities vested in provincial or national agencies. The United States, Canada, and European Commonwealth countries are in this category. Countries with predominantly threatened populations are those struggling with challenges such as high population growth, rural poverty, and political instability and are usually termed "developing." Though wildlife and national park departments and protected area networks may exist, law enforcement in these regions is usually considered marginally successful, at best.

The dividing line between these two categories is not sharp (Table 5.1) because range countries (those within the distribution of a species) vary considerably in the proportion of threatened (vulnerable, endangered, or critical) versus secure taxa. It seems, too, that the status ascribed to a spe-

TABLE 5.1

Conservation status of cervid species within two Asian countries

Status	China	India
Secure	Reeve's muntjac *(Muntiacus reevesi)*	Red muntjac *(Muntiacus muntjak vaginalis)* Sambar *(Cervus unicolor unicolor)* Axis deer *(Axis axis)*
Vulnerable	Chinese water deer *(Hydropotes inermis)* Black muntjac *(Muntiacus crinifrons crinifrons)* Thorold's deer *(Cervus albirostris)*	Hog deer *(Axis porcinus)* Barasingha *(Cervus duvauceli duvauceli)*
Endangered	Yarand stag *(Cervus elaphus yarkandensis)* Siamese brow-antlered deer *(Cervus eldi siamensis)* Sichuan sika *(Cervus nippon sichuanicus)* South China sika *(Cervus nippon kopschi)* Père David's deer *(Elaphurus davidianus)*	Montane musk deer *(Moschus* sp.) Kashmir stag *(Cervus elaphus hanglu)*
Critical	Mandarin sika *(Cervus nippon mandarinus)*	Brow-antlered deer *(Cervus eldi eldi)*
Unknown	Gansu stag *(Cervus elaphus macneillus)* Shou *(Cervus elaphus affinis)* Mongolian stag *(Cervus elaphus alashanicus)* Tufted deer *(Elaphodus cephalophus)* Fea's muntjac *(Muntjacus feai)*	None

cies comes closest to reality when its populations are fragmented, few, and small. China, with the largest complement of deer taxa, has 10 species and 13 subspecies, of which 4 are of unknown status and all the others are considered threatened. None appear to be secure. The situation in India, with 8 species and 10 subspecies, is not as alarming. Three species are secure and five are threatened. Overall, the status of Latin American species is less clear because a group of eight "mystery" species is largely unknown and variously represented in about 20 countries. This group of taxa includes the otherwise ubiquitous white-tailed deer and the pudu.

Trends in Population Endangerment of Deer

Some species, now so common as to have become nuisances, were in the past locally extirpated by hunting. The white-tailed deer, the European red deer *(Cervus elaphus),* and several other temperate species are well-known examples. These very same species in other parts of their range are (or may be) seriously threatened. If one dares to generalize about cervid endangerment, it would be that concentrate selectors of tree and shrub foliage and intermediate foragers, or mixed browse–grazers (Hofmann and Stewart 1972), show the greatest resilience to threats of habitat conversion (Table 5.2). Concentrate selectors, such as moose *(Alces alces),* sambar *(Cervus unicolor),* roe deer (*Capreolus* spp.), muntjac *(Muntiacus muntjak),* and perhaps even the Latin American brocket deer (*Mazama* spp.), have wide-ranging distributions and seem able to persist in disturbed habitats. The grazing deer on the other hand seem much more vulnerable to habitat modification. In Latin America this group contains the pampas deer *(Ozotoceros bezoarticus)* and swamp deer *(Blastocerus dichotomus),* whereas the Asian counterparts are the barasingha *(Cervus duvauceli)* and Eld's deer *(Cervus eldi).* The extinct Schomburgk's deer *(Cervus schomburgki)* was probably a grazer (related to the barasingha); the grazing Père David's deer *(Elaphurus davidianus)* long ago went extinct through most of its range.

Small-bodied grazing species, such as the hog deer *(Axis porcinus)* and water deer *(Hydropotes inermis),* seem less vulnerable, possibly because of their secretive habits. There also appear to be differences in tem-

TABLE 5.2

Foraging modes of select cervid species

Concentrate feeders on tree and shrub foliage	Mixed browser-grazer	Grazers
Sambar	Mule and white-tailed deer	Pampas deer
(Cervus unicolor)	*(Odocoileus* spp.)	*(Ozotoceros bezoarticus)*
Muntjac	Sika deer	Barasingha
(Muntiacus muntjak)	*(Cervus nippon)*	*(Cervus duvauceli)*
Moose	Red deer	Eld's deer
(Alces alces)	*(Cervus elaphus)*	*(Cervus eldi)*
Roe deer	Axis deer	Schomburgk's deer
(Capreolus spp.)	*(Axis axis)*	*(Cervus schomburgki)*
Brocket deer	Rusa deer	
(Mazama spp.)	*(Cervus timorensis)*	

perament. More open-habitat species seem to be timorous, high strung, and more dependent on flight as an antipredator ploy, whereas woodland species, particularly the smaller ones, seem more placid and prone to slink into the undergrowth. There seems to be a pattern, but the extent to which these behavioral characteristics are correlates of nutritional adaptations remains to be tested.

Last, mixed browser–grazers seem to be more adaptable to human populations and seem able to benefit from human landscapes. The sub-urban populations of white-tailed deer in North America have their counterpart in the axis deer of India, where, in the sweltering city of Madras, large numbers of this species invade the back streets nightly to consume refuse. But these thoughts are academic and don't get to the heart of the matter, which is identifying the causes of population rareness.

THREATS TO SPECIES SURVIVAL

Identifying the threats to declining wildlife populations is an enigmatic practice, often based more on opinions and impressions than on facts and data. Lurking in the backwaters of international conservation is an unmistakable attitude of antiscience—vestiges of imperial tradition, good-old-boy networks, and the protectionism of the new guard steeped in those traditions. The argument goes something like this: "The problem is immediate, and there is no time to do research" or "We need park guards, rangers, and beat officers who will protect the population; we can't afford the luxury of studying it." As time passes and the protection strategy falls short of the mark, we find we still don't understand the ecology of the species any better. Progress in single-species conservation is almost invariably slow unless there is an integrated multidisciplinary strategy.

In considering approaches to international wildlife conservation, it is instructive to focus on the differences dividing affluent and developing nations. Protected areas in affluent nations are relatively secure, and wildlife is managed and studied. Conservation biology—the multidisciplinary application of biology, sociology, and economics to the solution of conservation problems—plays a small but certain role in these countries. Its practitioners have strong academic roots and faith in the scientific method. In the developing world most conservationists have their roots in government bodies, as well as the military, business, or international organizations and agencies. It comes as little surprise that their perspective bears a strong resemblance to the resource conservation ethic that emerged in the United States earlier this century (Nash 1982). They advocate multidisciplinary solutions, but utilization is the bottom line, and science with its theoretical underpinnings is not a driving force. However, both approaches share certain beliefs: for example, the intrinsic value of wilderness for human welfare.

Conservation biology is concerned particularly with scientific analysis of problems, whereas developing world conservation is driven by the application of more traditional solutions. Most western practitioners of conservation in the developing world find themselves in a time warp in which research data analysis and the application of theory is viewed as "out of touch."

Science in the developing world often takes a back seat to conservation problem solving. Calls for conservation of large mammals are almost always based on inadequate ecological information. In general, prescriptions for conservation of large mammals bypass investigations of ecology, emphasize mitigation of often unverified threats, lean heavily on the expertise of western conservationists, and don't come to terms with developing local institutional capacity. Western conservationists' preachings on maximization of effective population size, minimum variance in population growth rate, and rapid fixation of viable population size, are lost on the unanointed congregations. Even if the presiding officials are philosophical converts, implementation is doomed unless a very different approach is adopted than the one usually taken—the production of a plan with limited follow-up.

THE PUZZLE OF OVERABUNDANCE

These issues of conservation biology often occur under very different circumstances when landscape and regulatory protection provide localized sanctuaries and deer populations—of both secure and threatened species—become locally abundant. Doubting Thomases ask to see the data attributing abundance, which is usually lacking because deer population sizes are not commonly estimated using valid methods. For both threatened and abundant species, when crop and property damage is reported, the validity of the complaint, identity of the culprit, and extent of damage is also questioned. When data and solid evidence do exist, their accuracy and validity are scorned by rival interest groups. Wildlife–human conflicts demand solutions now, and the aggrieved interest groups lack the patience to wait for advice borne on the slow and creaky wheels of science.

There can be no doubt that some, particularly specialized, deer species are unable to adapt to the kind of environmental change brought on by development. But what about the others? Would abundant species, such as the white-tailed deer of southern Texas, thrive if translocated to Argentina or Uruguay, where the pampas deer hangs on to life so tenuously? Would pampas deer recover their numbers if translocated to Texas? If Occam's razor is applied to the full range of explanatory hypotheses, populations of most threatened deer seem to be suffering from nothing more than intense human predation and competition. Removing these constraints, as is done in many protected areas of developed countries, may result in overabundance at the local geographical scale.

The North American rural versus urban dichotomy in wildlife attitudes is mirrored on a larger scale by North–South contrasts in conservation perspective. There are differences in defining the problems, attributing causes, and proposing solutions. In both microcosms, proximity to nature reinforces a utilitarian ethic of the "here and now." To people of the land, the conservation and development proposals of experts sound impractical and idealistic. In affluent societies, large-mammal charisma makes conservation fund-raising easy but guarantees strong opposition to actions seen as harmful to individual animals.

The final irony is that managing abundant wildlife is as daunting a challenge as managing threatened wildlife. There are times when science and technology seem unable to surmount human beliefs and attitudes. Factual information, as found in the following chapters of this volume, is a vital ingredient to bring about change, but dissemination of the information must be appropriately packaged for more audiences than have been traditionally addressed.

REFERENCES CITED

Ambruster, P., and R. Lande. 1993. A population viability analysis for African elephant (Loxodonta africana): How big should reserves be? Conservation Biology 7:602–610.

Brown, J. H., and A. Kodric-Brown. 1977. Turnover rates in insular biogeography: Effect of immigration on extinction. Ecology 58:445–449.

Caughley, G. 1970. Eruption of ungulate populations with emphasis on Himalayan Thar in New Zealand. Ecology 51:51–72.

Craighead, J. J., G. Atwell, and B. W. O'Gara. 1972. Elk Migrations in and near Yellowstone National Park. Wildlife Monographs 33, The Wildlife Society, Bethesda, MD.

Desai, A. A. 1991. The home range of elephants and its implications for management of the Mudumalai Wildlife Sanctuary, Tamil Nadu. Journal of the Bombay Natural History Society 88 (2): 145–156.

Eisenberg, J. F. 1980. The Mammalian Radiations. University of Chicago Press, Chicago.

Gould, S. J. 1974. The origin and function of bizarre structures, antler size and skull size in the Irish elk, *Megaloceros giganteus*. Evolution 28:191–220.

Harper, F. 1955. The Barren Ground Caribou of Keewatin. University of Kansas, Museum of Natural History Miscellaneous Publication 6.

Hofmann, R. R., and D. R. M. Stewart. 1972. Grazer or browser: A classification based on the stomach structure and feeding habits of East African ruminants. Mammalia 36:226–240.

Jayawardene, J. 1984. Elephant conservation amidst development. Tigerpaper 11 (4): 21–26.

Jayawardene, J. 1986. Elephant conservation amidst development (Part II). Tigerpaper 13 (3): 4–8.

Jayawardene, J. 1989. Elephant conservation amidst development (Part III). Tigerpaper 16 (2): 11–21.

Jayawardene, J. 1990. Elephant conservation amidst development (Part IV). Tigerpaper 17 (2): 16–21.

Khan, M. M. No date. The Malayan Elephant, a Species Plan for Its Conservation. Department of Wildlife and National Parks, Peninsular Malaysia.

Leuthold, W. 1977. African Ungulates, a Comparative Review of Their Ethology and Behavioral Ecology. Springer-Verlag, New York.

McNab, B. K. 1963. Bioenergetics and the determination of home range size. American Naturalist 97:130–140.

Meffe, G. K., and C. R. Carroll. 1994. Principles of Conservation Biology. Sinauer Associates, Sunderland, MA.

Nash, S. 1982. Wilderness and the American Mind. Yale University Press, New Haven, CT.

Saberwal, V. K., J. P. Gibbs, R. Chellam, and A. J. T. Johnsingh. 1994. Lion–human conflict in the Gir Forest, India. Conservation Biology 8:501–507.

Seidensticker, J. 1984. Managing Elephant Depredation in Agriculture and Forestry Projects. World Bank, Washington.

Simpson, G. G. 1953. The Major Features of Evolution. Columbia University Press, New York.

Soulé, M. R., ed. 1987. Viable Populations for Conservation. Cambridge University Press, New York.

Sukumar, R. 1992. The Asian Elephant: Ecology and Management. Cambridge University Press, Cambridge, United Kingdom.

Talbot, L. M., and M. H. Talbot, 1963. The Wildebeest in Western Masailand, East Africa. Wildlife Monographs 12, The Wildlife Society, Bethesda, MD.

Wing, L. D., and I. O. Buss. 1970. Elephants and Forests. Wildlife Monographs 19, The Wildlife Society, Bethesda, MD.

PART TWO

Population Effects of High-Density Deer Herds

6 Irruptive Behavior in Ungulates

DALE R. MCCULLOUGH

Overpopulation of ungulates is a common problem confronting nature conservation (Jewell and Holt 1981). Feeding by ungulates often heavily affects vegetation near the ground and indirectly affects a number of animal species dependent upon this vegetation. Commonly, these effects result in local extinction of some species of plants and animals and cause shifts in the species composition of the community (Leopold 1943; Klein 1981).

Of great concern in North America is the overabundance of deer (*Odocoileus* spp.) in parks, particularly in the eastern United States (Warren 1991; Porter 1992; Brown and Veirs 1993; Liberman, in press). Original, large natural predators of these communities, such as wolves *(Canis lupus)* and mountain lions *(Felis concolor),* have long been extirpated from most of these areas because of their incompatibility with human activities. When protected from human hunting, deer populations have commonly exhibited explosive population increases, and this phenomenon has usually been called irruptions.

The term "irruption" as used by Leopold (1943) is used here in preference to "eruption," as used by Caughley (1970). I agree with Caughley that eruption is a more descriptive word, but precedence should be followed. Ecology is full of poorly chosen terms, but we use them because the first author proposed them for that use. At least one dictionary (Neufeldt and Guralnik 1988) lists Leopold's (1943) definition. An irruption is defined as a sudden, explosive increase in population numbers, which if unchecked, will exceed the capacity of the resource base to sustain the population. Irruptions occur under circumstances in which a population of ungulates is at low density in favorable habitat conditions and lives in the absence of effective controlling factors. This circumstance can be created by a single, or combination of, variables. Earlier attempts in the wildlife literature to attribute irruptions to a single, predictable variable were misplaced and diverted attention from understanding the phenomenon first and then identifying causality.

Any number of factors can contribute to irruptive behavior. One set of factors works by increasing the carrying capacity of the habitat for the irruptive species. Sudden creation of habitat for subclimax species of ungulates often leads to Irruptive behavior. The habitat may be altered by natural (fire, windstorm, or flood) or anthropogenic (fire, logging, or cultivation) causes. Production of agricultural crops is a major contributor to irruptive behavior by white-tailed deer, and artificial feeding in the absence of habitat changes can lead to the same end.

Another set of factors contributes to irruptive behavior by reducing mortality. The major influences are reduction or elimination of predators or human hunting. Theoretically, control of pathogens and parasites could have the same effect.

Finally, irruptive behavior can be induced by confinement of populations, which restricts or eliminates dispersal and interrupts the source-sink dynamics typical in a larger, more complex environment. Natural confinement occurs when species reach previously unoccupied islands or circumvented barriers created by mountains, rivers, ice fields, or deserts to reach new habitat from which dispersal is restricted because of the natural barriers to movement. Confinement is caused anthropogenically by transplanting species to islands, isolating patches of habitat by development, and building barrier fences.

There is little question that in the modern world, anthropogenic causes are the major source of irruptive behavior of ungulate populations. But having said that, it is important to recognize that irruptions of ungulates are not exclusively a modern phenomenon and that irruptions likely occurred prior to the emergence of technological humankind. Islands and barriers have always existed, and zoogeography is replete with cases of isolated distributions. The Pleistocene was a time of particularly great upheaval. Its alternating glacial and interglacial periods produced sea level changes of up to 200 m and dramatic shifts in climate and distribution of communities that would have altered carrying capacity and population distribution drastically. Extinction and speciation were common because subpopulations were isolated from the parental population and populations were confined to relict areas.

Furthermore, the apparent stability of the current interglacial period is to a large extent an illusion created by the overselling by ecologists and environmentalists of the quasi-religious myth of the "balance of nature." The paradigm that nature has created stable equilibria which humans upset by unwise extraction and alteration is appealing. It harmonizes nicely with the "paradise lost" concept that is at the root of some religions. In addition to alienation from God (fallen angels), humankind was also alienated from nature (driven from the Garden of Eden). Perhaps the idealization of balance in nature subconsciously arose from these religious teachings of our early upbringing.

Certainly humankind has subjected the planet to extractions and alterations that are frequently excessive and unwise. But it is not necessary for nature to have been in equilibrium for that to be the case (although it may have been a necessary construct to convince a naive public that environmental problems were real). Recently many authors have questioned the stable equilibrium paradigm and have documented the prevalence of natural disturbances in shaping current natural communities (e.g., Sousa 1984; Pickett and White 1985; Whitlock 1993; Reice 1994; Russell 1994). It would be better if we recognized that change is ubiquitous, with only frequency, amplitude, and cause as variables of interest. Recognizing such would release us from the fetters of concepts such as subclimax and climax, stable versus unstable, gradual versus punctuated, and so on, that call for placing arbitrary, delimiting lines in time and space for processes that are occasionally discrete but typically continuous. Such demarcations may be useful for categorizing information for human comprehension over time (e.g., eras, periods, and epochs) or space (e.g., vegetation maps, rainfall isohyets, and species distributions), but these abstractions of the human mind to organize knowledge should not be confused with the realities in nature. They lead to biases by causing us to interpret nature according to what we expect to see, rather than maintain a skeptical attitude that requires rigorous hypothesis testing. And although at times nature is harmonious, at others it is abrupt, capricious, and destructive.

Natural disturbance processes in the past created the circumstances that fostered irruptive behavior of ungulates in the absence of human influence. Thus, the phenomenon we are discussing is not necessarily recent in origin or always attributable to human actions. Humans did not create the underlying population behavior; they only created the circumstances under which the behavior may be expressed.

These issues have important consequences for management policies in response to irruptions. If humans are responsible for an irruption of an ungulate population, then humans would bear clear responsibility to intervene to prevent environmental degradation due to anthropogenic causes. Conversely, if nature is responsible for an ungulate irruption, then the responsibility of humans to intervene is less clear. If some human value in a managed environment is involved (e.g., damage to forests or crops or hazard to vehicle traffic), the decision is reasonably obvious. However, if the irruption occurs in a park where the predominant human value is naturalness, the best course of action is problematic. If the irruption were caused by past actions of humans, intervention could be viewed as necessary mitigation for past human influences. Indeed, it could be argued that humans had an obligation to intervene to protect naturalness.

Conversely, if the irruption were caused by natural events, preserving naturalness would require humans not to intercede. Nature's experiment should be allowed to proceed even if effects on other elements of the ecosystem are upsetting to human sensibilities (Sinclair 1983). For example, there is continuing debate about the need for intervention in the herd of north Yellowstone elk *(Cervus elaphus canadensis)* in Yellowstone National Park, whose numbers are purported to be inducing changes in the vegetation (Sinclair 1983; Boyce 1991; Anonymous 1992; Porter 1992; Wagner et al. 1995). Although such cases are complex, an important first step is clear understanding of irruptive behavior and its consequences on the habitat in which it occurs.

In this chapter I will first explore the historical roots of the concepts of irruptions and the theoretical and empirical support of these concepts. I will next present three case histories of deer populations that show continuing tendencies for irruptive behavior. Finally, I will discuss our understanding of irruptive behavior and how we might clarify the issues it presents.

CONCEPTS OF IRRUPTIVE BEHAVIOR

Leopold (1943) was the first to conceptualize formally the irruptive phenomenon. He relied on early evidence from the mule deer *(Odocoileus hemionus)* population on the Kaibab Plateau (KP) in northern Arizona (Rasmussen 1941) and from white-tailed deer on the George Reserve (GR) in southeastern Michigan. Leopold's (1943) interpretation of these cases was put forward soon after the original results were published and was taken directly from his classroom notes in a wildlife ecology course offered at the University of Wisconsin in about 1942. He envisioned a population released from previous controls (KP) or introduced into a new environment (GR) that subsequently increased at nearly the theoretical potential until carrying capacity *(K)* was exceeded. Because of severe impacts upon their plant support base, these populations crashed (KP) or were expected to crash without control by hunting (GR). Damage to the vegetation was (or would be) expressed as the loss of *K* following the crash, and subsequently the population would grow to an equilibrium at a substantially lower number than the first population peak.

Results from KP were purported to show such a progression of events, and Leopold (1943) attributed the initiation of the process to the removal of large predators (wolves, mountain lions, and coyotes [*Canis latrans*]) by humans. For GR, only the initial increase (until 1933) was documented at the time. All subsequent projection of population numbers for GR was the prediction of Leopold (1943).

Leopold's (1943) paradigm for irruptions was widely accepted in the young field of ecology and adopted in several early text books (Allee et al. 1949; Davis and Golley 1963). Predator removal was seen as the critical variable in producing irruptions of ungulates, and this view was reinforced by Hairston et al. (1960) in their "the world is green" view of trophic dynamics, in which predators are the key to control of herbivores.

In an influential paper, Caughley (1970) showed how the case of the KP irruption evolved from some rough guesses of deer numbers to a series of mythical data points that gave undeserved credibility to the example as presented in ecology texts. Apparently the authors of these texts did not check the original sources, of which Rasmussen (1941) was the principal one, or evaluate the quality of the estimates of population size. These estimates were essentially guesses made by managers and were not based on sampling or surveys of the deer population. Perhaps it can be accepted on professional judgment alone that the population increased, peaked, and then declined, but the absolute numbers are without foundation. At best, the empirical data for the KP deer irruption were few and weak.

Caughley (1970) further pointed out that Leopold's (1943) attribution of the irruption to the removal of predators was complicated by the concurrent reduction of competition by removal of domestic livestock. Thus, the variable or combination of variables that contributed to the irruption could not be sorted out. Note, however, that Caughley presented no evidence that predators were not the sole cause; he only raised alternative hypotheses. In fact, none of the competing hypotheses could be rejected nor was correlative evidence presented to favor one hypothesis over any other.

Caughley (1970) rightly deflated an elaborate paradigm that had gained credibility by being repeated. Caughley, an exceptionally clear thinker, was good at this. May (1994), in a retrospective review of Caughley's career (Caughley died in February 1994), lauded him for exposing the KP irruption.

One would expect that having learned the lessons from the KP case, the field would proceed with development of a new paradigm (or modify the old paradigm) based on sound empirical evidence. This did not happen. Indeed, it can be argued that we have created a new myth of irruptions that differs from the old myth only in that it is based on no data whatsoever.

Caughley's (1970) paper is usually credited with firmly establishing the actual behavior of irruptive populations (May 1994). May restates the conventional view of irruptive population behavior to the effect that a low initial population increases rapidly, exceeds carrying capacity, crashes to a lower level, and then recovers and fluctuates around a size lower than the peak numbers. It should be noted that Caughley's (1976a) view differed from Leopold's only in dampened oscillation rather than growth to stability at reduced K following the initial crash. May (1994) further notes that Caughley believed that irruptions caused by secondary factors, such as removal of predators, were significantly less pronounced than those arising from new introductions. Finally, May stated that these concepts were based upon a "wealth of carefully analyzed empirical examples, and well within a broad theoretical framework." I agree with May about grounding in a theoretical framework, but I do not believe the empirical evidence is nearly as strong as implied.

It is not my intention to write a critical review of Caughley's (1970) paper. I fully agree with May (1994) that this was a landmark paper, a classic in the field. Nevertheless, it is pertinent to the issues here to remind ourselves that Caughley did not present direct empirical evidence of an irruption. He presented demographic (life table) data on four populations of introduced tahr *(Hemitragus jemlahicus)* in New Zealand that showed different rates of population growth. These differences were consistent with Riney's (1964) hypothesized expanding wavefront of irruptive behavior away from the point of introduction (which Caughley supported). In fact, the actual expansion of tahr was not documented, and the timing of the wavefront was Caughley's interpretation (essentially an argument), which he continually referred to as an hypothesis.

The circumstances of the tahr expansion would allow many alternative interpretations. The population at the introduction site existed for over 60 years before Caughley's study, during which time many events could have transpired. Of the three populations proposed to represent a wavefront of expansion from the site of introduction, one was in the opposite direction from the other two. This population was subjected to heavy hunting. The methods of analysis that Caughley (1970) applied to each population (time-specific life tables) are fraught with error, as Caughley himself was well aware (Caughley 1966, 1977). Caughley (1970) continually referred to "the hypothesis," and made numerous statements, such as "I would like to see our observations checked, preferably by someone skeptical of the hypothesis" (page 69); "The figured trend of density is not accurate" (page 70); and "While being unwilling to mount a spirited defense of this kind of estimate" (page 70). From personal conversation with Caughley I know he believed that his interpretation of irruptive behavior rested primarily on models and that he had misgivings about such models, including his own (Caughley 1976a, 1976b, 1977).

There is general acceptance in the field of the initial irruptive behavior; that is, a population at low level increases rapidly to a peak unsupportable by the vegetation, and a crash follows. However, there is disagreement over the variables that produce such irruptions, whether irruptions are greater for initial introductions than for secondary factors such as removal of predators, and whether subsequent recovery comes to dynamic equilibrium at a lower population level following an irruption. Cases such as reindeer *(Rangifer tarandus)* introduced to St. Matthew Island (Klein 1968) and South Georgia Island (Leader-Williams et al. 1989) are evidence of the buildup and crash of ungulates. However, postcrash population behavior has not been reported. Caughley (1976b) presented some evidence that domestic sheep introduced to Australia followed this irruptive paradigm, but it must be recognized that the data supporting the case are not strong and that husbandry, droughts, market forces, and other variables complicate the interpretation that sheep numbers conform to a vegetation–herbivore interaction.

Mathematical modeling of irruptions began with Caughley (1976a), and he presented the same model with permutations in later work (Caughley 1976b, 1977). Although this model was informed by Caughley's experience, it was not based upon empirical results from any given study. This model still forms the mental framework by which most ungulate ecologists think about irruptive behavior. McCullough (1979: Figure 11.2, page 169) produced a graphically modeled "irruption" and "recovery to a lower level" for the GR white-tailed deer herd. Although part of this example was based on data, the hypothesized crash and recovery were not. The crash and recovery experiment was not conducted on GR. Subsequently, this example was modified and presented in a basic textbook (Odum 1983: Figures 3–19, page 158). The evolution of these ideas through repetition is curiously similar to the KP case debunked by Caughley (1970) but with the difference this time of being based on no data at all.

Clearly the concept of ungulate irruptions (and their consequences) has a strong intuitive appeal, and it has prompted considerable theoretical and practical interest. But are we making progress? An elegant model in the absence of empirical support may well be fiction. This is a particular hazard when the fiction has intuitive appeal, and it teaches a moral of which many approve: (1) that humans upset a natural balance by removing predators or by introducing species where they do not belong; (2) that nature did not behave in this manner; and (3) that irruptive problems can be corrected only by intelligent intervention of humans.

THE FRAMING OF QUESTIONS

Paradigms (and often the models derived from them) are explanations of the interaction of complex variables and, as such, are not directly subject to rejection by single tests (McCullough 1992). Statement of hypotheses that derive from a paradigm reduces the paradigm to predictions that can be tested. The value of deconstruction in this fashion is the power to reject, a more powerful scientific method (Platt 1969; Romesburg 1981) than simply concluding that a time series of population point estimates "fits" a paradigm.

Rarely is a paradigm found to be totally lacking in value once empirical results allow testing of specific hypotheses. Consequently, complete discarding of a paradigm is rare. Commonly they evolve and become more elaborate as it becomes apparent that they are too simply constructed and that more variables must be included to account for the complex behavior observed in nature.

There are two needs in order to make progress. First, the paradigm needs to be decomposed into its separate elements, and these elements need to be restated as a series of testable hypotheses that are subject to possible rejection. This process reveals the complexity often contained in even simple models. Second, these hypotheses need to be tested by empirical research. Preferably this research would be by purposeful design. However, awareness of the hypotheses may allow natural perturbations, or artificial perturbations for other purposes, to be studied to the same end. Establishing the validity of paradigms by this process is slow and runs counter to demands for quick answers. Unfortunately quick answers may well be wrong, and uncertainty leads to continuing debates and a wide-spread perception that the field is based on shaky foundations.

There is little debate about the characteristics of the first irruptive sequence. The major questions are about the second irruptive sequence. What are the consequences to the population and habitat of having undergone the first irruptive sequence? Additionally, what are the continuing characteristics of the third, fourth, nth sequences? These questions pertain to the longer-term trends of irruptive behavior. Do irruptions eventually lead to stable equilibria, continue unabated, or attain some intermediate state?

The irruptive sequences of a hypothetical ungulate population are shown in Figure 6.1. Observe first the large issues. Three major paradigms are presented in Figure 6.1. The dotted line represents the conventional view as espoused by Caughley (1976a). It postulates a first irruption (shown as a solid line labeled 1A–E for all three paradigms), followed by a recovery to a reduced carrying capacity through a dampened oscillation to K. This is probably the predominant paradigm among ungulate biologists today. I will refer to this paradigm as the irruption, dampened oscillation to lowered K model (IDOLK).

The second paradigm (dashed line in Figure 6.1) was the Leopold (1943) view of irruptions. Although he did not include a second irruptive sequence in his diagrams, it is clear from his writings in this and later papers that he viewed the second sequence as likely to lead to a stable (give or take some environmental noise) equilibrium at a lowered K. This paradigm I will refer to as the irruption, stable lowered K model (ISLK).

A third paradigm has been put forward by Clutton-Brock and his colleagues (Clutton-Brock et al. 1991; Clutton-Brock 1994) for Soay sheep on Hirta Island in the St. Kilda Islands. This case involves repeated irruptions and crashes with no decline in K. This paradigm is shown in Figure 6.1 by the solid line and will be referred to as the continual irruptive, constant K model (CICK).

Other permutations could be proposed (e.g., gradually declining K following second and subsequent irruptive sequences), but this set is sufficient to illustrate the important questions about irruptive behavior of ungulates and allow framing hypothesis tests that will reject one or more of the alternatives in a given case.

Now consider the detailed difference shown in Figure 6.1. The first irruptive sequence is labeled with "1's." The first sequence is characterized by three important intervals in time, indicated by vertical dashed lines and Roman numerals, and two interesting population point values, the peak population (1C) and the population at the end of the first crash (1E). The

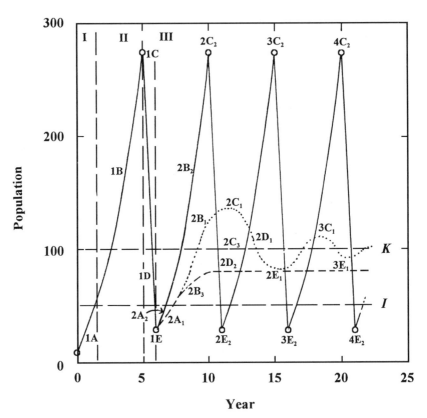

FIGURE 6.1. Schematic irruptive behavior of a hypothetical ungulate population. The three major paradigms are illustrated: Caughley (1976a) in dotted line, Leopold (1943) in dashed line, and Clutton-Brock et al. (1991) in solid line. Successive irruptions are labeled 1, 2, 3, and 4. The three sequences of an irruption are labeled I, II, and III in the first irruptive event, which is similar in all three paradigms, although Caughley's model yields curved trajectories more like that shown for subsequent irruptions. Timing is similar to the first irruption for the subsequent irruptive sequence of the Clutton-Brock et al. (1991) paradigm but variable for the other two. Label 1A is the initial growth below the inflection point *(I)* if the population were going to show logistic growth to carrying capacity *(K)* equal to 100; 1B is the subsequent growth to the peak population; 1C is the peak population; 1D is the the population crash phase; and 1E is the population low following the crash. Comparable points in the second and subsequent irruptive events are labeled 2 and 3, with the same letters. Models are indicated by subscripts (1 is Caughley, 2 is Clutton-Brock et al., and 3 is Leopold). See text for further explanation.

initial population at time 0 is another interesting point. In irruptive models it is relatively low, and in Figure 6.1, I arbitrarily selected 10.

Consider the first irruptive sequence. Time intervals I and II are characterized by exponential population growth, 1A and 1B. The reason for splitting the growth into two segments is the seldom-recognized phenomenon that the decoupling of herbivore population growth from the capacity of the vegetation for dynamic renewal to support the herbivore population's continued growth occurs at the expected inflection point (I in Figure 6.1), a point that does not occur with irruptive behavior (see McCullough 1987a: Figure 7). Thus, the time lag between dynamics of the ungulate population and dynamics of vegetation precedes the reaching of K. Caughley's (1976a) vegetation–herbivore dynamic model shows the earlier decoupling, but most ungulate biologists have a mental model with a more stable K.

Because the realized growth rate, $\bar{r}$, of the irruptive population does not decrease predictably at the expected inflection point of $K/2$, growth continues, and $\bar{r}$ on N, population size, has a different slope from that assumed by the logistic model. Consequently, these distinctions are shown in Figure 6.1 with reference to the inflection point ($I = 50$), given that K is 100 in this hypothetical case. The relationship of $\bar{r}$ on N with reference to I is important to appreciating the different paradigms about behavior of an ungulate population following the first irruptive sequence.

The major distinguishing feature of IDOLK and ISLK from CICK is the unaltered K in the latter. Lowered K over its value prior to the impact of the irruption for IDOLK and ISLK is obvious in the lowering of subsequent values of C, the peak population in Figure 6.1. However, the reduction of K is related also to a reduced $\bar{r}$ in the second and subsequent irruptive sequences. Consequently, the duration of the second and later irruptive sequences is longer in IDOLK and ISLK but remains unchanged in CICK. Because the length of the three intervals of an irruption is a variable for IDOLK and ISLK, they are not shown by vertical dashed lines or Roman numerals for second or later irruptive sequences in Figure 6.1. However, comparable points at different time intervals between the three models are given by peaks (C's) and lows (E's) for each model.

THE TESTING OF IRRUPTIVE HYPOTHESES

Figure 6.1 allows hypotheses to be stated in ways that can test various characteristics of these three major models to reject alternatives. In this section I will state the major questions about irruptive behavior and suggest the hypothesis test(s) that would apply. Ordinarily, the null hypothesis would be tested. However, for clarity of presentation, the hypothesis will be stated favorably to a given question, which sometimes results in the null hypothesis being the alternate hypothesis.

Question 1. *Is Leopold (1943) correct in his assumption that the overshooting of carrying capacity in the first irruption results in the lowering of K in subsequent population responses?*

Question 2. *Is Caughley (1970) correct that initial irruptions are more extreme than those produced by removal of competitors, predators, or other secondary events?*

I assume this difference is due to factors other than the initial population size being typically lower than the level to which the population crashes. It reflects a loss of K due to the ungulate population's impact on the habitat. The following hypotheses can be constructed.

Hypothesis 1. *The realized growth rate ($\bar{r}$) of the initial irruptive sequence is greater than those of the second or later irruptive sequences (i.e., in Figure 6.1, 1A > 2A$_1$ or 2B$_1$ and 1B > 2B$_1$ or 2B$_3$).*

Hypothesis 2. *The peak numbers reached in the initial irruptive sequence are greater than those reached in the second or later sequences (i.e., in Figure 6.1, 1C > 2C$_1$ and 2C$_3$).*

The same hypothesis test will address both questions 1 and 2. If the previous effects of ungulate feeding on the vegetation have been detrimental, then both the population growth rate and the population size achieved should be lower following the initial irruption. Although the second question may appear to be different, it becomes apparent that question 2 is subsumed by question 1 when the hypothesis needed to test both turns out to be the same. Questions 1 and 2 can be addressed by either hypothesis 1 or 2 alone; however, the strength of the test is greater if both hypotheses are tested together.

Question 3. *Can irruptive sequences repeat without loss of carrying capacity as proposed by Clutton-Brock et al. (1991) and Clutton-Brock (1994)?*

The following three hypotheses can be drawn.

Hypothesis 3. There is no difference in realized growth rate ($\bar{r}$) between successive irruptive sequences (i.e., in Figure 6.1, there is no difference between 1A, $2A_2$, . . . , $2A_n$ or 1B, $2B_2$, . . . , nB_2). This is the null hypothesis of hypothesis 1.

Hypothesis 4. There is no difference in peak population numbers achieved in successive irruptions (i.e., in Figure 6.1, 1C = $2C_2$, . . . , nC_2). This is the null hypothesis of hypothesis 2.

Hypothesis 5. There is no difference in the low population reached in successive irruptions (i.e., in Figure 6.1, 1E = $2E_2$, . . . , nE_2). This is a null hypothesis.

If only two irruptive sequences are observed, $\bar{r}$ (being an average) is probably a better measure than are the fixed values C or E, and all vary in response to local environmental stochasticity. Variance in $\bar{r}$ is dampened by the particular sequence of multiple years required to produce an irruption, whereas C and E are point values obtained only once in multiple years (4 years in Figure 6.1). Local conditions, particularly in the year prior to the peak, can significantly alter the value of C. Furthermore, C and E may be inversely related. A particularly great C results in a greater crash to a lower E, and vice versa. Consequently, for few irruptive sequences, no difference in $\bar{r}$ (hypothesis 3) is the strongest hypothesis test. Tests of hypotheses 4 and 5 are dependent on longer series of irruptions so that variance can be assessed. This leads to an additional hypothesis about question 3.

Hypothesis 6. There is no difference in the time interval between successive irruptions (the period is constant).

This is a null hypothesis, and it is illustrated in Figure 6.1 by the time between 1C, $2C_2$, . . . , nC_2 and 1E, $2E_2$, . . . , nE_2 being 4 years. Once again, because of local environmental stochasticity, and consequent variation in $\bar{r}$, the period between irruptions is not likely to be strictly constant. Greater amplitude of the peak and crash would be expected to extend the time of the irruption, much like starting from a low initial population took 5 years to peak rather than the subsequent 4 years in Figure 6.1. Similarly, a low peak and high population following the crash could lead to a 3-year interval. A longer time series would be required to evaluate if there was a predictable interval between irruptions.

That irruptive behavior of an ungulate population is sustained shows that there has been no reduction in habitat quality as measured by K. It does not say that there is no change in the habitat. There well may be elimination of some plant species and shift in species, age, or size-class composition of others. These changes may be detrimental to other values or bad by other standards. However, our concern here is confined to sustainability of the ungulate population as reflected by numerical responses only. Changes to the habitat are of concern but are a different problem (Caughley 1981).

Question 4. *After the first irruption, do populations show dampened oscillations to a constant K (Caughley 1976a) or do they achieve equilibrium at a reduced K as implied by Leopold (1943) and as commonly believed by ungulate biologists? Of course, equilibrium does not mean perfect stability but relatively small variation around the mean due to environmental stochasticity.*

In order to test this question, it is necessary to first reject one or more hypotheses under question 3, showing that the population does not continue to irrupt unabated. Once that is done, the following hypotheses can be tested.

Hypothesis 7. *On the second irruptive sequence, the population reaches a dynamic equilibrium.*

If hypothesis 7 is rejected, and the population continues to fluctuate over broad ranges, the following hypotheses can be tested.

Hypothesis 8. *The peak population becomes smaller with each subsequent irruptive sequence.*

Hypothesis 9. *The low population becomes greater with each subsequent irruptive sequence.*

If hypotheses 8 and 9 are tested simultaneously and accepted (i.e., the null hypothesis is rejected), the population peaks and lows would necessarily be converging towards equilibrium. If only one of the hypotheses were tested, it would be necessary to follow the irruptive sequences until equilibrium was achieved. Failure to reject the null hypothesis is a strong test only with sufficient statistical power (Peterman 1990), but other hypothesis tests suffer similar sample size problems.

Particularly troublesome is comparison of single values of peak population numbers in successive irruptive sequences, which inherently lack a measure of variance and are not amenable to statistical tests. Nevertheless, it must be borne in mind that variation in the peak values needs to be weighed against the purported reduction in K due to prior irruptive sequences. If the effects of prior irruptive sequences do not exceed the variation due to environmental stochasticity, then the purported irruptive effect must be weak indeed and deserving of no more concern than the yearly variation in weather or other environmental variables.

CASE HISTORIES

George Reserve, Michigan

The first case history comes from the white-tailed deer on GR, a 464-ha fenced research area of the University of Michigan, Ann Arbor, in southeastern Michigan. The GR deer herd is one of the most thoroughly studied deer populations in the world (McCullough 1979). This case, the first scientifically documented instance of an irruption by an introduced population of ungulates (Hickie 1937), was an important example in Leopold's (1943) description of irruptive behavior. The evidence on the initial irruption was reevaluated by McCullough (1979) to clarify the nature of the irruption.

Only the first two time intervals of the irruptive sequence (Figure 6.1, I and II) were studied in this case. The population grew from 6 deer introduced in 1928 to approximately 222 in 1935, but this cannot be accepted as the peak population (i.e., 1C of Figure 6.1). Because deer effects on vegetation were substantial and interfering with other studies on the reserve, the irruption was interrupted by culling in 1935. Further growth might have occurred if culling had not interceded. No significant mortality due to other causes was recorded, and culling averted a crash.

Moderate densities were maintained by culling until 1975. As a test of questions 1 and 2, McCullough (1982, 1983) reported on a severe reduction of the GR population to 10 animals in 1975. If Caughley (1970) was correct that initial irruptions are more severe than are secondary irruptions, then population growth rate following this second reduction should have been lower; that is, hypotheses 1 and 2, framed as null hypotheses, should have been rejected. Thus, 47 years of deer impact on vegetation would have had a depressing effect on $\bar{r}$ and, by inference, on K.

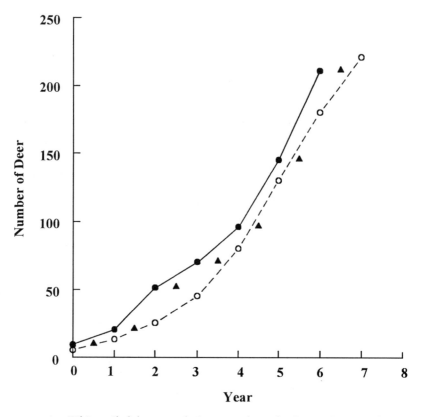

FIGURE 6.2. White-tailed deer population growth on the George Reserve. A comparison is made between the original introduction in 1928 (open points, dashed line) and the experimental growth from 1974–75 to 1980–81 (solid points, solid line); triangles show experimental growth offset to equalize starting population sizes (from McCullough 1982; used with permission of The Wildlife Society).

Population growth between 1975 and 1981 was essentially the same as between 1928 and 1935; so were the numbers if adjusted for the smaller initial population size (Figure 6.2). Even the high numbers reached were similar (222 for first irruption and 212 for the second), although culling interfered with measurement of ultimate peak numbers in both instances. McCullough (1982, 1983) concluded that the null hypotheses could not be rejected. Van Ballenberghe (1983) criticized that conclusion, but in an independent analysis, Eberhardt (1985) concluded that the null hypothesis could not be rejected.

All hypotheses predicting a lowered K and either dampening or growth to a stable K (hypotheses 3 through 5) were rejected for GR by these results.

From this case I conclude that loss of K (or "damage" to the vegetation) from an initial irruption is not inevitable and secondary irruptions are not necessarily less extreme than initial irruptions.

Certainly the vegetation of GR was not the same as that prior to the initial introduction of deer. Many effects on shape, size classes, and species composition of plants have been reported over many years (Brash 1947; Pengelly 1948; Meagher 1958; Walls 1962; Atzert 1969). These studies describe effects from moderate to severe, although there is also some mention of improvement with deer population reduction. The most dramatic effect of deer feeding was on two plantations of pines planted in 1928, one of red pine *(Pinus resinosa)*, an unpalatable species, and the other of white pine *(P. strobus)*, a palatable species. In 1975, 47 years later, the red pines were tall trees, 25–30 cm in diameter at breast height with a closed canopy, whereas the white pines that survived were permanent shrubs, essentially bonsai plants, hedged to less than 0.5 m in height by deer browsing.

Despite these effects, however, K as expressed by $\bar{r}$ did not seem to be lowered. Whereas some of the population growth on the second irruption might be attributed to short-term recovery of the vegetation due to lowered deer density, this would not alter the fact that many long-term changes had occurred (e.g., shift in species composition, plant shape, and plant density of woody species). These differences are apparent from aerial photos of the GR boundary fence, which show woody plant species density to be dramatically higher outside, where deer occur but are held to low density by heavy hunting pressure.

North Manitou Island, Michigan

North Manitou Island (NMI) is 5,968 ha and located about 11 km offshore in Lake Michigan. Currently it is part of the Sleeping Bear Dunes National Lakeshore administered by the U.S. National Park Service. North Manitou Island was the site of a white-tailed deer study reported by Case (1982) and Case and McCullough (1987a), from which this account is derived.

Deer were not native to NMI, having been introduced in 1926. Thereafter, the private owners of NMI managed the island as a deer hunting club. Deer were fed 54.3 metric tons of pelletized alfalfa annually in winter, which maintained an artificially high deer population. Effects on the woody vegetation were severe. A pronounced high line at maximum deer reach occurred throughout the forests (57.7% of the island), and regeneration of northern hardwood trees other than by the unpalatable beech

(Fagus grandifolia) was essentially eliminated. The island was severely lacking in winter thermal cover, with conifers, principally northern white cedar *(Thuja occidentalis),* occupying only 2.1% of the island.

When the National Park Service began acquisition of NMI in 1977, a high deer kill was taken by the private owners, and only 3.6 metric tons of winter feed (6.6% of normal) was distributed. No artificial feeding occurred thereafter. A massive die-off occurred in the winter of 1977–78. In summer 1978, during a visit to the island, I found deer carcasses concentrated under the canopy of the white cedar swamps and around the feeding stations. Even isolated juniper trees *(Juniperus communis)* had one or several carcasses under their crowns, and the floors of old, abandoned buildings were littered with deer carcasses. In the absence of anything to eat, deer sought whatever meager thermal cover was available.

On the basis of line-transect estimates of the surviving population (490), estimates of the number of carcasses of dead deer (882), and a fall 1977 hunting kill (507), we derived a conservative precrash population of 1,879 deer. Thus, around 74% of the population died in 1977–78 (Figure 6.3).

Based on the conventional wisdom of the time, and the impressive alteration of the woody vegetation on NMI, we expected a delayed recovery of the deer population. To our surprise, the population grew at an

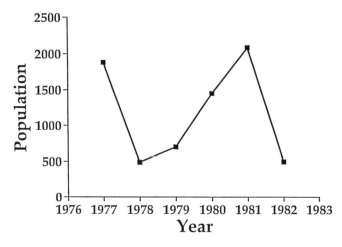

FIGURE 6.3. White-tailed deer population changes on North Manitou Island. An initial peak (1977) was followed by a crash (winter of 1977–78) to a low in 1978; a second irruptive event then occurred to a peak in 1981 and a second crash (winter of 1981–82).

unexpectedly high rate in the subsequent years (Figure 6.3, Table 6.1). It soon became apparent that deer were drawing most of their sustenance from grasses and forbs in the open lands, and an unexpected source, the annual die-offs of an exotic fish in Lake Michigan, the alewife *(Alosa pseudoharengus)* (Case and McCullough 1987b). As dead and dying alewives washed up on shore, the deer visited the beaches of NMI to consume large numbers. We estimated that the average deer made three visits to the beach per day and consumed 30 to 50% of its rumen volume in fish (Case and McCullough 1987b). We believe this rich energy and nutrient source, available for a variable time from May to July depending on the size of the alewife die-off, substantially fueled the rate of population growth.

The population continued to grow despite winter mortality that increased in the following years with population increase (Figure 6.4). The population peaked at an estimated 2,080 in 1981, and crashed in a second major die-off (76%) in the winter of 1981–82 (Figure 6.3). Thereafter, the population began increasing rapidly once again, and the National Park Service instituted public hunting to attempt to stabilize what promised to be a continuing sequence of booms and crashes.

The virtually cyclic nature of this population behavior is shown by the record of numbers over time (Figure 6.3) and the ovid of $\bar{r}$ plotted on population size (Figure 6.5). These are typical of the 4-year microtine cycle and similar to the population fluctuations shown by Soay sheep on Hirta Island in the St. Kilda Islands (Clutton-Brock et al. 1991; Clutton-Brock 1994).

As with the GR population, the deer population on NMI showed

TABLE 6.1

Three case histories of deer irruptions

Case history location and dates	Irruption period (years)	Population numbers	Realized growth rate $(\bar{r})$
George Reserve			
1928–35	8	6–222	0.516
1975–81	7	10–212	0.509
North Manitou Island			
1978–81	4	490–2,080	0.482
Angel Island			
1977–80	4	75–275	0.433
1981–84	4	44–260	0.566

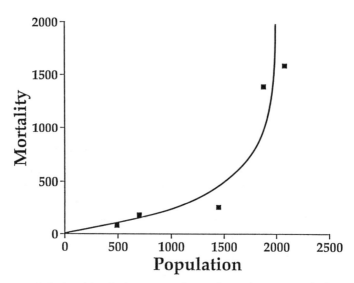

FIGURE 6.4. Relationship of winter mortality and population size of white-tailed deer on North Manitou Island. Winter mortality occurs in all winters but is exceptionally great in winters of crashes.

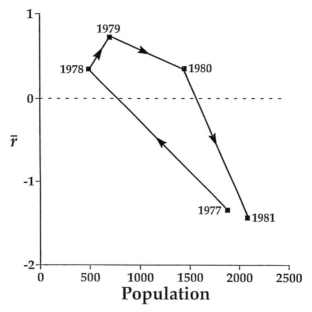

FIGURE 6.5. Relationship of rate of increase $(\bar{r})$ to population size of white-tailed deer on North Manitou Island through an irruptive cycle. The arrows indicate the direction of time. Note the ovid form, which indicates cyclic behavior with a time lag (McCullough 1992). Note also that $(\bar{r})$ was lower in the year following (1978) and preceding (1980) a crash than it was for the intervening year (1979).

behavior that contradicted questions 1 and 2 (IDOLK and ISLK) and supported Question 3 (CICK). This population peaked at comparable numbers (Figure 6.3), and all indications were that, unabated in the future, the system would continue to produce comparable oscillations. This behavior persisted despite severely altered vegetation that, from all indications, was stable in its altered state (Case and McCullough 1987b). Many ecologists would consider the shifted species composition of woody species to be degraded, but that is a value judgment (Caughley 1981; Sinclair 1983).

Would the absence of alewives have altered the deer irruptive behavior appreciably? I believe it would have lowered the amplitude of oscillation, and perhaps extended the period of the cycle, but probably not altered the basic behavior. The herbaceous forage in the open lands seemed sufficiently robust and resistant to degradation that NMI would have continued to support irruptive behavior of deer in the absence of alewives. This pattern is similar to the herbaceous vegetation-driven system for Soay sheep on Hirta Island (Clutton-Brock 1994). The following case history speaks to the same issue.

Angel Island, California

Angel Island (AI) is 220 ha and located in San Francisco Bay, California. Black-tailed deer *(Odocoileus hemionus columbianus)* were abundant on AI when the first Europeans arrived, but they became extinct in the later 1800s. They were reintroduced in 1915 by the U.S. military, which occupied the island for many years because of its strategic location facing the Golden Gate. Development of intercontinental ballistic missiles made AI obsolete as a military installation, so in 1955 it was given to California as Angel Island State Park. All hunting of deer stopped at that time.

Angel Island deer began to show irruptive behavior shortly following protection, and this led to enormous public controversy about how the problem should be handled (White 1981; Goldsmith 1982; Botti 1985; McCullough 1987b; and Mayer et al. 1995). Solutions attempted included feeding (Goldsmith 1982), relocation (O'Bryan and McCullough 1985), and contraception (Botti 1985), all of which failed. Introduction of a natural predator, the coyote, was rejected because of public opposition (McCullough 1987b). Finally, control by culling by park rangers was instituted, and this is the current method of control.

Early data on this population were weak, but the general behavior of the population was not disputed (Figure 6.6). The dispute concerned only what to do about the recurring peaks of abundance, which were followed

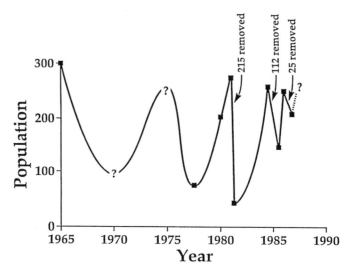

FIGURE 6.6. Population size of black-tailed deer on Angel Island. Shown is the repeated irruptive behavior and no apparent lessening of peak population sizes. Question marks represent qualitative estimates not based on data. See text for further explanation.

by crashes. The estimate of 300 deer in 1965 was made by a series of observers making simultaneous area counts. This estimate seemed improbable at first because it would have reflected a density of nearly 116 deer/km^2 (300/mi^2), whereas traditionally a density of 39 deer/km^2 (100/mi^2) has always been considered an extremely high density by deer biologists.

However, in 1980 a minimum population of 275 deer was determined by 215 being captured and removed live, 44 being counted in a drive census after the removal, and 16 carcasses recently dead being found. It is unlikely that either all of the deer remaining on the island were counted in the drive count or all of the dead deer carcasses were found because of steep slopes and dense brush. These results demonstrated that populations of the previously estimated magnitude were indeed being achieved on AI. The two estimates for the late 1970s in Figure 6.6 were made by California Department of Fish and Game biologists, and the estimates from 1980 onwards were made by my graduate students and me using a deer drive (1981) and mark–recapture (1984) and line-transect (1985 and later) methods.

In any event, there was no indication that the irruptive behavior of deer on AI was abating or that the height of the peaks were becoming lower. At least four peaks were observed between 1965 and 1984 (Figure 6.6). No data are available since 1987. The interval between peaks has varied in period length (Figure 6.1) for unknown reasons. However, drought and the pattern of rainfall are obviously important variables in coastal California. In this Mediterranean climate with winter precipitation, the low in food for deer occurs in late summer (August to October). Die-offs, when they happen, occur at this time as opposed to winter in colder climates. Rainfalls in autumn initiate germination of the annual grasses and forbs and end the summer food shortage period. Annual grasslands remain green until rains stop in late spring, usually April; herbaceous vegetation usually dries up in May. The green-growth period is a time of high availability of quality forage for deer. If the rains come early in the fall, or extend late into spring, they extend the time over which quality forage is readily available. Conversely, late rains in fall or early cessation in spring extend the dry period and place additional food stress on deer. Thus timing of rainfall is more critical than the amount in all but the severe drought years.

During the dry period, deer switch to woody browse. On AI, all of the favored browse species are heavily hedged, particularly at high deer population numbers. The situation on AI is analogous to NMI, except the bottleneck season is the summer instead of winter. But as with NMI, the deer forage system is driven primarily by the herbaceous layer, which suffers little carryover of deleterious effects of too many deer, so recovery (i.e., growth rate, Table 6.1) is rapid. Indeed, because AI herbaceous vegetation is predominantly annuals, there is almost no carryover, each annual crop being largely independent of the previous one.

Once again, as with NMI, the deer population at AI contradicts questions 1 and 2 (IDOLK and ISLK) and supports question 3 (CICK). The AI black-tailed deer showed four cyclic peaks and promised to continue irruptive behavior until controlled by humans. Once culling was begun in 1985, irruptive behavior stopped. Although the earlier peaks were less well measured, the indications are that peak numbers were not declining. Nor was there evidence of declining $\bar{r}$, although $\bar{r}$ for 1981 to 1984 (Table 6.1) seems too high to be accurate and probably reflects sampling error in one or both estimates.

DISCUSSION

The three case histories reviewed here show that the irruptive sequence proposed by Leopold (1943) and indicated by Caughley's (1976a) model is not inevitable. None of these populations showed a diminution of peak population in the second (GR and NMI) or subsequent (AI) peaks as being characteristic of irruptions.

These case histories illustrate the variety of factors that can produce irruptive behavior. For GR this was initial introduction and later heavy culling followed by protection. For NMI it was the combination of reduction of winter feeding, heavy hunting kill, and natural mortality in the first peak and crash. The second peak and crash occurred entirely due to natural processes. That the second peak was of the same approximate magnitude as the first shows that irruptive behavior can occur as a normal interaction of the climate–vegetation–herbivore system. This case suggests that the population crash due to three combined mortality factors (cessation of artificial feeding, hunting kill, and natural starvation) in the first irruption was virtually duplicated by natural starvation alone in the second case.

For the first two irruptions on AI natural starvation was solely involved in the crash. Although cessation of hunting (presumably; no data are available) contributed to the initial irruption, the second crash and peak were produced entirely by natural causes. The third decline was caused by capture and removal of deer plus natural mortality. It was apparent, given the poor condition of captured animals, that natural mortality would have decreased the population to comparable numbers if the removal program had not occurred.

That natural causes alone, or various mixes of natural and anthropogenic causes, can produce irruptive behavior points to the futility of searching for a single, generic cause of irruptive behavior. Any of an array of variables, including those entirely natural or anthropogenic (removal of competitors or predators, introduction, hunting imposition or cessation), in combination or alone can contribute to irruptive behavior (or, conversely, abate it). The role of these variables in individual cases continues to be of interest. But it is time to abandon the quest for a common root cause, which traditionally has been assumed to be anthropogenic in origin, because surely nature was more prudent than to foster such chaotic behavior in a grand design based on balance. In fact the root causes of irruptive behavior of ungulates is grounded firmly in the climate–vegetation–herbivore system. Anthropogenic factors influence the expression of the behavior but they do not create it.

All three cases were similar to the cyclic irruptive behavior of Soay sheep on Hirta Island (Clutton-Brock 1994). Indeed, even the period (4 years; Table 6.1) was comparable except for GR. Based on a wide range of animal sizes from a few grams to over 100 grams, Peterson et al. (1984) suggested this cycle period may be related to body size. However, deer and Soay sheep do not fit this scaling; their cycle lengths are much shorter than predicted from their body sizes. From Peterson et al.'s (1984) regression, a 60-kg deer should have a cycle period of approximately 24 years rather than the 4 years shown here.

Could it be that irruptive behavior is associated with secondary successional ungulate species in instances in which herbaceous vegetation predominates and irruptive behavior is a consequence of a high rate of increase compared with the body size of ungulate species (i.e., early maturation and multiple births per litter)? Are *Odocoileus* deer and Soay sheep the real norms for irruptive, perhaps even cyclic, behavior and reindeer on islands (Klein 1968) the unusual, extreme examples? Hirta Island Soay sheep are confined to feeding almost exclusively on herbaceous vegetation, virtually the only vegetation on the island. All three case histories with deer occurred in environments in which woody vegetation was abundant and effects of deer feeding on woody plants was pronounced. Still, the herbaceous layer in these areas played an extremely important role in deer dynamics. Most of the productivity of deer during the growing season was derived from herbaceous vegetation (plus alewives at NMI), and woody vegetation played the role of maintenance over the bottleneck season.

Only the GR population among these case histories showed cycle periods longer than 4 years (Table 6.1). Nevertheless, the $\bar{r}$'s at GR were roughly comparable (or higher) with those at NMI and AI (Table 6.1), so the longer period at GR is a reflection of the lower initial number of deer introduced (6) and the low number to which the population was artificially reduced (10). Natural die-offs would not be expected to reduce the population this low, so a period around 4 years for GR might be expected.

However, note that period of cycling ungulate populations will be dependent upon the amplitude of fluctuation, with period increasing with amplitude. Furthermore, $\bar{r}$ will depend upon the delay due to consequences of the peak population. Note that the NMI population showed a lower $\bar{r}$ in the year following the crash and the year preceding the next peak (Figure 6.5). Such delays will extend the period in given cases to a greater or lesser degree. Consequently, $\bar{r}$, during irruption, is probably a better measure of comparability between cases than is cycle period.

The results from these case histories do not mean that the irruptive paradigms of Leopold and Caughley do not occur. These paradigms have a strong intuitive appeal and are widely believed by deer biologists. There is much anecdotal support as well, but, curiously, well-documented cases are rare. There is major need to document unambiguously that the behavior exists and to elucidate its workings. Are the cases of reduced peaks in second and subsequent irruptions (or no second peak at all) a consequence of heavy dependence of the ungulate species on woody vegetation as opposed to herbaceous vegetation, as in the cases reviewed here?

Or could it be that the paradigm is simply not very applicable despite its great intuitive appeal? That the irruptive behavior of deer populations in these case histories continued unabated despite substantial alteration of the form and composition of the vegetation illustrates the robustness of some climate–vegetation–herbivore systems. Perhaps vegetation has resilience at a larger level than we have recognized (Sinclair 1983). Why do we have the strong intuition that irruptions inevitably lead to damage of the vegetation? Why are we so convinced that the effects are irreparable and the system will never recover? Isn't the continuance of irruptive sequences in some cases evidence for the sustainability of these systems, and doesn't sustainability suggest that nature has confronted this irruptive behavior sufficiently frequently in the past to have achieved this resilience? Might irruptive sequences not be one of multiple "equilibria" within the elasticity of these systems? Even African elephant *(Loxodonta africana)* populations that can have enormous effects on vegetation, converting woodlands to grasslands, have been suggested to show long-term (200 year) cycles (Caughley 1976c).

In my opinion it is time to confront the possibility that we have become enmeshed in a web of our own making. If we assume that nature always leads to balance, that plant communities are entities with specific components, and that human activity brings imperfection to a perfect nature, then the scene is set, the script is written, and the play of the irruptive paradigm will unfold. Perhaps we resist alternative paradigms because they conflict with our value system. However, if values are the basis of our paradigm, then inevitably our science will be compromised.

Fifty years of debate have not moved us much closer to the answers to these questions. It is possible to propose realistic scenarios that would result in any of the outcomes outlined in Figure 6.1. It is time to start testing the hypotheses outlined. These are feasible experiments. By making them explicit I hope to stimulate or provoke their testing. What I advocate is good science, objectively pursued and based upon good data.

Although I advocate objectivity to achieve understanding, I do not favor abandonment of subjective values for management. Yield of commercial products, recreation, and esthetics all are important to human societies. Irruptive behavior (whether natural or anthropogenically induced) can be stabilized by culling to achieve goals based upon given values. However, as pointed out in the introduction, the most problematic issues concern irruptive behavior of ungulates in parks and reserves where the values of nature are supposed to supersede those of humans. If the decisions are not informed by scientifically tested and empirically sound paradigms, the result will be that the human value system will shape parks and reserves in artificial ways rather than along the course of nature.

ACKNOWLEDGMENTS

The George Reserve studies reported here were supported by the National Science Foundation, the North Manitou Island studies by the U.S. National Park Service, and the Angel Island studies by the San Francisco Society for the Prevention of Cruelty to Animals, the California Department of Parks and Recreation, the California Department of Fish and Game, the California Agricultural Experiment Station (McIntire-Stennis), the A. Starker Leopold Endowed Chair, and the National Rifle Association. Numerous individuals contributed to these studies, but special thanks are due to Bruce Coblentz, David Hirth, Steve Newhouse, David Kitchen, R. Terry Bowyer, John Bissonette, Yvette McCullough, Paul Beier, David Case, Max Holden, Gene Fowler, Mary O'Bryan, Pam Mulligan, Tom Kucera, Mike Garguilo, and Bill Clark. For critical review of the manuscript I thank Richard Lancia and Mark Boyce.

REFERENCES CITED

Allee, W. C., A. E. Emerson, O. Park, T. Park, and K. P. Schmidt. 1949. Principles of Animal Ecology. W. B. Saunders, Philadelphia, PA.

Anonymous, 1992. Interim report, Yellowstone National Park Northern Range research. Park Research Division, Yellowstone National Park, WY.

Atzert, S. P. 1969. The effect of deer browsing on hickory and oak reforestation. Master's thesis, University of Michigan, Ann Arbor.

Botti, F. L. 1985. Chemosterilants as a management option for deer on Angel Island: Lessons learned. Cal-Neva Wildlife Transactions 1985:61–65.

Boyce, M. S. 1991. Natural regulations or control of nature? Pages 183–208 in The Greater Yellowstone Ecosystem: Redefining America's Wilderness Heritage. (R. B. Keiter and M. S. Boyce, eds.) Yale University Press, New Haven, CT.

Brash, J. G. 1947. Some late winter and spring relations of white-tailed deer to the ecological cover types of the Edwin S. George Reserve, Michigan. Master's thesis, University of Michigan, Ann Arbor.

Brown, W. E., and S. D. Veirs, Jr., eds. 1993. Proceedings of the Seventh Conference on Research and Resource Management in Parks and on Public Lands:
Partners in Stewardship. George Wright Society, Hancock, MI.

Case, D. J. 1982. The white-tailed deer of North Manitou Island, Michigan. Master's thesis, University of Michigan, Ann Arbor.

Case, D. J., and D. R. McCullough 1987a. The white-tailed deer of North Manitou Island. Hilgardia 55 (9): 1–57.

Case, D. J., and D. R. McCullough. 1987b. White-tailed deer forage on alewives.
Journal of Mammalogy 68:195–197.

Caughley, G. 1966. Mortality patterns in mammals. Ecology 47:906–918.

Caughley, G. 1970. Erruption of ungulate populations, with emphasis on Himalayan tahr in New Zealand. Ecology 51:51–72.

Caughley, G. 1976a. Wildlife management and the dynamics of ungulate populations. Pages 183–246 in Applied Biology. Vol. 1. (T. H. Coaker, ed.) Academic
Press, London.

Caughley, G. 1976b. Plant–herbivore systems. Pages 94–113 in Theoretical Ecology: Principles and Applications. (R. M. May, ed.) W. B. Saunders, Philadelphia, PA.

Caughley, G. 1976c. The elephant problem—an alternative hypothesis. East African Wildlife Journal 14:265–283.

Caughley, G. 1977. Analysis of Vertebrate Populations. John Wiley and Sons,
New York.

Caughley, G. 1981. Overpopulation. Pages 7–19 in Problems in Management of
Locally Abundant Wild Mammals. (P. A. Jewell and S. Holt, eds.) Academic
Press, New York.

Clutton-Brock, T. 1994. Counting sheep. Natural History 103 (3): 29–35.

Clutton-Brock, T., O. F. Price, S. D. Albon, and P. A. Jewell. 1991. Persistent instability and population regulation in Soay sheep. Journal of Animal Ecology
60:593–608.

Davis, D. E., and F. B. Golley. 1963. Principles in Mammalogy. Reinhold, New
York.

Eberhardt, L. L. 1985. Assessing the dynamics of wild populations. Journal of
Wildlife Management 49:997–1012.

Goldsmith, A. E. 1982. The Angel Island deer herd: A case history of wildlife
management controversy. Cal-Neva Wildlife Transactions 1982:78–82.

Hairston, N. G., F. E. Smith, and L. B. Slobodkin. 1960. Community structure,
population control, and competition. American Naturalist 94:421–425.

Hickie, P. 1937. Four deer produce 160 in six seasons. Michigan Conservationist
7:6–7, 11.

Jewell, P. A., and S. Holt, eds. 1981. Problems in Management of Locally Abundant Wild Animals. Academic Press, New York.

Klein, D. R. 1968. The introduction, increase, and crash of reindeer on St. Matthew Island. Journal of Wildlife Management 32:350–367.

Klein, D. R. 1981. The problem of overpopulation of deer in North America. Pages 119–127 *in* Problems in Management of Locally Abundant Wild Animals. (P. A. Jewell and S. Holt, eds.) Academic Press, New York.

Leader-Williams, N., D. W. H. Walton, and P. A. Prince. 1989. Introduced reindeer on South Georgia—a management dilemma. Biological Conservation 47: 1–11.

Leopold, A. 1943. Deer irruptions. Wisconsin Conservation Bulletin 8 (8): 3–11.

Liberman, S., ed. In press. Current Issues in Deer Management in Urbanizing Regions. U.S. Humane Society, Washington.

May, R. M. 1994. Graeme Caughley and the emerging science of conservation biology. Trends in Ecology and Evolution 9: 368–369.

Mayer, K. E., J. E. DiDonato, and D. R. McCullough. 1995. California urban deer management: Two case studies. Pages 51–57 *in* Urban Deer: A Manageable Resource? (J. McAnich, ed.) North Central Section of The Wildlife Society, Madison, WI.

McCullough, D. R. 1979. The George Reserve Deer Herd: Population Ecology of a K-Selected Species. University of Michigan Press, Ann Arbor.

McCullough, D. R. 1982. Population growth rate of the George Reserve deer herd. Journal of Wildlife Management 46: 1079–1083.

McCullough, D. R. 1983. Rate of increase of white-tailed deer on the George Reserve: A response. Journal of Wildlife Management 47: 1248–1250.

McCullough, D. R. 1987a. The theory and management of *Odocoileus* populations. Pages 535–549 *in* Biology and Management of the Cervidae. (C. M. Wemmer, ed.) Smithsonian Institution Press, Washington.

McCullough, D. R. 1987b. North American deer ecology: Fifty years later. Pages 115–122 *in* Aldo Leopold: The Man and His Legacy. (T. Tanner, ed.) Soil Conservation Society of America, Ankeny, IA.

McCullough, D. R. 1992. Concepts of large herbivore population dynamics. Pages 967–984 *in* Wildlife 2001: Populations. (D. R. McCullough and R. H. Barrett, eds.) Elsevier Science Publishers, London.

Meagher, M. M. 1958. A comparative browse and herd density study 1949–1958, on the George Reserve. Master's thesis, University of Michigan, Ann Arbor.

Neufeldt, V., and D. B. Guralnik. 1988. Webster's New World Dictionary, 3rd edition. Webster's New World, Cleveland, OH.

O'Bryan, M. K., and D. R. McCullough. 1985. Survival of black-tailed deer following relocation in California. Journal of Wildlife Management 49: 115–119.

Odum, E. P. 1983. Basic Ecology. Saunders College Publishing, Philadelphia, PA.

Pengelly, W. L. 1948. The effects of deer browsing on the upland hardwoods reproduction of the Edwin S. George Reserve, Michigan. Master's thesis, University of Michigan, Ann Arbor.

Peterman, R. M. 1990. Statistical power analysis can improve fisheries research and management. Canadian Journal of Fisheries and Aquatic Sciences 47: 2–15.

Peterson, R. O., R. E. Page, and K. M. Dodge. 1984. Wolves, moose, and the allometry of population cycles. Science 224:1350–1352.

Pickett, S. T. A., and P. S. White, eds. 1985. The Ecology of Natural Disturbance and Patch Dynamics. Academic Press, New York.

Platt, R. 1969. Strong inference. Science 146:347–353.

Porter, W. F. 1992. Burgeoning ungulate populations in national parks: Is intervention warranted? Pages 304–312 *in* Wildlife 2001: Populations. (D. R. McCullough and R. H. Barrett, eds.) Elsevier Science Publishers, London.

Rasmussen, I. D. 1941. Biotic communities of Kaibab Plateau, Arizona. Ecological Monographs 3:229–275.

Reice, S. R. 1994. Nonequilibrium determinants of biological community structure. American Scientist 82:424–435.

Riney, T. 1964. The impact of introductions of large herbivores on the tropical environment. International Union for the Conservation of Nature, Publication New Series Number 4: 261–273.

Roller, N. E. G. 1974. Airphoto mapping of ecosystem development on the Edwin S. George Reserve. Master's thesis, University of Michigan, Ann Arbor.

Romesburg, H. C. 1981. Wildlife science: Gaining reliable knowledge. Journal of Wildlife Management 45:293–313.

Russell, E. W. B. 1994. Land use history. (Review of a symposium on land use history and ecosystem processes: Inexorably connected.) Bulletin of the Ecological Society of America 75:35–36.

Sinclair, A. R. E. 1983. Management of conservation areas as ecological baseline controls. Pages 13–22 *in* Management of Large Mammals in African Conservation Areas. (R. N. Owen-Smith, ed.) Haum Educational Publishers, Pretoria, Republic of South Africa.

Sousa, W. P. 1984. The role of disturbance in natural communities. Annual Review of Ecology and Systematics 15:353–341.

Van Ballenberghe, V. 1983. Rate of increase of white-tailed deer on the George Reserve: A re-evaluation. Journal of Wildlife Management 47:1245–1247.

Wagner, F. H., R. Foresta, R. B. Gill, D. R. McCullough, M. R. Pelton, W. F. Porter, and H. Salwasser. 1995. Wildlife Policies in the U.S. National Parks. Island Press, Washington.

Walls, B. E. 1962. Deer utilization of grassland forbs. Master's thesis, University of Michigan, Ann Arbor.

Warren, R. J. 1991. Ecological justification for controlling deer populations in eastern national parks. Transactions of the North American Wildlife and Natural Resources Conference 56:56–66.

White, J. 1981. Trouble on Angel Island. Outdoor California 42 (5): 9–12.

Whitlock, C. 1993. Postglacial vegetation and climate of Grand Teton and southern Yellowstone National parks. Ecological Monographs 63:173–198.

7 Genetic Variation as a Predictor of Social Structure

Genetic Approaches for Studying Free-Ranging White-Tailed Deer

NANCY E. MATHEWS, J. ANDREW DEWOODY,
WILLIAM F. PORTER, LOREN C. SKOW, AND
RODNEY L. HONEYCUTT

GENETIC VARIATION WITHIN POPULATIONS

Numerous studies on genetic variation in mammals have revealed considerable geographic subdivision, reflecting reduced gene flow as a consequence of either geological or ecological barriers. Therefore, many mammalian species, including white-tailed deer, represent polytypic species that are subdivided into a series of geographic races distributed throughout the species' range. From a genetic standpoint, patterns of gene flow have a direct influence on the overall levels of genetic diversity seen within populations and divergence between populations. Although the degree of isolation and effective population size are major predictors of genetic variation, barriers to gene flow are generally considered to be a consequence of historical events associated with major climatic or geological events (e.g., glaciation). Patterns of genetic variation often denote a subdivision of a species throughout a major geographic area and are most likely a consequence of the evolutionary history of the species. Social organization also may have an influence on patterns of genetic variation in natural populations, yet the ability to evaluate changes in genetic variation among social groups is limited by the ability to detect enough genetic variation to evaluate changes on a microscale.

The influence of social organization on genetic variability of populations has received increasing attention over the past two decades (Selander 1970; Olivier et al. 1981; Chesser 1983; Melnick 1987). Various interpretations of genetic structure at the level of the social group have led to debates on the potential consequences of inbreeding and outbreeding (Chesser and Ryman 1986; Ralls et al. 1986; Templeton 1986). The classical presumption has been that small groups lead to lower genetic variability (e.g., excess homozygosity as expected from a Hardy–Weinberg equilibrium with random mating) within groups and greater variability among groups relative to that predicted from random mating (Chesser 1991a). Prout (1981), however, demonstrated mathematically that female philopatry in a polygynous species can lead to an increased level of heterozygosity within the population. Chesser's (1991a) mathematical models indicated that increased heterozygosity is expected within breeding groups of polygynous mammals. Further, the proportion of genetic variance among groups depends on the group size and number of males breeding within the group.

White-tailed deer provide an excellent example for detailed studies of genetic variation at both macro- and microgeographic levels. The species is subdivided into 30 subspecies distributed throughout most of the Nearctic and Neotropical biogeographic regions (Baker 1984), and the species demonstrates a social organization similar to most polygynous mammals. Although in theory (see Chesser 1991a and citations therein) social organization should have an effect on patterns of genetic variation observed within and between social groups, empirical evidence for this is lacking, especially on a microgeographic scale. One reason for the limited number of studies dealing with this issue is that, in most cases, the genetic markers used to examine macrogeographic patterns of genetic variation are not informative enough, in terms of genetic polymorphism, on a microgeographic scale. In this chapter, we review genetic variation in free-ranging white-tailed deer and provide an assessment of genetic markers that may prove useful to those interested in social structure and genetic structure in more local populations.

MACROGEOGRAPHIC VARIATION

Genetic studies (using both nuclear and mitochondrial DNA markers) have shown some genetic subdivision throughout the range of white-tailed deer and have even been useful in identifying regions of interspecific hybridization between white-tailed deer and mule deer *(Odocoileus hemionus)* (Carr et al. 1986; Derr 1991; Hughes and Carr 1993). In addition, both mitochondrial DNA (mtDNA) and allozyme studies (Ellsworth,

Honeycutt, Silvy, Bickham, et al. 1994; Ellsworth, Honeycutt, Silvy, Smith, et al. 1994) have shown that, for the most part, patterns of genetic subdivision in white-tailed deer from the southeastern United States do not correspond to taxonomic subdivision in terms of the recognized subspecies. This pattern of subdivision is very similar to that found in other organisms from this region (Avise 1994), suggesting the influence of a similar vicariant event that influenced gene flow patterns in unrelated species. Using restriction enzyme analysis of mtDNA, Cronin (1992) found that characteristic genotypes exist in white-tailed deer from different regions of North America. However, he also found that estimates of genetic divergence do not correspond with geographic distance. Cronin (1992) hypothesized that colonization following glacial recession resulted in the spread of similar genotypes over large geographic areas, implying that the deer he surveyed were structured on both macrogeographic and microgeographic levels.

MICROGEOGRAPHIC VARIATION

Patterns of allozymic variation within and between geographic populations of white-tailed deer have been documented throughout the United States (Hillestad 1984; Smith et al. 1984; Sheffield et al. 1985; Gavin and May 1988; Karlin et al. 1989; Carr et al. 1986). These studies suggest that levels of variability within populations appear to be associated with geographic location. Several authors (Manlove et al. 1978; Ramsey et al. 1979; Hillestad 1984; Sheffield et al. 1985; Kennedy et al. 1987) have revealed genetic variation and population subdivision on a microgeographic scale (e.g., less than 8 km²). Karlin et al. (1989) investigated the genetic variation of white-tailed deer in southern Arkansas. They attributed maintenance of genetic variation at the microgeographic level to differential dispersal, hunting, and dominance hierarchies, though they also suggested that restocking programs introduced the primary structure.

Ellsworth, Honeycutt, Silvy, Bickham, et al. (1994) and Ellsworth, Honeycutt, Silvy, Smith, et al. (1994) investigated the influence of historical biogeographical events on white-tailed deer by examining the patterns of mtDNA variation among white-tailed deer harvested from mainland and island populations in the southeastern United States. Populations greater than 60 km but less than 170 km apart had 35 composite mtDNA haplotypes. There was a high degree of geographic variation in the frequency of mtDNA haplotypes among groups, even neighbors. This finding was not consistent with the hypothesis of isolation by distance (Kennedy et al. 1987), nor were subspecies and groups defined by mtDNA consistent with previous phylogenetic designations (taxonomic subdivisions based on morphology), a pattern also observed by Cronin (1992). The observed patterns were more likely a result of historical biogeographic events and were maintained by sex-biased dispersal. The patterns suggested that spatially disjunct matrilineal groups restrict exchange of mtDNA among neighboring populations despite the potential ability of deer to disperse. Thus, through this mechanism, the historical patterns of intraspecific differentiation were preserved.

Similar to most polygynous mammals, the social organization of white-tailed deer is characterized by matrilineal groups consisting of adult females, several generations of female offspring, and predispersal subadult males (Behrend 1966; Behrend et al. 1970; Hawkins and Klimstra 1970; Hirth 1977). In general, female dispersal from a social group is rare (5–20%), whereas male dispersal is common (>85%; Hawkins and Klimstra 1970; Tierson et al. 1985; Nelson and Mech 1987; Mathews 1989; Nelson 1993). Working at the microgeographic scale and using radio telemetry data, Nelson and Mech (1987, 1992) identified probable genetic demes composed of clusters of matrilineal groups that were distributed throughout winter ranges in northern Minnesota. These authors hypothesized that deer using the same winter range should be more closely related because these deer breed primarily on their winter range. Nonetheless, Cronin et al. (1991) observed low levels of genetic subdivision (both mtDNA and allozymes) among distinct geographic subpopulations (demes) of deer representing the same Minnesota populations. Distinct mtDNA haplotypes were located within a single subpopulation, suggesting genetic structure on a microgeographic scale. Cronin et al. (1991) suggested that this genetic substructure may well result from the matrilineal structure created by highly philopatric females.

Although social structure has been demonstrated to influence geographic patterns of genetic variation in many social mammals (Chesser 1983; Melnick 1987), few empirical data are available to demonstrate a similar effect for white-tailed deer. In the first study of its type with white-tailed deer, Mathews and Porter (1993) investigated the relationship between social structure, genetic structure, and geographic proximity in social groups in the central Adirondacks of New York. They hypothesized that social structure, resulting from female philopatry, has led to genetic structure, leading to a greater amount of genetic variability among groups than within groups. They also hypothesized that the geographic location of social groups is related to the genetic distance among groups. Because these New York deer breed on their summer range, genetic characteristics should be more closely associated with summer range rather than with winter range.

GENETIC VARIATION AND SOCIAL ORGANIZATION: A CASE STUDY IN THE ADIRONDACK MOUNTAINS

Introduction and Methods

Mathews (1989) and Mathews and Porter (1993) assessed social structure and genetic variation within a white-tailed deer population in the Huntington Wildlife Forest in the central Adirondack Mountains of New York. Eight social groups were identified based on over 15,000 radiotelemetric relocations to determine home ranges. In all cases, individuals that were associated on summer range also were associated on winter range. In social groups with more than four radio-collared individuals ($n = 6$), home ranges of young (<2 years) females completely overlapped that of an older individual (Mathews 1989). Core-area analysis based on 50% minimum convex polygons on summer range provided better discrimination among social groups, although it indicated perhaps several core areas per group (Figure 7.1). Cumulative home range size of social groups (i.e., home range estimates from combined telemetry data for all group members based on 95% minimum convex polygons; $n = 3-9$ deer) varied ($1.6-7.2$ km^2). Maximum size was independent of the number of radio-collared individuals in the group ($P < 0.05$). Genetic characteristics of the social groups were assessed using starch gel electrophoresis (Mathews and Porter 1993).

Results

Mean heterozygosity, percent polymorphism, and mean number of alleles per locus were 7.6%, 23.4%, and 1.7%, respectively. Analysis of allelic frequencies, based on Fisher's exact test, indicated that one locus (transferrin) accounted for a significant amount of genetic variability among groups ($P = 0.04$; Table 7.1). Analysis of standardized variance of allele frequencies indicated that 12% ($P < 0.10$) of the relative variability was accounted for by variability among matrilineal social groups (mean F_{ST}; Table 7.1). Heterogeneity of allelic frequencies was significant ($P < 0.05$) for the peptidase (leucyl-glycyl-glycine) and transferrin loci. The overall

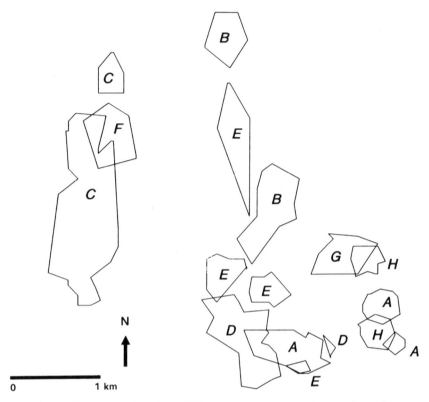

FIGURE 7.1. Core areas, based on 50% minimum convex polygons, for eight social groups of white-tailed deer in Huntington Wildlife Forest, Newcomb, New
York, 1986–1989. Multiple core areas per group are represented by the same
letter.

F_{ST} suggests that social groups have led to genetic partitioning among
groups. Sampling error accounted for 2% of the total variability explained by social groups. No significant deviations ($P > 0.05$) of observed from expected genotypic frequencies were observed within social
groups of greater than three radio-collared individuals. A negative F_{IT}
value (-0.10) indicated an excess of heterozygous individuals in the
population compared with that expected from Hardy–Weinberg equilibrium when data were pooled for all social groups. A negative F_{IS} value
(-0.25) also indicated an excess of heterozygous individuals within social
groups. We estimate that a large proportion (30–35%) of the females in
the population were radio-collared. Thus, even though our group sizes are

TABLE 7.1

Genetic differences among social groups

Locus	P^a	$F_{IS}{}^b$	$F_{IT}{}^b$	$F_{ST}{}^b$	H^c	n^d
Malate dehydrogenase	0.87	−0.29	−0.19	0.07	0.45	44
Malic enzyme 2	1.00	−0.07	−0.01	0.05	0.07	41
Mannose-6-phosphate isomerase	0.70	−0.18	−0.08	0.08	0.23	37
Peptidase-B	0.24	−0.02	0.16	0.17*	0.21	43
Phosphoglucomutase	0.74	−0.12	−0.05	0.06	0.07	44
Phosphogluconate dehydrogenase	0.15	−0.17	−0.04	0.12	0.07	38
Transferrin	0.04	−0.49	−0.18	0.21*	0.26	43
Mean		−0.25	−0.10	0.12**	0.16	41

Note: Genetic variability was assessed among eight social groups of radio-collared white-tailed deer from Huntington Wildlife Forest, Newcomb, New York, 1986–89.

[a] Probabilities based on Fisher's exact test of allele frequencies.

[b] Wright's F-statistics.

[c] Mean heterozygosity.

[d] Sample size by locus.

* $P < 0.05$.

** $P < 0.10$.

numerically small, they represent a large proportion of the population, hence a large proportion of the genetic and geographic variability. Caution should be exercised when interpreting the magnitude of the F-statistic values. Small within-group sample sizes may have influenced the values due to genetic drift. The near significance of the overall F_{ST} and the significance of three loci based on either Fisher's exact test or chi-square do, however, suggest genetic structure.

Mantel (1967) tests indicated an association between genetic characteristics and winter-range location but not between genetic characteristics and summer-range location. There was a significant association between genetic distance and location of winter range among social groups ($P = 0.028$) but not for individuals ($P = 0.06$). No statistically significant association ($P > 0.05$) was found between genetic distance and locations of the summer ranges for either the social groups or individuals. Groups using the same winter ranges (with the exception of groups G and H) were genetically more similar (Figure 7.2). Genetic differences among summer groups within wintering areas accounted for more of the total gene diversity (4%) than did winter or summer range alone. Relative to the total

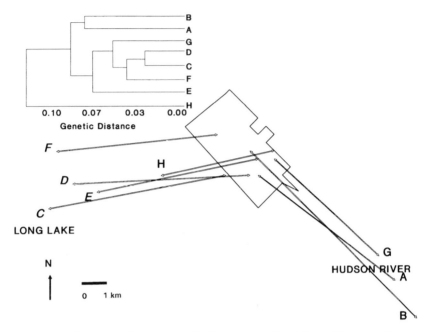

FIGURE 7.2. Location of summer and winter ranges for eight social groups (see Figure 7.1) of white-tailed deer. Dendrogram (inset) based on modified Rogers' genetic distance coefficients. (After Mathews and Porter 1993.)

population, winter-range location and summer-group location accounted for only 3% and 2% of total gene diversity, respectively; the transferrin and peptidase loci accounted for most of the variability.

Discussion

Given the presence of genetic structure at the level of a social group, we suggest that the probable mechanism accounting for the genetic structure is female philopatry. Because females rarely disperse and tend to establish home ranges adjacent to or overlapping their mother's (Mathews 1989), closely related females are juxtaposed spatially. Chesser (1991a, 1991b) demonstrated mathematically that the maximum effect on genetic differentiation among social groups, in the absence of inbreeding, occurs when a single, randomly selected male breeds with philopatric females. Although we lack sufficient information to evaluate the number of males breeding per matriline, previous studies suggest that a male may attempt to dominate up to 10 does within a group at one time (Marchington and

Hirth 1984). Increased male home range size during rut (Tierson et al. 1985) is an indication that males likely breed among several different social groups while on summer range. Previous studies of this same population indicate that, based on ovulation date, parturition date (Underwood 1986), and timing of migration (Tierson et al. 1985), the majority of deer breed on the summer range. Interbreeding among social groups would lead to high levels of gene flow among groups and potentially mask existing genetic structure resulting from female philopatry.

If a single male breeds within a social group for several generations, we would predict a higher level of relatedness or homozygosity within the group as indicated by classic measures of inbreeding (high, positive F_{IS} and F_{IT} values). In contrast to our prediction, we found negative values (although not significant) for F_{IS} and F_{IT}, suggesting excess heterozygosity relative to those values expected from Hardy–Weinberg proportions. Negative F_{IT} or F_{IS} values may indicate either a lack of inbreeding (e.g., outbreeding) or that individuals within a group are not close relatives. Given that female deer are philopatric, it is likely that the members of the social group are closely related. Thus, the negative F_{IS} and F_{IT} values are probably influenced by gene flow into the social group from genetically divergent individuals. Gene flow into a matriline may result from unrelated males breeding with philopatric females. Clutton-Brock et al. (1982) suggested that male dominance in red deer *(Cervus elaphus)* varies within and between years. A dominant breeding male in one year may lose his tenure the following year. Liberg et al. (1992) have documented this phenomenon in roe deer *(Capreolus capreolus)*. Possibly, male white-tailed deer behave in a similar manner and do not retain breeding tenure for successive years, thus allowing for constant influx of genes into each matriline. Consequently the rate of turnover among breeding males may have an important influence on the level of variability within a social group. However, Prout (1981) and Chesser (1991a, 1991b) demonstrated mathematically that, as a rule, some excess heterozygosity may be expected to occur within a matrilineal group even with complete philopatry and random selection of males with which to breed. Thus, the excess heterozygosity that we observed may be expected by chance alone.

If female philopatry is the underlying determinant of the magnitude of genetic variability among social groups, then we would predict an association between the genetic and geographic distance among groups. Further, we expect the closest association of genetic characteristics and geographic proximity to occur on the summer range where breeding occurs. Our findings indicate that social groups using the same winter range are more genetically similar than those using different winter ranges, even though deer breed on summer range. In the Adirondacks, wintering areas are traditional, and knowledge of them is passed on between generations of female deer. Female fawns accompany their dams throughout their first year and subsequently return with their offspring to the same winter range for the rest of their lives (Mathews 1989). This behavior appears to account for the association between winter range and genetic similarity among groups and individuals.

Contrary to our prediction of an association between genetic characteristics and breeding-range location, we found no association between genetic characteristics and summer range. We hypothesize that this expected association was obscured by the close proximity of social groups on summer range. Our definition of social groups and the determination of geographic centroid may have confounded the association as well. Correct identification of each social group is paramount to our interpretation of geographic and genetic associations. Clearly, the delineation of social groups based on summer or winter range alone would have greatly changed our interpretation. Had we not known that groups overlapping on summer range used separate winter ranges, we would have grossly misidentified group membership. The resolution needed to discern among social groups on summer range adequately, given the high amount of overlap, is probably higher than we were able to identify.

Other factors may have historically influenced the genetic similarity and geographic proximity of the social groups. Recent studies of red deer have indicated that, over time, lineages divide by fission (Clutton-Brock 1989). Small groups or propagules separate from the main matriline. Several of our groups possibly were part of another group at one time, and their current proximity on summer range fails to reflect their origin accurately. Because of the traditional use of winter ranges, these splinter groups would be expected to return to the same wintering area as their parent group. Although we lack direct evidence of social group development or long-term spatial dynamics in white-tailed deer, Chepko-Sade and Sade (1979) observed fissioning within matrilines of rhesus monkeys *(Macacca mulatta)*; older, subordinate females left their natal matriline and established a new group a short distance away.

The types of questions and hypotheses discussed in this study require long-term behavioral observations. Few studies of large ungulates have been designed to acquire such data. Although the results presented here should be viewed as somewhat preliminary, they are strongly suggestive of the importance of social structure and behavior in shaping the genetic structure of a virtually unharvested white-tailed deer population. These findings have important implications for the management and conservation of genetic diversity of numerous game and nongame species. They suggest that management for genetic diversity within a population should occur at a finer resolution than that of the population.

A REVIEW OF GENETIC TECHNIQUES

Where are we in terms of understanding social structure and genetic structure in deer and where do we need to go from here? One hypothesis is that female philopatry contributes heavily to genetic substructuring among social groups. Males disperse in and out of these female social groups; thus, heterozygosity can be high within the groups. If males disperse, breed with multiple females, and experience high turnover, then one would expect a high level of overall genetic cohesion among social groups compared with within-group cohesion, especially if female choice dictated that the most divergent males are chosen for breeding. Nevertheless, if one were to focus on females alone, a different story might arise. For instance, the use of mtDNA markers, a maternally inherited genome, tracks the history of the female lineage only. Therefore, one might expect males to have different mitochondrial haplotypes than those of local females. In addition, patterns of microgeographic variation along female genetic lines will be more pronounced than that seen for allozymes alone. The allozyme loci will probably not reflect much microgeographic subdivision of social groups. However, if one could obtain an accurate estimate of relatedness, based on highly variable genetic markers, then one would predict that females would be genetically more similar than would breeding-age males. Microsatellite loci offer an opportunity to test this hypothesis. In addition, a Y chromosome specific marker would offer an opportunity to test the overall pattern of genetic variation in the paternal lineage relative to that seen for a matrilineal marker (e.g., mtDNA).

Protein Electrophoresis

The conventional method of surveying genetic variability is protein electrophoresis. This technique involves separation of proteins in a gel matrix and histochemical staining; electrophoretic variants (allozymes) then are distinguished by differing rates of mobility. Several studies employing either allozymes, mtDNA, or both as genetic markers have been used to examine the population structure of white-tailed deer (Baccus et al. 1983; Breshears et al. 1988; Mathews and Porter 1993; Ellsworth, Honeycutt, Silvy, Bickham, et al. 1994). Baccus et al. (1983) showed that white-tailed deer have a much higher percentage of polymorphic loci, according to protein electrophoresis, than do other mammals. Breshears et al. (1988) compared allozyme polymorphisms in South Carolina to those in other published studies and found that white-tailed deer have significantly more heterozygous loci than do mammals in general.

Despite the available protein data, the lack of sufficiently polymorphic nuclear genetic markers has made it difficult to study the genetic structure of white-tailed deer on a microgeographic level. Although allozymes have been used successfully to study population subdivision in deer, allozymes have two major disadvantages. The first is the relatively low levels of polymorphism detectable using conventional electrophoretic techniques as compared with more advanced molecular techniques. The most extensive allozyme survey in the literature (Sheffield et al. 1985) examined 57 loci, only 18 of which were polymorphic (i.e., secondary allele present at a frequency of greater than 0.05); heterozygosity levels were reported at about 9%. Other allozyme studies report similar results (Baccus et al. 1983; Breshears et al. 1988). This makes studies of small populations difficult, and scoring of many loci is required to assess levels of heterozygosity and genetic variability.

The second obstacle associated with allozymes is that they are often expressed in a tissue-specific manner and are detectable by enzymatic activity. Consequently, the use of allozymes as molecular markers requires freshly collected tissues or body fluids (Manlove et al. 1976) that are often difficult to obtain and transport from animals in unmanaged populations. Additionally, the relatively large amounts of tissue require considerable storage space. The ideal genetic marker would be highly polymorphic, locus-specific, mapped to a linkage group, and easily typed from small quantities of fresh or postmortem tissue.

The Polymerase Chain Reaction

The advent of the polymerase chain reaction (PCR) circumvents many of the problems associated with protein electrophoresis. Polymerase chain reaction, first described by Saiki et al. (1988), is a method for enzymatic amplification of DNA. The method uses thermal cycling to synthesize millions of copies of a target DNA sequence from a few molecules of template DNA (Figure 7.3). Polymerase chain reaction has revolutionized molecu-

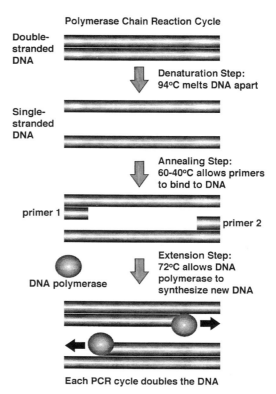

Polymerase Chain Reaction Cycle

Double-stranded DNA

Denaturation Step:
94°C melts DNA apart

Single-stranded DNA

Annealing Step:
60-40°C allows primers to bind to DNA

primer 1

primer 2

DNA polymerase

Extension Step:
72°C allows DNA polymerase to synthesize new DNA

Each PCR cycle doubles the DNA

FIGURE 7.3. Polymerase chain reaction cycle. (Figure presented here with permission of John Pfeifer, Perkin Elmer Corporation.)

lar biology (Erlich 1989) and population biology through the use of genetic markers such as microsatellites and mtDNA. The sensitivity of PCR allows DNA to be amplified from single cells; in fact, microsatellites have been typed from spermatocytes in humans (Weber 1990). Deoxyribonucleic acid also has been isolated and amplified from fossils that are over 80 million years old (Woodward et al. 1994). In a practical sense, this means that microsatellite markers can be typed from minute amounts of hair, tissue, blood, or bone. In fact, microsatellite DNA has been amplified from shed antlers that were over 20 years old (R. L. Honeycutt and L. C. Skow, unpublished data). Tissue can be collected in the field and stored in a lysis buffer at ambient temperature until transfer to the laboratory for DNA extraction.

MITOCHONDRIAL DNA   Traditionally, most of the mtDNA studies on natural populations have used restriction site variation to assess patterns of variation in white-tailed deer. In this approach, either total genomic DNA or purified mtDNA is digested with a series of restriction endonucleases that recognize unique sequences of DNA (consisting of either four or six nucleotides). The digested DNA is electrophoresed in an agarose gel, and the fragments resulting from the digestion are viewed either by ethidium bromide staining or with autoradiography (e.g., Cronin et al. 1991; Ellsworth, Honeycutt, Silvy, Bickham, et al. 1994). A composite haplotype is constructed for the digestion profiles obtained with all the restriction endonucleases. Alternatively, one can sequence PCR-amplified fragments of mtDNA known to be variable in deer (Hughes and Carr 1993). Recently, Travis and Keim (1995) showed that single-strand conformation polymorphisms of mtDNA can be used to differentiate between subpopulations of mule deer on the north and south rims of the Grand Canyon. This technique should be just as applicable in studies of white-tailed deer as well. Examples of mtDNA techniques are thoroughly reviewed in Avise (1994).

MICROSATELLITE LOCI   In 1989, microsatellites, a new class of DNA markers that circumvents the above criticisms of allozymes, were described (Litt and Luty 1989; Weber and May 1989). Microsatellites are short segments of DNA that contain a simple nucleotide repeat motif, such as the dinucleotide repeat d(GT)n or the trinucleotide repeat d(TCC)n (Weber 1990). Repeats of d(GT)n occur about 75,000 times in mammals and are spaced in a largely random pattern throughout the 3-billion-base genome (Stallings et al. 1991); other repeat motifs occur less often. Variation in microsatellite sequences is thought to arise in vivo from polymerase slippage during replication of the DNA molecule (Tautz and Renz 1984). The degree of polymorphism observed in a microsatellite sequence is usually correlated with the length of the repeating unit; microsatellites with more than 10 dinucleotide repeats tend to be highly informative (Weber 1990).

Microsatellites can be isolated by one of two general methods. The first involves constructing a genomic DNA library from the organism of interest. Briefly, genomic DNA is extracted from blood or tissue and digested with a specific restriction enzyme. The small ($<$500 base pair) fragments are collected and cloned into a plasmid vector. These vectors are then screened with the repeat motif of choice, and positive clones are isolated and sequenced. The regions of DNA immediately flanking the repeat provide specific sites for PCR primers to bind, and amplification via PCR provides millions of copies of the target microsatellite.

Microsatellites may also be obtained from data banks (e.g., Research Genetics, 2130 Memorial Parkway, SW, Huntsville, Alabama 35801) that contain microsatellite sequences which have been isolated from a related organism. Often the degree of primer conservation across taxa in the same family will allow amplification with a conserved set of primers (Moore et al. 1991). As more and more microsatellites are described, it will become possible to use microsatellites from related taxa to develope PCR primers, and doing so will avoid the tedious cloning and sequencing involved in the characterization of different microsatellites. In addition, the optimization of PCR primer pairs can be difficult; however, amplification conditions are usually described along with the sequence of the primers, another advantage of computer-based searches.

Microsatellites are randomly dispersed throughout the genome and exhibit extensive length polymorphisms (Stallings et al. 1991). These characteristics make them ideal for linkage studies; consequently, microsatellite markers have been used extensively in genome mapping studies of various mammals (Serikawa et al. 1992; Ellegren at al. 1993; Steffen et al. 1993; Barendse et al. 1994). Microsatellite markers have been used to a lesser extent in studies of natural populations, primarily due to their novelty, yet they offer a highly polymorphic suite of genetic markers that can potentially be obtained from every chromosome. The high level of polymorphism in most microsatellites, in combination with the ease of screening for genetic variation using PCR, provides a powerful tool for genetic typing of wild populations in a noninvasive and detailed manner. In addition, microsatellite loci circumvent more of the analytical problems (e.g., binning of alleles) associated with other classes of repetitive elements, such as minisatellites, and provide considerably more variation than can be detected with restriction fragment length polymorphisms (RFLP) or allozymes. In short, microsatellites are ideal for the study of genetics of natural populations (DeWoody 1994).

Highly polymorphic markers such as microsatellites have enormous potential as investigative tools due to the large number of genotypes that are possible. A high probability of different genotypes in different individuals means that the probability of exclusion is high, whereas the probability of coincidental match between individuals is very low (Chakraborty and Kidd 1991). For example, based on the microsatellite markers reported in DeWoody et al. (1995), the most conservative probability of any two individuals in a closed, pedigreed herd of white-tailed deer having the same genotype is on the order of 2.6×10^{-8} (assuming independent assortment and no sex linkage). These extremely low probabilities suggest that microsatellite markers will be useful in wildlife forensics as well as in management of white-tailed deer and related species.

Microsatellites have revealed population subdivision and differentiation in canids (Roy et al. 1994), extensive variation in a captive herd of white-tailed deer (DeWoody et al. 1995), and variation in a bottlenecked species, the hairy-nosed wombat (*Lasiophinus krefftii;* Taylor et al. 1994). The high levels of genetic variability detectable with microsatellites could benefit breeding programs designed to enhance genetic variability in endangered species. Microsatellites have great potential in the fields of population genetics and wildlife management. For example, some models of social structure (Sugg and Chesser 1994) depend on the accurate measurement of autozygosity (identity by descent). Autozygosity is most appropriately measured using a herd of known pedigree; however, this is seldom practical when studying an unmanaged population. Autozygosity can be estimated by the use of highly polymorphic markers that exhibit many alleles. Thus, microsatellites can be used to assess levels of coancestry in small populations and in studies of gene flow and population subdivision.

SUMMARY

We have reviewed both traditional genetic approaches and some new approaches that may prove useful in studies of social structure in white-tailed deer, especially with respect to studying genetic variation within and between local populations. Genetic variation as revealed by genetic markers can be used effectively as a predictor of social structure. The high levels of variation detectable with mtDNA and microsatellite markers should permit studies on a microgeographic (social group) scale, a level that has been difficult to analyze with less polymorphic markers. Management of deer from an ecosystem perspective should not overlook that genetic diversity on a microgeographic scale could have an enormous effect on genetic diversity on the macrogeographic scale.

ACKNOWLEDGMENTS

We thank our many field assistants. M. H. Smith, P. E. Johns, P. L. Leberg, J. Novak, K. Willis, and D. B. Wester assisted with electrophoretic or statistical analyses or both; R. L. Burgess, B. D. Chepko-Sade, R. K. Chesser, S. Demarais, E. Laca, P. L. Leberg, R. S. Lutz, K. Scribner, L. M. Smith, M. H. Smith, N. C. Parker, D. L. Ellsworth, and D. Sugg provided helpful critiques of the manuscript. The Huntington Wildlife Forest study was supported by the Adirondack Wildlife Program, funded by the New York State Legislature; the University of Georgia's Savannah River Ecology Laboratory, supported by contract DE-AC09-765R00-

819 with the U.S. Department of Energy; and the Oak Ridge Associated Universities Travel Contract T-457. We thank Texas Parks and Wildlife Department, S. Sibert, R. Sanderson, R. Saulsbury, D. Harmel, S. Williamson, B. Young, J. D. Williams, and J. Goy for their input and assistance. Manuscript preparation was supported by the National Biological Survey's Cooperative Research Unit Program at the Texas Cooperative Fish and Wildlife Research Unit and the Department of Biological Sciences, Texas Tech University.

REFERENCES CITED

Avise, J. C. 1994. Molecular Markers, Natural History, and Evolution. Chapman and Hall, New York.

Baccus R., N. Ryman, M. Smith, C. Reuterwall, and D. Cameron. 1983. Genetic variability and differentiation of large grazing mammals. Journal of Mammalogy 64:109–120.

Baker, R. H. 1984. Origin, classification and distribution. Pages 1–18 in White-Tailed Deer: Ecology and Management. (L. K. Halls, ed.) Stackpole Books, Harrisburg, PA.

Behrend, D. F. 1966. Behavior of white-tailed deer in an Adirondack Forest. Doctoral dissertation, State University of New York, College of Environmental Science and Forestry, Syracuse.

Behrend, D. F., G. F. Mattfeld, W. C. Tierson, and J. E. Wiley III. 1970. Deer density control for comprehensive management. Journal of Forestry 68:695–700.

Barendse W., and 22 others. 1994. A genetic linkage map of the bovine genome. Nature Genetics 6:227–235.

Breshears, D. D., M. H. Smith, E. G. Cothran, and P. E. Johns. 1988. Genetic variability in white-tailed deer. Heredity 60:139–146.

Carr, S. M., S. W. Ballinger, J. N. Derr, L. H. Blakenship, and J. W. Bickham. 1986. Mitochondrial DNA analysis of hybridization between sympatric white-tailed deer and mule deer in west Texas. Proceedings of the National Academy of Sciences of the USA 83:9576–9580.

Chakraborty, R., and K. Kidd. 1991. The utility of DNA typing in forensic work. Science 254:1735–1739.

Chepko-Sade, B. D., and D. S. Sade. 1979. Patterns of groups splitting within matrilineal kinship groups. Behavioral Ecology and Sociobiology 5:67–86.

Chesser, R. K. 1983. Genetic variability within and among populations of the black-tailed prairie dog. Evolution 37:320–331.

Chesser, R. K. 1991a. Gene diversity and female philopatry. Genetics 127:437–447.

Chesser, R. K. 1991b. Influence of gene flow and breeding tactics on gene diversity within populations. Genetics 129:573–583.

Chesser, R. K., and N. Ryman. 1986. Inbreeding as a strategy in subdivided populations. Evolution 40:616–624.

Clutton-Brock, T. H. 1989. Red Deer in the Highlands. BSP Books, Oxford, United Kingdom.

Clutton-Brock, T. H., F. E., Guiness, and S. D. Albon. 1982. Red Deer, Behavior and Ecology of Two Sexes. University of Chicago Press, Chicago.

Cronin, M. A. 1992. Intraspecific variation of mitochondrial DNA of North American cervids. Journal of Mammalogy 73:70–82.

Cronin, M. A., M. E. Nelson, and D. F. Pac. 1991. Spatial heterogeneity of mitochondrial DNA and allozymes among populations of white-tailed deer and mule deer. Journal of Heredity 82:118–127.

Derr, J. N. 1991. Genetic interactions between white-tailed and mule deer in the southwestern United States. Journal of Wildlife Management 55:228–237.

DeWoody, J. A. 1994. Isolation and characterization of microsatellite markers in white-tailed deer. Master's thesis, Texas A&M University, College Station.

DeWoody, J. A., R. L. Honeycutt, and L. C. Skow. 1995. Microsatellite markers in white-tailed deer. Journal of Heredity 86:317–319.

Ellegren, H., M. Johansson, B. P. Chowdhary, S. Marklund, D. Ruyter, L. Marklund, P. Brauner-Neilson, I. Edfors-Lilia, I. Gustavsson, R. K. Juneja, and L. Andersson. 1993. Assignment of 20 microsatellite markers to the porcine linkage map. Genomics 16:431–439.

Ellsworth, D. L., R. L. Honeycutt, N. J. Silvy, J. W. Bickham, and W. D. Klimstra. 1994. Historical biogeography and contemporary patterns of mitochondrial DNA variation in white-tailed deer from the southeastern United States. Evolution 48:122–136.

Ellsworth, D. L., R. L. Honeycutt, N. J. Silvy, M. H. Smith, J. W. Bickham, and W. D. Klimstra. 1994. White-tailed deer restoration to the southeastern United States: Evaluating genetic variation. Journal of Wildlife Management 58:686–697.

Erlich, H. 1989. Basic methodology. Pages 1–5 in PCR Technology: Principles and Applications for DNA Amplification. (H. Erlich, ed.) MacMillan Publishers, Basingstoke, United Kingdom.

Gavin, T. A., and B. May. 1988. Taxonomic status and genetic purity of Columbian white-tailed deer. Journal of Wildlife Management 52:1–10.

Hawkins, R. E., and W. D. Klimstra. 1970. A preliminary study of the social organization of the white-tailed deer. Journal of Wildlife Management 34:407–419.

Hillestad, H. O. 1984. Stocking and genetic variability of white- tailed deer in the southeastern United States. Doctoral dissertation, University of Georgia, Athens.

Hirth, D. 1977. Social Behavior of White-Tailed Deer in Relation to Habitat. Wildlife Monographs 53, The Wildlife Society, Bethesda, MD.

Hughes, G. A., and S. M. Carr. 1993. Reciprocal hybridization between white-tailed deer and mule deer in western Canada: Evidence from serum albumin and mtDNA sequences. Canadian Journal of Zoology 71:524–530.

Karlin, A. A., G. A. Heidt, and D. W. Sugg. 1989. Genetic variation and heterozygosity in white-tailed deer in southern Arkansas. American Midland Naturalist 121:273–284.

Kennedy, P. K., M. L. Kennedy, and M. L. Beck. 1987. Genetic variability in white-tailed deer *(Odocoileus virginianus)* and its relationship to environmental parameters and herd origin (Cervidae). Genetica 74:189–201.

Liberg, O., A. Axen, A. Johaansson, and K. Wahlström. 1992. Male roe deer territoriality, a rare mating tactic among the Cervidae. Page 353 *in* Biology of Deer. (R. D. Brown, ed.) Springer-Verlag, New York.

Litt, M., and J. Luty. 1989. A hypervariable microsatellite revealed by in vitro amplification of a dinucleotide repeat within the cardiac muscle actin gene. American Journal of Human Genetics 44:397–401.

Manlove, M. N., J. C. Avise, H. O. Hillestad, P. R. Ramsey, M. H. Smith, and D. O. Straney. 1978. Starch gel electrophoresis for the study of population genetics in white-tailed deer. Proceedings of the Southeastern Association of Game and Fisheries Commissioners 29 (1975): 392–403.

Manlove, M. N., M. H. Smith, H. O. Hillestad, S. E. Fuller, P. E. Johns, and D. O. Straney. 1978. Genetic subdivision in a herd of white-tailed deer as demonstrated by spatial shifts in gene frequencies. Proceedings of the Annual Conference Southeastern Association of Fish and Wildlife Agencies 30 (1976): 487–492.

Mantel, N. 1967. The detection of disease clustering and a generalized regression approach. Cancer Research 27:209–220.

Marchington, R. L., and D. L. Hirth. 1984. Behavior. Pages 129–168 in White-Tailed Deer: Ecology and Management. (L. K. Halls, ed.) Stackpole Books, Harrisburg, PA.

Mathews, N. E. 1989. Social structure, genetic structure and anti-predator behavior of white-tailed deer in the central Adirondacks. Doctoral dissertation, State University of New York, College of Environmental Science and Forestry, Syracuse.

Mathews, N. E., and W. F. Porter. 1993. Effect of social structure on genetic structure of free-ranging white-tailed deer in the Adirondack Mountains. Journal of Mammalogy 74:33–43.

Melnick, D. J. 1987. The genetic consequences of primate social organization: A review of macaques, baboons, and vervet monkeys. Genetica 73:117–135.

Moore, S. S., L. L. Sargeant, T. J. King, J. S. Mattick, M. Georges, and J. S. Hetzel. 1991. The conservation of dinucleotide microsatellites among mammalian genomes allows the use of heterologous PCR primer pairs in closely related species. Genomics 10:654–660.

Nelson, M. E. 1993. Natal dispersal and gene flow in white-tailed deer in northeastern Minnesota. Journal of Mammalogy 74:316–322.

Nelson, M. E., and L. D. Mech. 1987. Demes within a northeastern Minnesota deer population. Pages 22–40 *in* Mammalian Dispersal Patterns: The Effects of Social Structure on Population Genetics. (B. D. Chepko-Sade and Z. T. Halpin, eds.) University of Chicago Press, Chicago.

Nelson, M. E., and L. D. Mech. 1992. Dispersal in female white-tailed deer. Journal of Mammalogy 73:891–894.

Olivier, T., C. Ober, J. Buettner-Janusch, and D. S. Sade. 1981. Genetic differentiation among matrilines in social groups of rhesus monkeys. Behavioral Ecology and Sociobiology 8:279–285.

Prout, T. 1981. A note on the island model with sex dependent migration. Theoretical and Applied Genetics 59:327–332.

Ralls, K., P. H. Harvey, and A. M. Lyles. 1986. Inbreeding in natural populations of birds and mammals. Pages 35–56 *in* Conservation Biology: The Science of Scarcity and Diversity. (M. E. Soulé, ed.) Sinauer Associates, Sunderland, MA.

Ramsey, P. R., J. C. Avise, M. H. Smith, and D. F. Urbston. 1979. Biochemical variation and genetic heterogeneity in South Carolina deer populations. Journal of Wildlife Management 43:136–142.

Roy, M. S., E. Geffen, D. Smith, E. A. Ostrander, and R. K. Wayne. 1994. Patterns of differentiation and hybridization in North American wolf-like canids, revealed by analysis of microsatellite loci. Molecular Biology and Evolution 11 (4): 553–570.

Saiki, R. K., D. H. Gelfand, S. Stoffel, S. J. Scharf, R. Higuchi, G. T. Horn, K. B. Mullis, and H. A. Erlich. 1988. Primer-directed enzymatic amplification of DNA with a thermostable DNA polymerase. Science 239:487–491.

Selander, R. K. 1970. Behavior and genetic variation in natural populations. American Zoologist 10:53–66.

Serikawa, T., and 10 others. 1992. Rat gene mapping using PCR-analyzed microsatellites. Genetics 131:701–721.

Sheffield, S. R., R. P. Morgan II, G. A. Feldhamer, and D. M. Harman. 1985. Genetic variation in white-tailed deer *(Odocoileus virginianus)* populations in western Maryland. Journal of Mammalogy 66:243–255.

Smith, M. H., H. O. Hillestad, R. Baccus, and M. N. Manlove. 1984. Population genetics. Pages 119–128 *in* White-Tailed Deer: Ecology and Management. (L. K. Hall, ed.) Stackpole Books, Harrisburg, PA.

Stallings, R. L., A. F. Ford, D. Nelson, D. C. Torney, C. E. Hildebrand, and R. K. Moyzis. 1991. Evolution and distribution of (GT)n repetitive sequences in mammalian genomes. Genomics 10:807–815.

Steffen, P., A. Eggen, A. B Dietz, J. E. Womack, G. Stranzinger, and R. Fries. 1993. Isolation and mapping of polymorphic microsatellites in cattle. Animal Genetics 24:121–124.

Sugg, D. W., and R. K. Chesser. 1994. Effective population sizes with multiple paternity. Genetics 137:1147–1155.

Tautz, D., and M. Renz. 1984. Simple sequences are ubiquitous repetitive components of eukaryotic genomes. Nucleic Acids Research 12:6463–6471.

Taylor, A. C., W. B. Sherman, and R. K. Wayne. 1994. Genetic variation of micro-satellite loci in a bottlenecked species: The northern hairy-nosed wombat *Lasiorhinus krefftii*. Molecular Ecology 3:277–290.

Templeton, A. R. 1986. Co-adaptation and outbreeding depression. Pages 105–116 *in* Conservation Biology: The Science of Scarcity and Diversity. (M. E. Soulé, ed.) Sinauer Associates, Sunderland, MA.

Tierson, W. C., G. F. Mattfeld, R. W. Sage, Jr., and D. F. Behrend. 1985. Seasonal movements and home ranges of white-tailed deer in the Adirondacks. Journal of Wildlife Management 49:760–768.

Travis, S. E., and P. Keim. 1995. Differentiating individuals and populations of mule deer using DNA. Journal of Wildlife Management 59:824–831.

Underwood, H. B. 1986. Population dynamics of a central Adirondack deer herd: Responses to intensive population and forest management. Master's thesis, State University of New York, College of Environmental Science and Forestry, Syracuse.

Weber, J. 1990. Informativeness of human (dC-dA)n-(dG-dT)n polymorphisms. Genomics 7:524–530.

Weber, J., and P. May. 1989. Abundant class of human DNA polymorphisms which can be typed using the polymerase chain reaction. American Journal of Human Genetics 44:388–396.

Woodward, S. R., N. J. Wey, and M. Bunnell. 1994. DNA sequences from Cretaceous period bone fragments. Science 266:1229.

8 Density Dependence in Deer Populations

GARY C. WHITE AND
RICHARD M. BARTMANN

Density dependence in a deer population has major implications for management because the concepts of maximum sustained yield, compensatory mortality, and quality versus quantity assume density-dependent feedback in the population. Density dependence is generally defined as a negative relationship between population growth rate and population size (McCullough 1990). As McCullough (1990) pointed out, growth rate is a misnomer in the sense that its value can be positive, zero, or negative, the last resulting in a decreasing population. A positive growth rate is often associated with populations below carrying capacity, whereas a negative rate is more typical of populations above carrying capacity.

A concept closely tied to density dependence is compensatory mortality, or a change in the rate of remaining sources of mortality in response to a change in the rate of one mortality source. As Kautz (1990) stated, the only reasonable mechanism to explain compensatory mortality is density-dependent mortality.

In this chapter we (1) present models of how density dependence can operate in a population's dynamics, (2) review evidence in the literature of density dependence in deer populations, and (3) discuss some potential problems in experimental design and statistical analysis procedures in investigations of density dependence in deer populations.

MODELS INCORPORATING DENSITY DEPENDENCE

Population models can all be considered special cases of the model

$$N_{t+1} = N_t + B_t - D_t + I_t - E_t,$$

where N_t is population size at time t and, for the interval t to $t + 1$, B_t is number of new animals recruited to the population (births), D_t is number of deaths of animals alive at time t, I_t is number of immigrants into the population, and E_t is number of emigrants leaving the population. When the per capita rate of B_t, D_t, I_t, or E_t, changes with population size, then density-dependent population growth takes place (with population growth meaning either an increase or decrease). If B_t, D_t, I_t, and E_t, are replaced by their per capita rates, that is, $b_t = B_t/N_t$, then the above equation can be rewritten as

$$N_{t+1} = N_t + N_t(b_t - d_t + i_t - e_t)$$
$$= N_t(1 + b_t - d_t + i_t - e_t).$$

When the per capita rates b_t, d_t, i_t, and e_t are independent of population size, density-independent population dynamics result. That is, these rates do not change regardless of population density, or they change randomly with no correlation to population density (see McCullough 1990:534– 535 for definitions of density dependence, density independence, and inverse density dependence).

As a simplification of the above model, suppose $r_t = b_t - d_t + i_t - e_t$ so that all changes in the population between time t and $t + 1$ are modeled by one parameter. Here, r_t corresponds to the population growth rate of McCullough (1990). If r_t is modeled as a simple linear function of N_t, $r_t = r_0(1 - N_t/K)$, where the intercept is r_0 for an N_t of 0 and the slope is r_0/K, the usual logistic growth equation results. When N_t equals K, r_t is 0, and growth ceases because the population has reached carrying capacity, K (Macnab 1985).

Instead of modeling all density dependence in terms of r_t, the relationship can be split among the four components of population change. For example, suppose a population is closed ($i_t = e_t = 0$) all density dependence is in the mortality rate ($d_t = d_0[1 + N_t/K]$), and the per capita birth rate is constant across all population sizes ($b_t = b_0$ for all values of N_t). This simple model will also result in logistic growth because the per capita rate of change is still a linear function of population size. Thus, a density-dependent relationship between population size and any one or combination of the four components results in density-dependent population growth.

Two extensions to this framework are often applied. First, multiple age classes are modeled with the requirement of per capita rates for each age class. However, if relationships between per capita rates for all age classes and population size are assumed linear, growth equivalent to logistic growth still results.

Second, rather than modeling per capita rates of change as linear functions, more complex functions can be substituted. An example is the Richards' curve (Fowler 1981), for which per capita recruitment is

$$r_t = r_0[1 - (N_t/K)^m],$$

and the exponent m changes the shape of the relationship from linear to either concave or convex (Figure 8.1). For $m = 10$, density dependence is not invoked until the population approaches K. For $m = 1$, density dependence is invoked at a constant rate as the population grows. For $m = 0.1$, density dependence is invoked most strongly at low densities and relaxes as the population grows. Fowler (1981) argued that theory and empirical information support the conclusion that most density-dependent change occurs at high population levels (close to carrying capacity) for species with life history strategies typical of large mammals, such as deer ($m > 1$). The reverse is true for species with life history strategies typical of insects and some fishes ($m < 1$). McCullough (1990) also elaborated on this con-

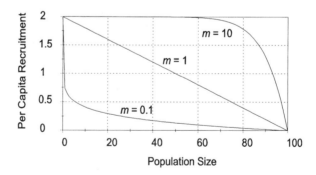

FIGURE 8.1. Forms of density dependence as modeled by the Richards' curve (Fowler 1981). For $m = 1$, logistic growth results; for $m > 1$, density dependence is strongest close to K; and for $m < 1$, density dependence is strongest at low densities.

cept and suggested that the spatial scale of the population being measured and the environmental heterogeneity affect the degree to which deer populations demonstrate density dependence near K.

EVIDENCE OF DENSITY DEPENDENCE
IN DEER POPULATIONS

The density-dependent process has been shown or implied to operate within various aspects of deer biology, for example, pregnancy rates and birth dates (Albon et al. 1983; Clutton-Brock et al. 1987). More important, however, are the cumulative and ultimate effects of these biological aspects as they are reflected in fawn survival and recruitment. Therefore, we considered these two parameters, fawn survival and recruitment, in reviewing four examples concerning density dependence in deer populations. These four studies incorporated one or more of the design requirements discussed by Kautz (1990): randomization, replication, and manipulation. Two other studies not meeting these requirements provided long-term data sets.

Most studies designed to detect density dependence in deer populations have been conducted on small, enclosed or well-defined, free-ranging populations. The George Reserve in Michigan contained a white-tailed deer population with a long and well-documented history (McCullough 1979). The population within the 4.64-km^2 enclosure was manipulated through planned reductions to explore the relationship between density and recruitment. Population size and the age and sex composition of the population during each year of study were reconstructed from age estimates for jaws collected from mortalities. Because nearly all mortalities of deer were from controlled shooting, or could otherwise be accounted for, birth and death dates were available for virtually all deer 6 months or older.

During the 19-year George Reserve study, prehunt populations varied from 16.1 to 34.1 deer/km^2 and posthunt populations from 5.0 to 11.9 deer/km^2. A significant negative relationship was found when recruitment rate (number of 6-month-old fawns per adult doe) was regressed on total posthunt females ($r^2 = 0.501$, $P < 0.01$). A similar regression replacing recruitment rate with total recruitment (total number of 6-month-old fawns) yielded a weaker ($r^2 = 0.317$) but still significant ($P < 0.05$) relationship. Application of this second regression equation supported a declining recruitment rate as the number of posthunt females increased to corroborate further a density-dependent relationship. As discussed below, the first regression has an increased type I error rate because including total females on both sides of the equation induces a correlation. The second regression should be significant for both density-dependent and density-independent populations because, even with density dependence, the number of young produced is a function of the number of adults present to produce them.

Bartmann et al. (1992) demonstrated density dependence in the winter survival of mule deer *(Odocoileus hemionus)* fawns stocked in large fenced pastures on a pinyon *(Pinus edulis)*–juniper *(Juniperus osteosperma)* winter range in northwest Colorado. During each of three winters, three pastures of 1.69, 1.01, and 0.69 km^2 were each stocked with 50 radio- collared fawns and enough adults to achieve densities of 44, 89, and 133 deer/km^2, respectively. These stocking rates represented densities that would have resulted from hunting removals of 67, 33, and 0%, respectively. An inverse relationship between fawn survival rates and density ($P < 0.001$) indicated a strong compensatory mortality process was operating in the population.

In a companion study with free-ranging mule deer fawns on an approximately 50-km^2 winter range, predation accounted for 49–77% of radio-collared fawn mortality over four winters (Bartmann et al. 1992). During the next three winters, coyotes *(Canis latrans)* were intensively removed. Predation rates decreased ($P = 0.004$) and starvation rates increased ($P = 0.042$), compared with the preremoval period, whereas survival rates were unchanged ($P = 0.842$). This study provided evidence of compensatory mortality, supporting results from the pasture study. However, as discussed below, Bartmann et al. (1992) did not correct for the year-to-year variation in predation, starvation, and survival rates. Reanalysis of these data suggests that Bartmann et al. concluded a compensatory mortality effect existed because of this temporal variation. Predation rate was likely not reduced ($P = 0.126$), and starvation rate was not shown to increase ($P = 0.552$).

Red deer *(Cervus elaphus)* on the 12-km^2 north block of the Island of Rhum, Scotland (Clutton-Brock et al. 1985) comprised a small free-ranging population that simulated confinement because of negligible immigration and emigration. Annual culling that occurred prior to the study was discontinued, and the population of hinds increased from 57 to 166. Because all deer could be individually identified and the population was intensively monitored during the 13-year study, fairly rigorous testing for density-dependent effects was possible. As hind density increased, proportions of hinds calving as 3-year-olds and of milk hinds calving decreased, whereas winter calf survival increased ($P < 0.01$). Consequently, calf to hind ratios in spring also decreased ($P < 0.01$). Again, these authors did not correct for temporal variation in their analysis, so they may have concluded that density dependence existed when it did not. However, year-to-year variation in climate and red deer survivorship in the maritime environment of the Island of Rhum is probably small compared with the temporal variation observed in a continental climate.

Hamlin and Mackie (1989) evaluated a 28-year data set on a nonmigratory mule deer population living on a 275-km^2 portion of the Missouri River Breaks in Montana. Fall population estimates ranged from 565 to 1,720, or 2.1 to 6.3 deer/km^2. Although hunting occurred, it was management oriented rather than a planned perturbation. Integrity of the data set was maintained over the 28-year period, but data collection procedures varied. Per capita fawn recruitment to 1 year of age (fawns per female 2 years old or greater) was not significantly related to total adults the previous spring ($r = -0.052, P > 0.05$). A stronger, but still nonsignificant, relationship resulted when total adults were replaced with breeding-age females ($r = -0.246, P > 0.05$). The authors concluded that any density dependence in the recruitment process was obscured by extreme environmental variation. However, such variation could not be separated from sampling variation that, although not quantified, was probably quite large.

The northern Yellowstone elk *(Cervus elaphus)* population has been extensively monitored for many years (Houston 1982). During all but the last 11 years in Houston's report, the elk herd was subjected to varying levels of removals by shooting and trapping within the national park to curb population growth. Public hunting adjacent to the park occurred all years. Calf recruitment to 6–9 months (proportion of cows with calves at heel) was inversely related to population size the previous year ($r^2 = 0.62$, $P < 0.001$). This density-dependent relationship was mostly attributed to calf mortality rather than to reproductive changes. Although the author acknowledged the questionable quality of data collected some years, the large span of years (24) and wide range in estimates of population size (3,000–13,000) were probably the main reasons density dependence was still detectable.

TESTS FOR DENSITY DEPENDENCE

Experimental Design

The need for adequate experimental design in order to detect density dependence operating in a species' population dynamics has been reviewed by Kautz (1990). As with inferences from any experiment, strength of the design directly affects the strength of inferences resulting from the experiment. We agree with Kautz (1990) that many tests of density dependence are flawed because design principles are ignored.

Probably the most commonly violated principle of experimental design is lack of replication. Most experiments to detect density dependence are too costly and time consuming for investigators to replicate the experiment to allow inferences across an entire species. Consequently, results of most experimental tests of density dependence cannot be extrapolated beyond the specific population being studied. None of the studies reported above had adequate replication to make their inferences widely applicable. Realistically, however, we cannot expect massive experiments to be replicated by the same investigators, so replication must be conducted by other investigators and reported in the literature. Also, we believe management by experimentation (Macnab 1985) and adaptive management (Walters 1986) provide state agencies the opportunity to test for density dependence by invoking different management strategies on different management units. Unfortunately, we perceive that most state agencies succumb to political pressure and invoke new management practices statewide rather than by an experimental approach to test new practices actively.

Statistical Tests

Two general methods of testing for density dependence have been developed. For a time series of population sizes, tests of a relationship between change in population size over an interval and population size at the start of the interval are commonly used. The second approach is to regress independently measured population rates, such as birth and death rates, against population size. For both types of tests, the null hypothesis is density independence and the alternative hypothesis is density dependence. Failure to reject the null hypothesis, however, does not constitute evidence of density independence in these cases. Instead, the evidence may suggest the test lacked sufficient sample size or that experimental variance was too high to reject the null hypothesis. In cases in which the null hypothesis of density independence is not rejected, the investigator should report the confidence interval on the parameter being tested. This confidence interval will include the parameter value that suggests density independence because the test failed to reject this hypothesis. A narrow confidence interval is evidence the true parameter value may not differ much from density independence. In contrast, a wide interval suggests the test lacked power to reject a false null hypothesis, and little information is contained in the data relative to the alternative hypothesis of density dependence.

A procedure for testing density dependence in a time series of population sizes was developed for the Hudson Bay trapping data on lynx *(Lynx lynx)* and snowshoe hares *(Lepus americanus)* by Bulmer (1975). Pollard et al. (1987) extended the procedure, and Dennis and Taper (1994) developed it further. These procedures have not been particularly useful in deer research because the long time series of population sizes needed to achieve reasonable power by these tests have not been available. Typically, more than 10 years of data are needed to achieve a power (probability of correctly rejecting the null hypothesis) greater than 0.5 for populations fluctuating around carrying capacity. Further, all procedures suffer increased type I errors when population sizes are estimated and include lognormally distributed sampling error (T. Shenk, Colorado State University, personal communication). Considerable controversy has developed over the usefulness of these tests (Hanski et al. 1993; Holyoak and Lawton 1993; Wolda and Dennis 1993; Wolda et al. 1993), so we will not consider them further.

Procedures to test for a relationship between recruitment (including per capita birth or death rates) and population size have been used extensively to test for density dependence (Tanner 1966; McCullough 1979). The approach is to regress population growth rate against population size. If population growth is density independent, the expected slope of the regression is 0. If density-dependent growth is occurring, the slope and correlation of the regression should be negative. However, as first pointed out by Eberhardt (1970), population growth rate (recruitment) must be estimated independently of population size. When population growth rate is estimated from the time series of population sizes as

$$\hat{r}_t = (N_{t+1} - N_t)/N_t,$$

and $\hat{r}_t$ is regressed against N_t, a correlation is induced because N_t occurs on both sides of the regression. Eberhardt (1970) pointed out that correlations of about -0.7 are expected for sequences of random numbers when tested with the regression procedure used by Tanner (1966).

The induced correlation problem also occurs when the number of new recruits (fawns, F_t) in the population is divided by N_t to obtain the per capita recruitment rate and then this rate is regressed against N_t. Here, N_t is in the denominator of the dependent variable (F_t/N_t) and is the independent variable. Hence, this simple linear regression is likely to suggest density dependence more often than it should. The appropriate analysis is to regress fawns against N_t and N_t^2 without an intercept, that is,

$$F_t = \beta_1 N_t + \beta_2 N_t^2,$$

and then test the null hypothesis of $\beta_2 = 0$. If the test rejects the null hypothesis and β_2 is less than 0, then fawn recruitment has been shown density dependent.

If the estimate of reproductive rate is independent of that of population size, then similar procedures can be used to assess density dependence in reproduction. The trap to avoid is a regression with the same variable on both sides of the equation, that is, creating an induced correlation.

A similar problem would occur if the number of animals dying in the population were divided by the population size and then regressed against population size. However, a more common procedure is to estimate the mortality rate in the population by means of radio tracking. A logistic regression procedure can then be used to regress the mortality rate (or equivalently, survival rate) against population size,

$$\text{logit}[n_{td}/(n_{tl} + n_{td})] = \beta_0 + \beta_1 N_t,$$

where n_{td} and n_{tl} are the number of radio-marked animals that died and lived, respectively, and $\text{logit}(p) = \log(p/[1 - p])$, where p is the proportion $n_{td}/(n_{tl} + n_{td})$. Note that the radio-marked sample and estimate of mortality rate are independent of population size, so no induced correlation is present in this logistic regression. A significant positive value of β_1 indicates density-dependent mortality, whereas, if the survival rate is regressed against N_t, density dependence is indicated by a negative value of β_1.

Power of Tests for Density Dependence

Power of a statistical test is defined as the probability the test will reject the null hypothesis given that the null hypothesis is false (or conversely, that the alternative hypothesis is true). Three factors are usually under the control of the experimenter and can be manipulated to increase the power of statistical tests for density dependence: increasing the size of the density-dependent response, decreasing sampling variation, and removing environmental variance.

To maximize the power of the tests of the slopes of recruitment rate, birth rate, or mortality rate against population size, the population should be manipulated over a range of values. For example, if the population is at K, the slope of the regression is expected to be zero, and failure to reject the null hypothesis that the coefficient is zero does not constitute evidence of density independence. To see if density dependence operates in the population, the population must be observed at densities less than K. The larger the difference between low and high densities at which observations are made, the greater the probability of detecting density dependence. McCullough (1982) provided an excellent example of manipulating a population to increase power of the experiment when he reduced the George Reserve white-tailed deer population to about 10 animals and then allowed them to increase unhindered.

Survival monitoring with small sample sizes of radio-tracked animals will result in low power because of a large sampling variance. For survival rates $(\hat{S})$, the variance of the estimate is inversely proportional to sample size. Thus, for $\hat{S}$ of 0.4, a sample of size 10 has a variance of $0.4(1 - 0.4)/10$, or 0.024, whereas a sample of size 100 has a variance of 0.0024. Bartmann et al. (1992) used 50 radio-marked mule deer fawns for each of three treatments in each of 3 years in their pasture study. Still, they had a power of less than 80% to detect a difference in survival of less than 0.1. To overcome the limitations of sample size, they attempted to maximize the treatment effect to increase the power of the experiment.

Another factor that influences power by means of increased sampling variation is precision of the estimate of population size. Most studies do not have a census of the population, so population size is estimated and this estimate includes sampling variation. The effect of sampling variation is to lower the power of the statistical test of density dependence.

Another source of variation that will lower the power of regression tests is temporal and spatial (environmental) variation in population growth rates, that is, the beta noise of McCullough (1990). For example, we monitored mule deer fawn survival in three study areas and obtained estimates of 30 annual survival rates in the Piceance Basin in northwest Colorado (see Bartmann et al. 1992 for a description of study areas and methods). The mean survival rate was 0.357 (standard error = 0.038). However, the survival rates among years and study areas varied from $\hat{S} = 0.03$ to $\hat{S} = 0.81$. Using the technique suggested by Burnham et al. (1987)

to estimate variation of the survival process (process variation) separately from sampling variation caused by a finite sample of radio-marked animals, we find a process variance of 0.040 (95% CI, 0.024 to 0.076). If the true survival rate for each year is drawn from a normal distribution with a mean 0.357 and a variance 0.040, then 95% of true survival rates would occur in the interval −0.035 to 0.749.

The following example demonstrates this calculation. Suppose survival rates of 0.3, 0.4, and 0.5 are estimated from 50 radio-marked fawns during three winters. The estimated total variance for these three estimates is

$$\sum_1^n (\hat{S}_i - \bar{S})^2/(n - 1) = 0.01.$$

However, this estimate includes both sampling and temporal variation. Sampling variation is a function of sample size and can be estimated for each estimate by the formula, variance $(\hat{S}_i) = \hat{S}_i(1 - \hat{S}_i)/n_i$. For an n_i of 50 each year, estimates of sampling variance are 0.0042, 0.0048, and 0.0050, respectively. Variation due to time, although unknown, is the variation in the true parameter across the 3 years. Variation in the process is not a function of sample size but a result of year-to-year differences in the true survival rate because of weather or other random effects. To estimate this process variation, a numerical optimization is required (Burnham et al. 1987): for this example, the estimate of process variation is 0.0054.

To overcome the loss of power because of high temporal (process) variation, a control area is needed to remove the effects of time. Thus, Bartmann et al. (1992) stocked deer in pastures at three different densities to test for density effects. Even though there were differences in survival across years, the pattern of density effects among pastures was consistent across years and allowed detecting a response in survival as a function of density.

Example of Power in a Test of Density Dependence

Although tests for density dependence based on regression analysis seem simple and easy to apply, little evidence of density dependence has been detected in deer populations. Here we demonstrate that even strong density-dependent effects will not be detected without experimental designs that remove environmental variation. Typically, data used in regression analyses are collected over some time period without a spatial control to account for environmental variation. Suppose fawn survival in a deer population is monitored for 5 years with 50 radio-marked fawns each year. Density is then reduced, and the population monitored for another 5 years, again with 50 radio-marked fawns each year. A test of density dependence would be whether the mean survival rate for the second 5-year period (low density) is greater than that for the first 5-year period (high density).

To evaluate the power of this approach, assume annual survival for the first 5 years is 0.357, a value based on survival for mule deer fawns in the Piceance Basin of northwest Colorado. Further assume the true survival for each year in the first 5 years is selected from a normal distribution with a mean of 0.357 and a variance of 0.040. Values were constrained to the range 0.02–0.99. Let mean annual survival in the second 5 years increase over the first 5 years by the amount Δ. The larger the value of Δ, the greater the mean annual survival and the stronger the density-dependent response.

The null hypothesis is that mean survival for the first 5-year period equals mean survival for the second 5-year period, which can be tested with logistic regression. The appropriate sampling unit for this study would be a year, so sample size is 10 years. However, most logistic regression procedures do not have methods to treat year as a random effect in order to construct the proper test of the null hypothesis stated above. Typically, users might specify the model

$$\text{logit}[n_{tl}/(n_{tl} + n_{td})] = P_i,$$

where P_i is a dummy variable specifying the 5-year period effect, that is, period 1 or period 2. However, this analysis treats the sample size as the total number of radio-marked fawns, or 500. The appropriate model is

$$\text{logit}[n_{tl}/(n_{tl} + n_{td})] = P_i + Y_i(P_i),$$

where $Y_i(P_i)$ is the year effect nested within the period effect. The appropriate test is then constructed as the ratio of the chi-square values divided by their respective degrees of freedom to form an F ratio:

$$F_{(1,8)} = [\chi^2_{(1)}/1]/[\chi^2_{(8)}/8].$$

The power of this test to reject the null hypothesis when appropriate is shown in Figure 8.2 for values of Δ from 0 to 0.6 and values of the process variation of survival from 0 to 0.04. Each estimate of power is based on 1,000 simulations. The power of the test to detect density dependence de-

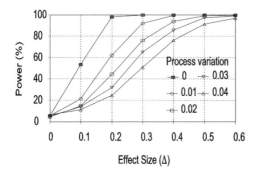

FIGURE 8.2. Power of *F*-test for fawn survival. Curves represent the power (probability of correctly rejecting the null hypothesis) of an *F*-test for fawn survival for seven effect sizes (Δ) and five values of process variation. Each plotted value is based on 1,000 simulations.

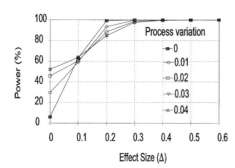

FIGURE 8.3. Power of χ^2 test for fawn survival. Curves represent the power (probability of correctly rejecting the null hypothesis) of a χ^2 test for fawn survival for seven effect sizes (Δ) and five values of process variation. Each plotted value is based on 1,000 simulations.

creases as the process variation increases. Even with no process variation, the probability of detecting density dependence with an increase in survival of 0.1 is only 0.53. For a Δ of 0.1, any process variation lowers the power substantially, down to 0.11 for a process variance of 0.04.

The problem with using a simple chi-square test is shown in Figure 8.3, in which the rejection rate (power) of the chi-square test is shown. For a Δ of 0, the rejection rate exceeds an α of 0.05 for values of process variance greater than 0. Particularly note that the type I error (probability of rejecting a true [Δ = 0] null hypothesis) rate reaches 0.54 for a process variance of 0.04. Thus, if process variance exists during the study, the chi-square test will reject a true null hypothesis more often than it should. Investigators would conclude that density dependence exists when it does not. When density dependence does exist, that is, Δ is greater than 0, this test suggests better power than does the *F*-test. However, the type I error rate of greater than 0.05 invalidates the simple chi-square test.

As this power calculation exercise demonstrates, even with a large number of radio-marked animals to estimate survival, a planned experiment that lacks a spatial control to remove environmental variation has little chance of detecting a reasonable (0.1–0.2) increase in survival. We doubt that increasing survival beyond an increment of 0.2 is biologically feasible. Therefore, we are not surprised density dependence is seldom detected by merely observing a population, that is, with no manipulation or temporal and spatial controls, when the correct statistical test is performed. Lack of a treatment to increase power of the statistical test, lack of spatial controls to remove temporal variation in the population process, and the usual lack of an exceptionally large sample size all preclude detecting density dependence even when a strong effect may be operating in the population.

CONCLUSIONS

Detection of density dependence in deer populations is complicated by the presence of process variation (including environmental variation.) Proper analysis methods correct for process variation, but none of the published tests for density dependence have used these methods. Other studies have concluded that density dependence exists in a population but have likely induced a correlation by including the same variable on both sides of the regression equation. Hence, investigators may have incorrectly concluded that density dependence exists in a population. Finally, studies that conclude density dependence does not exist in a deer population generally fail to reject the null hypothesis of density independence and then conclude that the null hypothesis is true. Given the difficulty of conducting large-scale, long-term studies to detect density dependence, it is not surprising that researchers are unable to provide conclusive evidence that density dependence commonly exists in deer populations.

For deer populations in environments with large year-to-year variation, detection of density dependence without a spatial control for temporal variation is unlikely. Thus, evidence for density dependence will be difficult to accumulate. Because tests for density dependence that lack a spatial control will have a low probability of detecting density dependence, managers will tend to be misled into thinking that density independence occurs in the population.

ACKNOWLEDGMENTS

This work was funded by Colorado Federal Aid in Wildlife Restoration Projects FW-26-P and W-153-R. We thank the numerous personnel from the Colorado Division of Wildlife, Los Alamos National Laboratory, and Colorado State University, and many other volunteers, who helped conduct the 15 years of mule deer research in the Piceance Basin. Constructive comments provided by Tanya Shenk, Ron C. Kufeld, and Warren Snyder are greatly appreciated.

REFERENCES CITED

Albon, S. D., B. Mitchell, and B. W. Staines. 1983. Fertility and body weight in female red deer: A density dependent relationship. Journal of Animal Ecology 52:969–980.

Bartmann, R. M., G. C. White, and L. H. Carpenter. 1992. Compensatory Mortality in a Colorado Mule Deer Population. Wildlife Monographs 121, The Wildlife Society, Bethesda, MD.

Bulmer, M. G. 1975. The statistical analysis of density dependence. Biometrica 31:901–911.

Burnham, K. P., D. R. Anderson, G. C. White, C. Brownie, and K. H. Pollock. 1987. Design and Analysis Methods for Fish Survival Experiments Based on Release–Recapture. American Fisheries Society Monograph 5, Bethesda, MD.

Clutton-Brock, T. H., M. Major, and F. E. Guinness. 1985. Population regulation in male and female red deer. Journal of Animal Ecology 54:831–846.

Clutton-Brock, T. H., M. Major, S. D. Albon, and F. E. Guinness. 1987. Early development and population dynamics in red deer. I. Density-dependent effects on juvenile survival. Journal of Animal Ecology 56:53–67.

Dennis, B., and M. Taper. 1994. Density dependence in time series observations of natural populations: Detecting stability in stochastic systems. Ecological Monographs 64:205–224.

Eberhardt, L. L. 1970. Correlation, regression, and density dependence. Ecology 51:306–310.

Fowler, C. W. 1981. Density dependence as related to life history strategy. Ecology 62:602–610.

Hamlin, K. L., and R. J. Mackie. 1989. Mule deer in the Missouri River Breaks, Montana: A study of population dynamics in a fluctuating environment. Montana Department of Fisheries, Wildlife, and Parks, Federal Aid in Wildlife Restoration, Project W-120-R-7-18, Final Report, Bozeman.

Hanski, I., I. Woiwod, and J. Perry. 1993. Density dependence, population persistence, and largely futile arguments. Oecologia 95:595–598.

Holyoak, M., and J. H. Lawton. 1993. Comment arising from a paper by Wolda and Dennis: Using and interpreting the results of tests for density dependence. Oecologia 95:592–594.

Houston, D. B. 1982. The Northern Yellowstone Elk: Ecology and Management. Macmillan Publishing Co., New York.

Kautz, J. E. 1990. Testing for compensatory responses to removals from wildlife populations. Transactions of the North American Wildlife and Natural Resources Conference 55:527–533.

Macnab, J. 1985. Carrying capacity and related slippery shibboleths. Wildlife Society Bulletin 13:403–410.

McCullough, D. R. 1979. The George Reserve Deer Herd: Population Ecology of a K-Selected Species. University of Michigan Press, Ann Arbor.

McCullough, D. R. 1982. Population growth rate of the George Reserve deer herd. Journal of Wildlife Management 46:1079–1083.

McCullough, D. R. 1990. Detecting density dependence: Filtering the baby from the bathwater. Transactions of the North American Wildlife and Natural Resources Conference 55:534–543.

Pollard, E., K. H. Lakhani, and P. Rothery. 1987. The detection of density dependence from a series of annual censuses. Ecology 68:2046–2055.

Tanner, J. T. 1966. Effects of population density on growth rates of animal populations. Ecology 47:733–745.

Walters, C. J. 1986. Adaptive Management of Renewable Resources. Macmillan Publishing Co., New York.

Wolda, H., and B. Dennis. 1993. Density dependence tests, are they? Oecologia 95:581–591.

Wolda, H., B. Dennis, and M. Taper. 1993. Density dependence tests, and largely futile comments: Answers to Holyoak and Lawton (1993) and Hanski, Woiwod and Perry (1993). Oecologia 98:229–234.

9 Density Effects on Deer Sociobiology

KARL V. MILLER AND JOHN J. OZOGA

Although still poorly understood, biologists have begun to investigate the relationships between white-tailed deer herd demographics, deer social behavior, and the effects of human-induced changes on deer biology and productivity. There have been numerous suggestions published as to the effects of deer herd management strategies, or nonmanagement, on deer social behavior and the effects of deer social behavior on deer population dynamics (Cowan 1972; Marchinton 1982; Ozoga et al. 1982; Ozoga and Verme 1985; Miller, Kammermeyer, et al. 1987; Bubenik 1988; Miller et al. 1995). Despite recent interest in the topic, relatively little is known about the interactions between deer social behavior and population demographics and dynamics. This lack of understanding is the result of a number of factors.

1. Although data on population attributes such as age-specific mortality rates or natality rates are relatively simple to collect, data pertaining to behavioral attributes such as an age-specific behavioral pattern as related to deer density, herd age structure, or adult sex ratio are much more difficult to obtain. Typical hypothetical–deductive experiments are essentially impossible to conduct. Rather, analysis and inference rely on observational data, correlational data, and syntheses of published accounts. These published accounts often are fragmentary, based on small sample sizes and anecdotal observations, or buried in the text of papers dealing with other aspects of deer management or biology.

2. The white-tailed deer's social organization originated as an adaptation to the ecosystems in which the animal evolved. However, some, or perhaps most, of our original concepts of deer behavior are based on studies of heavily exploited herds—herds that have been primarily male harvested. These herds have altered age structures and adult sex ratios that are heavily skewed toward females. Recent studies of deer herds suggest that the social patterns of deer are more complex than originally reported and that published descriptions of behaviors and their social significance may have been oversimplified (Ozoga et al. 1982; Ozoga and Verme 1984, 1985, 1986; Miller, Marchinton, et al. 1987; Mathews and Porter 1993).

3. Studies in the southern and midwestern United States of deer herds that have been restored in the relatively recent past suggest that behavioral patterns and their ecological significance may vary among regions and habitat types (Guynn et al. 1988; Marchinton, Miller, et al. 1990; Jacobson 1992; Jacobson and Kroll, in press). In many southern and midwestern regions deer herds do not experience dramatic seasonal shifts in habitat conditions typical of more northern regions (Nelson and Mech 1981; Tierson et al. 1985), and thus reproductive patterns are less constrained seasonally.

4. Colonization of habitat fragments and urban–suburban habitats has resulted in populations, or population fragments, that are essentially unmanaged. These small, isolated populations can differ dramatically from surrounding herds and therefore have quite different sociobiological patterns (Nixon et al. 1991). In fact, some of these populations appear to become self-regulating due to nutritional and sociobiological mechanisms that affect recruitment and emigration. They may even achieve a stable population level, although this level often is greater than what may be considered an ecological carrying capacity or greater than a human tolerance carrying capacity. In some cases, deer demographics in these fragment herds are very similar to high-density, heavily male-harvested herds. Due to sociobiological mechanisms, these unmanaged herds may mimic the unequal sex ratios and young male age structures found in many heavily exploited herds.

In this chapter, we review and synthesize some of the published data on deer sociobiology and suggest a conceptual model of the social life of deer in habitat fragments and in high-density herds in general. That sociobiological mechanisms can affect maturational and reproductive processes is widely accepted in a variety of vertebrate species (see reviews by Vandenbergh 1983; Bronson 1989). Our review includes the effect of high density on deer behavior, as well as the effects of behavior on population attributes in these populations.

FEMALE SUPPRESSION

Throughout their range, white-tailed deer generally have not been considered a territorial species (Smith 1976; Coblentz 1977). Rather, the basic social system is a dominance hierarchy, and the behavior of individuals is closely associated with their social status (Marchinton and Hirth 1984). Female social organization is considered to be a matriarchal group consisting of three to four generations of females and their offspring (Montgomery 1959; Nelson and Mech 1981; Mathews and Porter 1993).

Perhaps one of the most detailed and complete investigations of the influence of whitetail demographics on their biology was initiated in 1972 in the 252-ha enclosure at the Cusino Wildlife Research Station in Upper Michigan (Ozoga and Verme 1982). The major emphasis of this study was to explore the pros and cons of supplementally feeding deer to achieve densities higher than the habitat could support naturally. However, it also provided the opportunity to determine the consequences of density stress on deer presumably independent of their nutritional state, as herd size increased from 23 to 159 animals (Ozoga and Verme 1982; Ozoga et al. 1982; Seal et al. 1983). Follow-up investigations were designed to evaluate the possible reproductive consequences of simulated heavy exploitation of females (Ozoga and Verme 1984) and of males (Ozoga and Verme 1985).

Although supplemental nutrition allowed the herd to grow to approximately 10 times the area's normal carrying capacity, there were no behavioral or clinical signs of an impending population crash. High densities did not result in dramatic density-dependent changes in deer physiology (Seal et al. 1983) as has been proposed for other cervids (Christian 1980).

Even at high density, the productivity of yearling does was not sharply curtailed, although both yearlings and 2.5-year-old does bred later than normal. However, recruitment declined steadily as density increased; neonatal losses increased from 0 to 23%, despite does being provided high-quality supplemental feed ad lib.

Ozoga et al. (1982) reported that immediately pre- and postparturition, female deer isolated themselves and demonstrated territorial characteristics for approximately 4 weeks. These findings subsequentially were substantiated by Schwede et al. (1993). Matriarch does (≥4 years

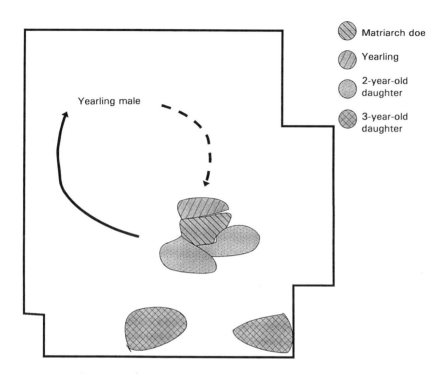

Matriarch doe

Yearling

2-year-old
daughter

3-year-old
daughter

Yearling male

FIGURE 9.1. Partuition home range of matriarch doe. Shown are the annual patterns in parturition home range of a matriarch doe and her offspring at the Cusino Wildlife Research Station in Upper Michigan (adapted from Ozoga et al. 1982). Most yearling males disperse from natal ranges, although a few return.

old) defended the same fawning area annually; primiparous (2-year-old) daughters occupied adjacent exclusive sites; and 3-year-olds established new grounds away from the family group (Figure 9.1). This territorial behavior had little effect on deer herd dynamics at low densities but became an important factor in decreasing neonatal survival rates once the herd size surpassed 38.6 deer/km².

Ozoga et al. (1982) suggested that increased neonatal mortality was due primarily to fawn abandonment and imprinting failure as a result of territorial behavior at high densities. Neonatal losses were related to social status and the ability to establish fawning territories. At high densities, prime-aged does lost only 6% of fawns born, 3-year-olds lost 24% (usually one of a pair of twins), and 2-year-olds lost 63% (usually both of a pair of twins and one-third of singletons). Apparently, density stress, presumably independent of nutritional stress, has little effect on in utero productivity among social classes but can have marked effects on the survival of neonates.

In the final years of the study, the enclosed herd was reduced from 159 to 44 deer to mimic severe exploitation of antlerless deer. In some matriarchal groups all but one member were removed (isolates), whereas in other groups 3–12 does were retained (socials) to determine responses of the surviving female to such drastic social change. Such repeated treatments over a 3-year period did not influence the date of breeding or number of fawns produced by yearling or 3.5-year-old or older does. However, 2.5-year-old isolates bred earlier, produced more fawns, and successfully reared more fawns than did socials of the same age (Ozoga and Verme 1984). Lack of maternal domination and access to uncontested fawning territory appeared to be important factors that modified the behavior and physiology of these does, hence improving their reproductive performance.

Compared with social does, isolate females also had higher plasma progesterone levels in March. This trend was consistent among age classes and was not dependent on fetal numbers. The authors hypothesized that adrenal progesterone secretion increased in isolates that had difficulty achieving compatible associations in winter, when sociability is highest and most vital to herd welfare on northern ranges.

In white-tailed deer, maternal success largely determines the primiparous doe's social standing. Those who fail to rear fawns at 2 years of age revert to yearling behavior by seeking their mother's leadership (Ozoga et al. 1982). Within the Cusino enclosure, maternally unsuccessful 2-year-old does bred an average of 1 week later than those having reared fawns and conceived more male progeny (64.7 versus 38.9%, respectively). Ozoga and Verme (1986) speculated that abnormally high levels of adrenal progesterone among socially subordinate 2-year-old does could block estradiol-induced luteinizing hormone surges during estrus (Plotka et al. 1983), which in turn could delay ovulation. In that event, delayed copulation could influence sex of the conceptus (Verme and Ozoga 1981) and explain the differential sex ratio among progeny conceived.

The Cusino enclosure studies clearly demonstrate that density stress and social subordination can alter a doe's rate of physical maturation and reproductive performance, probably independent of nutrition. Whether sociobiological mechanisms such as neonatal territoriality can regulate populations at high densities has not been demonstrated experimentally. However, anecdotal evidence suggests that some high-density, unhunted populations may achieve stable densities. Postparturition fawn mortality should be investigated as one mechanism regulating growth of these herds.

The prevalence and duration of territoriality during the neonatal period may vary among deer herds and among habitat types. Ozoga et al. (1982), for example, found a shorter period of territoriality expressed at high versus low herd density. Likewise, while Hirth's (1977) findings for northern white-tailed deer in forested habitats on the George Reserve in Michigan were similar to those of Ozoga et al. (1982) and Schwede et al. (1993), his observations of does on savannah grasslands of south Texas indicated little evidence of neonatal territoriality. Compared with deer in Michigan, however, unmarked and unhunted deer on Hirth's Texas study area lived at high density (twice that of the George Reserve) and probably experienced high neonatal mortality (Beasom 1974). Apparently, fawning white-tailed deer exhibit behavioral plasticity in response to prevailing social opportunities (and pressures) as well as habitat conditions.

Physiological development of males also was affected by increased density in the Cusino study. At high densities, yearling males had notably poor antler development. Twenty-two percent of yearlings (versus 0% at low densities) grew very short spike antlers (≤ 3 inches) despite being supplied high-quality nutrition. Ozoga and Verme (1982) suggested that socially stressed male fawns experienced a physiological setback and probable sex hormone imbalance that impaired antler pedicle development. Presumably, undersized pedicles resulted in smaller-than-normal antlers. Thus, the consequences of social stress at high densities on male physiological development is similar to those due to poor nutrition. Conversely, the Cusino study found that male fawns raised by social mothers had higher growth rates than did males raised by isolates, possibly the result of social facilitation (Clayton 1978).

DIFFERENTIAL DISPERSAL

Dispersal patterns of young white-tailed deer also can be affected by social pressures. Yearling males disperse at a much higher rate than do other age classes of males or females of any age (Hawkins et al. 1971; Kammermeyer and Marchinton 1976a; Downing and McGinnes 1976; Nixon et al. 1991). A number of reasons for the dispersal tendencies of young deer have been proposed: antagonism due to competition for food or space (Hawkins et al. 1971), hunting pressure, innate behavioral patterns, antagonism among males competing for breeding privileges (Kammermeyer and Marchinton 1976a), and antagonism of females toward maturing males, particularly sons. Downing et al. (1969) first suggested that movements by young males and females may be triggered by their mothers' antagonism toward them. Ozoga and Verme (1985) later suggested that yearling males leave familial range because of behaviorally stressful domination by older female relatives, plus a basic drive to seek fraternal membership in which to establish their dominance status.

That maternal domination is important in prompting dispersal among yearling males was demonstrated by Holzenbein and Marchinton (1992a), who compared the dispersal tendencies of males orphaned as weaned fawns with males who matured with their mothers. By 30 months of age, only 9% of orphans had dispersed whereas 87% of the control males had dispersed. Holzenbein and Marchinton suggested that differential dispersal evolved as a means to reduce inbreeding; the inclusive fitness of mothers may benefit most from dispersal of their male offspring, leading to a situation in which mothers force their male offspring to leave their natal range (Holzenbein and Marchinton 1992b).

Regardless of the underlying mechanism, differential dispersal by young males can have important effects on deer demography and social behavior, particularly in deer populations occupying habitat fragments. Marchinton (1982) suggested that adult sex ratios of herds within restricted geographical areas tend to become increasingly biased toward females as density increases. Furthermore, loss of yearling males from fragment populations likely will be much greater than ingress from adjacent source populations because larger populations usually are hunted and many young males may be harvested (Kammermeyer and Marchinton 1976a, 1976b). Ingress into the fragment likely will depend on the size of the fragment and the distance to the "continental" source population. Ingress of dispersing males into small, isolated fragments may be very limited, whereas egress may remove a significant portion of the yearling males (Figure 9.2). Thus, the demographics of many fragmented populations may mimic those of heavily male-harvested populations: young age structure among males and sex ratios heavily skewed toward females. Recent research has pointed to several important implications of such demographically altered herds (Gruver et al. 1984; Guynn et al. 1988; Jacobson 1992). However, as with most other aspects of deer social systems, the severity of the effects of young age structures and skewed sex ratios varies among regions of the country (Ozoga and Verme 1985; Marchinton, Miller, et al. 1990; Miller et al. 1995).

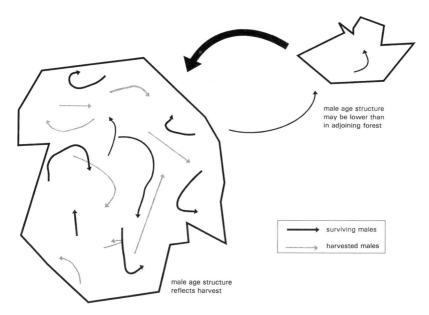

male age structure
may be lower than
in adjoining forest

surviving males

harvested males

male age structure
reflects harvest

FIGURE 9.2. Effect of yearling male dispersal on demographics. Shown are the effects of yearling male dispersal on male age structure of "continental" populations and isolated populations occupying habitat fragments. Dispersing males are indicated by arrows; relative emigration from and immigration to fragments are suggested by arrow size.

MALE SUPPRESSION AND BIOSTIMULATION

Under typical demographic conditions, male deer maintain a ritualized breeding system. Physically mature males dominate younger males, and a relatively small number of dominant males have preferential breeding rights in a given area (Marchinton and Hirth 1984). Males apparently do not normally join the breeding hierarchy until they are quite old (McCullough 1979). Thus, it appears likely that the most genetically and physically "fit" males will contribute disproportionately to future generations. In populations where few mature males remain, yearling males engage in breeding and courtship activities but fail to establish a strict dominance hierarchy (Ozoga and Verme 1985). The breeding system changes from a dominance competition to a "scramble" competition among the young males to breed estrous does. This lack of a dominance order suggests that most yearling males do some breeding under these demographic conditions and thereby may ultimately reduce the herd's genetic fitness in the long run (Ozoga and Verme 1985).

The presence of older males also tends to suppress aggressiveness and breeding competition among younger males, thereby helping to maintain the "agonistic balance" (Ozoga 1989). This suppressor effect (Marchinton, Miller, et al. 1990), caused by the presence of mature males and their signposts, may result in lowered testosterone levels in the younger males, thereby reducing the young male's aggressiveness and libido. Social aggression and the performance of certain ritualized rutting behaviors, such as scent marking, may be dependent on serum testosterone concentrations (Bubenik et al. 1977; Miller, Kammermeyer, et al. 1987). For a South Carolina herd, Miller et al. (1988) reported significantly higher and earlier testosterone peaks in 3.5-year-old or older males than in younger males. Reduced reproductive effort by young males, and subsequently reduced rut-related weight loss, likely leads to better overall physical development at maturity.

Young age structures and skewed sex ratios can also affect the timing of breeding, especially in herds in southern latitudes. Although the timing of the breeding season in white-tailed deer is directly influenced by photoperiod (Goss 1983), recent studies have suggested that herd demographics and resultant social factors can have pronounced effects on the timing, duration, and intensity of the rut. In a long-term study, Guynn et al. (1988) transformed a deer herd with a young male age structure and skewed sex ratio to a demographically more balanced herd by selective harvesting. Within 5 years, these changes resulted in a shorter breeding season (43 versus 96 days). In addition, the earliest breeding dates and the peak conception dates occurred much earlier. Mean conception dates shifted from 11 November in the first year of the study to 15 October during the fifth year. Similar shifts in breeding dates in response to changes in demography were reported by Jacobson (1992). In these studies, the increased proportion of mature males likely played a direct role in the earlier and more synchronous breeding season by reducing the number of females remaining unbred during their first and subsequent estrous cycles.

Miller et al. (1992) suggested that glandular secretions and urinary deposits left at antler rubs and scrapes act as a source of priming pheromones that assist in the termination of seasonal anestrus. Yearling males begin making antler rubs later than do mature males and make fewer rubs during the breeding season (Ozoga and Verme 1985; Miller, Kammermeyer, et al. 1987; Marchinton, Johansen, et al. 1990). Similarly, older males begin making ground scrapes approximately 2 months prior to the onset of breeding. Yearling males make very few scrapes and generally do not begin scraping until immediately prior to breeding begins (Ozoga and Verme 1985). In herds having mature males, signposting occurs much earlier and is more intense than in herds with young male age structures. Biostimulation through the presence of mature males (Verme et al. 1987) or their signposts (Miller et al. 1992) may affect timing of breeding, especially in southern herds that are not subject to severe seasonal fluctuations in habitat quality (Miller et al. 1995). Recent experimental studies in Eld's deer *(Cervus elaphus eldi)* have demonstrated that the presence of male Eld's deer, or their scent, can affect the reproductive physiology of Eld's deer hinds (Hosack et al., in press).

Prolonged breeding seasons due to unbalanced deer herds result in several negative effects. With a lengthy rut, males display rutting behaviors as long as females continue to enter estrus (Bubenik et al. 1977). Extended rutting activity likely can predispose males to higher than normal winter mortality rates in northern ranges or to reduced physical condition in southern ranges.

Natural selection has minimized the timing of births that deviate from the norm in northern environments, where a properly timed and brief rut is most conducive to good reproductive success (Verme 1965, 1969). In contrast, on southern ranges where winter climatic stress is not as severe, mean fawning dates for some herds occur outside the normal spring fawning period (Jacobson et al. 1980; Richter and Labisky 1985). However, Knox et al. (1993), Shea et al. (1994), and Jacobson (1995) have shown that body weight and antler development of yearling males is directly related to the male's date of birth. Thus, on southern ranges, a male's reproductive fitness may be related more to date of birth than to genetic background.

Delayed and protracted breeding seasons also can affect the female's fitness. White-tailed deer fawns are "hiders," relying on cryptic coloration and reduced scent to avoid predation. White-tailed deer use prey saturation to minimize predation by synchronizing fawning during a brief period in late spring. Prolonged breeding seasons in some deer herds may result in greater numbers of vulnerable fawns being at risk of predation (see Rutberg 1987). Additionally, late breeding among some matriarchal lineages appears to be a self-perpetuating phenomenon. Daughters of females bred late during the breeding season (and thus born late) appear to experience estrus later than do earlier-born members of their cohort (K. V. Miller, personal observation).

IMPLICATIONS

Numerous researchers have published findings describing the variability of deer social systems and management effects on this variability (Walther 1972; Geist 1981; Ozoga et al. 1982; Marchinton and Atkeson 1985; Miller et al. 1995). However, few aspects of deer sociobiology have been incorporated into population management principles. Mathews' (1989) "rose-petal" hypothesis is among the first to utilize information on deer social systems to provide management guidelines for controlling deer numbers. However, because white-tailed deer exhibit significant behavioral plasticity in response to differing habitat and demographic conditions, management strategies designed for a particular deer herd should not be applied universally.

ACKNOWLEDGMENTS

Publication of this paper was supported by McIntire-Stennis Project GEO-0049-MS-A and grants from Wellington Outdoors, Madison, Georgia, and Hunter's Specialties, Cedar Rapids, Iowa.

REFERENCES CITED

Beasom, S. L. 1974. Relationships between predator removal and white-tailed deer net productivity. Journal of Wildlife Management 38:854–859.

Bronson, F. H. 1989. Mammalian Reproductive Biology. University of Chicago Press, Chicago.

Bubenik, A. B. 1988. An immodest proposal. Bugle 1988:68–70.

Bubenik, G. A., A. B. Bubenik, G. M. Brown, and D. A. Wilson. 1977. Sexual stimulation and variations of plasma testosterone in normal, antiandrogen and antiestrogen treated white-tailed deer *(Odocoileus virginianus)* during the annual cycle. Proceedings of the International Congress of Game Biologists 13:377–386.

Christian, J. J. 1980. Endocrine factors in population regulation. Pages 55–116 *in* Biosocial Mechanisms of Population Regulation. (M. C. Cohen, R. J. Malpass, and H. G. Klein, eds.) Yale University Press, New Haven, CT.

Clayton, D. A. 1978. Socially facilitated behavior. Quarterly Review of Biology 53:373–392.

Coblentz, B. E. 1977. Comments on deer sociobiology. Wildlife Society Bulletin 5:67.

Cowan, I. M. 1972. Management implications of behaviour in the large herbivorous mammals. Pages 921–934 *in* The Behaviour of Ungulates and Its Relation to Management. (V. Geist and F. Walther, eds.) International Union for the Conservation of Nature and Natural Resources, Publication 24, Moiges, Switzerland.

Downing, R. L., and B. S. McGinnes. 1976. Movement patterns of white-tailed deer in a Virginia enclosure. Proceedings of the Annual Conference Southeastern Association of Game and Fish Commissioners 29 (1975): 454–459.

Downing, R. L., B. S. McGinnes, R. L. Petcher, and J. L. Sandt. 1969. Seasonal changes in movements of white-tailed deer. Pages 19–24 *in* White-Tailed Deer in the Southern Forest Habitat. U.S. Forest Service, Southern Forest Experiment Station, New Orleans, LA.

Geist, V. 1981. Behavior: Adaptive strategies in mule deer. Pages 157–223 *in* Mule and Black-Tailed Deer of North America. (O. C. Wallmo, ed.). University of Nebraska Press, Lincoln.

Goss, R. J. 1983. Deer Antlers: Regeneration, Function, and Evolution. Academic Press, New York.

Gruver, B. J., D. C. Guynn, Jr., and H. A. Jacobson. 1984. Simulated effects of harvest strategy on reproduction in white-tailed deer. Journal of Wildlife Management 48:535–541.

Guynn, D. C., Jr., J. R. Sweeney, R. J. Hamilton, and R. L. Marchinton. 1988. A case study in quality deer management. South Carolina White-Tailed Deer Management Workshop 2:72–79.

Hawkins, R. E., W. D. Klimstra, and D. C. Autry. 1971. Dispersal of deer from Crab Orchard National Wildlife Refuge. Journal of Wildlife Management 35:216–220.

Hirth, D. H. 1977. Social Behavior of White-Tailed Deer in Relation to Habitat. Wildlife Monographs 53, The Wildlife Society, Bethesda, MD.

Holzenbein, S., and R. L. Marchinton. 1992a. Emigration and mortality in orphaned white-tailed deer. Journal of Wildlife Management 56:219–223.

Holzenbein, S., and R. L. Marchinton. 1992b. Spatial integration of maturing-male white-tailed deer into the adult population. Journal of Mammalogy 73:326–334.

Hosack, D. A., D. L. Montfort, K. V. Miller, R. L. Marchinton, and C. M. Wemmer. In press. Male urinary chemosignals augment luteal function in Eld's deer hinds. *In* Biology of Deer. (H. A. Jacobson and J. C. Kroll, eds.)

Jacobson, H. A. 1992. Deer condition response to changing harvest strategy, Davis Island, Mississippi. Pages 48–55 *in* The Biology of Deer. (R. D. Brown, ed.) Springer-Verlag, New York.

Jacobson, H. A. 1995. Age and quality relationships. Pages 103–111 *in* Quality Whitetails: The Why and How of Quality Deer Management. (K. V. Miller and R. L. Marchinton, eds.) Stackpole Books, Harrisburg, PA.

Jacobson, H. A., D. C. Guynn, Jr., R. N. Griffin, and D. Lewis. 1980. Fecundity of white-tailed deer in Mississippi and periodicity of corpora lutea and lactation. Proceedings of the Annual Conference Southeastern Association of Fish and Wildlife Agencies 33 (1979): 30–35.

Jacobson, H. A., and J. C. Kroll. In press. The white-tailed deer—the most managed and mis-managed species. *In* Biology of Deer. (H. A. Jacobson and J. C. Kroll, eds.)

Kammermeyer, K. E., and R. L. Marchinton. 1976a. The dynamic aspects of deer populations utilizing a refuge. Proceedings of the Annual Conference Southeastern Association of Game and Fish Commissioners 29 (1975): 466–475.

Kammermeyer, K. E., and R. L. Marchinton. 1976b. Notes on dispersal of male white-tailed deer. Journal of Mammalogy 57:776–778.

Knox, W. M., M. O. Bara, and K. V. Miller. 1993. Effect of fawning date on physical development in yearling male white-tailed deer. Proceedings of the Annual Conference Southeastern Association of Fish and Wildlife Agencies 45 (1991): 30–36.

Marchinton, R. L. 1982. White-tailed deer dispersal: Population regulation and management implications. Transactions of the International Congress of Game Biologists 14:81–88.

Marchinton, R. L., and T. D. Atkeson. 1985. Plasticity of socio-spatial behaviour of white-tailed deer and the concept of facultative territoriality. Pages 375–377 *in* Biology of Deer Production. (P. F. Fennessy and K. R. Drew, eds.) The Royal Society of New Zealand, Bulletin 22, Wellington.

Marchinton, R. L., and D. H. Hirth. 1984. Behavior. Pages 129–168 *in* White-Tailed Deer: Ecology and Management (L. K. Halls, ed.) Stackpole Books, Harrisburg, PA.

Marchinton, R. L., K. L Johansen, and K. V. Miller. 1990. Behavioural components of white-tailed deer scent marking: Social and seasonal effects. Pages 295–301 *in* Chemical Signals in Vertebrates 5. (D. W. Macdonald, D. Muller-Schwarze, and S. E. Natynczuk, eds.) Oxford University Press, New York.

Marchinton, R. L., K. V. Miller, R. J. Hamilton, and D. C. Guynn. 1990. Quality deer management: Biological and social impacts on the herd. Pages 7–15 *in* Proceedings Tall Timbers Game Bird Seminar. (C. Kyser, D. C. Sisson, and J. L. Landers, eds.) Tall Timbers Research Station, Tallahassee, FL.

Mathews, N. E. 1989. Social structure, genetic structure and anti-predator behavior of white-tailed deer in the central Adirondacks. Doctoral dissertation, State University of New York, Syracuse.

Mathews, N. E., and W. F. Porter. 1993. Effects of social structure on genetic structure of free-ranging white-tailed deer in the Adirondack Mountains. Journal of Mammalogy 74:33–43.

McCullough, D. R. 1979. The George Reserve Deer Herd: Population Ecology of a K-Selected Species. University of Michigan Press, Ann Arbor.

Miller, K. V., K. E. Kammermeyer, R. L. Marchinton, and E. B. Moser. 1987. Population and habitat influences on antler rubbing by white-tailed deer. Journal of Wildlife Management 51:62–66.

Miller, K. V., R. L. Marchinton, K. J. Forand, and K. L. Johansen. 1987. Dominance, testosterone levels, and scraping activity in a captive herd of white-tailed deer. Journal of Mammalogy 68:812–817.

Miller, K. V., R. L. Marchinton, and W. M. Knox. 1992. White-tailed deer signposts and their role as a source of priming pheromones: A hypothesis. Pages 455–460 in Global Trends in Wildlife Management. Vol. I. (B. Bobek, K. Perzanowski, and W. L. Regelin, eds.) Transactions of the 18th Congress of the International Union of Game Biologists, Swiat Press, Krakow-Warszawa, Poland.

Miller, K. V., R. L. Marchinton, and J. J. Ozoga. 1995. Deer sociobiology. Pages 118–128 in Quality Whitetails: The Why and How of Quality Deer Management. (K. V. Miller and R. L. Marchinton, eds.) Stackpole Books, Harrisburg, PA.

Miller, K. V., O. E. Rhodes, Jr., T. R. Litchfield, M. H. Smith, and R. L. Marchinton. 1988. Reproductive characteristics of yearling and adult male white-tailed deer. Proceedings of the Annual Conference Southeastern Association of Fish and Wildlife Agencies 41 (1987): 378–384.

Montgomery, G. G. 1959. Social behavior in a refuge population of white-tailed deer (Odocoileus virginianus) studied with specially developed marking techniques. Master's thesis, Pennsylvania State University, University Park.

Nelson, M. E., and L. D. Mech. 1981. Deer Social Organization and Wolf Predation in North-Eastern Minnesota. Wildlife Monographs 77, The Wildlife Society, Bethesda, MD.

Nixon, C. M., L. P. Hansen, P. A. Brewer, and J. E. Chelsvig. 1991. Ecology of White-Tailed Deer in an Intensively Farmed Region of Illinois. Wildlife Monographs 118, The Wildlife Society, Bethesda, MD.

Ozoga, J. J. 1989. Scientific research: Whitetail (Odocoileus virginianus). North American Deer Foundation, Spring: 10–11, 16–19.

Ozoga, J. J., and L. J. Verme. 1982. Physical and reproductive characteristics of a supplementally-fed white-tailed deer herd. Journal of Wildlife Management 46:281–301.

Ozoga, J. J., and L. J. Verme. 1984. Effects of family-bond deprivation on reproductive performance in female white-tailed deer. Journal of Wildlife Management 48:1326–1334.

Ozoga, J. J., and L. J. Verme. 1985. Comparative breeding behavior and performance of yearling vs. prime-age white-tailed bucks. Journal of Wildlife Management 49:364–372.

Ozoga, J. J., and L. J. Verme. 1986. Initial and subsequent maternal success of white-tailed deer. Journal of Wildlife Management 50:122–124.

Ozoga, J. J., L. J. Verme, and C. S. Bienz. 1982. Parturition behavior and territoriality in white-tailed deer: Impact on neonatal mortality. Journal of Wildlife Management 46:1–11.

Plotka, E. P., U. S. Seal, L. J. Verme, and J. J. Ozoga. 1983. The adrenal gland in white-tailed deer: A significant source of progesterone. Journal of Wildlife Management 47:38–44.

Richter, A. R., and R. F. Labisky. 1985. Reproductive dynamics among disjunct white-tailed deer herds in Florida. Journal of Wildlife Management 49:964–971.

Rutberg, A. T. 1987. Adaptive hypotheses of birth synchrony in ruminants: An interspecific test. American Naturalist 130:692–710.

Schwede, G., H. Henrichs, and W. McShea. 1993. Social and spatial organization of female white-tailed deer, *Odocoileus virginianus*, during the fawning season. Animal Behavior 45:1007–1017.

Seal, U. S., L. J. Verme, J. J. Ozoga, and E. D. Plotka. 1983. Metabolic and endocrine responses of white-tailed deer to increasing population density. Journal of Wildlife Management 47:451–462.

Shea, S. M., T. A. Breault, and M. L. Richardson. 1994. Relationship of birth date and physical development of yearling white-tailed deer in Florida. Proceedings of the Annual Conference Southeastern Association of Fish and Wildlife Agencies 46 (1992): 159–166.

Smith, C. A. 1976. Deer sociobiology—some second thoughts. Wildlife Society Bulletin 4:181–182.

Tierson, W. C., G. F. Mattfield, R. W. Sage, Jr., and D. F. Behrend. 1985. Seasonal movements and home ranges of white-tailed deer in the Adirondacks. Journal of Wildlife Management 49:760–768.

Vandenbergh, J. G. 1983. Pheromonal regulation of puberty. Pages 95–112 *in* Pheromones and Reproduction in Mammals. (J. G. Vandenbergh, ed.) Academic Press, New York.

Verme, L. J. 1965. Reproduction studies on penned white-tailed deer. Journal of Wildlife Management 29:74–79.

Verme, L. J. 1969. Reproductive patterns of white-tailed deer related to nutritional plane. Journal of Wildlife Management 33:881–887.

Verme, L. J., and J. J. Ozoga. 1981. Sex ratio of white-tailed deer and the estrous cycle. Journal of Wildlife Management 45:710–715.

Verme, L. J., J. J. Ozoga, and J. T. Nellist. 1987. Induced early estrus in penned white-tailed deer does. Journal of Wildlife Management 51:54–56.

Walther, F. R. 1972. Territorial behavior in certain horned ungulates, with special reference to the examples of Thompson's and Grant's gazelles. Zoologica 7:303–307.

10 Profiles of Deer under Different Management and Habitat Conditions in Pennsylvania

WILLIAM L. PALMER, GERALD L. STORM,
RANDALL QUINN, WALTER M. TZILKOWSKI,
AND MATTHEW J. LOVALLO

Managers of public land are currently being challenged to minimize conflict between white-tailed deer and other natural resources (Porter 1991; DuBrock 1994; deCalesta, Chapter 16). The increased abundance of deer in Pennsylvania from 1970 to 1990 has concerned managers of reservations, parks, and refuges. Two federally managed areas in Pennsylvania experiencing conflicts between deer and other natural resources are (1) the historic areas at Gettysburg (the Gettysburg National Military Park and the Eisenhower National Historic Site in Adams County) and (2) the Letterkenny Army Depot in Franklin County; both areas are in south-central Pennsylvania.

Conditions at the 2,962-ha area at Gettysburg are similar to conditions in other parks and wildlife refuges in the mid-Atlantic region. Deer frequently move between public and private land, harvest of deer in the public areas is not permitted or is allowed under only special regulations, deer mortality on highways is high, and intensive browsing of vegetation is common in and adjacent to the public land.

Conditions at Letterkenny are quite different from those at Gettysburg. About 4,856 ha at Letterkenny are enclosed by a chain-link fence, deer are harvested on an annual basis, and vehicle collisions with deer are rare.

A common management goal for Gettysburg and Letterkenny is to maintain the deer herd at a size that is compatible with the levels of other natural resources and that can be tolerated by people who use the area.

To achieve this goal, managers must make a baseline assessment of the demographics and health of their deer herds, and they must monitor periodically thereafter to detect the responses of deer to the local environment and to management actions.

Demographic and health profiles of deer populations are needed to answer questions that managers, politicians, or public interest groups may ask concerning deer population dynamics, deer–habitat relationships, and the complex interactions among food availability, deer density, and deer physiological and behavioral states. For example, one likely question that has not been answered is whether deer populations in unhunted parks will experience self-regulation (Peterle 1975; Smith 1976) through physiological and behavioral mechanisms when abundance far exceeds levels acceptable to farmers and foresters.

We compare the demographic attributes of the deer populations in each public area (Gettysburg and Letterkenny) with those of the deer populations in surrounding Adams and Franklin counties, relate the demographic and health profiles of deer to current management programs, compare health profiles of deer at Letterkenny to those of local deer herds at Tyler State Park and Rockview State Prison in Pennsylvania, and make recommendations to managers of high-density deer herds for assessing trends in abundance and herd condition.

STUDY AREAS

The study area at Gettysburg (2,962 ha) comprised the Gettysburg National Military Park, the Eisenhower National Historic Site, and some adjacent private land. Twenty-six percent of the area was forest and 48% was cropland and pasture (Storm et al. 1992). The Gettysburg parks were not open to public hunting, but deer were killed each year on private lands adjacent to the parks. The Letterkenny Army Depot, near Chambersburg, encompassed 4,856 ha; about 10% of it was farmland and grassland and 42% forest. The depot was open to hunting by personnel associated with the facility, and the general public was allowed to hunt under special regulations during antlerless deer seasons. Adams and Franklin counties encompassed 134,917 ha and 220,324 ha, respectively. Both counties were open to hunting during statewide antlered and antlerless deer hunting seasons. Tyler State Park, near Newtown (southeastern Pennsylvania), encompassed about 700 ha and allowed deer hunting under special regulations. Forty-three percent of the area was being farmed and 41% was forested. Rockview State Prison, near Bellefonte (central Pennsylvania), encompassed about 1,400 ha, 12% of it in agriculture and 85% forested. The Rockview State Prison was open to the general public for deer hunting during the antlerless deer season.

METHODS

From 1987 to 1994, estimates of deer abundance at Gettysburg and Letterkenny were obtained from counts at dusk (Storm et al. 1992) and use of sighting indices (0.60 at Gettysburg and 0.40 at Letterkenny; G. L. Storm, unpublished data). Population estimates for Adams and Franklin counties from 1987 to 1993 were developed through population reconstruction modeling techniques (Roseberry and Woolf 1991). County population models were based on annual deer harvest statistics and related data such as reproductive rates. County harvests were calculated from the number of deer harvest report cards, corrected for reporting rates.

Estimates of age and sex composition of the deer population at Gettysburg were based on observations of 14,990 deer during fall spotlight surveys from 1985 to 1989. Age groups were determined for 22% (3,259) of the deer counted; these deer were classified as either fawns (<1 year old) or adults (>1 year old). In addition, although observers were unable to differentiate yearling females (1.5 years old) from older females (≥2.5 years old), they were able to differentiate yearling males from older males on the basis of body size and antler development. Observers were able to determine the sex of 13% (1,895) of the deer observed at Gettysburg. Data on 2,370 deer harvested during 1985, 1987, and 1989 were used to estimate age and sex composition at Letterkenny. Estimates of age and sex composition in Adams and Franklin counties were based on countywide harvest data and estimates of population structure from 1987 to 1993.

Counts of fawns of 61 radio-collared females from 1985 to 1987 were used to estimate productivity at Gettysburg, whereas counts of corpora lutea and fetuses from deer harvested during the 1984, 1988, and 1989 hunting seasons were used to estimate productivity at Letterkenny. Estimates of productivity for Adams and Franklin counties were based on Pennsylvania Game Commission's examinations of road-killed female deer, February–May each year from 1985 to 1993.

Mortality and survival estimates were derived from reports of marked deer killed by hunters and by vehicles from 1985 to 1994 for Gettysburg (Storm et al. 1989), from deer check stations monitored from 1987 to 1993 at Letterkenny, and from spring searches for dead deer at Gettysburg and Letterkenny during the 1993–94 winter. For Adams and Franklin counties, age-related survival was determined from road-killed female deer examined each year from February through May, 1985–93.

Field-dressed weights were recorded for, and kidneys were collected from, 6- to 7-month-old female deer killed by hunters at Letterkenny, Tyler State Park, and Rockview State Prison during two winters (December and January 1989–90 and 1990–91). Each kidney was separated from connective tissue and weighed with attached fat. Fat was then removed and the kidney was weighed again. The diameters of antler beams were measured (Severinghaus and Moen 1983) from a hunter-killed sample of yearling males from Letterkenny (1985–93), Adams County (1964–66), Franklin County (1964–66), and from a population of captive deer maintained at the Pennsylvania State University deer facility (1990–92).

RESULTS

Abundance

The estimated size of the deer herd at Gettysburg during spring (March–April) increased from about 700 in 1987 to over 1,200 in 1993 (Table 10.1). After the 1993–94 winter, the herd size had declined to about 900 deer. This reduction was not drastic because the number counted (589) in one of three surveys in 1994 was higher than the mean of three counts from both 1990 and 1991. Our population estimates based on the sighting index (Table 10.1) indicated an average preparturition herd size of over 1,000 deer for 1990–93. Mark–resight estimates of the Gettysburg herd supported these estimates. The density at Gettysburg was greater than 39 deer/km^2.

Postseason (mid-January) population estimates for Adams County ranged from 5,271 deer in 1991 to 7,272 deer in 1993. These population levels indicated a density between 4 and 5 deer/km^2. Thus, the density of deer at Gettysburg during 1990–93 was on average seven times the density in surrounding Adams County.

At Letterkenny, the mean number of deer counted increased from 841 in 1987 to 1,503 in 1992 (Table 10.1). Population size during 1992 was estimated at 3,758 deer (>58 deer/km^2). The number of deer counted in

TABLE 10.1

Estimates of deer population sizes at study areas in south-central
Pennsylvania

| Year | Gettysburg | | Letterkenny | | Adams County population size estimate[e] | Franklin County population size estimate[e] |
	Mean number counted[a]	Population size estimate[b]	Mean number counted[c]	Population size estimate[d]		
1987	427	712	841	2,103	8,245	16,439
1988	448	747	860	2,150	7,407	11,228
1989	—	—	897	2,243	6,841	9,716
1990	538	897	1,190	2,975	6,319	12,072
1991	582	970	1,407	3,518	5,271	8,980
1992	682	1,137	1,503	3,758	6,795	8,991
1993	765	1,275	850	2,125	7,272	9,639
1994	528	880	1,019	2,548	—	—

[a] Mean of three counts during April.

[b] Based on counts and sighting index of 0.60.

[c] Mean of three counts during March–April.

[d] Based on counts and sighting index of 0.40.

[e] Based on postseason reconstruction models.

1993 was 850 and in 1994 was 1,019, suggesting a decrease from the 1990–92 level.

Postseason population estimates for Franklin County decreased from 16,439 in 1987 to 8,980 in 1991. This reduction was in accordance with deer density goals established by the Pennsylvania Game Commission. Density of deer in Franklin County ranged from 4.6 to 8.1 deer/km^2. Density of deer at Letterkenny during 1990–93 was on average 12 times the abundance in surrounding Franklin County.

Age and Sex Composition

Forty-six percent of the adult bucks counted at Gettysburg from 1985 to 1989 were classified as yearlings (Table 10.2). In Adams County, prior to the hunting season, 83% of the adult bucks were yearlings and 30% of the adult females were yearlings from 1987 to 1993 (Table 10.2).

At Letterkenny, 67% of the adult bucks killed from 1985 to 1989 were yearlings, whereas 40% of the adult females killed were yearlings. In

TABLE 10.2

Deer herd attributes and management and habitat conditions, 1985–1994

Herd or habitat attribute	Gettysburg	Adams County	Letterkenny	Franklin County
Estimated postseason density (per km²)[a]	>35	4–5	>58	5–8
Management by deer harvest?	No[a]	Yes, annual	Yes, limited	Yes, annual
Relative carrying capacity	Moderate	High	Low	High
Population trend	Increasing	No change	Undetermined	Decreasing
Percent annual harvest	12[a]	32	34	24
Percentage of yearlings among:				
Adult males	46	83	67	79
Adult females	?[b]	30	40	34
Reproductive potential	High	High	Low	High
Adult sex ratio (females:males)	6.1	2.1	1.1	2.4
Fawns per pregnant adult female	1.7	1.7	1.1	1.8
Breeding by fawns?	Yes	Yes	No	Yes
Herd health declining?	No	No	Yes	No

[a] Deer were killed legally by hunters on private land adjacent to park boundaries; percentage is approximate.
[b] Unable to determine from spotlight surveys.

Franklin County, prior to the hunting season, 79% of the adult bucks were yearlings and 34% of the adult females were yearlings from 1987 to 1993 (Table 10.2).

The sex ratio of adult deer in Gettysburg (1985–89) was 6.1 females per male. The sex ratio of adult deer in Adams County (1987–93) was 2.1 females per male. The sex ratio for adult deer at Letterkenny (1985–89) was 1.1 females per male, whereas the sex ratio of adult deer in Franklin County (1987–93) was 2.4 females per male.

Reproductive Attributes

Eighty-two percent (50 of 61) of marked females at Gettysburg (1985–87) were observed with newborn offspring (Storm et al. 1989). The mean number of fawns per breeding female was 1.0 for marked females that bred at 6 months of age and 1.7 for marked females that bred as adults. Although we observed production by six marked females that bred as fawns, we did not estimate the proportion of females in the entire herd that bred at 6 months of age at Gettysburg. Embryo checks in Adams County indicated that 95% of adult female deer were pregnant. Adult deer ($n = 81$) checked in Adams County from 1985 to 1990 averaged 1.7 embryos per pregnant female (Table 10.2).

Production of offspring at Letterkenny was much lower than it was in Franklin County. Females at Letterkenny rarely bred at 6 months of age; only 1 of 48 females less than 1 year old was observed with a fetus. Mean counts of corpora lutea for females older than 1 year were 1.7 or less each year (1984, 1988, and 1989) and 1.5 for all years combined. For all three years combined, the number of fetuses produced per adult female averaged 1.1. Over 1985–90, 91% of the adult female deer checked in Franklin County were pregnant; the mean number of embryos was 1.8 per pregnant female.

Mortality and Survival

At Gettysburg, 125 deer were marked during 1985–87. Of these, 19 were shot by hunters on private land and 29 were killed by vehicles by 1988. The reported number of deer killed by vehicles at Gettysburg increased from 50 in 1985 to 108 in 1987. By 1994, 85 females and 21 males of the marked deer had been killed and reported to park personnel.

The number of deer reported killed annually on highways in Adams County averaged 562 and ranged from 377 to 749 during 1985–93. Of these deer, about 125–150 were killed on highways on or within 3.2 km of the Gettysburg area. Thus, 25% of the deer reported killed by vehicles were on or near Gettysburg even though the Gettysburg area represents only 2% of the Adams County area.

Landowners surrounding Gettysburg also killed deer for crop damage control. The number reported killed under the crop damage program was 117 during 1991, 90 during 1992, and 51 during 1993.

Hunters at Letterkenny killed, on average, 34% (range, 18–57%) of the herd each year from 1987 to 1993. The average proportions of the population harvested annually (1987–93) by hunters in Adams and Franklin counties were 32% (range, 26–37%) and 24% (range, 18–31%), respectively.

Survival of deer was significantly greater at Gettysburg during 1985–93 than at Letterkenny and Adams or Franklin counties. About 25% of the marked females that died at Gettysburg were older than 5 years, whereas only 3% of the females harvested during 1987–93 at Letterkenny were older than 5 years (Figure 10.1). Data on age-related survival for Adams and Franklin counties (1985–93) indicated that less than 3% of the females were more than 5 years old (Figure 10.1). Late-winter (March) searches for dead deer in 1994 indicated that a minimum of 50 deer died at Gettysburg (1.7 deer/km^2), whereas at least 435 died at Letterkenny (9 deer/km^2).

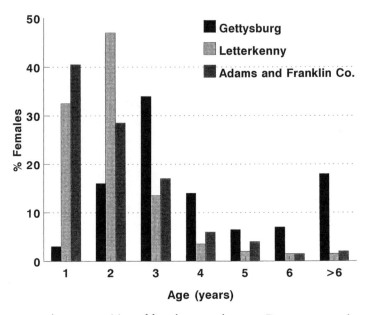

FIGURE 10.1. Age composition of females at study areas. Data represent the percentage of marked females at Gettysburg that survived 1 year or more (1985–94), the age composition of harvested females at Letterkenny (1987–93), and the age composition of road-killed females from Adams and Franklin counties combined (1985–93).

Health Profiles

Average field-dressed body weight of 6- to 7-month-old female deer at Letterkenny was less than 27 kg for 1989–91 (Ross 1994). Average weight of juvenile females at Letterkenny was lower than that of juvenile females harvested in 1989–91 at Tyler State Park, an area with high densities of deer (>77 deer/km^2), and at Rockview State Prison area (Figure 10.2). Among the three groups, the difference in averge body weight was significant ($P < 0.05$) only between the juvenile females from Letterkenny and those from Tyler State Park (Ross 1994).

Kidney fat indices were lower for juvenile females at Letterkenny than for juvenile females from the state park or the prison area. Average amount of kidney fat was significantly different ($P < 0.05$) between the juvenile females from Letterkenny and those from Tyler State Park (Figure 10.2).

Mean antler beam diameter for yearling males at Letterkenny (15.9 mm) was less than that from Adams and Franklin counties

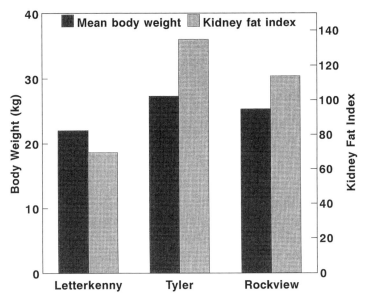

FIGURE 10.2. Health parameters for juvenile female deer at Letterkenny ($n = 19$), Tyler State Park ($n = 14$), and Rockview State Prison ($n = 13$).

(20.0 mm). Mean diameter of antler beams for a sample of captive yearling males at the Pennsylvania State University deer facility was 24.9 mm.

DISCUSSION

Our review of the recorded data indicated that herd sex and age composition and abundance, survival, and health of deer reflected the management programs in place at Gettysburg, Letterkenny, and Adams and Franklin counties (Table 10.2). The current population of more than 35 deer/km² at Gettysburg is considered excessive because of adverse effects on croplands and forest regeneration (Storm et al. 1989; Vecellio et al. 1994). It is conceivable that the herd size at Gettysburg could increase, given that areas such as Letterkenny have produced over 58 deer/km². The herd at Letterkenny and herds in other areas of Pennsylvania (e.g., Tyler State Park and Rockview State Prison) have shown the capacity to reach densities that cause serious problems for natural resource managers of public lands.

We did not observe a drastic decline in the deer herd at Gettysburg from 1987 to 1994 despite high initial densities of deer, lack of woody stems 1.5 m or less in height, and two consecutive winters (1993 and 1994) with above-normal snowfall and below-normal temperatures. Population size at Gettysburg appeared to change gradually rather than showing irruptive increases or drastic declines. The lack of drastic changes in the herd size at Gettysburg may be due to persistent annual mortality, high productivity, and the availability of annually renewed food supplies from agricultural areas in and around the park. Although deer were not harvested in the park, they were killed by farm machinery (e.g., machines harvesting hay), by vehicles on highways, and by hunters on private lands adjacent to the park. High productivity at Gettysburg was the result of (1) a high proportion of 3- to 5-year-old females that consistently produced more than one fawn per year, (2) breeding by females at 6 months of age, and (3) a heavily skewed adult sex ratio (>6 females to 1 male). On an annual basis, about 17% of the park was pasture, 7% was planted in corn and milo, 6% was planted in small grains (barley, oats, rye, and wheat), and 19% was in hay fields that provided winter forage.

The population at Letterkenny tended to reflect the annual harvest and has remained at relatively high levels despite habitat conditions that were of lower quality than those in Franklin County. Fluctuations in the herd at Letterkenny might be less drastic if hunters were to remove more than 30% of the herd annually. However, conditions at Letterkenny in recent years indicated significant alteration in the structure of the local deer population. These conditions were low production by adult females, lack of reproduction by juvenile females, and declining body condition (less kidney fat and lower body weight). Because the herd is enclosed in a deer-proof fence that restricts egress and ingress, the genetic profiles may be changing enough to influence the dynamics of the herd.

The notion that deer populations are highly influenced by self-regulatory mechanisms is not supported by the present conditions at Gettysburg. Despite a lack of small woody stems in forests during winter months, the annual renewal of food in croplands and pastures is adequate to support current and even higher densities. Farm–forest landscapes of southern Pennsylvania provided a suitable environment for deer to the extent that population irruptions and crashes are not yet evident and even seem unlikely (see McCullough, Chapter 6; Underwood and Porter, Chapter 12).

Demographic profiles based on abundance information can be useful for visualizing the status of a herd relative to carrying capacity. In this study, direct comparisons of each herd's size relative to carrying capacity were confounded by incomplete data on some demographic attributes and differences in procedures. However, some trends were apparent. First, the herd at Letterkenny appeared to be negatively influenced by a combination of high deer density and low-quality habitat, suggesting the herd has surpassed the inflection point of a sigmodial growth trajectory and that current trends in herd condition and population structure will continue. Second, the herd at Gettysburg has not shown signs of regulatory mechanisms and will continue to increase given current management and habitat conditions in the park. The herd at Gettysburg provides an example of the level of abundance that can be realized before changes in demographic profiles and declines in health become apparent.

Deer herds in public areas are affected by management programs in the surrounding region, but the degree of interaction, such as between the Gettysburg herd and the Adams County herd, is poorly understood. The high number of deer killed on highways in the park indicated that the Gettysburg herd made a significant contribution to the reported number of road kills for Adams County, though these figures are not corrected for traffic volume. High survival of deer in Gettysburg may result in more male deer with trophy-type antlers. That hunters have the opportunity to select and shoot trophy bucks on private land near the park and choose not to shoot females near the park may contribute to the skewed sex ratio and minimize the effect of hunting on the size of the Gettysburg herd. At Letterkenny, the challenges associated with high deer density and low-quality habitat should be addressed by managers to ensure the long-term maintenance of productive and diverse wildlife habitats. We suggest the following.

1. Estimates of abundance are needed to assess trends in local populations (Tzilkowski and Storm 1993) and the effectiveness of deer management programs. In farm–forest landscapes, we recommend counting deer at dusk (Storm et al. 1992) during late March and early April, when high proportions of the herd can be observed in relatively large groups in open, nonforested areas. If precise estimates of population size are desired, a proportion (White 1984) of the herd should be marked to implement mark–resight techniques, and estimates should be verified by other survey or census techniques such as remote sensing (Wiggers and Beckerman 1993) and removal methods (Eberhardt 1982).

2. Data should be collected to develop long-term demographic profiles and to assess herd productivity. Age and sex composition are important attributes to consider, particularly ratios of fawns to adult fe-

males and adult females to adult males. These data can be acquired in late October and early November by surveys conducted at dusk. Surveys should be conducted through all available land cover types to eliminate bias due to differential habitat preferences by females and males (McCullough et al. 1994).

3. Continued research on productivity (natality and recruitment), mortality, body condition, and survival are recommended for use in modeling, establishing annual harvest goals, and better understanding deer–habitat relationships. Accurate estimation of these parameters as they relate to deer density is essential to assess a herd's status relative to carrying capacity.

4. Deer populations in farm–forest landscapes will far exceed levels associated with conflicts (reduced biodiversity, increased agricultural damage, and frequent vehicle collisions with deer) before reduced productivity becomes apparent. In many situations, the cultural carrying capacity—the population level acceptable to people (Decker and Purdy 1988)—will be exceeded before a herd approaches the biological carrying capacity of farm–forest environments.

REFERENCES CITED

Decker, D. J., and K. G. Purdy. 1988. Toward a concept of wildlife acceptance capacity in wildlife management. Wildlife Society Bulletin 16:53–57.

DuBrock, C. W. 1994. Managing metro deer. Pennsylvania Game News 65 (9): 16–21.

Eberhardt, L. L. 1982. Calibrating an index by using removal data. Journal of Wildlife Management 46:734–740.

McCullough, D. R., F. W. Weckerly, P. I. Garcia, and R. R. Evett. 1994. Sources of inaccuracy in black-tailed deer herd composition counts. Journal of Wildlife Management 58:319–329.

Peterle, T. J. 1975. Deer sociobiology. Wildlife Society Bulletin 3:82–83.

Porter, W. F. 1991. White-tailed deer in eastern ecosystems: Implications for management and research in national parks. Natural Resources Report NPS/NRSUNY/NRR-91/05, Denver, CO.

Roseberry, J. L., and A. Woolf. 1991. A Comparative Evaluation of Techniques for Analyzing White-Tailed Deer Harvest Data. Wildlife Monographs 117, The Wildlife Society, Bethesda, MD.

Ross, A. S. 1994. Health profiles of white-tailed deer in different ecological conditions. Master of Forest Resources Paper, Pennsylvania State University, University Park.

Severinghaus, C. W., and A. N. Moen. 1983. Prediction of weight and reproductive rates of a white-tailed deer population from records of antler beam diameter among yearling males. New York Fish and Game Journal 30:30–38.

Smith, C. A. 1976. Deer sociobiology—some second thoughts. Wildlife Society Bulletin 4:181–182.

Storm, G. L., R. H. Yahner, D. F. Cottam, and G. M. Vecellio. 1989. Population status, movements, habitat use and impact of white-tailed deer at Gettysburg National Military Park and Eisenhower National Historic Site, Pennsylvania. National Park Service Technical Report NPS/MAR/NRTR-89/043, Philadelphia, PA.

Storm, G. L., R. H. Yahner, and J. D. Nichols. 1992. A comparison of 2 techniques for estimating deer density. Wildlife Society Bulletin 20:197–203.

Tzilkowski, W. M., and G. L. Storm. 1993. Detecting change using repeated measures analysis: White-tailed deer abundance at Gettysburg National Military Park. Wildlife Society Bulletin 21:411–414.

Vecellio, G. M., R. H. Yahner, and G. L. Storm. 1994. Crop damage by deer at Gettysburg Park. Wildlife Society Bulletin 22:89–93.

White, G. C. 1984. Ideas on estimating parameters for small isolated populations. Pages 124–127 in Deer in the Southwest: A Symposium. (P. R. Krausman and N. S. Smith, eds.) School of Renewable Natural Resources, University of Arizona, Tucson.

Wiggers, E. P., and S. F. Beckerman. 1993. Use of thermal infrared sensing to survey white-tailed deer populations. Wildlife Society Bulletin 21:263–268.

11 Health Characteristics and White-Tailed Deer Population Density in the Southeastern United States

WILLIAM R. DAVIDSON AND
GARY L. DOSTER

In this chapter we review the ecology of disease among "unmanaged" white-tailed deer populations on "protected areas" in the southeastern United States. In the context of this discussion, unmanaged means there is no hunting or any other form of population management. There are two types of protected areas: parks and similar settings, where human alterations of habitat are minimized, and urban–suburban settings, where habitat is highly altered and fragmented. The emphasis on population management is not intended to minimize the value of habitat management; however, benefits from habitat management eventually will be overcome by additional deer population growth in the absence of adequate population management (Eve 1981).

Compared with most deer populations subjected to regulated hunting harvest, these unmanaged populations are characterized by (1) a period of unrestricted population growth as a result of natural expansion from a population nucleus or the onset of hunting restrictions, (2) an eventual population density that exceeds nutritional carrying capacity, (3) an eventual age structure skewed toward older adults, (4) an eventual sex ratio in which both genders are more evenly represented, and (5) eventual declines in deer physiological indices and habitat quality. The degree to which these characteristics are manifest may vary with individual circumstances (e.g., size of the protected area, duration of protection, and type and selectivity of mortality factors). For example, relatively small protected areas surrounded by a region subjected to typical regulated deer hunting generally will develop a sex ratio skewed toward females. This will occur because larger home ranges of males and dispersal of yearling males will increase their vulnerability to harvest by hunters on surrounding lands, whereas young females will tend to occupy smaller home ranges near their natal range.

RELATIONSHIP OF DEER DENSITY TO HERD HEALTH

High deer density is generally accepted as favoring transmission of certain pathogens, which in turn leads to increased levels of disease-related morbidity or mortality (Hayes 1964; Eve 1981). Similarly, increased physiologic stress due to nutritional deficiencies is an important factor in increasing susceptibility of deer to disease by lowering their resistance (Eve 1981).

Eve (1981) presented a conceptual model of the relationship between deer population growth and changing levels of disease within populations at different densities relative to carrying capacity. This model partitioned herd health into three chronologic phases at various stages of a traditional sigmoid growth curve (Figure 11.1); it was noted that sharp demarcations did not exist between phases.

Eve's description of the three phases is as follows.

> Phase I: Virtual absence of disease. When the herd is in balance with the environment, relative population density is low to moderate; reproduction (R), yearling antler development (A), body weights (W), and nutritional levels (N) are high; abomasal parasite counts (APC) are low; and carrying capacity is well above herd density. The earliest indication of increasing density may be the slight, possibly undetectable, change in reproductive rate near point a.
>
> Phase II: Acute overpopulation. This is overpopulation of recent inception and short duration. Covert disease is present but usually can be demonstrated only through laboratory diagnostic procedures. After rapid herd growth, population density is relatively high and above carrying capacity; reproduction, antler development, body weights, and nutritional levels remain relatively high; APCs are high to very high; and carrying capacity is being progressively reduced. There may be a lag period of several years (b) after the carrying capacity is exceeded before physical deterioration can be seen in the deer.
>
> Phase III: Chronic overpopulation. Overt disease frequently is evident through gross observations of any or all of the following: unusual losses of adults or fawns, depleted fat reserves, general buildup of different species of

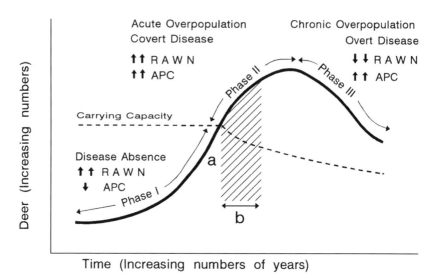

FIGURE 11.1. Disease levels associated with deer herds at different positions on a population growth curve. Symbols represent relative values of parameters that are believed to reflect disease levels in most southeastern white-tailed deer herds. Symbols are reproductive rate (R), yearling antler development (A), yearling body weights (W), nutritional level of herd (N), abomasal parasite counts (APC), point of earliest change in reproductive rate of herd (a), and period during which overpopulation is not accompanied by declining nutritional levels (b). (Redrawn from Eve 1981; used with permission from the Southeastern Cooperative Wildlife Disease Study, College of Veterinary Medicine, University of Georgia, Athens.)

internal and external parasites, and gross lesions of internal organs due to various pathologic conditions. Several years after carrying capacity has been exceeded, reproduction, antler development, body weights, and nutritional levels decline sharply; APCs are excessively high; and carrying capacity is greatly reduced. Population decline basically due to nutritional deficiencies in Phase III may be attributed to more visible agents that merely deliver the "coup de grace," such as parasites, predators, and infectious diseases.

In Eve's (1981) model, the principal parasite–disease aspect discussed was the level of infection by abomasal nematodes, which previously had been described using the term "abomasal parasite count (APC)" (Eve and Kellogg 1977). An APC was defined as the average number of adult abomasal parasites from five or more adult (>1-year-old) deer from a specific population collected at random within a short interval (<1 month), preferably during late summer or early fall (mid-July through September). In a 12-year test comparing APC values to biologists' evaluations of deer densities at 69 localities in 13 southeastern states, APC values were found to be positively correlated to biologists' estimates of deer density relative to carrying capacity (Eve and Kellogg 1977). The APC concept was based on the premise that parasites with certain biological characteristics (viz, a ubiquitous distribution, high host specificity, a direct life cycle, and absence of an effective host immune response) would be positively correlated with host density. To use this relationship as a management tool, Eve and Kellogg (1977) developed general guidelines for interpretation of APC data to estimate whether deer populations were below (APC < 500), near (APC = 500–1,500), or in excess of (APC > 1,500) carrying capacity. Later studies demonstrated that mean physical condition ratings (based on fat reserves) of deer populations varied inversely with these APC categories. On a scale of 1 to 4 (1 = poor and 4 = excellent), mean condition ratings were 3.15, 2.45, and 2.17 for herds with APC values of less than 500, 500–1,500, or greater than 1,500, respectively (Davidson et al. 1985). Citing examples from field investigations, Eve and Kellogg (1977) and Eve (1981) also indicated that in at least some instances high APC values appeared to presage mortality caused by other parasitic and infectious diseases.

DISEASES OF WHITE-TAILED DEER IN THE SOUTHEAST

Since 1957, the Southeastern Cooperative Wildlife Disease Study (SCWDS) at the University of Georgia's College of Veterinary Medicine has conducted disease diagnostic investigations on white-tailed deer and monitored population health status of white-tailed deer throughout the southeastern United States (Hayes 1981). This work has produced much of what is known regarding parasitism and disease among white-tailed deer in this region (Forrester 1992). Well over 100 different parasites, infections, or disease conditions, not counting traumatic injuries, have been identified in deer from the Southeast (Davidson et al. 1981; Forrester 1992). Of these, however, two distinct disease problems routinely result in morbidity or mortality of sufficient magnitude to be significant at the population level (Forrester 1992; SCWDS, unpublished data). These two herd health problems are hemorrhagic disease and a syndrome of malnutrition and parasitism.

Hemorrhagic Disease

The major infectious disease problem among southeastern white-tailed deer is hemorrhagic disease, which is due to infection by viruses in either of two orbivirus serogroups, epizootic hemorrhagic disease virus (EHDV) or bluetongue virus (BTV) (Prestwood et al. 1974; Couvillion et al. 1981; Nettles and Stallknecht 1992; Nettles et al. 1992, 1994). Episodes of mortality among southeastern white-tailed deer that are now attributed to hemorrhagic disease have occurred periodically from at least as early as 1901 through 1953 (Nettles and Stallknecht 1992), but it was not until 1955 that an EHDV was isolated during an epizootic in New Jersey (Shope et al. 1955, 1960). Bluetongue virus was first reported from white-tailed deer in Texas in 1967 (Robinson et al. 1967; Stair et al. 1968). Two serotypes of EHDV (EHDV-1, also known as the New Jersey strain, and EHDV-2, also known as the Alberta strain) and five serotypes of BTV (BTV-2, BTV-10, BTV-11, BTV-13, and BTV-17) occur in the United States (Pearson et al. 1992). Epizootic hemorrhagic disease virus appears to account for approximately twice as many of the occurrences of hemorrhagic disease among white-tailed deer as does BTV (Couvillion et al. 1981; Nettles and Stallknecht 1992; Nettles et al. 1992, 1994). Both viruses are transmitted by biting midges in the genus *Culicoides* (Thomas 1981); however, the overwintering mechanisms of EHDV and BTV are not known.

Since 1971, hemorrhagic disease has been detected annually during late summer or early fall among white-tailed deer in the southeastern United States (Nettles and Stallknecht 1992; Nettles et al. 1992, 1994). The distinct seasonality of hemorrhagic disease, primarily August through October but with chronically debilitated deer detected through January or later (Couvillion et al. 1981), has been attributed to vector-borne transmission during late summer followed by decreased transmission as midge vector populations decline with the onset of colder weather in the fall (Prestwood et al. 1974; Couvillion et al. 1981; Thomas 1981; Nettles et al. 1992).

Crude mortality rates among wild deer typically are relatively low (<15%), although rates over 50% have been reported. The initial concept that hemorrhagic disease viruses produce a very high case fatality rate appears to be an overestimate based on early experimental infection trials (Nettles and Stallknecht 1992), although data from certain localized epizootics indicate that case fatality rates can be high (Fox and Pelton 1974; SCWDS, unpublished data). Serologic surveys have documented that in much of the Southeast many deer survive natural infection and develop neutralizing antibodies (Nettles et al. 1992).

Annual surveys since 1980 to monitor clinical hemorrhagic disease among white-tailed deer and, more recently, serologic surveys of deer, have revealed distinct geographic patterns in the occurrence of EHDV and BTV and in the clinical severity of hemorrhagic disease (Couvillion et al. 1981; Stallknecht et al. 1991; Nettles and Stallknecht 1992; Nettles et al. 1994). In general, serologic surveys indicate that viral exposure and serotype diversity vary inversely with latitude (Stallknecht et al. 1991; SCWDS, unpublished data). In contrast, the severity of clinical disease generally increases with increasing latitude (Nettles and Stallknecht 1992; Nettles et al. 1992). Thus, consistently higher antibody prevalences coincide with absence of disease. For example, although deer populations from peninsular Florida typically have high prevalences of antibodies, often in excess of 80%, to multiple EHDV and BTV serotypes (Stallknecht et al. 1991; Forrester 1992), deer from this region almost never develop clinical signs or die due to hemorrhagic disease (Forrester 1992; Nettles and Stallknecht 1992; Nettles et al. 1994). In contrast, deer from the Appalachian Mountains and plateau regions immediately west of the Appalachians typically experience considerable mortality during sporadic epizootics (Nettles and Stallknecht 1992; Nettles et al. 1994) but have low prevalences of antibodies, usually only to a single serotype, during interepizootic intervals (Stallknecht et al. 1991; Nettles and Stallknecht 1992). Deer populations within the upper Coastal Plain and Piedmont physiographic provinces occupy intermediate positions with regard to both the severity of clinical disease and the occurrence of antibodies, although within these physiographic provinces the same general pattern of variance with latitude occurs (Couvillion et al. 1981; Stallknecht et al. 1991; Nettles and Stallknecht 1992; Nettles et al. 1994).

These geographic variations are believed to be due to an interaction of various epidemiologic factors (Nettles and Stallknecht 1992; Nettles et al. 1992, 1994). Among the potential factors are the seasonality, abundance, and competence of *Culicoides* midge vectors in various regions (Nettles et al. 1994); the serotype, strain, and pathogenicity of BTV and EHDV present (Nettles and Stallknecht 1992); the average levels of existing herd immunity to various virus serotypes or strains (Nettles and Stallknecht 1992); and possibly even genetic variations in susceptibility of deer in different regions (Nettles and Stallknecht 1992).

In the most southerly latitudes, vector populations have much longer annual periods of activity, which is thought to result in frequent exposure of deer to vectors, producing high prevalences of neutralizing antibodies (Nettles and Stallknecht 1992). Serotype diversity of both EHDV and BTV is higher in this region (Stallknecht et al. 1991; SCWDS, unpublished data), and many serotypes of both viruses appear to circulate annually. Young animals are thought to be exposed while protected by maternal antibodies, which precludes severe disease but boosts antibody response and thus produces populations with consistently high levels of herd immunity (Nettles and Stallknecht 1992). In contrast, vector populations in the more northerly latitudes and mountainous regions are limited by seasonal climatic changes; the potential for frequent (annual), high-intensity transmission of the viruses is diminished. Under this system of reduced potential for annual transmission, the viruses probably are not present each year, the diversity of virus serotypes present is lessened, and herd immunity among deer populations is not maintained. In fact, in the Appalachian Mountains and the plateau regions of the Southeast, hemorrhagic disease has been a sporadic event, occurring at intervals of approximately 10 years with limited or no evidence of virus transmission during the interepizootic intervals. Upper Coastal Plain regions have frequent (annual or nearly so) transmission and higher levels of mild clinical disease, whereas Piedmont regions have less frequent transmission and mild to moderately severe disease at approximately 3-year intervals.

The relationship of deer density to the occurrence of hemorrhagic disease is speculative and based on circumstantial evidence. Prestwood et al. (1974) noted that during a large-scale epizootic in 1971, mortality appeared to be related to host density. High mortality was reported in some captive herds and high-density wild populations, but deaths were thought to be fewer in nearby wild populations that were in balance with their habitats. As noted by Nettles and Stallknecht (1992), the transmissibility of infectious agents, including hemorrhagic disease viruses, theoretically is enhanced as host density increases; however, the role of deer density to hemorrhagic disease occurrence has not been critically evaluated. One important issue in resolving the role that deer density may have to epizootics centers on the detectability of sick and dead deer, which also is believed to vary with deer density (Nettles and Stallknecht 1992). In addition, the densities of *Culicoides* vectors and susceptible domestic ruminants are thought possibly to influence the exposure rates of sympatric white-tailed deer populations (Nettles and Stallknecht 1992).

Current epidemiologic information regarding hemorrhagic disease, recognizing that many details of the pathogenicity, transmission, and maintenance of EHDV and BTV are unknown, argues for the importance of epidemiologic factors other than deer density per se in governing the occurrence of hemorrhagic disease. These epidemiologic factors appear to be geographically variable within the southeastern United States. Thus, deer populations in different regions of the Southeast have different levels of risk for both infection by EHDV or BTV and for development of the clinical manifestations of hemorrhagic disease (Figure 11.2). High deer density in the hyperendemic lower Coastal Plain region would not be expected to increase risk of clinical disease significantly because deer populations in this region tend to maintain high levels of herd immunity. Conversely, high deer density in the Appalachian Mountains or plateau regions, which experience only sporadic incursions by hemorrhagic disease viruses, could be hypothesized to be at risk of higher morbidity or mortality because high host density would facilitate virus transmission within these typically nonimmune populations. However, during the usually lengthy interepizootic intervals characteristic of the Appalachian Mountains and plateau regions, high deer density would not incur higher risk

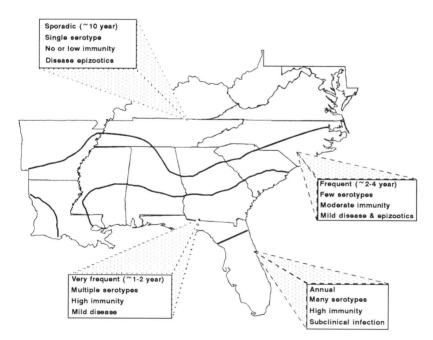

FIGURE 11.2. Generalized geographic pattern observed for hemorrhagic disease among white-tailed deer in the southeastern United States. Given are the typical frequency of viral activity, the usual level of serotype diversity, the general level of herd immunity, and the common outcome of infection.

because the viruses apparently are absent. A key to assessing risk for the regions that have infrequent viral incursions is an understanding of factors that precipitate the incursions; these factors are currently obscure.

Malnutrition–Parasitism Syndrome

NUTRITIONAL COMPONENTS   The nutritional component of the malnutrition–parasitism syndrome most often becomes limiting when deer foraging changes plant species composition, resulting in habitat degradation. As deer populations approach and exceed nutritional carrying capacity, ultimately the quantity and quality of forage is diminished due to overutilization by deer (Eve 1981). This situation has occurred on numerous occasions in various locations in the United States (Cowan and Clark 1981; Matschke et al. 1984) and is a basic axiom of the ecological relationship between white-tailed deer and their environment. As deer populations exceed nutritional carrying capacity, nutritional stresses resulting from habitat degradation due to overbrowsing begin to affect herd health by diminishing many physiologic functions (Eve 1981).

In addition to this traditional concept of the essential nature of overpopulation and malnutrition among white-tailed deer, recent work (Wood and Tanner 1985; Jacobson 1987; Osborne et al. 1992; Shea et al. 1992; Ford 1994; Shea and Osborne 1995) has focused on the inherent nutritional capabilities of certain habitats, a long-recognized (Lay 1957; Harlow and Jones 1965; Hesselton and Jackson 1974; Short 1975) but poorly documented aspect of nutritional stress among white-tailed deer. Regional variations in the inherent nutritional quality of habitats (plant communities) due to topography, soils, and climate predispose deer in certain locales to nutritional stresses that can be largely independent of the traditional concept of decreased nutritional status due to overbrowsing (Osborne et al. 1992; Shea et al. 1992; Petrick et al. 1994; Shea and Osborne 1995). These poor-quality habitats recently have been delineated, although somewhat arbitrarily, for the continental United States (Shea and Osborne 1995). A significant portion of the identified poor-quality habitat occurs in the southeastern United States (Figure 11.3), including much of the Appalachian, Ozark, and Quachita mountains; the pine flatwoods, pocosins, and Carolina bays in the Atlantic Coastal Plain; and the dry pine–oak uplands, such as the sand hills and scrub oak ridges, the Florida prairies, and most marshes in the Atlantic and Gulf coastal zones. Deer populations in these poor-quality habitats generally confront nutritional stresses regardless of population density, although extremely high-

FIGURE 11.3. Distribution of suboptimal habitats for white-tailed deer in the southeastern United States as reported by state wildlife agencies. (Redrawn from Shea and Osborne 1995; used with permission of Stackpole Books.)

density populations in these habitats also may compound the problem through habitat deterioration due to overbrowsing.

PARASITIC COMPONENTS   In the southeastern United States, white-tailed deer with significant nutritional stress usually have concomitant problems with parasitism (Eve and Kellogg 1977; Davidson et al. 1980; Anderson and Prestwood 1981; Eve 1981; Forrester 1992). Similarly, heavily parasitized deer nearly always originate from herds composed of unthrifty animals that are experiencing significant nutritional stress regardless of whether the nutritional stress is the result of inherently poor-quality habitat or degradation due to overbrowsing.

As noted above, deer in the Southeast are host to scores of species of parasites, many of which can result in disease under appropriate circumstances. However, because it is not feasible to evaluate all these species, selection of a relatively few species common throughout a large geographical area is the most feasible approach. The two most pathogenic species of parasites involved in the malnutrition–parasitism syndrome are the large stomach worm *(Haemonchus contortus)* and the large lungworm *(Dictyocaulus viviparus)* (Davidson et al. 1980; Forrester 1992). However, other parasites, including blood protozoans *(Theileria cervi)*, liver flukes *(Fascioloides magna)*, arterial worms *(Elaeophora schneideri)*, larvae of protostrongylid nematodes *(Parelaphostrongylus tenuis* and *P. andersoni)*, and ticks, especially lone star ticks *(Amblyomma americanum)*, may be important components of this syndrome in certain portions of the region. Epidemiologic characteristics of these parasites are presented below with emphasis on their ecological requirements and geographical distributions.

The large stomach worm *(Haemonchus contortus)*, which inhabits the abomasum of wild and domestic ruminants, is documented in deer from many locations in the Southeast. It has a direct life cycle; eggs shed in feces develop to infective third-stage larvae in the environment and are then ingested by ruminant hosts. High prevalences and intensities of infection and instances of haemonchosis occur primarily among deer populations in the Coastal Plain region (Davidson et al. 1980; Forrester 1992). Most cases occur between October and March, and predominantly young of the year are affected. Typical infections in clinically ill animals range from 1,000 to 15,000 large stomach worms per deer. Survivors develop immunity to subsequent massive infection, although they often retain low-intensity infections and serve as carriers, providing a source of infective larvae for subsequent cohorts (Davidson et al. 1980; McGhee et al. 1981). In coastal deer populations, 5–9-month-old deer had higher prevalences of infection and harbored as many as 140 times the number of large stomach worms as did adult (i.e., immune) deer (Davidson et al. 1980). In nearly all diagnosed cases of haemonchosis, large lungworms, ticks, or other parasites were involved as contributing factors (Davidson et al. 1980; Forrester 1992).

The large lungworm *(Dictyocaulus viviparus)* infects deer throughout the southeastern United States and has an overall prevalence of infection of approximately 30%. Large lungworms were found more often in young (<1 year) than in older deer and more frequently in males than females (Prestwood et al. 1971). Intensities of infection were higher during spring through fall than in winter, and there may be a general increase in prevalence and intensity from spring through fall (Prestwood et al. 1971). The life cycle of the large lungworm is direct. The first-stage larva is shed in the feces, and the infective third-stage develops in the environment and is then ingested by ruminant hosts. Dictyocaulosis has not been studied experimentally among deer, and there are no diagnostic guidelines relating infection intensity to disease. However, clinically affected animals may have hundreds of large lungworms, whereas apparently normal animals usually harbor 20 or fewer worms (Prestwood et al. 1971; Anderson and Prestwood 1981; Forrester 1992). Clinical dictyocaulosis has been recorded in deer from Alabama, Arkansas, Florida, Georgia, Louisiana, North Carolina, South Carolina, Virginia, and Maryland (Forrester 1992; SCWDS, unpublished).

Theileria cervi is a hemotrophic protozoal parasite that is transmitted by ticks. The lone star tick is considered to be the primary vector (Kingston 1981). The geographic distribution of *T. cervi* is associated with lone star tick infestations (Samuel and Trainer 1970; Davidson et al. 1983) and extends in a patchy and discontinuous fashion from Maryland to Florida and westward to Oklahoma and Texas (Kingston 1981; Davidson et al. 1983). In otherwise healthy deer, *T. cervi* has not been associated with overt disease. In deer with other significant parasitic or nutritional stresses, however, theileriosis has been reported to cause fever, anemia, dyspnea, emaciation, weakness, and general debility (Kingston 1981).

The geographic distribution of the liver fluke *(Fascioloides magna)* among white-tailed deer in the Southeast is restricted to certain major river drainage systems, including (1) the lower Mississippi and its tributaries, including the Arkansas, Cumberland, Ouachita, Red, White, and Yazoo rivers in Arkansas, Louisiana, Mississippi, and Tennessee; (2) the Mobile, Alabama, Tombigbee, and Black Warrior river systems in Alabama; (3) the Applachicola and Flint rivers in Florida and Georgia; (4) the Suwanee and Kissimmee rivers and the Everglades–Big Cypress Swamp region of Florida; (5) the Ogechee drainage in Georgia; (6) the Savannah, Edisto, Santee, Saluda, Wateree, and Pee Dee drainages in South Carolina; and (7) the Cape Fear and Roanoke rivers in North Carolina. In these locations, parasite transmission is restricted to those wetlands capable of supporting the obligatory intermediate host, the aquatic snail (*Lymnaea* spp.) (Pursglove et al. 1977; Foreyt 1981). Deer are the normal definitive host for the liver fluke and acquire infections by ingesting larvae (metacercariae) encysted on aquatic and semiaquatic vegetation. In enzootic locales, the prevalence of infection may be greater than 80% with adult deer

(>1 year) having higher prevalences of infection than do young deer (<1 year). Most infections involve 30 or fewer liver flukes, although intensities of over 100 liver flukes may occur. Deer that are otherwise healthy appear to tolerate the liver fluke without exhibiting clinical signs; however, subclinical disease characterized by a transitory anemia and chronic liver damage is common (Foreyt 1981).

White-tailed deer are the normal definitive host for two species of parelaphostrongylid nematodes, the meningeal worm *(Parelaphostrongylus tenuis)* and the muscleworm *(P. andersoni)*. Adult meningeal worms reside in the cranial vault, and adult muscleworms inhabit the major muscles of white-tailed deer (Anderson and Prestwood 1981). Both species require terrestrial gastropod intermediate hosts for completion of their life cycles. The meningeal worm is common in deer populations north of an arc extending from northeastern North Carolina to southwestern Louisiana; it is almost completely absent in the Coastal Plain southeast of that area (Comer et al. 1991). The distribution of the muscleworm is less well known, although it has been documented in most physiographic regions, including the southeastern Coastal Plain where the meningeal worm is absent. Adult parelaphostrongylid nematodes routinely do not cause clinical disease in white-tailed deer; however, their first-stage larvae, which temporarily inhabit the lungs upon their exit from deer, can produce verminous pneumonitis if present in large numbers.

The arterial worm *(Elaeophora schneideri)* inhabits the carotid arteries of native North American Cervidae and once was believed to occur only in high-elevation regions of the western United States, where it commonly infects mule deer *(Odocoileus hemionus)*, elk *(Cervus elaphus)*, and domestic sheep *(Ovis* spp.). In 1962 it was found in white-tailed deer on the Florida Gulf Coast (Prestwood and Ridgeway 1972) and later elsewhere in coastal habitats in Florida, Georgia, and South Carolina (Hibler and Prestwood 1981; Couvillion et al. 1985). These coastal foci of the arterial worm are believed to have persisted in remnant deer populations in coastal lowlands when deer were largely extirpated from the rest of the Southeast (Couvillion et al. 1985). The distribution now also includes areas in Arkansas and Louisiana, where it is thought to have recently spread naturally from Texas and Oklahoma (Couvillion et al. 1985; W. R. Davidson, unpublished data). Arterial worms are transmitted by horseflies, specifically *Tabanus lineola hinellus* in the southern Atlantic Coastal Plain (Couvillion et al. 1984; Couvillion, Nettles, Sheppard, et al. 1986). Arterial worms require at least one year per generation, which favors survival of *E. schneideri* in deer populations with older age structures, especially in locales with high densities of horseflies. The relationship of deer density to arterial worm abundance has not been specifically investigated; however, deer are the only known definitive hosts in the Southeast. Arterial worm infections cause pathologic changes within the carotid arteries (Titche et al. 1979) that may result in oral food impactions, tooth loss, and pathologic fractures of mandibles (Couvillion, Nettles, Rawlings, et al. 1986). These pathologic changes occur more often among older deer, suggesting that duration of infection is an important factor in the development of clinical signs and lesions.

Ticks are the most important group of arthropod parasites infesting deer, and 18 species have been reported from deer in the United States (Strickland et al. 1981). The lone star tick *(Amblyomma americanum)* is the most widely distributed tick frequently found on white-tailed deer in the Southeast (Smith 1977; Strickland et al. 1981; SCWDS, unpublished data). Lone star ticks occur in all states in the Southeast; however, high-density populations are locally patchy in Alabama, Arkansas, Florida, Georgia, Kentucky, Louisiana, Mississippi, Missouri, North Carolina, South Carolina, Tennessee, and Virginia. The Gulf Coast tick *(A. maculatum),* the black-legged tick *(Ixodes scapularis),* and the winter tick *(Dermacentor nigrolineatus)* also are relatively common on southeastern deer (Kellogg et al. 1971; Smith 1977; Strickland et al. 1981). Tick infestations are much lower in the Appalachian Mountain region than in the remainder of the Southeast. Coastal Plain areas typically have higher-intensity infestations of these common ticks, although high intensities of lone star ticks occur locally in the Piedmont, the Ozark and Quachita mountains, and the interior low plateaus. Up to 30% fawn mortality has been attributed to lone star tick infestations (Bolte et al. 1970; Hoch 1973), and lone star tick infestation has been a contributing factor in causing morbidity or mortality of heavily parasitized adult deer (Davidson et al. 1980; Forrester 1992). The generally lower-intensity infestations of other tick species usually have not been directly associated with deer morbidity or mortality (SCWDS, unpublished data). White-tailed deer are major hosts for the adult stages of the lone star tick (Patrick and Hair 1978; Haile and Mount 1987; Bloemer et al. 1988) and the black-legged tick (Wilson et al. 1988; Deblinger et al. 1992.), and deer also serve as important hosts for the larvae and nymphs of lone star ticks (Haile and Mount 1987; Bloemer et al. 1988).

In summary, because deer are the sole or at least a major definitive host for most of the aforementioned parasites, the intensity and pathologic consequences of infection by these species exhibit some degree of

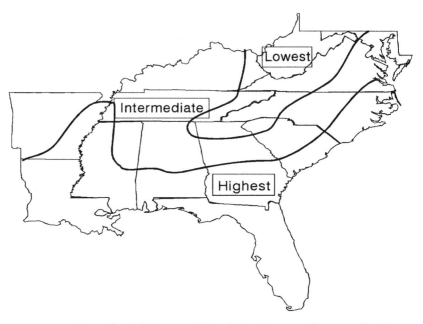

FIGURE 11.4. Generalized depiction of the relative diversity of species of pathogenic parasites among white-tailed deer in the southeastern United States.

density-dependent relationships to deer populations. How closely parasite abundance is tied to deer density varies among the species; however, the general phenomenon of density dependence is clear. Because deer populations in more southerly or Coastal Plain areas have a higher diversity of pathogenic species and therefore are subject to simultaneous infection with multiple species, the parasitic component of the malnutrition–parasitism syndrome tends to be more significant for deer populations in this region than for deer from more northerly latitudes or higher elevations (Figure 11.4). It is emphasized, however, that significant parasitic disease should be expected in high-density deer populations at any geographic location in the Southeast.

OVERVIEW

Significant disease-related morbidity and mortality among white-tailed deer in the southeastern United States are due to two major problems. One is hemorrhagic disease, which is caused by either EHDV or BTV. Both viruses are transmitted by *Culicoides* midges. The second is a syndrome of malnutrition and parasitism, with the principal parasitic agents being the large stomach worm and the large lungworm. Other infectious and parasitic agents may be important on a local scale or may serve as stressors compounding the syndrome of malnutrition and parasitism. Based on their epidemiologic features, these two disease problems were evaluated for compliance with the conceptual model presented by Eve (1981) of declining herd health attributable to increasing population density. Hemorrhagic disease is not necessarily related to deer density because its epidemiologic complexity (i.e., multiple virus serotypes, regulation of susceptibility by existing herd immunity, multiple species of *Culicoides* vectors, differing lengths of annual vector activity, and involvement of domestic ruminant hosts) results in distinct geographic patterns of viral activity and disease occurrence. In contrast, the syndrome of malnutrition and parasitism is fundamentally a density-dependent phenomenon, although the inherent nutritional quality of habitats and the identity of parasitic agents vary among geographic areas.

These two disease problems also exhibit markedly differing geographic patterns of occurrence within the region, and these geographic patterns are attributable to ecological requirements of the specific pathogens. Episodes of clinical hemorrhagic disease occur primarily in the upper Coastal Plain, Piedmont, or, occasionally, mountainous regions, whereas the malnutrition–parasitism syndrome, especially parasitism by multiple pathogenic species, is most prevalent in the Coastal Plain region.

Eve (1981) clearly recognized that variations such as those described for hemorrhagic disease and malnutrition–parasitism syndrome were to be expected among the infectious and parasitic disease processes that accrue with increasing deer density. Even though we conclude that hemorrhagic disease is not necessarily density dependent, we agree with the general tenet of Eve's model that deterioration in herd health is a consequence of high deer density. Thus, because high deer density, typically at a level that exceeds habitat carrying capacity, is characteristic of unmanaged deer populations, it follows that herd health of such populations can be predicted to be compromised when compared with those held at lower densities by regulated harvests.

ACKNOWLEDGMENTS

This work was conducted through the sponsorship of the fish and wildlife agencies of Alabama, Arkansas, Florida, Georgia, Kentucky, Louisiana, Maryland, Mississippi, Missouri, North Carolina, Puerto Rico, South Carolina, Tennessee, Virginia, and West Virginia. Funds were provided by the Federal Aid to Wildlife Restoration Act of 1937 (50 U.S. Statutes at Large 917) and through the National Biological Survey Grant Agreement 14-45-0009-94-906. Numerous past and present SCWDS coworkers contributed immensely to our knowledge and understanding of deer diseases and although individual thanks are not feasible, we recognize and appreciate their input. Special thanks are due to J. Hammond Eve, Forest E. Kellogg, and Donald J. Forrester for critical review of this manuscript.

REFERENCES CITED

Anderson, R. C., and A. K. Prestwood. 1981. Lungworms. Pages 266–317 *in* Diseases and Parasites of White-Tailed Deer. (W. R. Davidson, F. A. Hayes, V. F. Nettles, and F. E. Kellogg, eds.) Tall Timbers Research Station Miscellaneous Publication Number 7, Tallahassee, FL.

Bloemer, S. R., R. H. Zimmermann, and K. Fairbanks. 1988. Abundance, attachment sites, and density estimators for lone star ticks (Acari: Ixodidae) infesting white-tailed deer. Journal of Medical Entomology 25:295–300.

Bolte, J. R., J. A. Hair, and J. Fletcher. 1970. White-tailed deer mortality following tissue destruction induced by lone star ticks. Journal of Wildlife Management 34:546–552.

Comer, J. A., W. R. Davidson, A. K. Prestwood, and V. F. Nettles. 1991. An update on the distribution of *Parelaphostrongylus tenuis* in the southeastern United States. Journal of Wildlife Diseases 27:348–354.

Couvillion, C. E., W. R. Davidson, and V. F. Nettles. 1985. Distribution of *Elaeophora schneideri* in white-tailed deer in the southeastern United States, 1962–1983. Journal of Wildlife Diseases 21:451–453.

Couvillion, C. E., V. F. Nettles, W. R. Davidson, J. E. Pearson, and G. A. Gustafson. 1981. Hemorrhagic disease among white-tailed deer in the Southeast from 1971 through 1990. Proceedings of the United States Animal Health Association 85:522–537.

Couvillion, C. E., V. F. Nettles, C. A. Rawlings, and R. L. Joyner. 1986. Elaeophorosis in white-tailed deer: Pathology of the natural disease and its relation to oral food impactions. Journal of Wildlife Diseases 22:214–223.

Couvillion, C. E., V. F. Nettles, D. C. Sheppard, R. L. Joyner, and O. M. Bannaga. 1986. Temporal occurrence of third-stage larvae of *Elaeophora schneideri* in *Tabanus lineola hinellus* on South Island, South Carolina. Journal of Wildlife Diseases 22:196–200.

Couvillion, C. E., D. C. Sheppard, V. F. Nettles, and O. M. Bannaga. 1984. Intermediate hosts of *Elaeophora schneideri* Wehr and Dikmans, 1935 on South Island, South Carolina. Journal of Wildlife Diseases 20:59–61.

Cowan, R. L., and A. C. Clark. 1981. Nutritional requirements. Pages 72–86 *in*

Diseases and Parasites of White-Tailed Deer. (W. R. Davidson, F. A. Hayes, V. F. Nettles, and F. E. Kellogg, eds.) Tall Timbers Research Station Miscellaneous Publication Number 7, Tallahassee, FL.

Davidson, W. R., C. B. Crow, J. M. Crum, and R. R. Gerrish. 1983. Observations on *Theileria cervi* and *Trypanosoma cervi* in white-tailed deer *(Odocoileus virginianus)* from the southeastern United States. Proceedings of the Helminthological Society of Washington 50:165–169.

Davidson, W. R., F. A. Hayes, V. F. Nettles, and F. E. Kellogg, eds. 1981. Diseases and Parasites of White-tailed Deer. Tall Timbers Research Station Miscellaneous Publication Number 7, Tallahassee, FL.

Davidson, W. R., M. B. McGhee, V. F. Nettles, and L. C. Chappell. 1980. Haemonchosis in white-tailed deer in the southeastern United States. Journal of Wildlife Diseases 16:499–508.

Davidson, W. R., J. S. Osborne, and F. A. Hayes. 1985. Abomasal parasitism and physical condition in southeastern white-tailed deer. Proceedings of the Annual Conference Southeastern Association of Fish and Wildlife Agencies 36 (1982): 436–444.

Deblinger, R. D., M. L. Wilson, D. W. Rimmer, and A. Spielman. 1992. Reduced abundance of immature deer ticks following incremental removal of deer. Journal of Medical Entomology 30:144–150.

Eve, J. H. 1981. Management implications of disease. Pages 413–423 *in* Diseases and Parasites of White-Tailed Deer. (W. R. Davidson, F. A. Hayes, V. F. Nettles, and F. E. Kellogg, eds.) Tall Timbers Research Station Miscellaneous Publication Number 7, Tallahassee, FL.

Eve, J. H., and F. E. Kellogg. 1977. Management implications of abomasal parasites in southeastern white-tailed deer. Journal of Wildlife Management 41: 169–177.

Ford, W. M. 1994. Spring and summer nutrition of white-tailed deer in relation to site quality and timber in the southern Appalachians. Doctoral dissertation, University of Georgia, Athens.

Foreyt, W. J. 1981. Trematodes and cestodes. Pages 237–265 *in* Diseases and Parasites of White-Tailed Deer. (W. R. Davidson, F. A. Hayes, V. F. Nettles, and F. E. Kellogg, eds.) Tall Timbers Research Station Miscellaneous Publication Number 7, Tallahassee, FL.

Forrester, D. J. 1992. Parasites and Diseases of Wild Mammals in Florida. University of Florida Press, Gainesville.

Fox, J. R., and M. R. Pelton. 1974. Observations of a white-tailed deer die off in the Great Smoky Mountains National Park. Proceedings of the Annual Conference Southeastern Association of Game and Fish Commissioners 27 (1973): 297–301.

Haile, D. G., and G. A. Mount. 1987. Computer simulation of population dynamics of the lone star tick, *Amblyomma americanum* (Acari: Ixodidae). Journal of Medical Entomology 24:356–369.

Harlow, R. F., and F. K. Jones. 1965. The white-tailed deer in Florida. Florida Game and Fresh Water Fish Commission Technical Bulletin 9.

Hayes, F. A. 1964. Dig their graves Mr. Sportsman. Florida Wildlife 17 (10): 20–34.

Hayes, F. A. 1981. Preface. Pages vii–xii *in* Diseases and Parasites of White-Tailed Deer. (W. R. Davidson, F. A. Hayes, V. F. Nettles, and F. E. Kellogg, eds.) Tall Timbers Research Station Miscellaneous Publication Number 7, Tallahassee, FL.

Hesselton, W. T., and L. W. Jackson. 1974. Reproductive rates of white-tailed deer in New York State. New York Fish and Game Journal 21:135–152.

Hibler, C. P., and A. K. Prestwood. 1981. Filarial nematodes of white-tailed deer. Pages 351–362 *in* Diseases and Parasites of White-Tailed Deer. (W. R. Davidson, F. A. Hayes, V. F. Nettles, and F. E. Kellogg, eds.) Tall Timbers Research Station Miscellaneous Publication Number 7, Tallahassee, FL.

Hoch, A. L. 1973. Effects of lone star tick (Acarina: Ixodidae) parasitism and theileriasis on white-tailed deer fawn survival and hematology. Doctoral dissertation, Oklahoma State University, Stillwater.

Jacobson, H. A. 1987. Relationships between deer and soil nutrients in Mississippi. Proceedings of the Annual Conference Southeastern Association of Fish and Wildlife Agencies 38 (1984): 1–12.

Kellogg, F. E., T. P. Kistner, R. K. Strickland, and R. R. Gerrish. 1971. Arthropod parasites collected from white-tailed deer. Journal of Medical Entomology 8:495–498.

Kingston, N. 1981. Protozoan parasites. Pages 193–236 *in* Diseases and Parasites of White-Tailed Deer. (W. R. Davidson, F. A. Hayes, V. F. Nettles, and F. E. Kellogg, eds.) Tall Timbers Research Station Miscellaneous Publication Number 7, Tallahassee, FL.

Lay, D. W. 1957. Some nutrition problems of deer in the southern pine type. Proceedings of the Annual Conference Southeastern Association of Game and Fish Commissioners 10 (1956): 53–58.

Matschke, G. H., K. A. Fagerstone, F. A. Hayes, W. Parker, R. F. Harlow, V. F. Nettles, and D. O. Trainer. 1984. Population influences. Pages 169–188 *in* White-Tailed Deer: Ecology and Management. (L. K. Halls, ed.) Stackpole Books, Harrisburg, PA.

McGhee, M. B., V. F. Nettles, E. A. Rollor III, A. K. Prestwood, and W. R. Davidson. 1981. Studies on cross-transmission and pathogenicity of *Haemonchus contortus* in white-tailed deer, domestic cattle and sheep. Journal of Wildlife Diseases 17:353–364.

Nettles, V. F., W. R. Davidson, and D. E. Stallknecht. 1994. Surveillance for hemorrhagic disease in white-tailed deer and other wild ruminants, 1980–1989. Proceedings of the Annual Conference Southeastern Association of Fish and Wildlife Agencies 46 (1992): 138–146.

Nettles, V. F., S. A. Hylton, D. E. Stallknecht, and W. R. Davidson. 1992. Epidemiology of epizootic hemorrhagic disease viruses in wildlife in the USA. Pages

238–248 *in* Bluetongue, African Horse Sickness, and Related Orbiviruses. (T. E. Walton and B. I. Osborn, eds.) CRC Press, Boca Raton, FL.

Nettles, V. F., and D. E. Stallknecht. 1992. History and progress in the study of hemorrhagic disease of deer. Transactions of the North American Wildlife and Natural Resources Conference 57:499–516.

Osborne, J. S., A. S. Johnson, P. E. Hale, R. L. Marchinton, C. V. Vansant, and J. M. Wentworth. 1992. Population ecology of the Blackbeard Island white-tailed deer. Tall Timbers Research Station Bulletin 26, Tallahassee, FL.

Patrick, C. D., and J. A. Hair. 1978. White-tailed deer utilization of three different habitats and its influence on lone star tick populations. Journal of Parasitology 64:1100–1106.

Pearson, J. E., G. A. Gustafson, A. L. Shafer, and A. D. Alstad. 1992. Distribution of bluetongue in the United States. Pages 128–139 *in* Bluetongue, African Horse Sickness, and Related Orbiviruses. (T. E. Walton and B. I. Osborn, eds.) CRC Press, Boca Raton, FL.

Petrick, C. J., R. E. Vanderhoof, and S. M. Shea. 1994. Relationship of *in utero* productivity to population indices of white-tailed deer in the Florida sandhills. Annual Meeting of the Southeast Deer Study Group 17:30.

Prestwood, A. K., T. P. Kistner, F. E. Kellogg, and F. A. Hayes. 1974. The 1971 outbreak of hemorrhagic disease among white-tailed deer of the southeastern United States. Journal of Wildlife Diseases 10:217–224.

Prestwood, A. K., and T. R. Ridgeway. 1972. Elaeophorosis in white-tailed deer of the southeastern U.S.A.: Case report and distribution. Journal of Wildlife Diseases 8:233–236.

Prestwood, A. K., J. F. Smith, and J. Brown. 1971. Lungworms in white-tailed deer of the southeastern United States. Journal of Wildlife Diseases 7:149–154.

Pursglove, S. R., A. K. Prestwood, T. R. Ridgeway, and F. A. Hayes. 1977. *Fascioloides magna* in white-tailed deer in the southeastern United States. Journal of the American Veterinary Medical Association 171:936–938.

Robinson, R. M., T. L. Hailey, C. W. Livingston, and J. W. Thomas. 1967. Bluetongue in the desert bighorn sheep. Journal of Wildlife Management 31:165–168.

Samuel, W. M., and D. O. Trainer. 1970. *Amblyomma* (Acarina: Ixodidae) in white-tailed deer, *Odocoileus virginianus* (Zimmermann), from south Texas with implication for theileriasis. Journal of Medical Entomology 7:567–574.

Shea, S. M., T. A. Breault, and M. L. Richardson. 1992. Herd density and physical condition of white-tailed deer in Florida flatwoods. Annual Meeting of the Southeast Deer Study Group 12:9–10.

Shea, S. M., and J. S. Osborne. 1995. Poor quality habitats. Pages 193–209 *in* Quality Whitetails: The Why and How of Quality Deer Management. (K. V. Miller and R. L. Marchinton, eds.) Stackpole Books, Harrisburg, PA.

Shope, R. E., L. G. MacNamara, and R. Mangold. 1955. Deer mortality—epizootic hemorrhagic disease of deer. New Jersey Outdoors 6:17.

Shope, R. E., L. G. MacNamara, and R. Mangold. 1960. A virus-induced epizootic hemorrhagic disease of the Virginia white-tailed deer *(Odocoileus virginianus)*. Journal of Experimental Medicine 111:155–170.

Short, H. L. 1975. Nutrition of southern deer in different seasons. Journal of Wildlife Management 39:321–329.

Smith, J. S. 1977. A survey of ticks infesting white-tailed deer in 12 southeastern states. Master's thesis, University of Georgia, Athens.

Stair, E. L., R. M. Robinson, and L. P. Jones. 1968. Spontaneous bluetongue in Texas white-tailed deer. Pathologia Veterinaria 5:164–173.

Stallknecht, D. E., J. L. Blue, E. A. Rollor III, V. F. Nettles, W. R. Davidson, and J. E. Pearson. 1991. Precipitating antibodies to epizootic hemorrhagic disease and bluetongue viruses in white-tailed deer in the southeastern United States. Journal of Wildlife Diseases 27:238–247.

Strickland, R. K., R. R. Gerrish, and J. S. Smith. 1981. Arthropods. Pages 363–389 *in* Diseases and Parasites of White-Tailed Deer. (W. R. Davidson, F. A. Hayes, V. F. Nettles, and F. E. Kellogg, eds.) Tall Timbers Research Station Miscellaneous Publication Number 7, Tallahassee, FL.

Thomas, F. C. 1981. Hemorrhagic disease. Pages 87–96 *in* Diseases and Parasites of White-Tailed Deer. (W. R. Davidson, F. A. Hayes, V. F. Nettles, and F. E. Kellogg, eds.) Tall Timbers Research Station Miscellaneous Publication Number 7, Tallahassee, FL.

Titche, A. R., A. K. Prestwood, and C. P. Hibler. 1979. Experimental infection of white-tailed deer with *Elaeophora schneideri*. Journal of Wildlife Diseases 15:273–280.

Wilson, M. L., S. R. Telford III, J. Piesman, and A. Spielman. 1988. Reduced abundance of immature *Ixodes dammini* (Acari: Ixodidae) following elimination of deer. Journal of Medical Entomology 25:224–228.

Wood, J. M., and G. W. Tanner. 1985. Browse quality response to forest fertilization and soils in Florida. Journal of Range Management 38:432–435.

12 Reconsidering Paradigms of Overpopulation in Ungulates

White-Tailed Deer at Saratoga National Historical Park

H. BRIAN UNDERWOOD AND
WILLIAM F. PORTER

Recent decades have seen the dramatic growth of populations of white-tailed deer throughout the eastern United States (Cypher and Cypher 1988; Warren 1991). Biologists have limited experience with the high population densities that occur in many places today. These populations are especially interesting because they cause us to question the basic principles associated with growth of ungulate populations. This growth sequence is characterized by three phases: (1) initial upsurge and overshoot of carrying capacity, (2) the crash, and (3) the recovery to intermediate density (Caughley 1979). Though a paucity of evidence exists, this characterization has become widely accepted (Leopold 1943; Caughley 1970, 1976, 1979), supported in large measure by two spectacular and enigmatic cases: the mule deer *(Odocoileus hemionus)* on the Kaibab Plateau in Arizona (Rasmussen 1941) and the reindeer *(Rangifer tarandus)* of St. Paul Island off the coast of Alaska (Scheffer 1951). The details notwithstanding, these two examples stand as hallmarks in the indoctrination of several generations of wildlife professionals.

For the purpose of this chapter, we elevate this basic characterization of the growth of ungulate populations to a paradigm. This paradigm is especially relevant to National Park Service (NPS) managers, for it was singularly identified as the justification for active intervention in a seminal and influential report advocating an otherwise light-handed approach to wildlife management in the national parks (Leopold et. al. 1963). Based on our own experiences at New York's Saratoga National Historical Park

(SNHP) and elsewhere, we propose that the classic paradigm of deer population growth needs to be reconsidered.

BACKGROUND

In the mid-1980s, SNHP was one of many eastern parks in which increasing deer populations were garnering a lot of attention (Underwood et al. 1994). Managers were concerned that deer were causing damage to vegetation and inflicting harm to themselves by overbrowsing and exhausting their food supply. In other parks, high densities of deer also raised concern about risks of deer–vehicle collisions and the spread of Lyme disease (Porter et al. 1994). Active management of deer populations was not ongoing in most parks, but managers were getting pressure to do something to alleviate the concerns. At SNHP, the issue came to a head when neighboring landowners contacted the local congressional delegation about damage "park deer" were causing to crops.

The NPS was concerned about the problems that burgeoning deer populations were creating but were hesitant to take direct action to control deer because of existing legislation, policies, and directives. Details of these regulatory concerns can be found in Underwood and Porter (1991) and Porter et al. (1994). Few parks had the legislative framework in place to undertake hunting as a means of reducing deer densities, and NPS was wary of legal challenges to other forms of direct population reduction. Although considerable research was available to describe the biology of white-tailed deer, little was known about the ecology of free-ranging deer populations at high densities. Consequently, the NPS sought to understand better the deer at SNHP as the basis for the development of a responsible management program. As part of this research program, we conducted studies of various aspects of deer and vegetation ecology at SNHP from 1985 through 1994, most of which can be found in Austin (1992) and Underwood et al. (1994).

STUDY AREA

Saratoga National Historical Park is located in eastern Saratoga County, New York, 32 km north of Albany along the Hudson River (latitude 43°00′, longitude 73°78′). The park encompasses approximately 1,100 ha. Elevations range from 122 m above sea level in the west to 30 m in the east on the floodplain of the Hudson River. The western part of the park consists of low, elongated hills oriented northeast–southwest that alternate with broad, flat-bottomed valleys. To the east, there are two large terraces cut in an east–west direction by deep ravines.

The climate is humid continental with long, cold winters, short, warm summers, and heavy precipitation. Average temperatures range from a low of −7°C in January to a high of 21°C in July. Mean annual precipitation is 960 mm and is evenly distributed throughout the year.

The land-use history of SNHP is primarily agricultural. Prior to the Revolutionary War battles in 1776, the forested landscape was being cleared for farming. Clearing continued throughout the next century (Russell 1994), and agricultural fields formed the core of the designated Revolutionary War battlefield site in the late 1880s. Land acquisition to incorporate the entire battlefield is ongoing. The present landscape is a mosaic of mowed fields, old fields in various successional stages, and second-growth woodland. Most of the second-growth forests are relatively young (<65 years). There are no old-growth forest stands at SNHP.

METHODS

The history of the deer population at the park was gleaned from interviews with past superintendents and chief rangers, other park staff, long-term residents familiar with the local deer population, and filed official correspondence. These were not formal surveys but rather polls to gain impressions about how serious deer-related issues were in the minds of managers during the decades following the park's federal designation in 1938. In addition, the New York State Department of Environmental Conservation (NYSDEC) has maintained records of the reported adult male harvest since 1954 for the townships now constituting Deer Management Unit 40 (DMU 40). Most of the park lies within the township of Stillwater, and a small portion of the park lies within Saratoga Township. Collectively, the two townships constitute approximately 11% of DMU 40's total land area.

For our analysis, the reported buck harvest for Stillwater Township was assumed to represent the influence of the park on local deer harvests. For comparison, data for Saratoga Township and all other townships of DMU 40 were plotted and rates of increase (Caughley and Birch 1971) were computed by regression (Freund et al. 1986) of the natural logarithm of the reported harvest on time (1954 was time index 0). Only data from

1954 to 1983 were used in the analysis to exclude years of significant harvests of antlerless deer (i.e., fawns and yearling and adult does).

In conjunction with a field laboratory exercise for undergraduate students, we conducted counts of deer on three areas of SNHP from 1985 to 1994 by means of the drive method (Behrend et al. 1970; McCullough 1979; deCalesta and Witmer 1990). Drivers marched from one side of each area to the other while watchers observed boundaries; the objective was to count all animals exiting the sample area. Participants were given explicit instructions in order to avoid duplicate counts. Areas were selected based on general cover type and juxtaposition to well-defined boundaries such as field edges. Each area was surveyed and ground control was established to facilitate navigation through dense vegetation. The three units totaled 87 ha (area A = 42 ha, B = 27 ha, and C = 18 ha) and represented about 10% of the total land area available within the administrative park boundary in 1985. Parkwide population estimates were derived from the counts by prorating the observed density to the total area for each cover type in the entire park and then dividing that number by the total land area within the park's administrative boundary. Because some cover types were not represented in the three areas, this estimate must be considered a minimum.

Finally, we characterized deer herd productivity from 1984 to 1987 by (1) recording the reproductive performance of marked females, (2) predicting reproductive rates (i.e., fetuses per pregnant and nonpregnant female) from mean yearling male antler beam diameters (Severinghaus and Moen 1983), and (3) examining reproductive tracts from a small sample of carcasses.

RESULTS

Based on our informal telephone interviews and reading of file correspondence, deer at SNHP were not noticeably visible until the early 1960s (Table 12.1). By the 1970s, the deer population was large enough to warrant correspondence between the chief ranger, regional chief scientist, and the NYSDEC. The first park superintendent (1940–47) reported very infrequent sightings of deer, whereas one of his successors three decades later estimated a population of around 200 deer. Additional anecdotes by local hunters suggest that deer sightings in the early days of the park were indeed rare events. These observations are corroborated by local harvest statistics (Figure 12.1). Percentage rate of increase computed from the

TABLE 12.1

Informal interviews with past managers of Saratoga National Historical Park

Manager name and title	Years in service	Comments
Warren Hamilton, Superintendent	1940–47	Did not recall seeing any deer at all
Howard Chapman, Chief Ranger	1950–52	Characterized sightings of deer as a rare event, only three or four deer at the most; found remains in Mill Creek ravine—assumed poached
Dixon Freeland, Superintendent	1964–67	Recalled heavy hunting pressure on boundary but reported infrequent personal sightings of deer
Harold L. Grafe, Chief Ranger	1970–72	Estimated a relatively stable population of about 200 deer at the time
Stephan Butterworth, Chief Ranger	1973–78	Noticed seasonal changes in numbers (greatest in autumn); counted 60–70 deer on a typical park closing
William Gibson, Chief Ranger	1978–88	Witnessed an increasing deer population through-out the decade

Note: All interviews were conducted from 1987 to 1989.

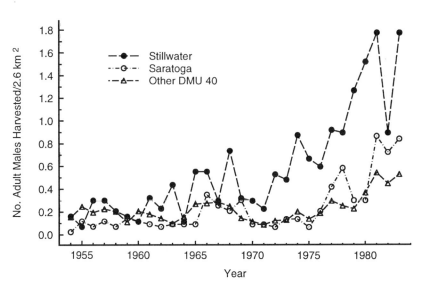

FIGURE 12.1. Reported adult male white-tailed deer harvest for Stillwater, Saratoga, and other Deer Management Unit (DMU) 40 townships in New York, 1954–1983.

slopes of reported harvest regressed on time were 8, 8, and 2% per year for Stillwater, Saratoga, and other DMU 40 townships, 1954–83. The linear model was significant ($P < 0.0001$) and adequate for describing the combined trends ($r^2 = 68\%$). An analysis of covariance indicated that while the rates of increase (i.e., slopes) in harvest for the towns of Stillwater and Saratoga were different ($P < 0.05$) from the rest of DMU 40, the initial levels of harvest in 1954 (i.e., intercepts) were not.

For the interior 10.9 km^2 of SNHP, mean density of deer for the 10-year period, 1985–94, was 53 deer/km^2. Parkwide population estimates derived from sampled area densities during this time period ranged from 409 to 732 deer ($\bar{x} = 576$, coefficient of variation = 20%; Table 12.2). Trends in the deer population estimate indicated a general decline from 1985 through 1989 and then an increase from 1990 to 1994. With the effect of year removed, we found no relationship between residual density and the number of participants on any given drive.

The proportion of reproductive yearlings in our marked sample was higher than that estimated from a small number of reproductive tracts (Table 12.3). Reproductive rates predicted from mean antler beam diameters of yearling males ($n = 75$) harvested throughout the townships of Stillwater and Saratoga were 1.76, 1.39, and 0.27 fetuses per adult, yearling, and fawn females, respectively.

TABLE 12.2

Parkwide deer population estimates derived from surveys of three areas (A–C) of Saratoga National Historical Park

Year	Deer count			Deer density[a]			Parkwide population estimate[b]
	A	B	C	A	B	C	
1985	34	55	5	0.81	2.04	0.28	659
1986	63	22	5	1.50	0.81	0.28	441
1987	73	35	6	1.74	1.30	0.33	603
1988	57	37	0	1.36	1.37	0.00	526
1989	69	19	2	1.64	0.70	0.11	409
1990	81	24	0	1.93	0.89	0.00	481
1991	106	20	1	2.52	0.74	0.06	530
1992	80	37	18	1.90	1.37	1.00	731
1993	76	43	1	1.81	1.59	0.06	649
1994	42	50	18	1.00	1.85	1.00	732

[a] Deer densities are given as number per hectare, based on 42 ha sampled in area A, 27 ha in area B, and 18 ha in area C.

[b] To derive estimate, sampled density was prorated to the total area of each cover type represented. Total area of cover type represented by area A was 133 ha; area B, 252 ha; and area C, 133 ha.

TABLE 12.3

Reproductive rates for female white-tailed deer in Saratoga National
Historical Park, 1985–1987

| Age of group | Percent of female population[a] | Percent of age group breeding | | Fetuses per female[c] | Reproductive rate[d] | |
		Marked females[b]	Reproductive tracts[c]		Marked females[b]	Reproductive tracts[c]
Adult	63	100	100	2.00	2.00	2.00
Yearling	14	64	42	1.00	0.64	0.42
Fawn	23	2	3	1.00	0.02	0.03

[a] Estimated from October population ratios in 1985–87; number of deer classified was 695, 612, and 424, respectively. See Underwood et al. (1994) for details.

[b] Estimated from a marked sample of female deer, 1984–87 ($n = 11$).

[c] Estimated from a sample of reproductive tracts, 1984–87: $n = 4$ for adults, 12 for yearlings, and 34 for fawns.

[d] Product of the percent of the age group breeding and the fetuses per female for that age group.

DISCUSSION

Populations of deer on SNHP during this study were crudely estimated to be between 400 and 800 animals, or about 37 to 74 deer/km^2 (96 to 192 deer/mi^2) over a 10-year period. This density is similar in magnitude to those observed in other parks where hunting is prohibited or severely restricted (Burst and Pelton 1979; O'Connell and Sayre 1988; Christie and Sayre 1989; Storm et al. 1989; Warren and Ford 1990). Harvests of antlered males in the town of Stillwater did not depart from those in adjacent townships until about 1960. We attribute the timing of this departure to the presence of a burgeoning park deer population. Because much of SNHP lies within the township of Stillwater (constituting about 22% of the total township land area), we believe that by the late 1950s dispersal movements of young males from SNHP were sufficient to boost local deer harvests. However, dramatic increases in regional deer harvests did not occur until about two decades later. Causes for the delay remain a matter for speculation, though differences in land-use patterns among park and adjacent property are compelling possibilities. Abandonment of farmland and associated old-field succession in the park predates that on adjacent lands (Russell 1994) by several decades or more. The park was probably capable of supporting a deer population much earlier than were surrounding lands, which were devoid of large (>50 ha) areas of escape cover just a few decades ago. Regional increases in buck harvests ultimately resulted in the implementation of an antlerless deer permit system in the early 1980s. Because differences in vegetation characteristics among townships are much less dramatic now, the sustained difference in harvest between the towns surrounding the park and elsewhere can only be attributed to the allure that a so-called protected population has to hunters. Hunting pressure along the park boundary is intense by any standard and does account for very high deer mortality within a short distance from the park (Schaberl 1994).

Reproductive characteristics of the deer herd studied at SNHP are consistent with a population that, from a demographic sense, is nearing its upper limit imposed by environmental pressures. McCullough (1979) refers to this upper limit as K-carrying capacity, or just K. In theory, K includes all the components that might limit further population growth, including food, water, and shelter. However, rarely are any of these components measured directly. Instead, biologists index these components' combined effects by the number of animals that survive through critical shortages (Hamlin and Mackie 1989). Though it could be argued that the existence of K has never been "proven," there are several demographic milestones that appear to indicate reliably the likelihood that a deer population will sustain further growth (McCullough 1979; Downing and Guynn 1985) and lend credence to the K concept.

It is generally accepted that the principal mechanism limiting deer population growth near K is declining recruitment of young (McCullough 1979, 1984). Because of their small size and greater energetic demands relative to adults, deer 6–11 months of age are disadvantaged both socially and physically during periods of low resource availability (Hirth 1977; McCullough 1979). As deer populations approach K, competition for resources intensifies. Because they are poor competitors, young animals tend to show the first signs of physiological stress, which manifests itself in various forms (e.g., decreased reproductive performance, physical stature, survival, and other measures of well-being). Yearling females at SNHP were sufficiently stressed such that 36% ($n = 11$) of our marked sample failed to breed, and recruitment of young to 11 months was consistently low (i.e., 50 fawns per 100 does; Underwood et al. 1994). The reproductive rates of yearling and adult females observed in our study suggest, based on the criteria of McCullough (1979) and Downing and Guynn (1985), that the deer population at SNHP fluctuates in the range of 65–90% of K. These characteristics contrast with those of populations on surrounding lands, where about 30% of fawn and nearly all yearling females conceive and produce offspring, indicating a lower density and increased biotic potential for increase.

Will the deer population at SNHP overshoot K and then crash to low abundance? We do not believe so. Caughley (1976) and McCullough (1983) argued that the overshoot and crash phases of the eruption sequence can be eliminated through a controlled harvest beginning at low to intermediate population density. Our data and historical regional harvest statistics indicate that population growth at SNHP is frequently arrested by severe winter weather. Because the frequency of severe winters exerts a constant and sometimes intense backdrop of mortality, a classic eruption sequence that includes a high-amplitude overshoot and subsequent crash is unlikely. In addition, depending upon the level of chronic natural mortality, the eruption sequence can be extended in duration beyond what might be predicted in the absence of chronic natural mortality. For example, what might be about a 20-year process from start to end for deer (Calder 1984) might take twice as long in chronically harsh climates. A slower trajectory toward K, in theory, would also change the nature of the biotic effects of deer on vegetation and other animal communities. By avoiding a high-amplitude overshoot, the population crash would be averted and an overall reduction in range quality—predicted by the classic paradigm—would not occur. Our analysis begs asking where, over the distribution of deer, might a high-amplitude overshoot and crash sequence likely be encountered? An answer, though perhaps not an entirely useful one, is in areas where deer populations do not experience moderate to high levels of chronic natural mortality.

Our experience thus far has led us to conclude that the details surrounding how a population gets from low density to high are important because they determine the very nature of overabundance. To complicate matters even more, the capricious hand of nature in some areas of deer range might, through a run of unusual years (e.g., winter severity or drought), deal an entirely different picture of overabundance and associated problems than we now face, making generalizations about the growth sequence difficult to find. Consequently, use of the classic paradigm for the purpose of predicting future conditions of either deer or the populations of plants and other animals they affect is probably not justified.

A CONTEXT FOR OVERABUNDANCE

Caughley (1981) defined four classes of overabundance that warrant some reflection, particularly with respect to public land management policies.

1. The animals threaten human life or livelihood.
2. The animals depress the densities of favored species.
3. The animals are too numerous for their own good.
4. In the case of large herbivorous mammals, the system of plants and animals is off its equilibrium.

Caughley (1981) further notes that class 1 contains only conflicts with human interests, which are real enough but not of ecological importance. Class 2 problems are purely technical. That is, the goal is to reduce the density of animals to a level (through whatever means is necessary) that allows the favored species to flourish. Overabundance as defined by class 3 is a rejection of current conditions in favor of an opinion about what is best for the animal population. This clearly represents a judgement of value. Caughley (1981) indicates that the class 4 problem is the only one to which ecology is central and about which a relatively objective and scholarly discussion is possible. In our judgement, a good place to start that discussion is to evaluate the usefulness of the classic paradigm carefully in framing specific issues of overabundance. Next, a concerted effort to define the class 4 problem precisely is essential; to our knowledge its definition is sketchy and diffuse at best. Only when the paradigm has been evaluated and the problem of overabundance defined will a synthetic view of overabundance be attained and a specific course of management action be indicated.

The classic paradigm currently predicts a system of plants and herbivores that achieves equilibrium through first an herbivore overshoot of K and crash and then a series of dampened oscillations. In contrast, the system we have described for SNHP may be one in which the equilibrium is approached asymptotically, without overshoot and crash. Still another possibility is a system that oscillates within a stable-limit cycle, though this trajectory has not been confirmed for ungulates. Current mathematical constructs of simple plant–herbivore systems are capable of producing all of these variants (and more) depending upon the value of input parameters (Caughley 1976, 1979). Adopting the classic paradigm as a means for framing specific issues of overabundance ignores alternative system trajectories and, hence, system states. Two plant–herbivore systems differing only in their respective trajectories would appear very different at equilibrium. Not only would the suite of concomitant effects on other system biota be different but also the standing crop of herbivores and plants at each time interval would be different. Thus, these two hypothetical herbivore populations measured at 60% of K-carrying capacity, for example, would indicate little else in common in terms of other system component states. Because overabundance by definition is vague, it transcends the details of the herbivore eruption predicted by the classic paradigm. Therefore, the development of a meaningful framework for evaluating overabundance in ecological terms will be very difficult.

Determining just when a plant–herbivore system is off its equilibrium is a vexing problem. What standard should be used in making that judgement? Technically speaking, any point along the trajectory other than the equilibrium represents a system off its equilibrium. By this definition, the entire herbivore eruption would be considered an ecological aberration except at equilibrium. Not only is this definition logically inconsistent, but it also denies that there is a process involved. Our view is that the definition must have a temporal scope suggesting that a comparison of trajectories is appropriate. For example, when compared with an asymptotic trajectory, the overshoot is potentially the most deleterious phase in the classic paradigm. It is in the overshoot phase that dramatic effects on plant populations and other biota occurs. According to the classic paradigm, it is in the overshoot phase that the carrying capacity is irrevocably lowered as long as the herbivore remains in the system, though evidence in support of this observation is lacking (McCullough, Chapter 6). However, the overshoot and subsequent crash appear to be the rule rather than the exception in most ungulate eruptions. Is a comparison to a system without these elements meaningful? In considering the scope of potential ecological change throughout an ungulate eruption, we believe that such a comparison is valid. Until a more rigorous evaluation of past eruptions and analysis of contemporary studies is done, a precise definition of the class 4 problem will remain elusive.

In national parks the burden of ecological proof for any decision to remove or cull deer is heavy (Porter et al. 1994), and in some contexts will be unbearable because the state of the science is inadequate. This places the manager on the horns of a dilemma. On one hand, without the benefit of solid science, management will be more difficult to justify. On the other hand, there are many valid and nonscientific reasons to move forward in spite of the uncertainty. In specific cases such as these, we suggest a dual thrust for action. First, realistic objectives for management need to be cast. Those objectives must be explicit about the nature of uncertainty inherent in the ecological problem. For example, on NPS lands, indigenous species may be actively managed as "pests" in order to (1) prevent the loss of another species, (2) preserve the integrity of cultural resources, and (3) protect human safety (USDI 1988). These objectives are clearly statements of value, having little to do with ecology. However, they are no less valid than any other objective when the ecology is uncertain. Most scientists would agree that these mandates indicate research approaches from which concrete answers to questions are attainable. Most managers would agree that they could do worse than to aspire to meet these mandates. Second, any management action should be undertaken with the intent of learning more about the ecological problem. In this way, management feeds back into the scientific process of understanding.

ACKNOWLEDGMENTS

Special thanks are due to the staff, past and present, of Saratoga National Historical Park, the Systems Support Office of the National Park Service (formerly the North Atlantic Regional Office), and the State University of New York for their support of this project. K. A. Austin, R. L. Burgess, and R. W. Sage, Jr., conducted portions of the research and provided important input to the ideas presented here. We thank an anonymous reviewer for improving an earlier version of this paper.

REFERENCES CITED

Austin, K. A. 1992. Gray dogwood (*Cornus racemosa* Lam) as a refuge from herbivory in old fields of Saratoga National Historical Park, New York. Doctoral dissertation, State University of New York, College of Environmental Science and Forestry, Syracuse.

Behrend, D. F., G. F. Mattfeld, W. C. Tierson, and J. E Wiley III. 1970. Deer density control for comprehensive forest management. Journal of Forestry 68: 695–700.

Burst, T. L., and M. R. Pelton. 1979. Some populations parameters of the Cades Cove deer herd, Great Smoky Mountains National Park. Proceedings of the Annual Conference Southeastern Association of Fish and Wildlife Agencies 32 (1978): 339–347.

Calder, W. A. III. 1984. Size, Function, and Life History. Harvard University Press, Cambridge, MA.

Caughley, G. 1970. Eruption of ungulate populations, with emphasis on Himalayan thar in New Zealand. Ecology 51:53–72.

Caughley, G. 1976. Wildlife management and the dynamics of ungulate populations. Pages 183–246 *in* Applied Biology. Vol. 1. (T. H. Cocker, ed.) Academic
Press, London.

Caughley, G. 1979. What is this thing called carrying capacity? Pages 2–8 *in*
North American Elk: Ecology, Behavior and Management. (M. S. Boyce and
L. D. Hayden-Wing, eds.) University of Wyoming Press, Laramie.

Caughley, G. 1981. Overpopulation. Pages 7–19 *in* Problems in Management of
Locally Abundant Wild Mammals. (P. A. Jewell and S. Holt, eds.) Academic
Press, New York.

Caughley, G., and L. C. Birch. 1971. Rate of increase. Journal of Wildlife Management 35:658–663.

Christie, R., and M. W. Sayre. 1989. Status of the white-tailed deer population
on the Morristown National Historical Park, New Jersey. Final Report to the
National Park Service. System Support Office for the Northeast Field Area of
the National Park Service, Boston.

Cypher, B. L., and E. A. Cypher. 1988. Ecology and management of white-tailed
deer in northeastern coastal habitats: A synthesis of the literature pertinent to
National Wildlife Refuges from Maine to Virginia. U.S. Fish and Wildlife Service Biological Report 88(15).

deCalesta, D. S., and G. W. Witmer. 1990. Drive-line census for white-tailed deer
within fenced enclosures. U.S. Forest Service Research Paper NE-643.

Downing, R. L., and D. C. Guynn, Jr. 1985. A generalized sustained yield table
for white-tailed deer. Pages 95–103 *in* Game Harvest Management. (S. L. Beasom and S. F. Roberson, eds.) Ceasar Kleberg Wildlife Research Institute,
Kingsville, TX.

Freund, R. J., R. C. Littell, and T. C. Spectoret. 1986. SAS Systems for Linear
Models. SAS Institute, Inc., Cary, NC.

Hamlin, K. L., and R. J. Mackie. 1989. Mule deer in the Missouri River Breaks,
Montana: A Study of Population Dynamics in a Fluctuating Environment.
Montana Department of Fish, Wildlife and Parks, Helena, MT.

Hirth, D. H. 1977. Social Behavior of White-Tailed Deer in Relation to Habitat.
Wildlife Monographs 53, The Wildlife Society, Bethesda, MD.

Leopold, A. 1943. Deer irruptions. Wisconsin Conservation Bulletin 321:3–11.

Leopold, A. S., S. A. Cain, C. M. Cottam, I. N. Gabrielson, and T. L. Kimball.
1963. Wildlife management in the national parks. Transactions of the North
American Wildlife and Natural Resources Conference 28:29–42.

McCullough, D. R. 1979. The George Reserve Deer Herd: Population Ecology of
a K-Selected Species. University of Michigan Press, Ann Arbor.

McCullough, D. R. 1983. The theory and management of *Odocoileus* populations. Pages 535–549 *in* Biology and Management of the Cervidae. (C. M.
Wemmer, ed.) Smithsonian Institution Press, Washington.

McCullough, D. R. 1984. Lessons from the George Reserve, Michigan. Pages
211–242 *in* White-Tailed Deer: Ecology and Management. (L. K. Halls, ed.)
Stackpole Books, Harrisburg, PA.

O'Connell, A. F., and M. W. Sayre. 1988. White-tailed deer management study: Fire Island National Seashore. Final Report to the National Park Service. System Support Office for the Northeast Field Area of the National Park Service, Boston.

Porter, W. F., M. C. Coffey, and J. Hadidian. 1994. In search of a litmus test: Wildlife management on the U.S. national parks. Wildlife Society Bulletin 22: 301–306.

Rasmussen, D. I. 1941. Biotic communities of Kaibab Plateau, Arizona. Ecological Monographs 3:229–275.

Russell, E. W. B. 1995. Cultural landscape report for Saratoga National Historical Park: Land use history and cultural landscape analysis. Draft Final Report to the National Park Service. System Support Office for the Northeast Field Area of the National Park Service, Boston.

Schaberl, J. P. 1994. Assessment of hunting adjacent to park boundaries on the survival and population dynamics of white-tailed deer. Master's thesis, State University of New York, College of Environmental Science and Forestry, Syracuse.

Scheffer, V. B. 1951. The rise and fall of a reindeer herd. Science Monthly 73: 356–362.

Severinghaus, C. W., and A. N. Moen. 1983. Prediction of weight and reproductive rates of a white-tailed deer population from records of antler beam diameter among yearling males. New York Fish and Game Journal 30:30–38.

Storm, G. L., R. H. Yahner, D. F. Cottom, and G. M. Vecellio. 1989. Population status, movements, habitat use, and impact of white-tailed deer at Gettysburg National Military Park and Eisenhower National Historic Site, Pennsylvania. National Park Service Technical Report NPS/MAR/NRTR-89/043.

USDI (U.S. Department of Interior). 1988. Natural Resources Management Policies. U.S. Department of Interior, Washington.

Underwood, H. B., K. A. Austin, W. F. Porter, R. L. Burgess, and R. W. Sage, Jr. 1994. Interactions of white-tailed deer and vegetation at Saratoga National Historical Park. National Park Service Technical Report NPS/NAROSS/NRTR/95-28.

Underwood, H. B., and W. F. Porter. 1991. Values and science: White-tailed deer management in eastern national parks. Transactions of the North American Wildlife and Natural Resources Conference 56:67–73.

Warren, R. J., and C. R. Ford. 1990. Population and ecological characteristics of white-tailed deer on Catoctin Mountain Park. U.S. National Park Service Final Report. Southeast Regional Office, National Park Service, Atlanta, GA.

Warren, R. J. 1991. Ecological justification for controlling deer in eastern national parks. Transactions of the North American Wildlife and Natural Resources Conference 56:56–66.

PART THREE

Ecosystems and High-Density Deer Herds

13 Rethinking the Role of Deer in Forest Ecosystem Dynamics

OSWALD J. SCHMITZ AND A. R. E. SINCLAIR

Ecologists often conceptualize natural ecosystems as having three interacting components: (1) primary producers (plant trophic level) that convert sunlight and nutrients from biogeochemical cycling into energy, (2) primary consumers (herbivore trophic level) that convert plant energy into animal protein, and (3) secondary consumers (carnivore trophic level) that prey on primary consumers. In addition to developing this largely static model, ecologists have devoted considerable effort to formalizing theory that explains the dynamical interactions among the three trophic levels. A particularly influential theory of trophic interactions was proposed by Hairston et al. (1960; hereafter the HSS model). This theory explains how the direct effects of herbivores on plants are mediated by carnivores and, how carnivores, by doing such, indirectly benefit plants by preying on herbivores.

The HSS model predicts that herbivores seldom overexploit plant resources because their population sizes are limited by their predators to the extent that they seldom reach sufficient densities to consume most of the available plant biomass. The HSS model has been called a "top-down" model of ecosystem dynamics (McQueen et al. 1986; DeAngelis 1992) because it proposes that carnivores are the primary controlling force determining the abundance and dynamics of plants and herbivores in lower trophic levels. This same theory predicts that there would be a dramatic increase in herbivore abundance with a concomitant decrease in plant abundance if the carnivore trophic level were removed from the ecosystem.

The kind of thinking embodied in the HSS model has formed the basis for a considerable amount of wildlife management aimed at enhancing deer abundance by means of predator control programs. Accordingly, management, by disrupting the functional structure of natural ecosystems, has unwittingly created the kind of perturbation needed to test the HSS model. Predator control programs often result in unusually high densities of large herbivores, such as white-tailed deer. Correlated with changes in deer abundance are unexpected changes in forest-stand structure and plant biodiversity (Alverson et al. 1988; Tilghman 1989). In addition, numerous experiments in which deer are excluded from certain areas and allowed to exist in others have demonstrated that white-tailed deer can have dramatic effects on both the abundance and biological diversity of woody plant species (Frelich and Lorimer 1985; see review in Alverson et al. 1988; Tilghman 1989). The result of these observations is that deer have been implicated as the major "controlling" influence in forest ecosystem dynamics in the absence of carnivores (Sullivan et al. 1990). In turn, it is often recommended that management should lower deer numbers to restore woody species production and diversity. Basically, management sees itself as substituting for the effects of carnivores in controlling deer numbers and hence forest regeneration (Sullivan et al. 1990).

However, the notion that management substitutes for natural predators presupposes that the simple dynamics embodied in the HSS model are operating in all ecosystems. Yet, the HSS model has rarely been tested explicitly in terrestrial systems and not at all in forest ecosystems. Consequently, the HSS model may ascribe a dynamic that does not accord with reality. The observation that deer are the major controlling force in forest ecosystem dynamics is often confounded by land-use or silvicultural practices that indirectly enhance habitat suitability for deer. Moreover, there is now a large body of research (Sinclair 1975; White 1978; Price et al. 1980; Leibold 1989; Weis and Berenbaum 1989; Dublin et al. 1990; Louda et al. 1990; Huntly 1991; Power 1992; Schmitz 1992a, 1993, 1994; Abrams 1993) that questions whether natural ecosystems are generally top-down controlled to begin with. In many cases, the degree to which herbivores exploit plants may be more contingent on plant nutritional quality and abundance than on direct limitation by carnivores. The implication of this for management is that the practice of lowering deer numbers to enhance plant productivity and diversity may be based on an incomplete understanding of the role of deer in forest ecosystem dynamics. Hence management may fail to reach its goal in ecosystems in which top-down mechanisms are not operating.

Our aim here is to revisit the idea that large herbivores, such as white-tailed deer, alone are the dominant controlling influence in forest ecosystem dynamics in the absence of carnivores. We begin by showing how simple, but conceptually accurate, theory on plant–herbivore dynamics can be used to suggest how deer might directly affect forest tree abundance and production. We then discuss the role of deer under greater degrees of real-world complexity. We present several hypotheses about the way deer and other large forest herbivores might interact with woody plants. Our intention is to raise a host of new research questions in order to convince ecologists and managers that more research needs to be aimed at exploring the alternative ways in which large herbivores may affect forest ecosystems. Hopefully, this will encourage more collaboration between basic research and management, as we foresee that management, if treated as scientific experimentation (MacNab 1983; Sinclair 1991), offers the best, and perhaps only, opportunity to test the various hypotheses at ecologically relevant spatial and temporal scales.

PLANT–HERBIVORE INTERACTIONS: AN EXCURSION INTO THEORY

We present here a simple consumer–resource model to describe the dynamical interaction between plants and herbivores. Individual wildlife ecologists and managers would undoubtedly offer different opinions about the kind of information and precise ecological detail that should be included in such a model. Our model abstracts much of real-world complexity by casting an ecosystem as a linear chain of trophic levels, in much the same way as ecosystems are conceptualized by ecologists (e.g., the HSS model). The model is intended to generate thinking about the potential role of deer in forest ecosystems by providing insight into the elementary processes involved in the plant–herbivore interaction. In doing so, we hope to illustrate an elementary point that is not appreciated in the management of overabundant deer: the degree to which deer control forest ecosystems hinges directly on the functional relationship between tree species abundance, the consumption rate of trees by deer as a function of tree species abundance, and deer abundance—not simply between plant abundance and deer abundance.

A very simple model of plant–herbivore interactions has two basic elements, plant production and loss of plant production due to consumption by herbivores.

Plant Production

The main factors limiting woody plant production are nutrient supply and space (which determines the density of emergent stems and ability to absorb solar radiation). These limiting factors lead to competition at high plant population density, which results in self-thinning within stands. We appreciate that plant ecologists and foresters alike might disagree on the particular mechanisms involved in self-thinning. We suggest that a suitable first approximation, which at least captures the essence of the process, is a simple logistic population growth model. Based on this model, plant production (or plant population growth rate, dV/dt) can be described by the familiar equation

$$dV/dt = rV[1 - (V/K)], \tag{13.1}$$

where r is the intrinsic rate of increase, V is plant density, and K is the carrying capacity of the plant population, which is set by the limiting factors. This equation describes a population that grows exponentially at low density (primarily density independent). As density increases, competitive (density dependent) interactions (e.g., self-thinning) become increasingly important. This causes net plant population growth rate to decrease until the plant population reaches a steady state or carrying capacity, at which point net plant population growth (production) is zero. Under this assumption, a plot of net plant population growth rate in relation to plant density produces the classic, hump-shaped growth curve (Figure 13.1).

Loss of Plant Production to Herbivores

The effect of herbivores on plant production can be incorporated by subtracting a term from equation (13.1) that describes the consumption rate of plants by the herbivore population (i.e., the consumer total response [Sinclair 1989] or the consumption function [May 1977]). The consumer total response is the product of two elements, (1) the functional relationship between consumption rate of plants by herbivores and plant density (the consumer functional response) and (2) the relationship between herbivore offspring production and plant density (the numerical response).

The functional response of herbivores is often assumed to increase with increasing resource abundance up to a certain level of plant biomass. Beyond this level, herbivore consumption of plant biomass is no longer limited by the availability of plants. Instead, herbivore consumption rate saturates because individuals are physically incapable of consum-

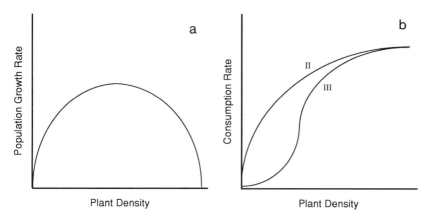

FIGURE 13.1. Classical growth rate and functional response curves. Curves describe the classical relationships between (a) plant population growth rate (plant production) and plant population density and (b) herbivore consumption rate and plant density. Figure 13.1b presents shapes of curves for a Type II (II) and Type III (III) functional response. A Type II functional response is inversely density dependent with plant density. The ascending portion of the Type III response is density dependent; the response then switches to being inversely density dependent at high plant density.

ing greater amounts of food per unit time. This saturation effect is typical of Type II or Type III functional responses (Figure 13.1). The functional response has been measured for a variety of large herbivore species feeding on a host of plants (Wickstrom et al. 1984; Hudson and Watkins 1986; Hudson and Frank 1987; Lundberg and Danell 1990; Gross et al. 1993). However, there are, to our knowledge, no published measures of the functional response of white-tailed deer feeding on natural woody plants. This is ironic considering the imperative to solve the "deer impacts on forests problem" and that white-tailed deer are one of the most intensely studied wildlife species. In the absence of empirical information, we proceed by considering the implications of both types of consumer functional response. Below we show that the particular form of the functional response can have a crucial bearing on how we interpret the effects of deer in forest ecosystems and on the management solutions we devise.

The total response of deer ($g[V]$) combines the numerical response and the functional response. A summary of data on reproductive performance of white-tailed deer under controlled feeding conditions indicates that deer will have a nonlinear numerical response that saturates at high food intake (Schmitz 1992b). This saturation is an artifact of the feeding experiments because deer were provided substantially more feed than they would encounter in natural environments. The numerical response will be linear over the range of intake rates that deer would experience under natural conditions (Schmitz 1992b). Thus, a Type II or Type III functional response multiplied by a linear numerical response produces a total response curve that retains the particular shape of the functional response curve (Figure 13.1b).

The total response curve can then be described by the function (May 1977)

$$g(V) = \beta HV/(\alpha + V), \tag{13.2a}$$

when the functional response is Type II, and

$$g(V) = \beta HV^2/(\alpha^2 + V^2), \tag{13.2b}$$

when the functional response is Type III. In the above functions, H represents deer density, β is the maximum consumption rate of plants, and α is the plant density at which half the maximum consumption rate is reached.

A Model of Deer–Plant Interactions

We obtain a simple mathematical model of deer–plant interactions that quantifies gains and losses in plant production by subtracting equation (13.2a) or (13.2b) from (13.1). This subtraction gives rise to

$$dV/dt = rV[1 - (V/K)] - \beta HV/(\alpha + V); \tag{13.3a}$$

$$dV/dt = rV[1 - (V/K)] - \beta HV^2/(\alpha^2 + V^2). \tag{13.3b}$$

A first step in analyzing the dynamics of equation (13.3a) or (13.3b) is to identify steady state equilibrium points, that is, points at which the removal rate of plants by herbivores exactly balances the production of plants. By this definition, steady state equilibria must satisfy the condition dV/dt equals 0. Applying this to equations (13.3a) and (13.3b) produces

$$r[1 - V/K)] - \beta H/(\alpha + V) = 0; \tag{13.4a}$$

$$r[1 - (V/K)] - \beta HV/(\alpha^2 + V^2) = 0. \tag{13.4b}$$

Equations (13.4a) and (13.4b) can be decomposed into two parts. The first term, $r[1 - (V/K)]$, represents the per capita production rate of plants (i.e., percent increase in plant population growth). The second term, $\beta H/(\alpha + V)$ or $\beta H/(\alpha^2 + V^2)$, represents the per plant loss rate of plant tissue (i.e., percent loss of plant growth). These components can be plotted separately on the same graph relating percent gain or loss in per capita growth rate to plant density. Intersections of these curves indicate where equilibrium solutions will occur (Sinclair 1989).

The first term of equations (13.4a) and (13.4b) produces the "recruits" curve, which decreases continuously with increasing plant density owing to density-dependent competitive interactions among plants, that is, self-thinning (Figure 13.2). The equilibrium plant density, in the absence of herbivores, is denoted by point K, the carrying capacity.

The second term produces the "herbivore response" curve. There will be different shapes of this curve depending on the type of functional response and the relative magnitudes of per capita plant production and herbivore total response rate. If the herbivore functional response is Type II (equation 13.4a), then the herbivore response curve will decrease nonlinearly with increasing plant density (Figure 13.2a). This curve will always intersect the recruits curve at high plant density (K_l) and may intersect the recruits curve at low plant density (B), depending on the magni-tude of the consumption parameters. If the herbivore functional response is Type III (equation 13.4b), then we obtain a hump-shaped herbivore response curve that can give rise to three possible scenarios (Messier 1994). The curve could intersect the plant recruits curve at high plant density only (Figure 13.2b, point K_l), owing to inefficient consumption by herbivores or a very slow numerical response to food intake. The curve could intersect the plant recruits curve three times (Figure 13.2c, at points K_l, B, and K_r). These intersection points represent different equilibrial conditions, or multiple states, of the same plant–herbivore system. Finally, if the herbivores are extremely efficient foragers or exhibit a fast numerical response to food intake, we may see the herbivore response curve intersect the plant recruits curve only once and at low plant density (Figure 13.2d, point K_r).

Stability of the Model's Equilibria

In analyses of equilibria, there are two important conditions that must be evaluated. First, we wish to know if a particular equilibrium will be in a steady state (i.e., stable) or unstable. This will indicate whether we should expect deer and plants to coexist in an ecosystem (i.e., steady state conditions). Second, we wish to know which factor (e.g., plant recruitment or herbivore total response) is driving the system to a steady state. A steady state equilibrium will exist only when there is a negative feedback on population growth due to density-dependent interactions; that is, the system must be regulated (Sinclair 1989). It is crucial to identify which

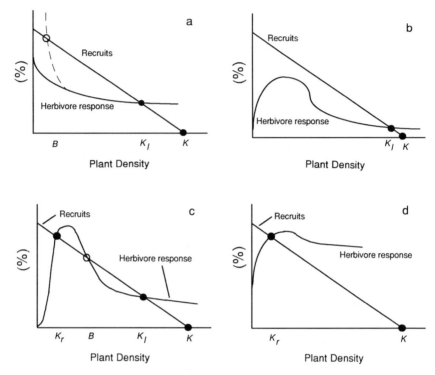

FIGURE 13.2. Recruits and herbivore response curves. Curves describe the relationships between per capita plant growth (%) and plant density (recruits) and per plant effect of herbivores (%) and plant density (herbivore response) for cases with a herbivore Type II functional response (a) or Type III functional response (b–d). In the absence of herbivores, the equilibrium plant population density will be K, the carrying capacity. Intersections of the recruits and herbivore response curves indicate equilibrium plant population densities when herbivores are present. In 13.2a, the herbivore response curve could intersect the recruits curve once (solid line) or twice (dashed line and solid line), depending on the magnitude of the herbivore response. Points denoted by K_l represent cases in which herbivores only limit plant production; the stability of the steady state is driven by plant competition. Points denoted by K_r represent cases in which herbivores regulate production and hence ecosystem dynamics. The steady state points K_r and K_l are separated by point B, an unstable equilibrium representing a boundary between the alternative stable states.

component exerts the density-dependent feedback because this component will be the "controlling" factor in ecosystem dynamics.

In Figure 13.2a, there is one steady state equilibrium (K_l); the second (B) will be unstable (Noy-Meir 1975). In this case, the herbivore total response curve varies with plant density in an inversely density-dependent manner. This implies that as plant density increases, herbivores will eat proportionally less plant biomass. Consequently, herbivores do not exert the negative feedback needed to stabilize the equilibrium; herbivores are limiting plant production but they are not regulating it. Herbivores cannot, therefore, be implicated as the major control of ecosystem dynamics. Indeed, it is the negative feedback due to plant self-thinning that is the regulating factor stabilizing the equilibrium.

The same scenario also can arise when the herbivore response curve is based on a Type III functional response and the herbivore total response curve intersects the recruits curve only once, at high plant density (Figure 13.2b). As the herbivore response curve progresses right beyond the peak of the hump, it also decreases in an inversely density-dependent manner with increasing plant density. Point K_l will be stable, but the stability arises due to plant competition.

When the herbivore total response curve intersects the plant recruits curve three times we obtain a system with multiple steady state equilibria (Figure 13.2c). Point B will be an unstable equilibrium (Noy-Meir 1975) and represents a boundary or breakpoint of the system (May 1977). If plant density is decreased (left of B), the system will drift to K_r. Likewise, if plant density is increased (right of point B), the system will drift to K_l. The points K_l and K_r will be stable (Noy-Meir 1975; May 1977; Ludwig et al. 1978; Sinclair 1989), but the factors leading to stability will differ. At K_r, density-dependent interactions among plants are comparatively weak. Consequently, stability is determined largely by the strong density-dependent total response of herbivores on plants; that is, as plant abundance increases, herbivores will consume proportionately more plant biomass, thereby driving plant abundance to low levels. In this case, herbivores will regulate or "control" plant production and hence ecosystem dynamics. At K_l, herbivores again have an inverse density-dependent effect on plants and therefore can only limit plant production. The regulating, or controlling factor stabilizing ecosystem dynamics in this case is plant competition for nutrients or space.

Finally, the intersection of the herbivore response curve and the plant recruits curve at low plant density produces a single steady state equilibrium (Figure 13.2d). In this case, the stability is determined by the strong density-dependent total response of herbivores on plants. Accordingly, herbivores will regulate or control plant production and hence ecosystem dynamics.

The above analysis shows that herbivores can be implicated as the major controlling factor in ecosystem dynamics only in a subset of cases, those in which they exert a density-dependent negative feedback on plant production. Therefore, it would be incorrect to control deer abundance in all cases in which deer appear to reduce plant biomass. In instances in which the stability of the system is determined by plant competition, it is more appropriate to enhance plant production by reducing competitive interactions through, for example, commercial thinning or the application of fertilizers.

RELATIONSHIPS BETWEEN PLANT AND HERBIVORE ABUNDANCE

Theoretical Relationships

One of the limitations of analyzing system dynamics based on the curves presented in Figure 13.2 is that information about ecosystem states is presented in terms of plant density only. This is not directly useful for management because management aimed at controlling deer numbers needs to know the relationship between plant density and herbivore density. Moreover, precise details about the exact plant density at an equilibrium in Figure 13.2 are not that useful for management because reaching a single-point equilibrium is, in practice, difficult (Dublin et al. 1990). From a practical standpoint, one is more interested in the potential combinations of stable plant and herbivore densities.

In the introduction we suggested that the practice of lowering deer numbers to decrease the effect that deer exert on forest production and tree species diversity presumes that there is an inverse relationship between deer abundance and tree species abundance. We now examine whether such a simple relationship is to be expected. In order to generate a curve describing the relationship between plant density and herbivore density we must rewrite equations (13.4a) and (13.4b) in a form that expresses plant density as a function of herbivore density (Noy-Meir 1975; May 1977). A plot of these relationships (Figure 13.3) indicates that we should not always expect simple inverse relationships to exist (Figure 13.3a). When they do exist (e.g., Figure 13.3b, d), the relationships do

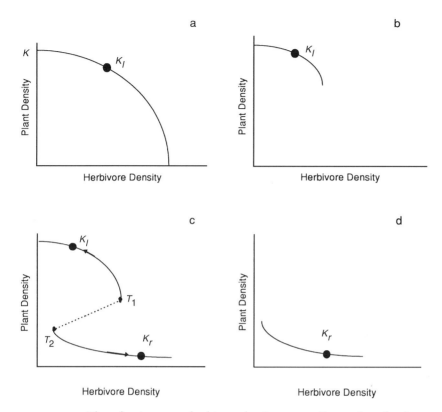

FIGURE 13.3. Plant density versus herbivore density curves. Curves describe the relationship between stable plant and stable herbivore density when herbivores have a Type II functional response (a) or a Type III response (b–d). Simple inverse relationships between deer density and plant density in natural systems occur under two conditions, b and d. In case b, ecosystem dynamics are largely controlled by plant competition for resources, so controlling deer abundances will only cause weak responses in plant abundances. Strong plant responses occur in case d, where herbivores are controlling ecosystem dynamics. In a multiple steady states system (c) there will be two domains, the first depicted by the solid line K_l–T_1, and the second by the solid line T_2–K_r and extending outward. The dashed line represents the unstable boundary between the two stable domains. T_1 and T_2 are unstable threshold points. The attractors K_r and K_l (see Figure 13.2 for description), depicted as open circles, correspond to fixed equilibrium points. In this case, the system will tend to drift to one or the other attractor (indicated by arrows).

not arise solely when deer are the major controlling force in ecosystem dynamics; deer stabilize ecosystem dynamics only in the case represented by Figure 13.3d.

We may also obtain more complex situations in which we obtain two different domains of stable densities (Figure 13.3c). Between these domains is an intermediate region, bounded by threshold points T_1 and T_2, that is unstable (the breakpoint or boundary) in the relationship between plant and herbivore density. The existence of thresholds is reminiscent of alternative ecosystem states observed or hypothesized to occur in other plant–herbivore systems, including spruce budworm *(Choristoneura fumiferana)* in the boreal forest of Canada (Ludwig et al. 1978; Holling 1992), elephants *(Loxodonta africana)* in African savanna (Dublin et al. 1990; Prins and Van der Jeugd 1993; Sinclair 1995), and managed rangelands (Noy-Meir 1975; Laycock 1991). In a multiple-states system, herbivores would regulate, or control, woody plant production over certain densities of woody biomass, in which case excluding those herbivores is warranted. However, at different densities of woody browse (i.e., alternative states of the same ecosystem), herbivores would only limit plant production, in which case management that enhances plant growth rates, rather than lowering herbivore numbers, is more appropriate.

In multiple steady state systems we may obtain complex and even counterintuitive outcomes if we apply management to restore woody tree production under conditions of high deer densities. In the first domain of Figure 13.3c, determined by the line K_l-T_1, plant population size is regulated by plant competition. In the second domain, determined by the line T_2-K_r and extending beyond, plant population size is regulated by herbivores. If deer and plant density in the lower domain (T_2-K_r) are perturbed towards T_2, further continuous increases in plant density are not possible beyond T_2. If perturbed at T_2 by a temporary reduction in deer numbers, the system will quickly jump to T_1 (Noy-Meir 1975; May 1977). Conversely, if the system were at or near T_1, reductions in deer density could indeed result in increased plant density as the system drifts toward point K. However, there is the disconcerting possibility that if there were a stochastic event (e.g., drought) or if wildlife management aimed at controlling deer abundances was confounded by forest management that reduced plant density through harvesting, the system could jump back to T_2 from T_1. This would cause the entire plant–herbivore system to collapse to very low plant densities, at which point deer would regulate plant dynamics. In essence, the management would realize the opposite result of that anticipated.

Conclusive evidence for multiple states in deer–forest plant systems is largely nonexistent because the proper field experiments needed to detect this dynamical property have yet to be conducted: simple exclosure experiments do not give sufficient insight because they do not manipulate plant and herbivore densities in the manner needed to detect multiple states. It is clear from Figure 13.3, however, that management aimed simply at lowering deer numbers will not always prevent deer from limiting the regeneration capacity of forest ecosystems. The outcome of management (i.e., the state a system reaches following a perturbation [e.g., a density change]) may be highly dependent on initial conditions and, if multiple states exist, the relationship of the initial conditions to the boundary or breakpoints.

The above theory suggests that the role of large herbivores such as deer in forest ecosystem dynamics may be quite complex. Therefore, in order to mediate the effects of deer on forest ecosystems, one must first understand the precise relationship between plant density and herbivore density, which is determined by the relationship between plant density and the total response of the herbivore population. A simple, systematic reduction in deer density will not be sufficient. The theory, if correct, makes the strong case that we require a radical change in thinking about the way deer and forest plant populations are to be managed if we want to enhance woody tree production. But to what extent does the theory explain real-world ecosystem dynamics?

Empirical Relationships

The potential for different kinds of dynamics in deer–forest plant interactions rests primarily on the form of the functional response of deer feeding on woody browse. To our astonishment, there seem to be no published estimates for the functional response of deer feeding on woody browse.

Data that could be used to estimate the functional response were collected as part of a larger study examining the foraging behavior of white-tailed deer in a northern wintering area in Canada (Schmitz 1990, 1991, 1992b). At the beginning of the winter and at three 30-day intervals throughout the winter, browse abundance (number of woody twigs) was inventoried in 54 random 1-m-radius plots that contained a variety of woody species. This inventory allowed an estimate of twig removal by deer over a 30-day window under conditions in which initial twig density was known for each time period. A crude estimate of functional response can be obtained from this data set by means of nonlinear regression of

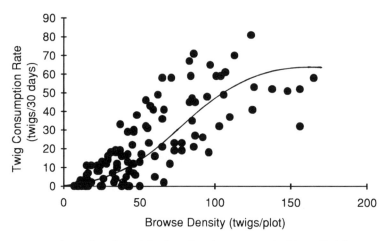

FIGURE 13.4. An estimation of the functional response of white-tailed deer. Data from Schmitz (1990, 1991, 1992b) were used to generate the functional response for white-tailed deer in a northern wintering area in Canada ($n = 162$). Models describing a Type II functional response, $f(v) = \beta V/(\alpha + V)$, and a Type III response, $f(v) = \beta V^2/(\alpha^2 + V^2)$, were fit to the data by means of nonlinear regression. Both models were highly significant (analysis of variance, $P < 0.001$). However, the model for a Type III response explained a greater amount of variation in the data set (Type III, $r^2 = 0.83$, versus Type II, $r^2 = 0.71$). Therefore, a Type III response was judged to be the best model.

twig removal at the end of 30 days on twig abundance at the beginning of the 30-day period. Statistical analysis indicates that the trend in the data (Figure 13.4) appears more S-shaped, the signature of a Type III functional response, rather than concave downward, typical of a Type II response. In the context of the above theory, this suggests that there is the potential for multiple steady states to exist in deer–forest plant systems.

A proper test of the theory of a multiple-states system would require an experiment in which the major influencing factor of ecosystem dynamics (i.e., deer or plant density or both) is manipulated in such a way as to cause a change in state (Sinclair 1989; Dublin et al. 1990). If multiple states exist, the system should not return to its original state once the manipulation on the influencing factor is relaxed or if the influencing factor reverts to its previous level (Sinclair 1989; Dublin et al. 1990). Essentially, the system must cross a boundary or breakpoint to detect a multiple state. Virtually all experiments on deer–forest systems simply exclude deer and do not manipulate deer or plant density. Thus, the requisite manipulative experiment that tests for a boundary or breakpoint has not been done. However, a survey of the literature has produced two studies that, when the data are reanalyzed, offer indirect evidence that there is not a simple inverse relationship between herbivore abundance and tree abundance and that multiple states may indeed exist in large herbivore–forest systems.

The first study could be considered a natural experiment that examined interactions between moose *(Alces alces)* and balsam fir *(Abies balsamea)* on Isle Royale, Michigan (Brandner et al. 1990). The study was conducted to assess moose herbivory in relation to natural population densities of both moose and fir. The study was a 3 × 3 design involving three qualitative densities of moose and fir respectively (low, medium, and high). In addition, the exact densities of trees, broken down by height class (seedling, sapling, and tree), were reported. We plotted the combined measure of seedling and sapling density in relation to moose density in Figure 13.5a. The height classes chosen were those most likely to be exploited by moose. (Potentially edible components of larger trees usually are beyond the browse line.) Consistent with our simple model for a multiple-states system, Figure 13.5a indicates that there may be two stable domains of tree density for the same range of moose density. These domains are indicated by the solid vertical and solid horizontal lines.

The second study was an enclosure experiment in the Allegheny Na-

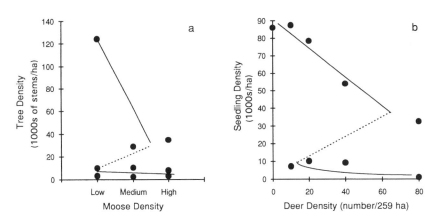

FIGURE 13.5. Empirical relationships between tree density and large herbivore density. The curves are based on two studies exploring the effects of large herbivores on forest-stand structure: (a) moose (Brandner et al. 1990; data used with permission of the Ecological Society of America) and (b) white-tailed deer (Tilghman 1989; data used with permission of The Wildlife Society). Curves are fit to the data by eye merely to suggest the possibility of multiple states in these systems.

tional Forest, Pennsylvania, in which deer and hardwood tree densities were manipulated by the researchers (Tilghman 1989). The aim of the study was to explore the relationship between plant species density and composition and height growth of new stems at five different densities of white-tailed deer (0, 10, 20, 40, and 80 deer/259 ha) following three different kinds of silvicultural treatments (clear-cut, thinned, and uncut). The study reported tree densities (response variable) in different height classes as a function of commercial value. We pooled data across commercial value classes but used only those densities from height classes below 0.9 m, reflecting trees that were likely to be below the browse line. We present only data for clear-cut (manipulated) and uncut (control) treatments to evaluate extremes in seedling manipulation (i.e., clear-cuts represent cases with high seedling production and abundance and uncut areas have low seedling production and abundance). Figure 13.5b presents a plot of tree density in relation to deer density. Again, when both plant and herbivore density are manipulated in a systematic way, the data cluster into two domains with what appears to be an intermediate boundary or breakpoint. These data are also consistent with the observation that northeastern hardwood forests likely will not regenerate unless deer densities are perturbed to extremely low densities (i.e., <5 deer/km^2 and held there for some time (Alverson et al. 1988). These low levels are speculated to have occurred prior to European settlement (Alverson et al. 1988).

Note, however, that the curves in Figure 13.5 are drawn by eye merely to raise the possibility of a trend consistent with the hypothesis of a multiple-states system. Obviously, this theory needs to be explored more formally, using the kind of perturbation experiment outlined above, before we may state conclusively that multiple states exist. Nevertheless, the possibility of a consistent trend suggests that such experiments would be extremely worthwhile to conduct.

Greater Complexity: Individual Plant Species Abundance

The above theory assumes that all plant species are ecologically equivalent and can, therefore, be treated as a single functional unit or trophic level. In reality, of course, different plant species are not identical ecologically. We now consider, briefly, the implications of examining the effects of deer on individual tree species abundances.

In our previous analyses we explored the direct effects of consumers (deer) on resource abundance. Under a completely new hypothesis, the direct effects of deer on woody plant species in an ecosystem could be quite subtle. Even so, this subtle effect may have profound indirect consequences on ultimate plant community structure of an ecosystem.

Consider the case for hardwood forests of the northeastern United States (the following is based on our own experience at the Yale University Research Forest and personal communication with S. Stout, U.S. Forest Service, Warren, Pennsylvania). Following harvesting, a natural successional pathway of a hardwood forest, in the absence of deer, begins with the invasion by herbaceous annuals and early successional woody species such as *Rubus* spp. (Figure 13.6). These species, in turn, create light environments suitable for the development of commercially valuable, shade-tolerant woody species such as oaks (*Quercus* spp.) and maples (*Acer* spp.). These strong light competitors preempt the invasion of shade-intolerant, commercially less valuable tree species such as cherry (*Prunus* spp.) and American beech *(Fagus grandifolia),* which are strong nutrient competitors.

Deer could alter this successional pathway without even consuming the commercially valuable tree species by browsing on the early successional herbaceous and woody species (Figure 13.6). The browsing changes the light environment, making it more suitable for the invasion of the shade-intolerant nutrient competitors.

This scenario represents a case in which there will never be a simple inverse relationship between deer abundance and plant species abundance. Consequently, no amount of management aimed at controlling deer numbers to improve forest tree production will be successful. Creative solutions to this problem will require management aimed at manipulating deer behavior in order to deflect the effect deer have on early successional plant species and consequently the successional pathway of the

FIGURE 13.6. Hypothetical successional pathways of eastern hardwood forests in the presence and absence of deer. The figure illustrates the indirect effect deer may have on forest tree species abundances. Heavy arrows indicate the direction of the successional pathway.

forest (see also DeSteven 1991). Such manipulation will require a level of mechanistic understanding of deer-mediated competitive interactions of plant species, in space and time, that we unfortunately do not yet have.

DISCUSSION

A natural tendency in management is to seek straightforward solutions to resource management problems. The rationale is that if one could find the single, dominant controlling variable in system dynamics, then management becomes a matter of manipulating that controlling variable in ways that achieve a desired outcome or endpoint. However, we are becoming increasingly aware that natural systems are more complex than we would like to admit. A growing body of theory and empirical work supports the idea that it will be the norm rather than the exception that natural systems will reconfigure toward alternative steady states following perturbations (Kneidel 1983; Robinson and Dickerson 1987; Barkai and McQuaid 1988; Dublin et al. 1990; Knowlton et al. 1990; Pech et al. 1992; Drake et al. 1993; Law and Morton 1993; Luh and Pimm 1993). If so, this reality requires a radical change in the way we manage ecosystems. Specifically, theory on complex systems should play an increasing role in decision making.

To illustrate the utility of theory in decision making, we have developed a simple model of ecosystem dynamics that gives insight into the kind of management that may be needed to solve forest regeneration problems in systems containing large herbivores. The model abstracts many biological details and yet produces fairly complex dynamics. Our model suggests that a continuous change in a control variable (e.g., deer density) can have discontinuous effects on a response variable (plant density) (Noy-Meir 1975; May 1977). This implies that manipulating deer densities alone, without some appreciation for the original state of the system, can produce discontinuous effects on plant density. In order to manage effectively, one needs to know what those initial states are by identifying where possible breakpoints occur. We therefore caution that, in the absence of adequate empirical understanding of forest ecosystem dynamics, management should not continue to reduce deer numbers systematically in order to enhance woody tree production because this may have dire consequences for the entire ecosystem.

The fact that systems may be complex in no way implies that management of natural systems is a hopeless prospect. It means, rather, that one has to become more sophisticated in the approach to management. We should use models to guide us through the complexity; models can help identify where the different domains of attraction might occur in natural systems. Identification of domains will allow us to judge where systems are likely to drift following perturbations introduced by management. More importantly, however, models force us to explore empirically the precise relationships between interacting components while we carry out management. In other words, we must make a greater effort to treat management as a scientific experiment that has proper controls and treatments (MacNab 1983; Sinclair 1991) rather than treat it simply as an endpoint of a scientific process.

If natural, unmanaged forest ecosystems appear to regenerate successfully, then why is it that managed systems have a deer problem? What has led to the widespread acknowledgment (Alverson et al. 1988; Tilghman 1989) that deer are preventing forests from regenerating, especially northeastern U.S. hardwood forests? Based on our theory, we suggest that the deer problem has arisen through two management processes that have conflicting goals. From the perspective of forest management, silvicultural practices, such as patch cuts or clear-cuts aimed at providing an economic return to the industry, have essentially perturbed the natural ecosystem to low levels of tree abundance. At the same time, game management, primarily for sport hunting, has improved habitat for deer to the extent that population sizes may be an order of magnitude higher than historical levels (Alverson et al. 1988). The consequence is that human activity may have created an environment in which any forest harvesting strategy in the face of an overabundance of deer causes the system to cross a boundary, from a state in which tree production is self regulated (i.e., merely limited by deer) to a state in which production is regulated by deer. In essence, there is a large-scale ecosystem perturbation that causes the system to shift to a state in which another factor, which usually only limits system dynamics, now becomes the major regulatory force (Sinclair 1989).

An analogous scenario has been proposed for parts of the Serengeti ecosystem (Dublin et al. 1990; Sinclair 1995), in which increased incidence of grass fires has caused a radical shift from woodlands to grasslands. This shift has created a condition in which tree abundance has become low relative to existing large herbivore populations. Consequently, elephants and other larger herbivores are now able to regulate tree regeneration when they only limited production previously, making it impossible for the woodlands to be restored through natural processes. Essentially, fire has caused the system to cross the boundary or breakpoint. (A similar scenario may be operating in a predator–prey system [Knowlton et al. 1990].)

We emphasize that our ideas on the roles of deer in forest ecosystems are still untested hypotheses; they are not reliable knowledge sensu Romesburg (1981). Indeed, the models presented here are highly deterministic and therefore may not apply when there is a high amount of environmental stochasiticity. If any of the models are incorrect, then the predictions will not be supported by data. Again, it is crucial that we begin testing trophic interaction models to evaluate their utility.

We are now in a position to test various hypotheses about the linkages among deer foraging, overabundant deer populations, and forest tree production. Given the urgency to restore the regeneration capacity of many eastern hardwood forests it is entirely possible to design management aimed at restoring production as a scientific experiment. Such an experiment would involve management treatments that systematically manipulate deer abundance, tree abundance through silviculture, and tree production through changes in factors limiting the growth of trees.

If our hypotheses are supported by empirical testing, then the results have important implications for the way we perceive the problem of deer overabundance. The traditional view, consistent with a top-down or the HSS model, holds that deer populations have erupted because predators, which normally limit their prey populations, no longer have a functional role in ecosystem dynamics. Consequently, if deer populations remain unmanaged they will increase to unnaturally high levels. However, according to our hypothesis, the deer overabundance problem does not result from lack of management but rather stems from intensive management for conflicting goals (i.e., silviculture for forest tree production versus habitat manipulation for game animal production). The source of the problem may be, in reality, a land management and land-use issue rather than an issue of overabundance because systems are unmanaged.

ACKNOWLEDGMENTS

We thank M. Ashton, A. Beckerman, B. Patten, and V. Van Ballenberghe for helpful comments.

REFERENCES CITED

Abrams, P. A. 1993. Effect of increased productivity on the abundances of trophic levels. American Naturalist 141:351–371.

Alverson, W. S., D. M. Waller, and S. L. Solheim. 1988. Forests too deer: Edge effects in northern Wisconsin. Conservation Biology 2:248–258.

Barkai, A., and C. McQuaid. 1988. Predator–prey role reversal in a marine benthic ecosystem. Science 242:62–64.

Brandner, T. A., R. O. Peterson, and K. L. Risenhoover. 1990. Balsam fir on Isle Royale: Effects of moose herbivory and population density. Ecology 71:155–164.

DeAngelis, D. L. 1992. Dynamics of Nutrient Cycling and Food Webs. Chapman and Hall, New York.

DeSteven, D. 1991. Experimental mechanisms of tree establishment in old-field succession: Seedling survival and growth. Ecology 72:1076–1088.

Drake, J. A., T. E. Flum, G. J. Witteman, T. Voskuil, A. M. Holyman, C. Creson, D. A. Kenny, G. R. Huxel, C. S. Larue, and J. R. Duncan. 1993. The construction and assembly of an ecological landscape. Journal of Animal Ecology 62:117–130.

Dublin, H. T., A. R. E. Sinclair, and J. McGlade. 1990. Elephants and fire as causes of multiple stable states in the Serengeti–Mara woodlands. Journal of Animal Ecology 59:1147–1164.

Frelich, L. E., and C. G. Lorimer. 1985. Current and predicted long-term effects of deer browsing in Michigan, USA. Biological Conservation 34:99–120.

Gross, J. E., L. A. Shipley, N. T. Hobbs, D. E. Spalinger, and B. A. Wunder. 1993. Functional response of herbivores in food-concentrated patches: Tests of a mechanistic model. Ecology 74:778–791.

Hairston, N. G., F. E. Smith, and L. B. Slobodkin. 1960. Community structure, population control and competition. American Naturalist 94:421–425.

Holling, C. S. 1992. The role of forest insects in structuring the boreal landscape. Pages 170–191 in A Systems Analysis of the Global Boreal Forest. (H. H. Sugart, R. Leemans, and G. B. Bonan, eds.) Cambridge University Press, Cambridge, United Kingdom.

Hudson, R. J., and S. Frank. 1987. Foraging ecology of bison in aspen boreal habitats. Journal of Range Management 40:71–75.

Hudson, R. J., and W. G. Watkins. 1986. Foraging rates of wapiti on green and cured pastures. Canadian Journal of Zoology 64:1705–1708.

Huntly, N. 1991. Herbivores and the dynamics of communities and ecosystems. Annual Review of Ecology and Systematics 22:477–503.

Kneidel, K. A. 1983. Fugitive species and priority during colonisation in carrion-breeding diptera communities. Ecological Entomology 8:163–169.

Knowlton, N., J. C. Lang, and B. D. Keller. 1990. Case study of natural population collapse: Post-hurricane predation on Jamaican staghorn corals. Smithsonian Contributions to the Marine Sciences 31:1–25.

Law, R., and R. D. Morton. 1993. Alternative states of ecological communities. Ecology 74:1347–1361.

Laycock, W. A. 1991. Stable states and thresholds of range conditions on North American rangelands: A viewpoint. Journal of Range Management 44:427–433.

Leibold, M. A. 1989. Resource edibility and the effects of predators and productivity on the outcome of trophic interactions. American Naturalist 134:922–949.

Louda, S. M., K. H. Keeler, and R. D. Holt. 1990. Herbivore influences on plant performance and competitive interactions. Pages 414-444 *in* Perspectives on Plant Competition. (J. B. Grace and D. Tilman, eds.) Academic Press, New York.

Ludwig, D., D. D. Jones, and C. S. Holling. 1978. Qualitative analysis of insect outbreak systems: The spruce budworm and forest. Journal of Animal Ecology 47:315–332.

Luh, H., and S. L. Pimm. 1993. The assembly of ecological communities: A minimalist approach. Journal of Animal Ecology 62:749–765.

Lundberg, P., and K. Dannell. 1990. Functional response of browsers: Tree exploitation by moose. Oikos 58:378–384.

MacNab, J. 1983. Wildlife management as scientific experimentation. Wildlife Society Bulletin 11:397–401.

May, R. M. 1977. Thresholds and breakpoints in ecosystems with a multiplicity of stable states. Nature 269:471–477.

McQueen, D., J. R. Post, and E. L. Mills. 1986. Trophic relationships in freshwater pelagic ecosystems. Canadian Journal of Fisheries and Aquatic Sciences 43:1571–1581.

Messier, F. 1994. Ungulate population models with predation: A case study with North American moose. Ecology 75:478–488.

Noy-Meir, I. 1975. Stability of grazing systems: An application of predator graphs. Journal of Ecology 63:459–481.

Pech, R. P., A. R. E. Sinclair, A. E. Newsome, and P. C. Catling. 1992. Limits to predator regulation of rabbits in Australia: Evidence from a predator removal experiment. Oecologia 89:102–112.

Power, M. 1992. Top-down and bottom-up forces in food webs: Do plants have primacy? Ecology 73:733–746.

Price, P. W., C. E. Bouton, P. E. Gross, B. A. McPheron, J. A. Thompson, and A. E. Weis. 1980. Interactions among three trophic levels: Influence of plants on interactions between insect herbivores and natural enemies. Annual Review of Ecology and Systematics 11:41–65.

Prins, H. H. T., and P. Van der Jeugd. 1993. Herbivore population crashes and woodland structure in East Africa. Journal of Animal Ecology 81:305–314.

Robinson, J. V., and J. E. Dickerson. 1987. Does invasion sequence affect community structure? Ecology 68:587–595.

Romesburg, H. C. 1981. Wildlife science: Gaining reliable knowledge. Journal of Wildlife Management 45:293–313.

Schmitz, O. J. 1990. Management implications of foraging theory: Evaluating deer supplemental feeding. Journal of Wildlife Management 54:522–532.

Schmitz, O. J. 1991. Thermal constraints and optimization of winter feeding and habitat choice in white-tailed deer. Holarctic Ecology 14:104–111.

Schmitz, O. J. 1992a. Exploitation in model food webs with mechanistic consumer–resource dynamics. Theoretical Population Biology 41:161–183.

Schmitz, O. J. 1992b. Optimal diet selection by white-tailed deer: Balancing reproduction with starvation risk. Evolutionary Ecology 6:125–141.

Schmitz, O. J. 1993. Trophic exploitation in grassland food webs: Simple models and a field experiment. Oecologia 93:327–335.

Schmitz, O. J. 1994. Resource edibility and trophic exploitation in an old-field food web. Proceedings of National Academy of Sciences of the USA 91:5364–5367.

Sinclair, A. R. E. 1975. The resource limitation of trophic levels in tropical grassland ecosystems. Journal of Animal Ecology 44:479–520.

Sinclair, A. R. E. 1989. Population regulation in animals. Pages 197–241 *in* Ecological Concepts. (J. M. Cherett, ed.) Blackwell Scientific, Oxford, United Kingdom.

Sinclair, A. R. E. 1991. Science and the practice of wildlife management. Journal of Wildlife Management 55:767–772.

Sinclair, A.R.E. 1995. Population limitation of resident herbivores. Pages 194–219 *in* Serengeti II: Dynamics, Management and Conservation of an Ecosystem. (A. R. E. Sinclair and P. Arcese, eds.) University of Chicago Press, Chicago.

Sullivan, T. P., A. S. Harestad, and B. M. Wilkeem. 1990. Control of mammal damage. Pages 8–34 *in* Regenerating British Columbia Forests. (D. P. Lavender, R. Parish, C. M. Johnson, G. Montgomery, A. Vyse, R. A. Willis, and D. Winston, eds.) University of British Columbia Press, Vancouver.

Tilghman, N. G. 1989. Impacts of white-tailed deer on forest regeneration in northwestern Pennsylvania. Journal of Wildlife Management 53:524–532.

Weis, A. E., and M. R. Berenbaum. 1989. Herbivorous insects and green plants. Pages 123–162 *in* Plant–Animal Interactions. (W. G. Abrahamson, ed.) McGraw-Hill, New York.

White, T. C. R. 1978. The importance of relative shortage of food in animal ecology. Oecologia 33:71–86.

Wickstrom, M. L., C. T. Robbins, T. A. Hanley, D. E. Spalinger, and S. M. Parish. 1984. Food intake and foraging energetics of elk and mule deer. Journal of Wildlife Management 48:1285–1301.

14 Vertebrate Abundance and the Epidemiology of Zoonotic Diseases

MARK L. WILSON AND JAMES E. CHILDS

The abundance of vertebrates and the presence of their associated parasites influence the epidemiology of many human diseases. The term *zoonosis* designates those diseases of humans caused by infectious agents that normally circulate among nonhuman vertebrates considered to be their natural hosts (Acha and Szyfres 1988). The complement is an *anthroponosis*, in which humans are the natural reservoir. Zoonotic diseases result when viruses, bacteria, protozoa, or other microorganisms (microparasites) or helminths (macroparasites) occasionally spill over as "dead-end" infections of humans. Because people typically play no role in the transmission cycle of these parasites, their persistence depends on other processes involving the vertebrate host and its environment. Factors such as the rate of transmission, development of immunity, and reproduction or death rates in the vertebrate host population are critical to the continued existence of these microorganisms. Analogous to *endemic* diseases in humans that occur with stable incidence of infection, persistent transmission of infectious agents within animal populations is termed *enzootic*. Enzootic transmission of zoonotic disease agents allows for their perpetuation in nature; correspondingly, *epizootic* transmission means that new infections among vertebrate hosts are occurring more frequently than normal. The following discussion addresses some of the relationships among these transmission factors and risk of zoonotic diseases and, with various examples, illustrates the complex interactions of vertebrate abundance and pathogen transmission.

RESERVOIR–PARASITE INTERACTIONS
AND ZOONOTIC DISEASES

As distinguished from *vector,* which identifies an invertebrate or vertebrate animal that carries a pathogen toward another host, the term *reservoir* indicates the passive host to which an infectious organism is transported. The reservoir is frequently a site of parasite replication or development, but the functions of reservoir and definitive host (a host in which sexual stages of a parasite are found) may be distinguished (e.g., *Toxoplasma gondii* below). Reservoir hosts may harbor microorganisms as commensals (in which neither causes harm to the other while one organism may benefit), as mutualists (in which mutual benefit is derived from the association of the two organisms), or as parasites (in which one organism benefits at some cost to the other) (Whitfield 1979). Although these organisms may be pathogenic to humans, they rarely cause much harm to their reservoir host. This observation illustrates the important distinction between infection and disease. Infections usually do not provoke disease in the reservoir host, whereas infection in humans may be recognized due to resulting zoonotic disease.

Reservoir host *abundance* represents a dimensionless relative measure of the number of individuals in a population. Greater abundance usually implies greater *density,* a more useful measure that reflects the number of individuals per unit area. Both the density of vertebrate reservoirs and the pattern of their spatial distribution influence proximity among individuals, a variable affecting the probability that infectious organisms will be transmitted. Infectious contacts, whether direct, by aerosol, or by arthropod vector, partly depend on sufficient density and proximity of vertebrate hosts (Wilson 1994a).

Another factor influencing transmission is the relative abundance of susceptible, infected, infectious, and immune individuals in the population. Individuals move in defined directions among these compartments, depending on the nature of the interactions between host and parasite. The level of immunity, which defines the entirety of the reservoir host's production of humoral or cellular defense responses to infection by a foreign organism, is influenced by many variables, including the site, timing, and quantity of inoculum. Immunity can be complete, partial, or nonexistent, which in turn determines the flow of infected individuals to the immune compartment or back to the susceptible compartment from either the infected, infectious, or immune stages. In addition, variation in the immunogenic properties of the infecting organism may alter the effect of the host's immune response. Thus, maintenance of transmission in the vertebrate reservoir, as well as risk of zoonotic spillover to humans, partly depends on the density of immune, infectious, and susceptible vertebrate reservoirs. The term *herd immunity* defines that proportion of a population in the immune category. Various demographic processes influence herd immunity, particularly the death rate of immune individuals and the introduction of new susceptibles through births. This turnover among susceptible, infectious, and immune individuals represents an important demographic component in the maintenance of zoonotic disease agents (Anderson and May 1991).

One characteristic contributing to overabundance of a species that can influence transmission parameters of zoonoses is relatively rapid population growth. As a consequence of rapid population growth, shifts in the age structure toward younger age groups may change the manner in which the population responds to infection with a parasite (e.g., *T. gondii*). In general, a growing host population with proportionally more young individuals should experience relatively more infection, and perhaps disease, although pathogenesis often is less severe in younger than in older hosts.

Human risk of zoonotic disease is partly a function of the mode of transmission of the infectious organism. Humans usually are infected in the same manner in which transmission normally occurs among vertebrate hosts. Particular behaviors, however, may expose people who would otherwise be at little risk. Thus, zoonotic disease risk may be reduced by behavioral changes that decrease exposure regardless of the abundance of infectious reservoirs. These principles are best illustrated by examples of diverse zoonoses that represent a variety of vertebrate reservoir host species, modes of transmission, and associated human disease.

DIRECTLY TRANSMITTED ZOONOTIC AGENTS: SOME EXAMPLES

Many zoonoses are caused by infectious agents that normally are transmitted by water, excreta, or physical contact. The role of host population density generally is more direct and detectable for such infections. Cryptosporidiosis is a water-borne intestinal infection caused by a protozoa of the genus *Cryptosporidium* (Fayer and Unger 1986). Potentially a severe human illness, cryptosporidiosis is particularly a problem in the immunocompromised. In 1993, contamination of the water supply in Milwaukee resulted in an outbreak in which over 400,000 people became ill and

47 died (MacKenzie et al. 1994). Human cryptosporidiosis tends to be underdiagnosed (Gallaher et al. 1989; Skeels et al. 1990). A study of patients with acute infectious diarrhea in England found that *Cryptosporidium* infection was almost as common as *Salmonella* infection and nearly three times more common than that of *Shigella* (Public Health Laboratory Service Study Group 1990). Many vertebrates, but particularly domestic and wild ungulates, appear to be naturally infected and frequently infectious (Navin and Juranek 1984). The quantity of fecal shedding of *Cryptosporidium* oocysts or spores, and hence the extent to which surface water will be infected, probably is proportional to the abundance of infected hosts. While farm animals are believed to be important reservoirs, various deer species also harbor this agent (Tzipori et al. 1981; Simson 1992). Thereby, deer density may be related to human risk of cryptosporidiosis in certain regions.

Toxoplasma gondii is a coccidian parasite that infects numerous species of mammals and birds and causes one of the most common zoonoses of humans worldwide. This parasite has received increasing attention since the early 1980s because of the dire consequences of toxoplasmosis in immunodeficient persons, most notably those with human immunodeficiency virus (HIV)-related acquired immundeficiency syndrome (AIDS). Members of the family Felidae are definitive hosts for *T. gondii* and shed oocysts in their feces (Frenkel et al. 1970). Many vertebrates other than felids, including humans, develop only tissue cysts after ingestion of sporulated oocysts or cysts present in the tissues of other animals. Tissue cysts may persist for extended periods, perhaps lifelong, and if reactivated produce toxoplasmosis. Epidemics of human toxoplasmosis have been linked directly to oocyst exposure through infected cats and their feces (Stagno et al. 1980) or, more commonly, indirectly through the ingestion of undercooked meat (Kean et al. 1969). Food animals harboring tissue cysts therefore may act as the primary reservoir of this parasite for humans. In either case, the ultimate source of the infecting parasite is the sexually reproductive forms of *T. gondii* living in the epithelium of the cat intestine; where cats are not present, *T. gondii* infections are absent or fail to perpetuate (Wallace 1972, 1973).

The abundance of cats, therefore, is inferred as critical in the extent of environmental contamination with oocysts and ultimately in the risk of direct or indirect transmission of this parasite to humans. However, the dynamics of parasite acquisition and shedding among cats is influenced by the age at which individuals are infected, hence the demographic characteristics of the reservoir population. Young cats typically acquire *T. gondii* infections by approximately 5 to 6 months of age, when they have started to feed on prey animals that harbor tissue cysts (Ruiz and Fraekel 1980; Childs and Seegar 1986). Kittens less than 2 months are more susceptible to extraintestinal invasion by *T. gondii* and resulting disease but rarely, if ever, are found infected in nature (Dubey 1973; Wallace 1973). Following acute infection, young cats less than 1 year typically shed oocysts more frequently and in greater numbers than do older cats (Dubey et al. 1977; Ruiz and Fraenkel 1980). Thereby, young cats may play a crucial role in maintaining high levels of environmental contamination. Studies of the demographic characteristics of owned-cat populations in the United States indicate a high percentage of young animals, suggesting a rapidly expanding population or high population turnover (e.g., Childs 1990). Human preference for young companion animals and the willingness to dispose of pets that are no longer young should promote demographic characteristics favoring high levels of *T. gondii* transmission, in addition to contributing to an overabundance of cats.

Other examples of direct transmission systems include certain hantaviruses (Johnson 1989) and arenaviruses (Childs and Peters 1994) that are maintained in particular rodent reservoirs. These agents are usually transmitted via aerosols or bites that contain viruses shed in excreta or saliva. Hantavirus-associated zoonotic diseases, such as Korean hemorrhagic fever and nephropathia epidemica (NE), now generically grouped as hemorrhagic fever with renal syndrome, have been known for decades throughout much of Asia and Europe (LeDuc et al. 1994). A new member of this group of hantaviruses, sin nombre virus (Elliot et al. 1994), has been identified as the agent of a recently recognized, often fatal disease in the United States termed hantavirus pulmonary syndrome (HPS) (Duchin et al. 1994). The causative viruses of each of these syndromes are related taxonomically; however, each is maintained in different rodent reservoir hosts. Hantaan and Seoul viruses, associated with hemorrhagic fever with renal syndrome, circulate among field mice (*Apodemus* spp.) and Norway rats *(Rattus norvegicus),* respectively (Lee et al. 1978, 1982). Puumala virus (causative agent of NE) is maintained in bank voles *(Clethrionomys glareolus)* and occurs primarily in Europe and western Russia (LeDuc 1987; Gavrilovskaya et al. 1990). Although details of the cycles of these hantaviruses differ among the various virus–reservoir combinations (Leduc et al. 1994), transmission to individuals of the primary reservoir species typically produces chronic infection that persists for life (Lee et al. 1981; Yanagihara et al. 1985; Gavrilovskaya et al. 1990).

Over broad geographic regions, the abundance of rodents has been linked to outbreaks of hantavirus disease. In the southwestern United States, heavy rains contributed to lush vegetation and increased rodent food resources during the spring and summer of 1993. It was then that the first recognized outbreak of HPS occurred. Data from the Sevilleta research station in Socorro County, New Mexico (south of the geographic location of most HPS cases) indicated that populations of the deer mouse *(Peromyscus maniculatus)* in some locations increased 10-fold between May 1992 and May 1993 (Parmenter et al. 1993). Deer mouse populations of 30 mice/ha in May 1993, during the HPS epidemic, declined to less than 3 mice/ha by August (Parmenter and Vigil 1993) when the outbreak of HPS was waning, suggesting that rodent abundance may have contributed to the large number of HPS cases during the spring and summer (Childs et al. 1994). At a finer spatial scale, local rodent abundance also may influence the risk of human acquisition of hantaviral disease. One of the only environmental variables that distinguished those households in which patients with HPS resided from those selected as control dwellings was a significantly greater abundance of rodents, as indicated by trapping success (Childs et al. 1995).

Several studies in Sweden have convincingly linked the abundance of rodents to patterns in the incidence of NE among humans. The number of cases of NE was significantly correlated with estimates of small rodent abundance between 1959 and 1975 (Nyström 1982). However, this early analysis was hampered by lack of systematic rodent trapping data and the unavailability of reagents to confirm serologically cases of NE. From 1985 to 1993, the number of serologically confirmed cases of NE in Västerbotten County, Sweden, was positively correlated with rodent abundance. Time series analysis revealed that the incidence of NE in humans during the autumn was positively correlated with corresponding density estimates of bank voles for each season and year (Niklasson et al. 1995). Populations of bank voles in northern Sweden fluctuate cyclically, with peak densities occurring every 3 to 4 years; density can increase to 300-fold greater than that of the nadir (Hansson and Hettonen 1985; Hörnfeldt 1994). Obviously, the conditions resulting in human outbreaks of this zoonotic disease are closely coupled to the abundance of the reservoir species. The factors contributing to cyclic "overabundance" in these rodent populations, however, are incompletely understood and controversial.

Arenaviruses, such as the Argentine Junin virus in the corn mouse *(Calomys musculinus)* and the Bolivian Machupo virus in *C. callosus,* also establish chronic infections in their respective rodent hosts. Although much of the evidence is anecdotal, there appears to be a clear link between reservoir density and human arenaviral disease. During an outbreak of Bolivian hemorrhagic fever in San Joaquín, nearly 3,000 C. *callosus* (about 10 per household) were removed during a 3-week period (Mercado 1975), apparently contributing to the rapid decline in new Bolivian hemorrhagic fever cases. A longitudinal study of corn mouse populations in the area of Argentine hemorrhagic fever documented a dramatic increase in rodent density during the third year of the study. The number of human cases of Argentine hemorrhagic fever reached a 20-year high during the epidemic season following the increase in rodent density (Mills et al. 1992).

Rabies is perhaps a better-known directly transmitted zoonosis. Unlike most zoonotic disease agents, rabies virus is highly pathogenic in virtually all vertebrate species. It kills most hosts, thereby creating the conundrum of its persistence in nature. Various rabies virus variants have coevolved with particular mammalian carnivore or bat reservoir species that are considered natural hosts (Smith et al. 1992), although all variants are pathogenic in most mammals. The role of reservoir host abundance in this disease has not been clearly delineated in field settings. However, rabies has been extensively modeled, and the population dynamics of wildlife reservoir hosts is regarded as critical to understanding the temporal and spatial dynamics of transmission (Bacon 1985). Measures of mammalian carnivore abundance, such as hunting indices of red foxes (*Vulpes vulpes* L.) in Germany, indicate that the incidence of animal rabies is positively associated with increasing density of this dominant reservoir species (Steck and Wandeler 1980). Following the appearance of epizootic rabies, red fox populations are diminished and reports of animal rabies in a given locale decline precipitously; evidence of disease may disappear from given regions for some time. A threshold density (K_T of Anderson et al. 1981) is apparently required for rabies to perpetuate in red fox populations; below this threshold, infectious contacts appear too few to maintain transmission. As red fox density increases, models suggest that an increasingly larger percentage of the red fox population would have to be vaccinated or culled to eradicate rabies (Anderson et al. 1981).

Control of rabies in animals is key to reducing the incidence of human disease. Risk of human exposure to rabid animals in North America is due primarily to contact with terrestrial wildlife, although bat-associated rabies variants have been the source of most human cases of rabies in the United States over the last decade (Krebs et al. 1993, 1994). Wildlife density, such as that of raccoons *(Procyon lotor)*, appears related to human risk of exposure (Winkler and Jenkins 1992). Elevated densities of mammal reservoirs at the onset of epizootic rabies transmission therefore represent the greatest risk to humans. The extent of postexposure treatment of humans with rabies immunoglobulin and vaccine is a measure of human contact with potentially rabid animals. In New York State, the number of humans receiving antirabies treatment increased from 1,125 to 2,905 from 1992 to 1993 (CDC 1994), at the same time that the number of rabid raccoons rose from 1,355 to 2,320 (Krebs et al. 1993, 1994). By vaccinating pets, restricting movement of domestic animals, and intentionally reducing free-ranging urban dog populations (Beran and Firth 1988), human risk of rabies has declined in many parts of the world. Future efforts aimed at reducing human and domestic animal rabies probably will combine traditional domestic animal prevention methods with distribution of oral vaccine in baits (Brochier et al. 1991). Culling of animals may play a role in reducing wildlife rabies in certain specific applications but is unlikely to be effective as the sole control method (Debbie 1991).

For directly transmitted zoonoses, the importance of vertebrate reservoir density largely is influenced by the population-level effects of the microorganism on its vertebrate host (Figure 14.1). Whether the microorganism functions as a commensal, mutual, or parasite of its vertebrate host largely determines the outcome of interactions among density, transmission rate, and infection prevalence. In general, human risk should be greatest when both reservoir density and infection prevalence are maximal. Although many other biotic and abiotic factors intervene, the primary function of vertebrate density can be viewed within this general theoretical framework (Figure 14.1).

INDIRECTLY TRANSMITTED ZOONOTIC AGENTS: SOME EXAMPLES

Most recognized zoonotic disease agents are transmitted by an arthropod, in this context, a vector. Arthropod vectors generally require a blood meal from a vertebrate to survive and reproduce. Uptake and transfer of microrganisms occurs during such blood feeding. Transmission to humans may result when infected arthropods feed on people. Risk to humans is, thereby, a function of vector abundance and vector infection prevalence, both of which often are related to the density of reservoir hosts (Wilson 1994b). Examples of some North American vector-borne zoonoses include tick-borne Rocky Mountain spotted fever *(Rickettsia*

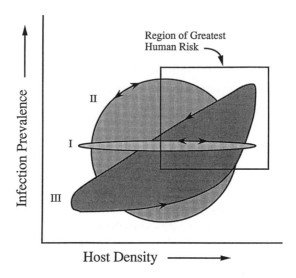

FIGURE 14.1. Vertebrate reservoir host density and the prevalence of infection. Figure depicts theoretical interaction between vertebrate reservoir host density and the prevalence of infection in that reservoir by various types of microorganisms. Type I represents local or transovarial (mother to offspring), host-density-independent transmission of a nonpathogenic microorganism that functions as a commensal (e.g., *Cryptosporidium* in cattle or herpes virus in humans). Factors other than the microorganism influence host density. Type II represents host-density-dependent transmission of a nonpathogenic microorganism that may function commensally or mutualistically with the host (possibly sin nombre virus in the deer mouse); host density changes influence transmission and therefore infection prevalence. Type III represents host-density-dependent transmission of a parasitic microorganism that reduces survival or reproduction of the host (e.g., rabies virus in most terrestrial vertebrates).

rickettsii), mosquito-transmitted viral diseases such as St. Louis encephalitis or eastern equine encephalitis, flea-vectored plague *(Yersinia pestis),* and sandfly-borne leishmaniasis (*Leishmania* spp.). The arthropod vector acquires the infectious organism while feeding on an infected reservoir host and subsequently transmits during a later blood meal. Again, humans are dead-end hosts for the microorganism, as well as atypical sources of blood for the arthropod vector.

The role of reservoir abundance in vector-borne zoonoses is confounded by the addition of other variables, in particular the vector and its host(s). Not only do previously mentioned factors such as host proximity or immunity influence human risk of vector-borne zoonoses, but additional variables such as vector abundance, feeding behavior, infection rate, and alternative hosts must be considered. For example, a contradiction exists between efficient vector-borne maintenance of an infectious agent among reservoirs and its zoonotic transmission to humans (Spielman and Kimsey 1991). Human blood meals that produce dead-end infections deny new infections in the vertebrate reservoir. Alternatively, efficient vector-borne transmission in the reservoir population would rarely spill over to humans if the vector were not partially anthropophilic. Thus, the presence of nonhuman hosts suitable to the vector would provide a measure of zooprophylaxis by absorbing infectious spillover blood meals from the vector. Nevertheless, zoonotic transmission still may occur if additional "bridge" vector species that feed both on the reservoir and on humans are sufficiently abundant; such appears to explain the transmission of urban yellow fever (Monath 1989). Thus, the effect of vertebrate density on risk of zoonotic disease is complicated by numerous additional variables that influence the force of transmission.

ZOONOSES THAT INVOLVE WHITE-TAILED DEER

All recognized North American zoonotic disease agents that use white-tailed deer as their natural reservoir are vector borne. Jamestown Canyon virus (JCV) produces a mild to severe illness in humans, including central nervous system dysfunction, meningitis, and encephalitis in some cases. Antibody to this mosquito-borne virus is found in white-tailed deer at prevalences that are correlated positively with those in humans residing in the region (Boromisa and Grimstad 1987). Numerous *Aedes* mosquito species appear able to transmit JCV, some of which also transmit the virus vertically from female mosquitoes to their eggs (Grimstad 1989). Evidence implicating white-tailed deer in transmission of the virus is strong (Issel 1973), and increased deer abundance has been linked to greater prevalence of JCV in mosquitoes (Grayson et al. 1983). Infected deer develop JCV-specific antibody (Grimstad et al. 1987), which may inhibit transmission to uninfected mosquitoes. Regardless of whether viremic white-tailed deer frequently infect vectors, deer abundance is likely to influence that of the mosquitoes which use them as blood sources necessary for egg laying.

Since 1986, when the first U.S. case of human ehrlichiosis was recognized (Maeda et al. 1987), both the distribution and incidence of disease from *Ehrlichia* spp. infections have increased (Fishbein et al. 1994). Previously considered a disease of domestic animals, human ehrlichiosis is now believed to result from infection by at least three separate species, including *E. sennetsu* (in Japan and eastern Asia), *E. chaffeensis,* and the agent of the newly described agent of human granulocytic ehrlichiosis (HGE). Infection by *E. chaffeensis* is responsible for the 237 serologically confirmed human cases of human monocytic ehrlichiosis from 27 states in the United States between 1985 and 1990 (Fishbein et al. 1994). A new species closely related to *E. phagocytophila* or *E. equi* was recently implicated in 12 cases of HGE in the northern Midwest and Northeast, of which 2 were fatal (Bakken et al. 1994). Human risk differs among *Ehrlichia* species, seasons, and locations but certainly involves exposure to ticks (CDC 1990; Goldman et al. 1992).

White-tailed deer populations over much of the southern and eastern United States have a high prevalence (overall 43% of 1,269 deer) of antibody reactive to *E. chaffeensis* antigens (Dawson, Childs, et al. 1994). Although it is not apparent that this antibody is specific for the human pathogen, white-tailed deer infected in the laboratory with *E. chaffeensis* remained rickettsemic for 2 weeks (Dawson, Stallknecht, et al. 1994). Based on polymerase chain reaction methods (Anderson et al. 1993), *Amblyomma americanum,* the lone star tick, has been incriminated as vector of *E. chaffeensis* by demonstration of specific DNA in field-collected specimens. Laboratory study has indicated that deer may be competent reservoirs for *E. chaffeensis,* passing the organism to lone star tick larvae and nymphs, which then are capable of subsequent transmission to naive deer (Ewing et al. 1995). Limited data, based on polymerase chain reaction findings, incriminate the black-legged tick (*Ixodes scapularis* Say) as a possible vector of the HGE agent in the northeastern United States (Pancholi et al. 1995).

Deer presence and density exert a powerful influence on risk of other tick-borne zoonoses, not because deer are reservoirs of the pathogen but because they strongly affect the distribution and abundance of the pathogen's vector. The best studied example of this in North America involves the black-legged tick (Spielman et al. 1979) and closely related *I. pacificus.* The adult stages of these species, members of a group related to the European *I. ricinus,* are recognized for their predilection for feeding on cervids. Furthermore, their capacity as vectors of important viral, bacterial, and protozoal zoonotic disease agents is extensive. Because a female tick lays thousands of eggs following the single adult blood meal, the availability of suitable hosts, notably deer, is critical to the abundance of these vectors (Wilson and Deblinger 1993).

Northern *I. scapularis* (black-legged tick) populations, also referred to as *Ixodes dammini* (Spielman et al. 1979), are found primarily in the northeastern and northern midwestern United States, whereas other populations of *I. scapularis* occur in the Southeast. An effort has been made to synonomize *I. dammini* and *I. scapularis* under the latter (Oliver et al. 1993), but debate continues. Although the behavior, ecology, and epidemiologic features of the northern *I. dammini* differ significantly from those of the southeastern *I. scapularis,* and although most previously published studies have used the name *I. dammini,* we refer to both populations as *I. scapularis.* The related *I. pacificus* is found primarily in the Pacific coastal states.

Risk to humans of at least two zoonoses, Lyme disease and human babesiosis, is a function of the abundance of these *Ixodes* ticks. In addition, the agents of Powassan encephalitis (Artsob 1989) and the aforementioned HGE agent may be transmitted by the black-legged tick in the northeastern United States (Pancholi et al. 1995; Telford et al. 1996). With the possible exception of HGE, the reservoirs for these agents are mammals other than deer. Deer do not become infectious for ticks following exposure and therefore are not considered competent reservoirs for contributing to transmission cycles (Telford et al. 1987). The abundance of deer solely influences the population dynamics of the tick vector. Both the bacterial spirochete *Borrelia burgdorferi* (Lyme disease) and the protozoal piroplasm *Babesia microti* (human babesiosis) are reservoired by white-footed mice *(Peromyscus leucopus)* (Spielman et al. 1981; Piesman and Spielman 1982; Levine et al. 1985; Donahue et al. 1987). Immature northern black-legged ticks abundantly infest this rodent, permitting efficient enzootic transmission of both microorganisms. Powassan virus (Flaviviridae) is less well studied but appears to be transmitted by *I. cookei, I. marxi,* and possibly northern black-legged ticks that feed on small mammals, especially rodents (Costero 1994).

Ecology of *I. ricinus*-Group Ticks

Particular life history characteristics of *I. ricinus*-group ticks *(I. dammini, I. scapularis,* and *I. pacificus)* contribute to their role as vectors of agents of deer-associated zoonoses. As obligate hematophagous ectoparasites, each of the three motile stages (larva, nymph, and adult) must take one blood meal from a vertebrate host to survive and mature or reproduce. Engorged females lay a single egg batch and die. These *Ixodes* species typically attach, engorge, and detach from a different individual host during each of their three blood meals. Such a three-host feeding pattern creates particular options and constraints for transmission of microorganisms. Larval and nymphal stages infest a large variety of vertebrates, including mammals, birds, and reptiles. Adults, however, typically are more restricted in host species diversity; large mammals, especially cervids, are most often fed upon (Lane et al. 1991). The common names "deer tick" for northern *I. scapularis* (Spielman et al. 1985) and European "sheep tick" for *I. ricinus* (e.g., Gray 1984) reflect the feeding predilection of the adults. In North America, the density of deer exerts a profound influence on the abundance of these *Ixodes* ticks, hence risk of the zoonoses for which they are vectors. In addition to white-tailed deer abundance, environmental variables that may influence tick survival can be informative for predicting the abundance of black-legged ticks on deer (Glass et al. 1994).

Ecology of Northern Black-Legged Ticks and Deer

Considerable evidence demonstrates that adult black-legged ticks feed predominantly on white-tailed deer (Piesman et al. 1979; Carey et al. 1980; Schulze et al. 1984; Wilson, Litwin, et al. 1990). Other hosts such as canids, raccoons, and opossums (*Pidelphis virginiana* Kerr) also may be infested by adult ticks (Carey et al. 1980; Main et al. 1981; Schulze et al. 1986; Fish and Dowler 1989), yet white-tailed deer feed many more female ticks than do these other vertebrates (Wilson, Litwin, et al. 1990). Similarly, female *I. pacificus* primarily engorge upon Columbian black-tailed deer *(Odocoileus hemionus columbionus)* (Westrom et al. 1985). Because ticks are flightless and crawl over only a scale of meters, their spatial distribution should depend largely on local host movement. Thus, within its range in the northeastern United States, the mesogeographic distribution of black-legged ticks is correlated with the abundance of white-tailed deer (Wilson et al. 1985; Anderson et al. 1987; Duffy et al. 1994). Furthermore, by monitoring radio-collared white-tailed deer at a black-legged-tick-infested site on Long Island, New York, we demonstrated that deer density over the scale of 0.25-ha plots was correlated with the abundance of immature stages of this tick (Wilson, Ducey, et al. 1990). Adult ticks reproduce at the site where they detach from hosts following engorgement, apparently resulting in this fine-scale spatial relationship with white-tailed deer density.

Recognition of the microgeographic relationship between white-tailed deer density and black-legged tick abundance led to studies that examined the effect of the exclusion of white-tailed deer on tick distribution. Not surprisingly, relative abundance of immature ticks declined inside plots where deer were excluded shortly after the intervention occurred (Daniels et al. 1993; Stafford 1993). In general, fewer larval and nymphal ticks were found as the distance inward from the fence increased; ticks found inside but near the barrier probably were transported short distances by small mammal hosts. Again, tick reproduction in the absence of white-tailed deer declined, leading to local reduction of immature stages.

REPRODUCTION OF BLACK-LEGGED TICKS AND DEER DENSITY   In contrast to most other hematophagous arthropods, ticks are relatively long lived. They ultimately die, however, if unable to obtain a blood meal. For this reason, the density of suitable hosts directly influences tick survival. Reduced host density generally should increase the time spent questing or resting, thereby increasing tick mortality and reducing reproduction. The limited host range of adult black-legged ticks in the northern United States indicates that reproduction might be reduced when access to white-tailed deer is reduced. An experiment to test this hypothesis was undertaken in which white-tailed deer were virtually eradicated from a 240-ha coastal island off Cape Cod, Massachusetts (Wilson et al. 1988). Between 1982 and 1985, estimated deer abundance was decreased by more than 10-fold when a total of 52 deer were shot. During a 5-year period before and after deer removal, immature black-legged tick abundance was monitored. The abundance of immature ticks declined drastically following deer elimination: larval black-legged tick abundance was diminished the first year following intervention, whereas nymphal tick abundance did not decline until 1 year later (Wilson et al. 1988). Because northern populations of black-legged ticks typically exhibit a 2-year life cycle (Yuval and Spielman 1990), reduced abundance of nymphs should lag 1 year behind that of larvae. Adult tick densities, in turn, should not decline until at least 2 years after larval abundance is reduced. During the decade since the effect was first observed, deer density has been maintained at less than 10% of that when the study was begun, and immature black-legged tick abundance also has remained low; furthermore, adult tick abundance has continued to be sparse (S. R. Telford III, Harvard University, personal communication).

A second study examined the effect of gradual reduction of white-tailed deer density on the abundance of black-legged ticks at a heavily infested site in coastal northeastern Massachusetts (Deblinger et al. 1993).

By means of controlled hunting, deer abundance at the 530-ha Crane Reservation was reduced by about 40% each year from approximately 350 to approximately 60 deer during 1985 through 1991. Throughout this period, abundance of immature black-legged ticks fluctuated, but the average number of larval ticks following the intervention declined to about one-half of that prior to deer removal. Nymphal tick abundance also diminished, though less dramatically. Interestingly, the average number of adult ticks per deer increased as deer density declined. Apparently, the remaining deer encountered adult black-legged ticks at a rate sufficient to compensate partially for the decreased abundance, lessening the immediate effect of host removal on tick feeding and reproduction. The effect of host removal may be further compromised by the timing of deer reduction. Hunting seasons in the northeastern United States occur after the majority of fall-feeding adult ticks already have engorged: adult black-legged tick feeding commences during September, peaks during October and November, and declines thereafter (Watson and Anderson 1976; McEnroe 1977; Piesman et al. 1979; Carey et al. 1980; Wilson, Ducey, et al. 1990). A second, minor period of feeding also is apparent during the spring (Fish and Dowler 1989; Wilson, Litwin, et al. 1990).

DEER ABUNDANCE AND INCIDENCE OF LYME DISEASE   Within the present range of black-legged ticks in the northeastern United States, elevated white-tailed deer density appears necessary but not sufficient for tick abundance to be great. Although white-tailed deer do not function as a reservoir for *Borrelia burgdorferi* (Telford et al. 1987), we know of no sites where the tick vector is abundant but not infected. Accordingly, risk of Lyme disease should be associated with white-tailed deer density within the range of the vector. Lastavica et al. (1989) examined this relationship among persons residing near the Crane Reservation in Massachusetts. Of residents living within 5 km of the reservation, one-third had contracted Lyme disease. The attack rate increased with proximity to the reservation and was positively correlated with various measures of deer density.

The experimental removal of white-tailed deer on Great Island, Massachusetts (Debling et al. 1993), also permitted observation of changes in annual incidence of Lyme disease among residents there. Lyme disease rates ranged upwards of 3 cases per 100 per year prior to deer removal (Steere et al. 1986) but declined as the abundance of nymphal ticks decreased following deer removal (Wilson et al. 1988). Indeed, the annual incidence now averages less than 0.2 cases per 100 per year (Telford, personal communication). The mesogeographic correlation of white-tailed deer density and Lyme disease incidence observed near the Crane Reservation (Lastavica et al. 1989) is consistent with the reduction in Lyme disease incidence following experimental decrease in deer density on Great Island. One possible caveat in reducing deer density is that deer reduction may temporarily increase the number of questing, unfed nymphal and adult ticks. Thereby, humans may briefly experience greater risk of tick bite during a few years.

CONCLUSIONS

The importance of vertebrate density to human risk of zoonotic disease is a complex function of many factors that depend on the natural mode of transmission of the microorganism (Table 14.1). Risk generally increases as reservoir density increases but not necessarily in a linear manner. Under certain circumstances, increased density may not alter human risk or may even decrease risk; the actual risk depends on the transmission dynamics among reservoirs and the mode of transfer to humans.

Directly transmitted mutuals or commensals produce interactions that are more likely to lead to a positive relationship between reservoir density

TABLE 14.1
Vertebrate density and human risk of zoonoses for various types of transmission

Role of vertebrate in transmission	Correlation between host density and human risk	Example
Direct transmission (no vector involved)[a]		
Reservoir	Positive	Cryptosporidiosis
Bridge to reservoir	Indeterminant	Argentine hemorrhagic fever
Indirect transmission (vector-mediated)		
Reservoir and vector	Positive	Malaria (anthroponoses)
Reservoir and bridge to vector	Indeterminate, often positive	Sylvan yellow fever
Vector only	Indeterminate, may be negative	Lyme disease

[a] Transmission via aerosol, excreta, water, or contact.

and human risk. As the complexity of transmission or reservoir interactions increases, the density-to-risk relationship becomes more tenuous. No simple formula can predict how changes in reservoir density will affect zoonotic diseases. The particular transmission characteristics of each microorganism and its usual interaction with the vertebrate reservoir(s) must be analyzed. Then, processes involving vectors, immunity, alternative hosts, and other factors may lead to counterintuitive results.

The relationships between microorganisms and their vertebrate hosts have resulted from lengthy coevolution (Ewald 1993). Human-infection-producing zoonotic disease plays no role in the natural selection of these interactions. Thus, research into zoonotic disease risk should focus on reducing exposure. The new category of "emerging" zoonoses (Lederberg et al. 1992; Wilson et al. 1994) may represent true increases in disease incidence, perhaps due to increased reservoir density or human exposure, or may reflect better surveillance and recognition of cases. Regardless, the biological determinants of human disease risk lie in the interactions among microorganism, possible vectors, and vertebrate reservoirs, of which vertebrate density often plays an important part.

ACKNOWLEDGMENTS

The work presented here was supported in part by a grant from the National Institutes of Health (AI34409) to M. L. Wilson.

REFERENCES CITED

Acha, P. N., and B. Szyfres. 1988. Zoonoses and communicable diseases common to man and animals. Pan American Health Organization, Scientific Publication 354, Washington.

Anderson, B. E., K. G. Sims, J. G. Olson, J. E. Childs, J. F. Piesman, C. M. Happ, G. O. Maupin, and B. J. B. Johnson. 1993. *Amblyomma americanum*: A potential vector of human ehrlichiosis. American Journal of Tropical Medicine and Hygiene 49:239–244.

Anderson, J. F., R. C. Johnson, L. A. Magnarelli, F. W. Hyde, and J. E. Myers. 1987. Prevalence of *Borrelia burgdorferi* and *Babesia microti* in mice on islands inhabited by white-tailed deer. Applied Environmental Microbiology 53: 892–894.

Anderson, R. M., H. C. Jackson, R. M. May, and A. M. Smith. 1981. Population dynamics of fox rabies in Europe. Nature 289:765–771.

Anderson, R. M., and R. M. May. 1991. Infectious Disease of Humans: Dynamics and Control. Oxford University Press, New York.

Artsob, H. 1989. Powassan encephalitis. Pages 29–49 *in* The Arboviruses, Epidemiology and Ecology. Vol. 4. (T. P. Monath, ed.) CRC Press, Boca Raton, FL.

Bacon, P. J., ed. 1985. Population Dynamics of Rabies in Wildlife. Academic Press, New York.

Bakken, J. S., J. S. Dumler, S. M. Chen, M. R. Eckman, L. L. Van Etta, and D. H. Walker. 1994. Human granulocytic ehrlichiosis in the upper midwest United States. Journal of the American Medical Association 272:212–218.

Beran, G. W., and M. Firth. 1988. Domestic animal rabies control: An overview. Reviews of Infectious Diseases 10:S672–S677.

Boromisa, R. D., and P. R. Grimstad. 1987. Seroconversion rates to Jamestown Canyon virus among six populations of white-tailed deer *(Odocoileus virginianus)* in Indiana. Journal of Wildlife Diseases 23:23–33.

Brochier, B., M. P. Kieny, F. Costy, P. Coppens, B. Baudin, J. P. Lecocq, B. Languet, G. Chappuis, P. Desmettre, K. Afiademyo, R. Libois, and P.-P. Pastoret. 1991. Large-scale eradication of rabies using recombinant vaccinia-rabies vaccine. Nature 354:520–522.

Carey, A. B., W. L. Krinsky, and A. J. Main. 1980. *Ixodes dammini* (Acari: Ixodidae) and associated ixodid ticks in south-central Connecticut, USA. Journal of Medical Entomology 17:89–99.

CDC (Centers for Disease Control). 1990. Rocky Mountain spotted fever and human ehrlichiosis—United States, 1989. Morbidity and Mortality Weekly Report 39:281–284.

CDC (Centers for Disease Control). 1994. Raccoon rabies epizootic—United States, 1993. Morbidity and Mortality Weekly Report 43:269–273.

Childs, J. E. 1990. Urban cats: Their demography, population density, and owner characteristics in Baltimore, Maryland. Antrozoös 3:234–244.

Childs, J. E., J. W. Krebs, T. G. Ksiazek, G. O. Maupin, K. L. Gage, P. Rollin, P. S. Zeitz, J. Sarisky, R. E. Enscore, J. C. Butler, J. E. Cheek, G. E. Glass, and C. J. Peters. 1995. A household based case-control study of environmental factors associated with hantavirus pulmonary syndrome in the southwestern United States. American Journal of Tropical Medicine and Hygiene 52:393–397.

Childs, J. E., T. G. Ksaizek, C. F. Spiropoulou, J. W. Krebs, S. Morzunov, G. O. Maupin, K. L. Gage, P. E. Rollin, J. Sarisky, R. E. Enscore, J. K. Frey, C. J. Peters, and S. T. Nichol. 1994. Serologic and genetic identification of *Peromyscus maniculatus* as the primary rodent reservoir for a new hantavirus in the southwestern United States. Journal of Infectious Diseases 169:1271–1280.

Childs, J. E., and C. J. Peters. 1994. Ecology and epidemiology of arenaviruses and their hosts. Pages 345–401 *in* The Arenaviridae. (M. Salvato, ed.) Plenum Press, New York.

Childs, J. E., and W. S. Seegar. 1986. Epidemiologic observations on infection with *Toxoplasma gondii* in three species of urban mammals from Baltimore, Maryland, USA. International Journal of Zoonoses 61:249–261.

Costero, A. 1994. Experimental transmission of Powassan virus (Flaviviridae) by *Ixodes dammini* Spielman, et al., 1979 ticks (Acari: Ixodidae). Doctoral dissertation, McGill University, Montreal, Quebec.

Daniels, T. J., D. Fish, and I. Schwartz. 1993. Reduced abundance of *Ixodes scapularis* (Acari: Ixodidae) and Lyme disease risk by deer exclusion. Journal of Medical Entomology 30:1043–1049.

Dawson, J. E., J. E. Childs, K. L. Biggie, C. Moore, D. Stalknecht, J. Shaddock, E. Hofmeister, and J. G. Olson. 1994. White-tailed deer as a potential reservoir of *Ehrlichia* spp. Journal of Wildlife Diseases 30:162–168.

Dawson J. E., D. E. Stallknecht, E. W. Howerth, C. Warner, K. Biggie, W. R. Davidson, J. M. Lockhart, V. F. Nettles, J. G. Olson, and J. E. Childs. 1994. Susceptibility of white-tailed deer to infection with *Ehrlichia chaffeensis*, etiologic agent of human ehrlichiosis. Journal of Clinical Microbiology 32:2725–2728.

Debbie, J. G. 1991. Rabies control of terrestrial wildlife by population reduction. Pages 477–484 *in* The Natural History of Rabies. 2nd edition. (R. G. Baer, ed.) CRC Press, Boca Raton, FL.

Deblinger, R. D., M. L. Wilson, D. W. Rimmer, and A. Spielman. 1993. Reduced abundance of immature *Ixodes dammini* (Acari: Ixodidae) following incremental removal of deer. Journal of Medical Entomology 30:144–150.

Donahue, J. G., J. Piesman, and A. Spielman. 1987. Reservoir competence of white-footed mice for Lyme disease spirochetes. American Journal of Tropical Medicine and Hygiene 36:94–98.

Dubey, J. P. 1973. Feline toxoplasmosis and coccidiosis: A survey of domiciled and stray cats. Journal of the American Veterinary Medical Association 162: 873–877.

Dubey, J. P., E. A. Hoover, and K. W. Walls. 1977. Effect of age and sex on the acquisition of immunity to toxoplasmosis in cats. The Journal of Protozoology 24:184–186.

Duchin J. S., F. T. Koster, C. J. Peters, G. L. Simpson, B. Tempest, S. R. Zaki, T. G. Ksiazek, P. E. Rollin, S. Nichol, E. Umland, R. L. Moolenaar, S. E. Reef, K. B. Nolte, M. M. Gallaher, J. C. Butler, R. F. Brieman, and the Hantavirus Study Group. 1994. Hantaviral pulmonary syndrome: Clinical description of disease caused by a newly recognized hemorrhagic fever virus in the southwestern United States. New England Journal of Medicine 330:949–955.

Duffy, D. C., S. R. Campbell, D. Clark, C. DiMotta, and S. Gurney. 1994. *Ixodes scapularis* (Acari: Ixodidae) deer tick mesoscale populations in natural areas: Effects of deer, area, and location. Journal of Medical Entomology 31: 152–158.

Elliott, L. H., T. G. Ksiazek, P. E. Rollin, C. F. Spiropoulou, S. Morzunov, M. Monroe, C. S. Goldsmith, C. D. Humphrey, S. R. Zaki, J. W. Krebs, G. Maupin, K. Gage, J. E. Childs, S. T. Nichol, and C. J. Peters. 1994. Isolation of the causative agent of hantavirus pulmonary syndrome. American Journal of Tropical Medicine and Hygiene 51:102–108.

Ewald, P. W. 1993. The evolution of virulence. Scientific American 268:86–93.

Ewing, S. A., J. E. Dawson, A. A. Kocan, R. W. Barker, C. K. Warner, R. J. Panciera, J. C. Fox, K. M. Kocan, and E. F. Bloun. 1995. Experimental transmission of *Ehrlichia chaffeensis* (Rickettsiales: Ehrlichieae) among white-tailed deer by *Amblyomma americanum* (Acari: Ixodidae). Journal of Medical Entomology 32:368–374.

Fayer, R., and B. L. P. Ungar. 1986. *Cryptosporidium* spp. and cryptosporidiosis. Microbiological Reviews 50:458–483.

Fish, D., and R. C. Dowler. 1989. Host associations of ticks (Acari: Ixodidae) parasitizing medium-sized mammals in a Lyme disease endemic area of southern New York. Journal of Medical Entomology 26:200–209.

Fishbein, D. B., J. E. Dawson, and L. E. Robinson. 1994. Human ehrlichiosis in the United States, 1985 to 1990. Annals of Internal Medicine 120:736–743.

Frenkel, J. K., J. P. Dubey, and N. L. Miller. 1970. *Toxoplasma gondii* in cats: Fecal stages identified as coccidian oocysts. Science 167:893–896.

Gallaher, M. M., J. L. Herndon, L. J. Nims, C. R. Sterling, D. J. Grabowski, and H. F. Hull. 1989. Cryptosporidiosis and surface water. American Journal of Public Health 79:39–42.

Gavrilovskaya, I. N., N. S. Apekina, A. D. Bernshtein, V. T. Demina, N. M. ˙Okulova, Y. A. Myasnikov, and M. P. Chumakov. 1990. Pathogenesis of hemorrhagic fever with renal syndrome virus infection and mode of horizontal transmission of hantavirus in bank voles. Archives of Virology, Supplement 1: 57–62.

Glass, G. E., F. P. Amerasinghe, J. M. Morgan III, and T. W. Scott. 1994. Predicting *Ixodes scapularis* abundance on white-tailed deer using geographic information systems. American Journal of Tropical Medicine and Hygiene 51:538–544.

Goldman, D. P., A. W. Artenstein, and C. D. Bolan. 1992. Human erlichiosis. American Family Physician 46:199–208.

Gray, J. S. 1984. Studies on the dynamics of active populations of the sheep tick, *Ixodes ricinus* L. in Co. Wicklow, Ireland. Acarologia 25:167–178.

Grayson, M. A., S. Srihongse, R. Deibel, and C. H. Calisher. 1983. California serogroup viruses in New York State: A retrospective analysis of subtype distribution patterns and their epidemiological significance, 1965 to 1981. Pages 257–267 *in* California Serogroup Viruses. (C. H. Calisher and W. H. Thompson, eds.) Allen R. Liss, New York.

Grimstad, P. R. 1989. California serogroup viruses. Pages 99–139 *in* The Arboviruses, Epidemiology and Ecology. Vol. 2. (T. P. Monath, ed.) CRC Press, Boca Raton, FL.

Grimstad, P. R., D. G. Williams, and S. M. Schmitt. 1987. Infection of white-tailed deer *(Odocoileus virginianus)* in Michigan with Jamestown Canyon virus (California serogroup) and the importance of maternal antibody in viral maintenance. Journal of Wildlife Diseases 23:12–22.

Hansson, L., and H. Hentonnen. 1985. Gradients in density variations of small rodents: The importance of latitude and snow cover. Oecologia 67:394–402.

Hörnfeldt, B. 1994. Delayed density dependence as a determinant of vole cycles. Ecology 75:791–806.

Issel, C. J. 1973. Isolation of Jamestown Canyon virus (a California group arbovirus) from a white-tailed deer. American Journal Tropical Medicine and Hygiene 22:414–417.

Johnson, K. M. 1989. Hantaviruses. Pages 341–450 in Viral Infections of Humans: Epidemiology and Control. 3rd edition. (A. S. Evans, ed.) Plenum Press, New York.

Kean, B. H., A. C. Kimball, and W. N. Christenson. 1969. An epidemic of acute toxoplasmosis. Journal of the American Medical Association 208:1002–1004.

Krebs, J. W., T. W. Strine, and J. E. Childs. 1993. Rabies surveillance in the United States during 1992. Journal of the American Veterinary Medical Association 203:1718–1731.

Krebs, J. W., T. W. Strine, J. S. Smith, C. E. Rupprecht, and J. E. Childs. 1994. Rabies surveillance in the United States during 1993. Journal of the American Veterinary Medical Association 205:1695–1709.

Lane, R. S., J. Piesman, and W. Burgdorfer. 1991. Lyme borreliosis: Relation of its causative agent to its vectors and hosts in North America and Europe. Annual Review of Entomology 36:587–609.

Lastavica, C. C., M. L. Wilson, V. P. Barardi, A. Spielman, and R. D. Deblinger. 1989. Rapid emergence of a focal epidemic of Lyme disease in coastal Massachusetts. New England Journal of Medicine 320:133–137.

Lederberg, J., R. E. Shope, and S. C. Oaks, eds. 1992. Emerging Infections: Microbial Threats to Health in the United States. National Academy Press, Washington.

LeDuc, J. W. 1987. Epidemiology of Hantaan and related viruses. Laboratory Animal Science 37:413–418.

LeDuc, J. W., G. E., Glass, J. E. Childs, and A. J. Watson. 1994. Hantaan virus and rodent zoonoses. Pages 149–158 in Emerging Viruses: Evolution of Viruses and Viral Diseases. (S. S. Morris, ed.) Princeton University Press, Princeton, NJ.

Lee, H. W., L. J. Baek, and K. M. Johnson. 1982. Isolation of Hantaan virus, the etiologic agent of Korean hemorrhagic fever, from wild urban rats. Journal of Infectious Diseases 146:638–644.

Lee, H. W., P. W. Lee, L. J. Baek, C. K. Song, and I. W. Seong. 1981. Intraspecific transmission of Hantaan virus, etiologic agent of Korean hemorrhagic fever, in the rodent Apodemus agrarius. American Journal Tropical Medicine and Hygiene 30:1106–1112.

Lee, H. W., P. W. Lee, and K. M. Johnson. 1978. Isolation of the etiologic agent of Korean hemorrhagic fever. Journal of Infectious Diseases 137:298–308.

Levine, J. F., M. L. Wilson, and A. Spielman. 1985. Mice as reservoirs of the Lyme disease spirochete. American Journal of Tropical Medicine and Hygiene 34:355–360.

MacKenzie, W. R., N. J. Hoxie, M. E. Proctor, M. S. Gradus, K. A. Blair, D. E. Peterson, J. J. Kaxmierczak, D. G. Addiss, K. R. Fox, J. B. Rose, and J. P. Davis. 1994. A massive outbreak in Milwaukee of *Cryptosporidium* infection transmitted through the public water supply. New England Journal of Medicine 331:161–177.

Maeda, K., N. Markowitz, R. C. Hawley, M. Ristic, D. Cox, and J. E. McDade. 1987. Human infection with *Ehrlichia canis*, a leukocytic rickettsia. New England Journal of Medicine 316:852–856.

Main, A. J., K. O. Sprance, K. O. Kloter, and S. E. Brown. 1981. *Ixodes dammini* (Acari: Ixodidae) on white-tailed deer *(Odocoileus virginianus)* in Connecticut. Journal of Medical Entomology 18:487–492.

McEnroe, W. D. 1977. The restriction of the species range of *Ixodes scapularis* Say, in Massachusetts by fall and winter temperature. Acarologia 18:618–625.

Mercado, R. R. 1975. Rodent control programmes in areas affected by Bolivian haemorrhagic fever. Bulletin of the World Health Organization 52:691–696.

Mills, J. M., B. A. Ellis, K. T. McKee, Jr., G. E. Calderon, J. I. Maiztegui, G. O. Nelson, T. G. Ksiazek, C. J. Peters, and J. E. Childs. 1992. A longitudinal study of Junin virus activity in the rodent reservoir of Argentine hemorrhagic fever. American Journal of Tropical Medicine and Hygiene 47:749–763.

Monath, T. P. 1989. Yellow fever. Pages 139–231 *in* The Arboviruses, Epidemiology and Ecology. Vol. 5. (T. P. Monath, ed.) CRC Press, Boca Raton, FL.

Navin, T. R., and D. D. Juranek. 1984. Cryptosporidiosis: Clinical, epidemiological, and parasitologic review. Review of Infectious Diseases 6:313–327.

Niklasson, B., B. Hörnfeldt, Å. Lundkvist, S. Björsten, and J. W. LeDuc. 1995. Temporal dynamics of Puumala antibody prevalence in voles and of nephropathia epidemica incidence in humans. American Journal of Tropical Medicine and Hygiene 53:134–140.

Nyström, K. 1982. Epidemiology of HFRS (endemic benign nephropathy—EBN) in Sweden. Scandinavian Journal of Infectious Diseases, Supplement 36: 92.

Oliver, J. H., Jr., M. R. Owsley, H. J. Hutcheson, A. M. James, C. Chen, W. S. Irby, E. M. Dotson, and D. K. McLain. 1993. Conspecificity of the ticks *Ixodes scapularis* and *Ixodes dammini* (Acari: Ixodidae). Journal of Medical Entomology 30:54–63.

Pancholi, P., C. P. Kolbert, P. O. Mitchell, K. D. Reed, Jr., J. S. Damler, J. S. Bakken, S. R. Telford III, and D. H. Persing. 1995. *Ixodes dammini* as a possible vector of human granulocytic ehrlichiosis. Journal of Infectious Diseases 172: 1007–1012.

Parmenter R. R., J. W. Brunt, D. I. Moore, and S. Ernest. 1993. The hantavirus epidemic in the southwest: Rodent population dynamics and the implications for transmission of hantavirus-associated adult respiratory distress syndrome

(HARDS) in the Four Corners region. University of New Mexico, Sevilleta Long-Term Ecological Research Publication 41, Albuquerque, NM.

Parmenter R. R., and R. Vigil. 1993. The HARDS epidemic in the southwest: An assessment of autumn rodent densities and population demographics in central and northern New Mexico, October, 1993. University of New Mexico, Sevilleta Long-Term Ecological Research Publication 45, Albuquerque, NM.

Piesman, J., and A. Spielman. 1982. *Babesia microti*: Infectivity of parasites from ticks for hamsters and white-footed mice. Experimental Parasitology 53: 242–248.

Piesman, J., A. Spielman, P. Etkind, T. K. Ruebush, and D. D. Juranek. 1979. Role of deer in the epizootiology of *Babesia microti* in Massachusetts, USA. Journal of Medical Entomology 15:537–540.

Public Health Laboratory Service Study Group. 1990. Cryptosporidiosis in England and Wales: Prevalence and clinical and epidemiological features. British Medical Journal 300:774–777.

Ruiz, A., and J. K. Frenkel. 1980. *Toxoplasma gondii* in Costa Rican cats. American Journal of Tropical Medicine and Hygiene 29:1150–1160.

Schulze, T. L., G. S. Bowen, M. F. Lakat, W. E. Parkin, and J. K. Shisler. 1986. Seasonal abundance and hosts of *Ixodes dammini* (Acari: Ixodidae) and other ixodid ticks from an endemic Lyme disease focus in New Jersey, USA. Journal of Medical Entomology 23:105–109.

Schulze, T. L., M. F. Lakat, G. S. Bowen, and J. K. Shisler. 1984. *Ixodes dammini* (Acari: Ixodidae) and other ixodid ticks collected from white-tailed deer in New Jersey, USA. I. Geographical distribution and its relation to selected environmental and physical factors. Journal of Medical Entomology 21:741–749.

Simson, V. R. 1992. Cryptosporidiosis in newborn red deer *(Cervus elaphus)*. Veterinary Record 130:116–118.

Skeels, M. R., R. Sokolow, C. V. Hubbard, J. K. Andrus, and J. Biasch. 1990. *Cryptosporidium* infection in Oregon public health clinic patients 1985–88: The value of statewide laboratory surveillance. American Journal of Public Health 80:305–308.

Smith, J. S., L. A. Orciari, P. A. Yager, H. D. Seidel, and C. K. Warner. 1992. Epidemiologic and historical relationships among 87 rabies virus isolates as determined by limited sequence analysis. Journal of Infectious Diseases 166: 296–307.

Spielman, A., C. M. Clifford, J. Piesman, and M. D. Corwin. 1979. Human babesiosis on Nantucket Island, USA: Description of a vector, *Ixodes (Ixodes) dammini*, n. sp. (Acarina: Ixodidae). Journal of Medical Entomology 15:218–234.

Spielman, A., P. Etkind, J. Piesman, T. K. Ruebush, D. D. Juranek, and M. Jacobs. 1981. Reservoir hosts of human babesiosis on Nantucket Island. American Journal of Tropical Medicine and Hygiene 30:560–565.

Spielman, A., and R. B. Kimsey. 1991. Zoonosis. Pages 891–900 *in* Encyclopedia of Human Biology. Vol. 7. Academic Press, New York.

Spielman, A., M. L. Wilson, J. F. Levine, and J. Piesman. 1985. Ecology of *Ixodes dammini*-borne human babesiosis and Lyme disease. Annual Review of Entomology 30:439–460.

Stafford, K. C. III. 1993. Reduced abundance of *Ixodes scapularis* (Acari: Ixodidae) with exclusion of deer by electric fencing. Journal of Medical Entomology 30:986–996.

Stagno, S., A. L. Dykes, C. S. Amos, R. A. Head, D. D. Juranek, and K. Walls. 1980. An outbreak of toxoplasmosis linked to cats. Pediatrics 65:706–712.

Steck, F., and A. Wandeler. 1980. The epidemiology of fox rabies in Europe. Epidemioloigcal Review 2:71–96.

Steere, A. S., E. Taylor, M. L. Wilson, J. F. Levine, and A. Spielman. 1986. Clinical and epidemiological features of Lyme disease in a defined community. Journal of Infectious Diseases 154:295–300.

Telford, S. R. III, J. E. Dawson, P. Katavolos, C. K. Warner, C. P. Kolbert, and D. H. Persing. 1996. Perpetuation of the agent of human granulocytic ehrlichiosis in a deer tick–rodent cycle. Proceedings of the National Academy of Sciences of the USA. 93:6209–6214.

Telford, S. R. III, T. N. Mather, S. I. Moore, M. L. Wilson, and A. Spielman. 1987. Incompetence of deer as reservoirs of the Lyme disease spirochete. American Journal of Tropical Medicine and Hygiene 39:105–109.

Tzipori, S., K. W. Angus, I. Campbell, and D. Sherwood. 1981. Diarrhea in young red deer associated with infection with *Cryptosporidium*. Journal of Infectious Diseases 144:170–175.

Wallace, G. D. 1972. Cats, rats and toxoplasmosis on a small Pacific island. American Journal of Epidemiology 95:475–482.

Wallace, G. D. 1973. The role of the cat in the natural history of *Toxoplasma gondii*. The American Journal of Tropical Medicine and Hygiene 22:313–322.

Watson, T. G., and R. C. Anderson. 1976. *Ixodes scapularis* Say on white-tailed deer *(Odocoileus virginianus)* from Long Point, Ontario. Journal of Wildlife Diseases 12:66–71.

Westrom, D. R., R. S. Lane, and J. R. Anderson. 1985. *Ixodes pacificus* (Acari: Ixodidae): Population dynamics and distribution on Columbian black-tailed deer *(Odocoileus hemionus columbianus)*. Journal of Medical Entomology 22:507–511.

Whitfield, P. J. 1979. The Biology of Parasitism: An Introduction to the Study of Associating Organisms. University Park Press, Baltimore, MD.

Wilson, M. E., R. Levins, and A. Spielman, eds. 1994. Disease in Evolution: Global Changes and the Emergence of Infectious Diseases. New York Academy of Sciences, New York.

Wilson, M. L. 1994a. Population ecology of tick vectors: Interaction, measurement and analysis. Pages 20–44 *in* Ecological Dynamics of Tick-Borne Zoonoses. (D. E. Sonenshine and T. N. Mather, eds.) Oxford University Press, New York.

Wilson, M. L. 1994b. Rift Valley fever virus ecology and the epidemiology of disease emergence. Pages 169–180 *in* Disease in Evolution: Global Changes and the Emergence of Infectious Diseases. (M. E. Wilson, R. Levins, and A. Spielman, eds.) New York Academy of Sciences, New York.

Wilson, M. L., G. H. Adler, and A. Spielman. 1985. Correlation between abundance of deer and that of the deer tick, *Ixodes dammini* (Acari: Ixodidae). Annals of the Entomological Society of America 78:172–176.

Wilson, M. L., and R. D. Deblinger. 1993. Vector management to reduce the risk of Lyme disease. Pages 126–156 *in* Ecology and Environmental Management of Lyme Disease. (H. S. Ginsberg, ed.) Rutgers University Press, New Brunswick, NJ.

Wilson, M. L., A. M. Ducey, T. S. Litwin, T. A. Gavin, and A. Spielman. 1990. Microgeograhpic distribution of immature *Ixodes dammini* (Acari: Ixodidae) correlated with that of deer. Medical and Veterinary Entomology 4:151–160.

Wilson, M. L., T. S. Litwin, T. A. Gavin, M. C. Capkanis, D. C. MacLean, and A. Spielman. 1990. Host-dependent differences in feeding and reproduction of Ixodes dammini (Acari: Ixodidae). Journal of Medical Entomology 27: 945–954.

Wilson, M. L., S. A. Telford III, J. Piesman, and A. Spielman. 1988. Reduced abundance of immature *Ixodes dammini* (Acari: Ixodidae) following elimination of deer. Journal of Medical Entomology 25:224–228.

Winkler, W. G., and S. R. Jenkins. 1992. Raccoon rabies. Pages 325–340 *in* The Natural History of Rabies. 2nd edition. (R. G. Baer, ed.) CRC Press. Boca Raton, FL.

Yanagihara, R., H. L. Amyx, and D. C. Gajdusek. 1985. Experimental infection with Puumala virus, the etiologic agent of nephropathia epidemica, in bank voles *(Clethrionomys glareolus)*. Journal of Virology 55:34–38.

Yuval, B., and A. Spielman. 1990. Duration and regulation of the developmental cycle of *Ixodes dammini* (Acari: Ixodidae). Journal of Medical Entomology 27:196–201.

15 Influence of Deer on the Structure and Composition of Oak Forests in Central Massachusetts

WILLIAM M. HEALY

Interactions among white-tailed deer and forest plant communities are of interest as ecosystem processes (Naiman 1988) and from the standpoint of conserving plant species diversity, especially species that are sensitive to browsing (Alverson et al. 1988). Management of deer and forests will become more complex as wildlife biologists and public land managers adopt an ecosystem approach to management. Basic data on plant–animal interactions will be needed to balance the current needs of society with the need to sustain ecosystem productivity.

The widespread failure of oak *(Quercus)* to replace itself on better sites throughout the East presents a serious challenge to managers (Crow 1988). Oaks are the dominant genus through much of the eastern deciduous forest (Braun 1950), and a decline in the relative abundance of oak will have important economic and ecologic consequences. Deer can cause regeneration failures (Trumbull et al. 1989), but the role of deer in limiting oak regeneration throughout the region is unclear.

The Quabbin Reservoir in central Massachusetts provided an opportunity to study an oak ecosystem in which the same forest management has been applied for about 50 years to areas with hunted and protected deer herds. My goal was to describe the effects of deer and forest management within the context of land-use history, past deer abundance, and the stage of stand development. The first phase of the study compared forest structure and composition among two levels of deer density and two cutting treatments. It addressed questions about the ability of existing stands to replace themselves and the likely species composition of future stands. The second part of the study measured the effect of excluding deer for 7 years on regeneration in stands with a history of deer abundance. I wanted to know how long it might take oak regeneration to develop if deer numbers were reduced.

STUDY AREA

The study was conducted within the watershed of the Quabbin Reservoir in Franklin, Hampshire, and Worcester counties in central Massachusetts. The watershed contains a 9,713-ha reservoir and 22,663 ha of surrounding uplands. The area immediately adjacent to the reservoir (approximately 19,625 ha) was set aside as a wildlife sanctuary, and public access has been controlled since 1938. The property is managed by the Metropolitan District Commission (MDC) to provide municipal water, forest products, wildlife, and recreation.

Potential study stands were identified from MDC forest inventory data. All stands met the following criteria: white pine *(Pinus strobus)*– northern red oak *(Quercus rubra)*–red maple *(Acer rubrum)* forest type (Society of American Foresters type 20; Eyre 1980); even-aged trees, 60– 100 years old; sawtimber-sized trees, the dominant trees having a diameter at breast height (dbh) greater than 30 cm; and location not on extremely steep or rocky sites. Four stands were selected in each of four categories: (1) unthinned and 3–6 deer/km²; (2) unthinned and 10–17 deer/km²; (3) thinned and 3–6 deer/km²; and (4) thinned and 10–17 deer/ km² (Table 15.1). High-deer-density stands were in the wildlife sanctuary and low-deer-density stands were outside the sanctuary but on contiguous portions of the Quabbin Reservation where public hunting was permitted.

Thinning had been conducted to promote the growth of quality sawtimber according to the guidelines for upland oaks (Roach and Gingrich 1968; Hibbs and Bentley 1983). Thinning removed trees of poor form or quality and generally left a residual stocking of 50–60% (Roach and Gingrich 1968; Hibbs and Bentley 1983). This type of thinning, called improvement cutting, is one of the most common practices employed in previously unmanaged hardwood stands in the eastern United States (Smith 1986:165–167). Among the thinned stands, timber harvest had occurred from 9 to 17 years before this study, and four stands had been thinned twice (Table 15.1). Stands were selected for treatment by MDC foresters primarily on the basis of stand condition, access, and market conditions.

TABLE 15.1

Mature oak stands sampled on the Quabbin Reservation, central
Massachusetts

Stand	Hectares	Year of origin	Cutting treatment
			3–6 deer/km^2
1	14.1	1929	None, some residuals >100 years old
2	13.3	1922	None
3	18.2	1916	None
4	8.5	1935	None
5	57.6	1910	Thinning 1968, sawlogs; 1980–81, cordwood
6	50.0	1907	Thinning 1982, sawlogs and cordwood
7	8.9	1895	Thinning 1962, sawlogs; 1982, sawlogs and cordwood
8	13.4	1904	Thinning 1982–83, sawlogs and cordwood
			10–17 deer/km^2
9	13.0	1919	None
10	21.8	1921	None
11	10.0	1923	None
12	51.9	1913	None
13	13.8	1924	Thinning 1971 and 1982, cordwood
14	10.0	1882	Thinning 1981, sawlogs and cordwood
15	5.6	1889	Thinning 1974, ½ volume removed
16	18.4	1924	Thinning 1969, sawlogs; 1979 sawlogs and cordwood

These stands were characteristic of southern New England oak forests in
terms of age, species composition, and management.

Several aspects of past land use are pertinent to understanding the
current effects of deer on the Quabbin forest. The original forests of central Massachusetts were cut and the land cleared for agriculture between
1700 and 1830 (Hosley and Ziebarth 1935; Foster 1992). At the peak of
land clearing in the mid-1800s, more than 80% of the arable land was
cleared. Reforestation of abandoned pastures and fields began about 1850
and continued into the early 1900s. The major pattern of reforestation
included establishment of white pine on abandoned agricultural land. Less
commonly, successional hardwoods such as aspens (*Populus* spp.), gray
birch *(Betula populifolia),* red maple, and cherries (*Prunus* spp.) became
established on abandoned fields. Commercial harvest of old-field white

pine began about 1885 and continued through the early 1900s. As the white pine was cut and the successional hardwoods died, the modern forest dominated by northern red oak, red maple, and white pine emerged.

Today the Quabbin Reservation is 93% forested; 99% of the forest is older than 50 years and 59% is older than 90 years (MDC 1994:13). Oak cover types occupy 48% of the forested acreage. The other forest cover types include white pine (21%), birch (*Betula* spp.)–red maple (11%), red pine *(Pinus resinosa)* plantations (7%), northern hardwoods (7%), eastern hemlock *(Tsuga canadensis)* (5%), and spruce (*Picea* spp.) plantations (1%).

Deer were not abundant at the time the modern forests were initiated, and outside the Quabbin Sanctuary deer populations have been maintained at low densities throughout this century (Shaw and McLaughlin 1951; McDonough and Pottie 1979). Deer were extirpated from central Massachusetts by 1850. Deer hunting was prohibited statewide from 1892 through 1909, and relict populations expanded rapidly during this period of protection. Modern hunting seasons began in 1910, and from 1910 through 1966 hunters were permitted to kill one deer of either sex during the first full week of December. From 1967 until the present hunters have been allowed to harvest antlered deer, but the harvest of antlerless deer has been limited to a specific quota through a permit system (McDonough and Pottie 1979). Deer populations outside the Quabbin Sanctuary have probably averaged 1 deer/km^2 or less during most of this century (Hosley and Ziebarth 1935; Shaw and McLaughlin 1951). Population estimates based on legal harvest suggest densities of 3–6 deer/km^2 from 1984 through 1991. Hunting has been prohibited on the Quabbin Sanctuary since 1938; an increase in deer numbers and the signs of overbrowsing were evident by 1946 (Shaw and McLaughlin 1951:34–35). Thus, deer densities have been greater in the sanctuary than in the hunted portions of the Quabbin watershed since the mid-1940s.

Oliver and Larson's (1990:140–147) model of stand development is useful for viewing this history of deer abundance. The model, based primarily on stand structure, has wide applicability and is easy to relate to silvicultural guidelines for managing oaks (Roach and Gingrich 1968; Hibbs and Bentley 1983). The model describes four general stages of stand development: stand initiation, stem exclusion, understory reinitiation, and old growth. Deer were uncommon during the stand initiation stage (1880–1940). Deer became abundant on the sanctuary during the stem exclusion stage (1940–80) and have remained abundant as stands progressed into the understory reinitiation stage (1980 to present).

METHODS

Vegetation Composition and Structure

In 1984 I established in each stand sampling transects that ran parallel to the long axis of each stand. Two or more transects were established depending on the size and shape of the stand. The minimum distance between transects was 40 m. The first point was established randomly, and subsequent points were marked at 20-m intervals along the line until 30 total points were established in each stand. Points were permanently marked to locate the center of two concentric circular plots that were used to sample understory (4-m^2 plot) and overstory (250-m^2 plot) vegetation. In high-deer-density stands the understory sampling point was surrounded in 1985 with a 1.5-m-tall woven-wire fence that enclosed an area of 7 m^2. An alternative sampling point was established at right angles to the transect 3.4 m east of the first point.

Overstory characteristics were measured during the dormant seasons in 1986 and 1987. Species and dbh were tallied for all live trees with a dbh of greater than 2.5 cm on the 250-m^2 plots. Undergrowth characteristics were measured during July and August 1991. Woody stems less than 2.5 cm dbh, including tree seedlings and shrubs, were tallied by species and height class on the 4-m^2 plots. On the smaller plots, herbaceous cover was estimated by species. In the high-deer-density stands undergrowth was measured both inside the fence and at the alternative sampling point.

Deer Density

I estimated deer density in the sanctuary with line-transect sampling (Burnham et al. 1980). Surveys were conducted in late October–early November, 1983 through 1992, by means of six or seven 3-km transects. Transects were searched six or more times each year (see Healy and Welsh 1992 for details of the field procedures). Transect data were analyzed with Distance software (Buckland et al. 1993).

Outside the sanctuary, deer density was estimated from harvest data collected from 1983 through 1992 by the Massachusetts Division of Fisheries and Wildlife and analyzed with the deer-sheet population model (Gary M. Vecellio, Massachusetts Division of Fisheries and Wildlife, personal communication). Estimates of density inside and outside the sanctuary were obtained annually to represent the average fall deer density in the high-deer-density and low-deer-density areas, respectively.

Percentage estimates of vegetative cover were subject to arcsine transformation before analysis (Zar 1974:185–186). The effects of deer density and thinning on vegetation structure characteristics were compared with analysis of variance (ANOVA).

RESULTS

Overstory Structure

Stands in the high-deer-density area had fewer stems per hectare and a larger mean dbh than did stands in the low-deer-density area (Table 15.2; $F = 7.9$ for stems/ha, $F = 8.8$ for dbh, $P < 0.05$). The reduction in stem density occurred primarily among sapling size trees in the 5- and 10-cm-dbh classes. The reduction in the number of small trees in high-deer-density stands was responsible for the observed increase in mean stand dbh. As expected, thinning reduced both overstory stem density and basal area. Thinning did not affect mean stand dbh ($F = 0.1$, $P = 0.53$). There

TABLE 15.2

Overstory structure by deer density and silvicultural treatment

	UNTHINNED STANDS				THINNED STANDS		
Stand	Stem density (number/ha)	Basal area (m²/ha)	Dbh[a] (cm)	Stand	Stem density (number/ha)	Basal area (m²/ha)	Dbh[a] (cm)
	3–6 deer/km²				3–6 deer/km²		
1	1,209	21.1	11.9	5	671	16.1	12.7
2	984	27.9	15.7	6	1,109	15.9	9.3
3	1,112	24.0	12.3	7	997	13.1	9.8
4	2,029	25.0	10.7	8	725	17.7	12.3
$\bar{x}$	1,334	24.5	12.7	$\bar{x}$	876	15.7	11.0
	10–17 deer/km²				10–17 deer/km²		
9	935	20.8	13.3	13	900	18.4	12.7
10	1,216	21.7	11.1	14	313	14.4	20.4
11	873	23.7	15.3	15	392	16.4	18.8
12	873	25.0	15.3	16	976	13.6	9.8
$\bar{x}$	974	22.8	13.8	$\bar{x}$	645	15.7	15.4

Note: Data collected from 16 mature oak stands, Quabbin Reservation, central Massachusetts, 1986 and 1987.

[a] Diameter at breast height.

was no significant interaction between deer density and thinning on either tree density or mean stand dbh.

Seedling Density

High-deer-density stands had fewer tree seedlings of all species in two size classes than did low-deer-density stands ($F = 8.76$ for stems 30–99 cm tall, $F = 8.46$ for stems greater than 100 cm tall, $P < 0.05$). Thinning increased the abundance of tree seedlings in both size classes, regardless of deer density ($F = 13.28$ for stems 30–99 cm tall, $F = 7.92$ for stems greater 100 cm tall, $P < 0.05$). The interaction between deer density and thinning was not significant.

No oak seedlings taller than 100 cm were observed in the high-deer-density stands, and only two of eight of these stands had any oak seedlings 30–99 cm tall (Table 13.3; ANOVAs were not performed because of the

TABLE 15.3

Density of tree seedlings by deer density and silvicultural treatment

	UNTHINNED STANDS					THINNED STANDS			
	Density oak seedlings		Density all tree seedlings			Density oak seedlings		Density all tree seedlings	
Stand	30–99 cm	>100 cm	30–99 cm	>100 cm	Stand	30–99 cm	>100 cm	30–99 cm	>100 cm
		3–6 deer/km²					3–6 deer/km²		
1	1,167	83	12,083	4,833	5	6,250	8,083	13,167	16,583
2	750	0	6,667	917	6	750	167	21,917	32,416
3	167	0	2,500	2,250	7	4,250	2,333	24,417	16,833
4	833	0	2,833	167	8	583	83	12,083	4,583
$\bar{x}$	729	21	6,021	2,042	$\bar{x}$	2,958	2,667	17,896	17,604
		10–17 deer/km²					10–17 deer/km²		
9	167	0	5,250	1,250	13	917	0	8,250	2,250
10	0	0	4,250	1,667	14	0	0	917	83
11	0	0	83	0	15	0	0	11,833	583
12	0	0	166	0	16	0	0	9,500	4,250
$\bar{x}$	42	0	2,437	729	$\bar{x}$	229	0	7,625	1,792

Notes: Data collected from 16 mature oak stands, Quabbin Reservation, central Massachusetts, 1991. Density represents number of seedlings per hectare. "All tree seedlings" includes oak seedlings.

large number of empty data cells). Oak seedlings were not abundant in the unthinned, low-deer-density stands. Only one of four of these stands had oak seedlings taller than 100 cm. Oak seedlings were most abundant in the thinned, low-deer-density stands, but there were differences among stands within this treatment. Two stands (5 and 7) had abundant oak regeneration, whereas two others (6 and 8) had relatively few oak seedlings (Table 15.3).

Seedling Distribution

The distribution of seedlings within a stand is generally a better indicator of the ability of a stand to replace itself following disturbance than is mean density of seedlings. There was good distribution of seedlings only in the thinned, low-deer-density stands, in which 87–93% of the plots had seedlings 30–99 cm tall and 70–90% of the plots had a seedling greater than 100 cm tall (Table 15.4). Oaks were well distributed in two of these stands

TABLE 15.4
Distribution of tree seedlings by deer density and silvicultural treatment

	UNTHINNED STANDS					THINNED STANDS			
	Density oak seedlings		Density all tree seedlings			Density oak seedlings		Density all tree seedlings	
Stand	30–99 cm	>100 cm	30–99 cm	>100 cm	Stand	30–99 cm	>100 cm	30–99 cm	>100 cm
	3–6 deer/km²					3–6 deer/km²			
1	8	1	26	16	5	23	17	27	23
2	4	0	18	4	6	5	2	27	27
3	2	0	16	8	7	15	12	28	24
4	4	0	14	2	8	4	1	26	21
	10–17 deer/km²					10–17 deer/km²			
9	1	0	14	8	13	7	0	19	6
10	0	0	11	5	14	0	0	7	1
11	0	0	1	0	15	0	0	12	4
12	0	0	2	0	16	0	0	10	14

Notes: Data collected from 16 mature oak stands, Quabbin Reservation, central Massachusetts, 1991. Data represent number of 4-m² plots per stand (n = 30 plots/stand) that had at least one oak seedling or one seedling of any tree species.

(50–77% of the plots had seedlings 30–99 cm tall) and poorly distributed in two others (13–15% of the plots had seedlings 30–99 cm tall).

Unthinned, low-deer-density stands had a wide distribution of small seedlings of all species (47–87% of plots had at least one seedling 30–99 cm tall). Small oaks, however, were poorly distributed within these stands (7–27% of plots).

Tree seedlings of all species were poorly distributed in high-deer-density stands. Two unthinned, high-deer-density stands (3 and 4) had small seedlings on only 1 or 2 of 30 plots and no seedlings greater than 100 cm tall. Thinned stands had a more uniform distribution of seedlings (23–63% of plots had seedlings 30–99 cm tall and 3–47% had seedlings greater than 100 cm tall).

Deer Exclosures

Fencing excluded deer from one set of undergrowth sampling plots on the Quabbin Sanctuary from 1985 through 1991. Vegetation within these plots was not browsed for six growing seasons. Unfenced plots used for comparison were exposed to deer populations estimated at 10–17 deer/km^2 during these years (Table 15.5).

Excluding deer led to an increase in the density of tall seedlings (>100 cm) of all species (Table 15.6; $F = 7.44$, $P < 0.05$). The interaction

TABLE 15.5
Deer density on the Quabbin Sanctuary, central Massachusetts, 1983–1992

Year	Deer/km^2 $\bar{x}$	95% CI	Transects (n)	Effort (km)	Deer observed
1983	10.5	5.7–19.4	6	51	69
1984	13.0	8.7–19.5	6	94	157
1985	15.4	11.5–20.6	7	132	268
1986	16.6	9.2–30.1	7	126	257
1987	14.7	11.1–19.5	7	114	182
1988	9.8	6.0–16.1	7	249	312
1989	15.0	9.2–24.4	7	116	187
1990	14.6	10.4–20.4	7	123	211
1991	10.9	7.1–16.6	7	141	182
1992	10.8	6.6–17.6	7	126	172

Notes: Transects were searched in late October and early November each year. Density estimates were obtained using Distance software and the Fourier series estimator (Buckland et al. 1993).

TABLE 15.6

Density of tree seedlings on fenced and open plots

	UNTHINNED STANDS					THINNED STANDS			
	Density oak seedlings		Density all tree seedlings			Density oak seedlings		Density all tree seedlings	
Stand	30–99 cm	>100 cm	30–99 cm	>100 cm	Stand	30–99 cm	>100 cm	30–99 cm	>100 cm
	Fenced plots					*Fenced plots*			
9	750	0	12,917	3,167	13	7,750	1,167	34,917	7,333
10	167	0	5,583	1,667	14	583	0	8,750	4,667
11	917	0	10,000	500	15	750	0	17,083	14,167
12	83	0	917	83	16	1,083	0	13,167	5,583
$\bar{x}$	479	0	7,354	1,354	$\bar{x}$	2,542	292	18,479	7,938
	Open plots					*Open plots*			
9	167	0	5,250	1,250	13	917	0	8,250	2,250
10	0	0	4,250	1,667	14	0	0	917	83
11	0	0	83	0	15	0	0	11,833	583
12	0	0	167	0	16	0	0	9,500	4,250
$\bar{x}$	42	0	2,438	729	$\bar{x}$	229	0	7,625	1,792

Notes: Data collected from 16 mature oak stands, Quabbin Reservation, central Massachusetts, 1991. Density represents number of seedlings per hectare. "All tree seedlings" includes oak seedlings. Seedlings on open plots were exposed to deer populations of 10–17 deer/km^2. Deer were excluded from fenced plots, 1984–91 (six growing seasons).

between thinning and excluding deer had a significant effect on the density of small seedlings (30–99 cm), and small seedlings were most abundant in fenced plots in thinned stands (Table 15.6; $F = 7.47$, $P < 0.05$). Considering all species, tree seedlings were well distributed in fenced plots in thinned stands; 70–87% of plots had small seedlings and 53–60% plots had large seedlings (Table 15.7). Seedlings were poorly distributed in all other treatments.

Oak seedlings were more abundant in fenced than in open plots (Table 15.6). Small oak seedlings were found in fenced plots in all eight stands but in open plots in only two stands (Table 15.7). Oak seedlings had grown to a large size (>100 cm) and were reasonably well distributed in fenced plots only in one of the eight stands. Oak seedlings were small and poorly distributed in fenced plots in the other seven stands.

TABLE 15.7
Distribution of tree seedlings on fenced and open plots

	UNTHINNED STANDS					THINNED STANDS			
	Density oak seedlings		Density all tree seedlings			Density oak seedlings		Density all tree seedlings	
Stand	30–99 cm	>100 cm	30–99 cm	>100 cm	Stand	30–99 cm	>100 cm	30–99 cm	>100 cm
	Fenced plots					Fenced plots			
9	7	0	24	12	13	18	8	26	16
10	1	0	20	10	14	3	0	22	16
11	3	0	23	2	15	4	0	21	18
12	1	0	7	1	16	6	0	23	18
	Open plots					Open plots			
9	1	0	14	8	13	7	0	19	6
10	0	0	11	5	14	0	0	7	1
11	0	0	1	0	15	0	0	12	4
12	0	0	2	0	16	0	0	10	14

Notes: Data collected from 16 mature oak stands, Quabbin Reservation, central Massachusetts, 1991. Data represent number of 4-m^2 plots ($n = 30$ plots/stand) that had at least one oak seedling or one tree seedling of any tree species. Seedlings on open plots were exposed to deer populations of 10–17 deer/ km^2. Deer were excluded from fenced plots, 1984–91 (six growing seasons).

Seedling Species Composition

Importance values (IV) that reflect seedling density and distribution were calculated to suggest the composition of the forest that would emerge if the stands were regenerated in their present condition. A species' IV equals the sum of that species' frequency of occurrence and relative density divided by two. Frequency is equal to the percentage of plots with a given species. Relative density expresses the stem count for each species as a percentage of the sum of the stem counts for all species. Large seedlings are more likely to contribute to future stands than are small ones (Sander et al. 1984), so seedling counts were weighted by height class based on weighting factors developed by McWilliams et al. (1993) for forest regeneration in Pennsylvania. The weighting factors were 1 for stems 30–99 cm tall, 10 for stems 100–150 cm tall, and 25 for stems greater than 150 cm tall. Importance values were calculated by species and stand and then

TABLE 15.8

Mean importance values ($\pm s$) of tree seedlings

Tree species	Unthinned stands			Thinned stands		
	3–6 deer/km²	10–17 deer/km²	Deer excluded	3–6 deer/km²	10–17 deer/km²	Deer excluded
Red maple (*Acer rubrum*)	25.3 ± 13.4	14.9 ± 23.5	28.8 ± 25.9	28.1 ± 8.0	3.3 ± 4.6	15.8 ± 12.0
Sugar maple (*Acer saccharum*)	12.6 ± 25.2	—	—	—	—	0.3 ± 0.5
Serviceberry (*Amelanchier* spp.)	5.3 ± 7.9	—	2.3 ± 2.7	2.4 ± 1.0	1.4 ± 2.8	3.0 ± 2.7
Yellow birch (*Betula alleghaniensis*)	—	—	—	2.0 ± 3.3	5.6 ± 7.1	7.9 ± 9.6
Sweet birch (*Betula lenta*)	7.3 ± 6.4	50.3 ± 38.1	22.0 ± 30.9	19.4 ± 21.2	50.8 ± 39.5	39.3 ± 21.5
Paper birch (*Betula papyrifera*)	—	—	0.6 ± 1.2	2.4 ± 1.6	2.4 ± 4.8	3.5 ± 4.7
Gray birch (*Betula populifolia*)	—	—	—	0.8 ± 1.1	1.5 ± 2.9	1.5 ± 0.6
Hickory (*Carya* spp.)	0.8 ± 1.6	1.0 ± 2.0	1.0 ± 1.2	1.2 ± 1.0	—	0.2 ± 0.4
American chestnut (*Castanea dentata*)	15.0 ± 17.4	6.7 ± 13.5	10.0 ± 17.9	10.6 ± 7.3	6.1 ± 9.0	0.4 ± 0.5
American beech (*Fagus grandifolia*)	0.7 ± 1.5	0.9 ± 1.8	3.1 ± 6.2	0.2 ± 0.4	—	—
White ash (*Fraxinus americana*)	1.5 ± 1.8	—	1.1 ± 2.2	1.0 ± 1.6	—	2.5 ± 3.1
White pine (*Pinus strobus*)	0.5 ± 1.0	—	19.7 ± 19.4	2.5 ± 1.1	20.9 ± 24.2	10.0 ± 6.0
Big tooth aspen (*Populus grandidentata*)	—	—	—	0.2 ± 0.4	—	—
Pin cherry (*Prunus pensylvanica*)	—	—	—	—	—	0.2 ± 0.4
Black cherry (*Prunus serotina*)	13.2 ± 6.0	25.0 ± 50.0	3.7 ± 6.6	8.3 ± 7.1	4.8 ± 9.6	3.1 ± 2.7
White oak (*Quercus alba*)	3.8 ± 5.3	1.2 ± 2.3	5.2 ± 4.0	6.3 ± 6.7	2.1 ± 4.1	3.4 ± 3.7
Scarlet oak (*Quercus coccinea*)	—	—	—	0.5 ± 1.0	—	—
Red oak (*Quercus rubra*)	9.1 ± 3.5	—	2.2 ± 2.6	12.9 ± 13.8	1.1 ± 2.1	5.8 ± 4.5
Black oak (*Quercus velutina*)	—	—	0.3 ± 0.6	0.9 ± 1.8	—	1.8 ± 3.0
Sassafras (*Sassafras albidum*)	—	—	—	0.2 ± 0.4	—	—
Eastern hemlock (*Tsuga canadensis*)	4.8 ± 5.5	—	—	0.2 ± 0.3	—	1.4 ± 2.4

Note: Data collected from 16 mature oak stands, Quabbin Reservation, central Massachusetts, 1991.

averaged for the four stands in each treatment. Mean seedling IVs are shown in Table 15.8 for six combinations of thinning and deer density, including fenced plots from which deer were excluded. The standard deviations suggest great variation in the importance of individual species among stands within a treatment, but some patterns are evident among the treatments.

Oaks (including red, white [*Q. alba*], black [*Q. velutina*], and scarlet [*Q. coccinea*]) are most important in thinned, low- deer-density stands (combined IV = 19%). Oaks are also well represented in unthinned, low-deer-density stands (IV = 13%). Oaks are poorly represented in high-deer-density stands (IV < 3.2%) and intermediate in importance in plots from which deer had been excluded for six growing seasons (IV = 7.4% unthinned, 9.2% thinned).

Regeneration in the unthinned, low-deer-density stands is dominated by red maple, American chestnut *(Castanea dentata)*, black cherry *(Prunus serotina)*, sugar maple *(Acer saccharum)*, red oak, and eastern hemlock (IV = 80%). In thinned, low-deer-density stands the most important regeneration includes red maple, sweet birch *(Betula lenta)*, red oak, American chestnut, black cherry, and white oak. Regeneration in high-deer-density stands was dominated by sweet birch, which had an IV of 50% in both thinned and unthinned stands. The important regeneration in unthinned, high-deer-density stands included sweet birch, black cherry, and red maple (IV = 90%), and in thinned, high-deer-density stands it included sweet birch, white pine, American chestnut, and yellow birch *(Betula alleghaniensis)*. The regeneration in fenced plots in these stands was dominated by red maple, sweet birch, and white pine (IV = 70% unthinned, 65% thinned).

Seedling species richness was greater in low-deer- than in high-deer-density stands. The numbers of seedling species encountered in each stand category were 19 (thinned, low deer density); 17 (thinned, fenced); 13 (unthinned, low deer density); 13 (unthinned, fenced); 11 (thinned, high deer density); and 7 (unthinned, high deer density).

DISCUSSION

Feeding by white-tailed deer has interrupted the sequence of stand development in the Quabbin Sanctuary. Maturing stands are not passing from the stem exclusion phase to the understory reinitiation phase and are not developing understories with adequate numbers of seedlings and saplings. The lack of adequate understory development precludes the use of silviculture to initiate new stands or new age classes within existing stands.

The paucity of seedlings will also prevent these stands from maturing into an old growth condition (sensu Oliver and Larson 1990:153).

Browsing by deer seems to be directing succession on the Quabbin Sanctuary toward parklike or savanna conditions. Trees that die are replaced by herbaceous species and shrubs that are unpalatable to deer. Natural and human disturbance accelerates the process of savanna formation. The largest area of open land on the sanctuary (919 ha, 4%) consists of nonforested wetlands created by beaver *(Castor canadensis)* activity and maintained by deer browsing (MDC 1994:143). Reduced tree and seedling density observed in unthinned, high-deer-density stands suggests that succession toward savanna is also occurring in stands that have been free from disturbance.

Outside the sanctuary, where deer numbers have ranged from 1 to 6 deer/km² throughout this century, stands are following the expected sequence of development. Silvicultural treatments designed to improve stand quality have increased seedling abundance and accelerated the process of understory reinitiation. The numbers and distribution of seedlings in thinned stands are sufficient to ensure the regeneration of these stands following either silvicultural treatment or natural disturbance.

Deer populations and vegetation have not reached an equilibrium relationship in the sanctuary during the more than 50 years since hunting has been prohibited. Deer numbers have fluctuated while forested habitats have changed continuously toward savanna conditions. The lack of a deer–habitat equilibrium may be partly explained by the natural maturation of the forest and the relative importance of acorns and undergrowth in determining carrying capacity for deer (K of the logistic equation; McCullough 1979:149–155).

Theoretically, browse and forage supplies should have remained stable and mast production should have increased steadily since the sanctuary was established in 1938. The youngest stands originated shortly after 1938, and since then less than 1% of the area has been regenerated to new stands. Today, half of the forest is more than 90 years old. Acorn production begins when oaks are about 40 years old and increases as trees increase in diameter (Goodrum et al. 1971). The oldest stands had just reached seed-bearing age in 1938. Since then, acorn production should have increased as seed-producing stands matured and younger stands attained seed-bearing age. Over the whole area, browse and forage production should have remained stable because declines in browse production as young stands entered the stem exclusion phase should have been offset by increased production as older stands entered the understory reinitiation phase.

Once oak stands begin producing seed, acorn production often exceeds winter browse production (Liscinsky 1984). I measured acorn crops in eight oak stands on the Quabbin from 1989 to 1993 and observed mean oven-dry weights of sound acorns ranging from 7 to 680 kg/ha. Production of sound acorns exceeded 100 kg/ha in 4 of 5 years. Comparable acorn production has been reported for Missouri (60–800 kg/ha; Christisen and Kearby 1984:9) and Virginia (3–396 kg/ha; McShea and Schwede 1993). Where acorns and browse have been measured on the same sites, mean annual acorn production has been 3–10 times greater than mean winter browse production (Watts 1964; Segelquist and Green 1968; Rogers et al. 1990). In the absence of canopy disturbance, browse production is relatively constant from year to year, and acorn production is erratic (Segelquist and Green 1968; Rogers et al. 1990).

Annual fluctuations in acorn crops may be the most important factor preventing an equilibrium relationship between deer and vegetation on the sanctuary. Acorn crops are independent of deer density, and carrying capacity varies with the size of the acorn crop. Competition for food acts to regulate deer populations, and deer populations adjust to a constantly changing carrying capacity determined by mast crops rather than a relatively stable point determined by winter forage availability. Deer prefer acorns to most other foods in oak forests and generally consume woody browse in fall and winter only when the acorn supply is depleted (Wentworth et al. 1991). Acorn crops on the sanctuary seem to be sufficient to maintain deer populations that can consume most of the growth of palatable woody species during the growing season or in winters when acorns are unavailable.

CONCLUSIONS

The interactions among deer populations, acorn crops, and seedling populations have important implications for managing oak ecosystems. First, the average carrying capacity of oak forests probably increases as they mature from seedling to old growth because older forests have an abundance of mast-producing trees and a well-developed understory. The variance of carrying capacity, however, also increases as oak forests mature because of the erratic nature of seed production.

Second, the regeneration of oak forests depends on developing vigorous oak seedlings in the understory before the overstory is removed (Crow 1988). Oak seedlings that have survived in the understory for several years and have well-developed root systems are most capable of competing with seedlings of more rapidly growing species when the canopy is removed. This type of oak regeneration usually develops over several decades. Thus, oak seedlings must survive deer browsing during the relatively long stage of understory reinitiation.

In oak forests in central Massachusetts, deer populations of 10–17 deer/km² interrupted the process of understory reinitiation and prevented regeneration. At these deer densities, maturing oak stands developed an open, parklike structure with poorly developed understory and midstory layers. Future stands will be dominated by fewer species, notably white pine, red maple, and sweet birch. Oaks and other species that are common now will be less abundant in the future. If these oak forests are to be managed to maintain the current array of species and levels of diversity, deer populations will have to be reduced below the recent densities of 10–17 deer/km². In areas of the forest where deer numbers have been limited to 3–6 deer/km², understory vegetation is abundant and diverse. At these lower deer densities, stands follow the expected sequence of development and regenerate when given the appropriate silvicultural treatment. Thus, deer densities of 3–6 deer/km² have been compatible with maintaining these oak forests and deer densities above 10 deer/km² have not.

REFERENCES CITED

Alverson, W. S., D. M. Waller, and S. L. Solheim. 1988. Forests too deer: Edge effects in northern Wisconsin. Conservation Biology 2:348–358.

Braun, E. L. 1950. Deciduous Forests of Eastern North America. The Blakeston Co., Philadelphia, PA.

Buckland, S. T., D. R. Anderson, K. P. Burnham, and J. L. Laake. 1993. Distance Sampling: Estimating Abundance of Biological Populations. Chapman and Hall, London.

Burnham, K. P., D. R. Anderson, and J. L. Laake. 1980. Estimation of Density from Line Transect Sampling of Biological Populations. Wildlife Monographs 72, The Wildlife Society, Bethesda, MD.

Christisen, D. M., and W. H. Kearby. 1984. Mast Measurement and Production in Missouri (with Special Reference to Acorns). Missouri Department of Conservation, Terrestrial Series 13, Jefferson City.

Crow, T. R. 1988. Reproductive mode and mechanisms for self-replacement of northern red oak. Forest Science 34:19–40.

Eyre, F. H., ed. 1980. Forest Cover Types of the United States and Canada. Society of American Foresters, Washington.

Foster, D. R. 1992. Land-use history (1730–1990) and vegetation dynamics in central New England, USA. Journal of Ecology 80:753–772.

Goodrum, P. D., V. H. Reid, and C. E. Boyd. 1971. Acorn yields, characteristics, and management criteria of oaks for wildlife. Journal of Wildlife Management 35:520–532.

Healy, W. M., and C. J. E. Welsh. 1992. Evaluating line transects to monitor gray squirrel populations. Wildlife Society Bulletin 20:83–90.

Hibbs, D. E., and W. R. Bentley. 1983. A Management Guide for Oak in New England. Connecticut Cooperative Extension Service, University of Connecticut, Storrs.

Hosley, N. W., and R. K. Ziebarth. 1935. Some winter relations of the white-tailed deer to the forests of north central Massachusetts. Ecology 4:535–553.

Liscinsky, S. 1984. Tree seed production. Pennsylvania Game News 55 (8): 23–25.

McCullough, D. R. 1979. The George Reserve Deer Herd. University of Michigan Press, Ann Arbor.

McDonough, J. J., and J. J. Pottie. 1979. A successful antlerless deer hunting permit system in Massachusetts. Transactions Northeast Section Wildlife Society 36:110–119.

McShea, W. J., and G. Schwede. 1993. Variable acorn crops: Responses of white-tailed deer and other mast consumers. Journal of Mammalogy 74:999–1006.

McWilliams, W. H., S. L. Stout, T. W. Bowersox, and L. H. McCormick. 1993. Can we regenerate Pennsylvania's hardwood forests? Pages 23–36 in Penn's Woods—Change and Challenge. (J. C. Finley and S. B. Jones, eds.) Proceedings of the Penn State Forest Resources Issues Conference, Pennsylvania State University, University Park.

MDC (Metropolitan District Commission). 1994. MDC Land Management Plan, Quabbin Watershed. MDC, Division of Watershed Management, Boston.

Naiman, R. J. 1988. Animal influences on ecosystem dynamics. Bioscience 38: 750–752.

Oliver, C. D. and B. C. Larson. 1990. Forest Stand Dynamics. McGraw-Hill, New York.

Roach, B. A., and S. F. Gingrich. 1968. Even-Aged Silviculture for Upland Central Hardwoods. U.S. Forest Service, Agriculture Handbook 355, Washington.

Rogers, M. J., L. K. Halls, and J. G. Dickson. 1990. Deer habitat in the Ozark Forests of Arkansas. U.S. Forest Service, Southern Forest Experiment Station, Research Paper SO-259, New Orleans, LA.

Sander, I. L., P. S. Johnson, and R. Rogers. 1984. Evaluating oak advance repro duction in the Missouri Ozarks. U.S. Forest Service, North Central Forest Experiment Station, Research Paper NC-251, St. Paul, MN.

Segelquist, C. A., and W. E. Green. 1968. Deer foods in four Ozark forest types. Journal of Wildlife Management 32:330–337.

Shaw, S. P., and C. L. McLaughlin. 1951. The management of white-tailed deer in Massachusetts. Bureau of Wildlife Research and Management, Research Bulletin 13, Boston.

Smith, D. M. 1986. The Practice of Silviculture. 8th edition. John Wiley and Sons, New York.

Trumbull, V. L., E. J. Zielinski, and E. C. Aharrah. 1989. The impact of deer browsing on the Allegheny forest type. Northern Journal of Applied Forestry 6: 162–165.

Watts, C. R. 1964. Forage preference of captive deer while free ranging in a mixed oak forest. Pennsylvania Cooperative Wildlife Research Unit, Paper Number 112, University Park.

Wentworth, J. M., A. S. Johnson, P. E. Hale, and K. E. Kammermeyer. 1991. Seasonal use of clearcuts and food plots by white-tailed deer in the southern Appalachians. Proceedings of the Annual Conference Southeastern Association of Fisheries and Wildlife Agencies 44 (1990): 215–223.

Zar, J. H. 1974. Biostatistical Analysis. Prentice-Hall, Englewood Cliffs, NJ.

16 Deer and Ecosystem Management

DAVID S. DECALESTA

Within the last decade, managers of public and private forestlands have contemplated managing forest resources in ways that address the desired (future) condition (outcomes) of these resources (Society of American Foresters 1993), which include all plant and animal species, noncommercial as well as commercial. Such management necessitates dealing with ecosystems and dovetails with an emerging management concept identified as "ecosystem management" (Society of American Foresters 1993; Grumbine 1994; Salwasser 1994).

According to Grumbine (1994), ecosystem management integrates knowledge of ecological relationships within a sociopolitical values framework. The goal of ecosystem management is to protect native ecosystem integrity over the long term. Grumbine (1994) identified a dominant theme of ecosystem management as that of managing to preserve diversity of communities (species and populations) and ecosystems as well as ecological patterns and processes. Such management will shape the future age, structure, species composition, and abundance of forest resources, which together constitute forest condition.

Ecosystem diversity and ecological patterns and processes constitute ecosystem integrity. Ecosystem integrity and forest condition form the building blocks, or biological components, of ecosystem management as defined by Grumbine (1994). These biological components of ecosystem management are affected by weather and by patterns and composition of vegetation that occur within landscapes. Weather and composition and pattern of vegetation change over time as does the spatial arrangement of vegetative patterns. Human sociological, economic, and political events influence, for example, harvest of timber and subsequent landscape patterns of vegetation. Forest health factors (insect and disease) and browsing by deer also affect the landscape pattern and composition of vegetation. Interactions among these factors, and the effects of these interactions on landscape patterns of vegetation, constitute ecosystem management contexts that influence the status of ecosystem components.

Ecosystem management is defined as a strategy by which, in aggregate, the full array of forest values and functions is maintained at the landscape level over long periods of time (Society of American Foresters 1993; Irland et al. 1994), suggesting the importance of spatial and temporal scales.

Definitions of ecosystem management do not include identification of plant or animal species that can affect ecosystem management components profoundly enough to be identified as keystone species, which by Hunter's (1990:240–241) definition includes species upon which the integrity of whole ecosystems rely. In this context, McShea and Rappole (1992) identified the white-tailed deer as a keystone species. The premise of this chapter is that the effect of white-tailed deer, a keystone species, on vegetation can be of a magnitude sufficient to influence (1) ecosystem integrity, (2) future condition of forest resources, and, (3) the conduct and outcome of ecosystem management.

CONCEPTUAL FRAMEWORK

The interrelationships among ecosystem management components and contexts and deer impact may be expressed by a flow diagram (Figure 16.1). Ecosystem management contexts influence ecosystem management components as mediated by deer impact. Marquis et al. (1992) and Redding (1995) defined deer impact as a joint function of deer density and forage availability, suggesting that as forage availability increases, the impact of deer on forest resources decreases. Deer density is affected primarily by mortality associated with winter severity, hunting harvest, and deer–vehicle collisions (Witmer and deCalesta 1992).

Forage availability and deer density are affected by landscape patterns of vegetation and deer harvest as they vary through space and time. Severe winter can limit the ability of deer to move to find forage under deep snow and can induce winter mortality. Natural (windstorm) and

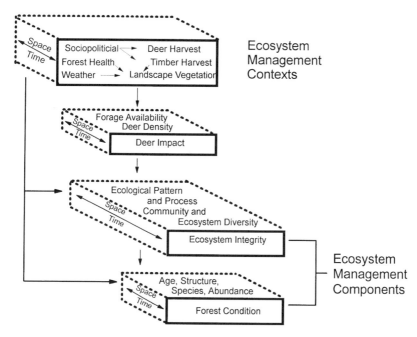

FIGURE 16.1. Relationships among deer impact and ecosystem management components and contexts.

human-induced (timber harvest) disturbance creates patterns and amounts of forest openings that produce deer forage. Mortality of trees from insect and disease organisms (forest health factors) can result in increased deer forage production by increasing the amount of light reaching the forest floor. Social and political values concerning use of natural resources affect timber and deer harvests.

Factors that affect forage availability and deer density vary through time and space, creating stochasticities of forage availability and deer density that are integrated as deer impact. Deer impact, in turn varying through space and time, contributes to stochasticities of ecosystem integrity and forest condition. Managing for deer impact on ecosystem management requires an understanding of the relationships among deer impact and ecosystem management components and contexts.

The following discussion of the effects of white-tailed deer on ecosystem management is based on research conducted in northern hardwood forest type in northwestern Pennsylvania at the Warren Laboratory, Northeastern Forest Experiment Station, U.S. Forest Service. The effect of varying white-tailed deer densities on regeneration of woody vegetation and on songbird and herbaceous communities was evaluated during 1980–91 (Tilghman 1989; deCalesta 1992, 1994; Jones et al. 1993). In the 10-year study, deer density was controlled within four 65-ha fenced enclosures and optimal timber harvest levels (10% clear-cutting, 30% thinning) were practiced.

DEER AND ECOSYSTEM MANAGEMENT CONTEXTS

Biological Contexts That Affect Deer Impact

Presettlement forests of northwestern Pennsylvania were characterized by large areas of maturing timber and large and small openings created by natural disturbance (e.g., hurricanes, tornadoes, fire, and ice storms). These openings contained vegetation in various seres from regenerating to subclimax and climax communities (Braun 1964; Marquis 1975; de-Calesta 1989). Young timber stands approaching canopy closure supported understories of herbaceous and shrubby species, but even mature stands (characterized by uncut, virgin forests in the 1920s) were endowed with these plants (Lutz 1930; Bjorkbom and Larson 1977; Whitney 1984). Climax and subclimax forests probably dominated, but areas from less than an acre to thousands of acres contained early successional vegetation because of local and regional disturbances. This produced a "landscape of patches at different ages and stages of succession rather than a uniform climax forest" (Millers et al. 1989).

These patches created a landscape of deer forage that increased and decreased in quality and quantity in relation to the amount of light reaching the forest floor. No quantitative data exist relative to associated pre-European settlement deer densities, but McCabe and McCabe (1984) estimated white-tailed deer densities of 3–4 deer/km^2 within the range of the species in the eastern United States. Alverson et al. (1988) suggested that white-tailed deer densities may have approximated 4 deer/km^2 in undisturbed eastern hemlock *(Tsuga canadensis)* forests in Wisconsin. Deer density likely was affected by available forage in extensive tracts of mature forest and by predation (wolf [*Canis* spp.], mountain lion [*Felis concolor*], and Native Americans) (Marquis 1975; McCabe and McCabe 1984; Ellingwood and Caturano 1988; Witmer and deCalesta 1992).

By the end of the nineteenth century much of Pennsylvania's forests had been completely cut over, and the white-tailed deer herd nearly eliminated by unregulated harvest (Redding 1995). By the early twentieth century, large amounts of deer forage were produced by the extensive timber harvest, deer hunting was prohibited, and major deer predators were extirpated from Pennsylvania. The result was an irruption of the deer population from 1907 to 1939: deer density exceeded 20 deer/km^2 in northwestern Pennsylvania (Clepper 1931; Redding 1995). The expanding deer herd depleted its food supply and, during a series of hard winters in the late 1930s, declined to around 4–6 deer/km^2 by the early 1940s. Coincidentally, timber harvest began anew in the 1950s as forests harvested 50–80 years earlier approached commercial maturity. The deer population again increased, averaging over 12 deer/km^2 in the ensuing 40 years, even after sustaining a population decline following a series of harsh winters in 1978–79 (Figure 16.2; Redding 1995).

Hough (1965) and Whitney (1984) documented the loss of herbaceous and shrub species from unmanaged mature forests in northwestern Pennsylvania since the 1930s and attributed the declines to herbivory by deer. Composition of understory vegetation shifted from shrubs and herbs to grasses and ferns during this period (Marquis and Grisez 1978; Horsley and Marquis 1983), and species richness and abundance of seedlings of woody plants were reduced.

Thus, biological contexts of ecosystem management have shifted qualitatively and quantitatively since pre-European settlement and most

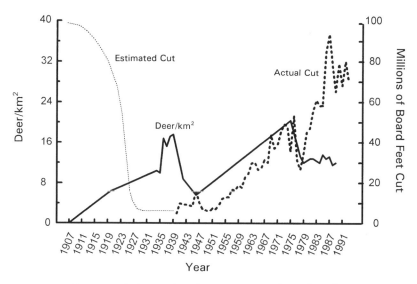

FIGURE 16.2. Deer population and timber cutting trends on the Allegheny National Forest, Pennsylvania, 1907–1991 (from Redding 1995; used with permission of author).

appreciably during the twentieth century. Deer densities have been higher, and understory vegetation has shifted from a diverse assemblage of woody and herbaceous plants to a reduced number of species dominated by fern, grass, and woody vegetation not preferred by deer. Social and political contexts, in the form of values and economies assigned to resources, have been defined by the above biological contexts, again most appreciably during the twentieth century.

Social and Political Contexts That Affect Deer Impact

Deer are valued positively as an economic and recreational resource. Deer are valued negatively as an agent of significant damage to forest and agricultural interests and to private citizens in the form of deer–vehicle collisions and depredation of urban–suburban gardens and landscaping (Witmer and deCalesta 1992).

Over 400,000 deer were harvested annually in Pennsylvania over 1988–93: average statewide posthunt deer density was 11 deer/km^2; average harvest level was 6 deer/km^2 (W. Palmer, Pennsylvania Game Commission, personal communication). Posthunt deer density has been greater than 12 deer/km^2 in northwestern Pennsylvania since the late 1920s (excepting two notable crashes; Redding 1995; Figure 16.2), and the last three generations of deer hunters have come to expect these deer densities and associated harvests as normal and sustainable. Hunters have numbered over one million in Pennsylvania for the last three decades (Witmer and deCalesta 1992) and represent a significant lobbying force for maintaining these high deer densities and harvests.

Income generated by deer hunting activities in Pennsylvania amounts to at least one billion dollars annually (Kosack 1991). Both business and hunting interests have benefited from the high deer densities and harvests experienced over the last 70 years; these interests exert considerable pressure to maintain posthunt deer densities in excess of 11 deer/km^2.

Since the second-growth forest in Pennsylvania became commercially mature in the late 1950s, there has been an increasing amount of timber harvested (Redding 1995; Figure 16.2). Expectations of the industry are that timber harvests can be sustained at a level comparable to that of the past decades. However, timber stands cannot be harvested if advance regeneration is inadequate to produce replacement trees. McWilliams et al. (1993) reported that only 4–20% of forested lands surveyed across Pennsylvania in 1990 had advance regeneration sufficient to provide adequate regeneration of diverse woody species under conditions ranging from unfavorable to favorable. Overabundant white-tailed deer populations were hypothesized as the primary cause for failure of advance regeneration. In 1994 only 33% of maturing forestland within the Allegheny National Forest carried sufficient advance regeneration to permit removal of over-story timber with reasonable expectation of successful regeneration (L. DeMarco, Allegheny National Forest, Warren, Pennsylvania, personal communication).

Thus, management of deer and timber has been driven by social and political values and has resulted in creation of deer densities and forage production over the last 70 years that have exceeded levels created by natural disturbance and deer mortality. Changes in species composition of floral communities have been associated with these changes in deer density and forage production.

DEER AND ECOSYSTEM MANAGEMENT COMPONENTS

Deer Impact on Process: Regeneration

When overstory forest trees are removed by natural processes (e.g., fire, windstorm, or insect and disease mortality) or by timber harvest, the succeeding forest is promulgated by seeds and vegetative reproduction from overstory trees. Seedlings constituting the advance regeneration are present at the time of overstory removal and form the nucleus of the emerging timber stand. Failure of advance regeneration (inadequate seedling abundance, height, and species richness) following timber harvest in the mid-1950s in northwestern Pennsylvania prompted research to determine causes of the failure (Tilghman 1989; Redding 1995).

This 10-year study in northwestern Pennsylvania demonstrated that species richness, abundance (expressed as percent plots fully stocked), and height of saplings (small trees with diameter at breast height less than 2.5–14 cm) declined significantly once deer density exceeded 7.9 deer/km^2 (Tilghman 1989; deCalesta 1992). At deer densities greater than 7.9 deer/km^2, seedlings of six woody tree species were missing or prevented by deer browsing from becoming incorporated into the overstory (deCalesta 1992). As deer densities exceeded 7.9 deer/km^2, clear-cut sites approached monocultures of black cherry *(Prunus serotina);* on uncut sites, American beech *(Fagus grandifolia)* and striped maple *(Acer pensylvanicum)* dominated (Tilghman 1989). Deer negatively affected the regeneration process and future overstory when populations exceeded estimated pre-European settlement deer density (Tilghman 1989; deCalesta 1992).

Deer Impact on Community

SONGBIRDS   Deer browsing can affect vegetation that songbirds use for foraging surfaces, escape from predators, and nesting. By significantly reducing the height of woody vegetation, white-tailed deer affected habitat for songbirds that fed, nested, and sought cover in the 0–7.6-m height interval (deCalesta 1994). The bird community that uses this intermediate foliage canopy exhibited a significant reduction in species richness and abundance when deer density exceeded 7.9 deer/km², and five songbird species were no longer observed on study sites. Some songbird species that remained at higher deer densities did not exhibit reduced abundance; they increased in dominance as abundance of other species declined.

HERBS AND SHRUBS   Scientists noted that species richness and abundance of herbaceous and shrubby vegetation began to decline in northwestern Pennsylvania in the 1920s (Hough 1965; Whitney 1984), when white-tailed deer density exceeded approximately 7.9 deer/km² (Redding 1995). Species richness and abundance (expressed as percent ground cover) of shrubs and herbaceous plants (excepting ferns, grasses, and mosses) were negatively affected when deer density exceeded 3.7 deer/km² (Jones et al. 1993). Two shrub species and one herbaceous species disappeared when deer density exceeded 7.9 deer/km².

Species composition and abundance of plants in the herb–shrub layer shifted when deer densities exceeded 7.9 deer/km²: percent ground cover of ferns, grasses, and mosses increased while that of shrubs and other herbs decreased (deCalesta 1992). Many herb and shrub species noted in earlier (pre-1950; Jennings 1953) surveys were not found (deCalesta 1992), having been eliminated by 70 years of browsing pressure by deer populations in excess of 7.9 deer/km². Species richness and abundance of plants in the herb and shrub communities, like that of songbirds, declined when deer population density exceeded estimated pre-European settlement density.

Deer Effects on Biodiversity

Most definitions of biodiversity include variety of genetic material within species, variety of species, and variety of communities over time and space (Thorne et al. 1995). Reduction of abundance of individuals within a species and reduction of number of species when deer density exceeds 7.9 deer/km², as documented in the studies cited above, results in reduction and elimination of genetic material. Three communities (songbird, herb and shrub, and tree) were affected by deer, exhibiting changes in species composition, dominance, and abundance within communities. The loss of some species (herbs and shrubs) occurred over approximately 70 years, reflecting a temporal aspect of biodiversity.

Deer Effects on Forest Condition

The effect of deer on forest condition is largely a function of how deer influence biodiversity—the abundance and richness of the various species composing the many forest communities, floral and faunal—over time and space. Deer impact is a long-term influence: species richness and abundance of tree seedlings determine the composition and structure of stands that develop following natural or human disturbances and that will persist for decades or longer. Characteristics of understory vegetation (species richness and abundance and vertical habitat structure) and associated wildlife communities are likewise affected by deer and by the nature of the overstory vegetation as influenced by deer.

Unmanaged mature forests in northwestern Pennsylvania consist primarily of eastern hemlock, American beech, and sugar maple *(Acer saccharum)* (Braun 1964; Marquis 1975). Retention of these forests depends on continual seed supply and regeneration success of trees. Deer can prevent successful regeneration of eastern hemlock by eliminating seedlings in the understory (Alverson et al. 1988). Beech bark disease, an introduced scale insect and fungus complex, can eliminate American beech from the overstory (Houston 1975) and remove it as a reliable seed supplier. Sugar maple decline syndrome is associated with a general failure of sugar maple regeneration in parts of northwestern Pennsylvania (R. White, Allegheny National Forest, personal communication). It is possible that deer can eliminate eastern hemlock regeneration and that overstory American beech and sugar maple trees may become unreliable seedling producers as a result of disease and parasitic organisms. This scenario could result in no replacement of eastern hemlock, American beech, or sugar maple trees to provide the seed source for future forests. The resulting forest might then be populated by species resistant to deer browsing (black cherry and striped maple) or others not affected by the disease and parasitic organisms. Composition, structure, and age of such forests, as affected by deer, may be quite different from past and present forests. Wildlife communities associated with these deer-affected forests may also differ.

Second-growth Allegheny hardwood forests in northwestern Pennsylvania, characterized by black cherry, American beech, eastern hemlock, red maple *(Acer rubrum)*, white ash *(Fraxinus americana)*, cucumbertree *(Magnolia acuminata)*, yellow poplar *(Liriodendron tulipifera)*, and black *(Betula lenta)* and yellow *(Betula alleghaniensis)* birch overstories, could regenerate to near monocultures of black cherry with remnants of red maple, American beech, and striped maple if deer browsing were sufficient to prevent establishment of tree species preferentially browsed by deer. Understories in old- and second-growth stands could be composed primarily of ferns, grasses, mosses, and seedlings of American beech, striped maple, and black cherry.

CONCLUSIONS

The ecosystem management scenarios presented in this chapter were developed within the context of deer density and forage availability found in northwestern Pennsylvania where forage production occurs primarily as a function of logging and natural disturbance. Other places in the Northeast, notably national parks and other deer refugia (Storm et al. 1989; Palmer et al., Chapter 10), have considerably higher deer densities (25 – 62 deer/km²) and greater forage production resulting from interspersion of old and current agricultural and forest lands. Deer densities higher than those of pre-European settlement may be required to produce negative effects on ecosystem management components because of the counter-effect of greater deer forage provided by agricultural fields. Unfortunately, studies that relate deer impact to ecosystem management components within agricultural–forested landscapes are lacking.

Providing for sustained ecosystem integrity and future forest condition will require understanding and proactive management of deer impact. Studies in northwestern Pennsylvania provide evidence of the pervasive effect of deer on ecological integrity and forest condition under ecosystem management contexts that are typical of heavily forested ecosystems.

This chapter demonstrates how deer impact, as influenced by ecosystem management contexts, can affect ecosystem integrity and forest condition. Passive, reactive deer management may well result in continued reductions in species richness and abundance and shifts in composition of plant and animal communities, effectively thwarting the main goal of ecosystem management (preservation of ecosystem integrity). Future conduct of ecosystem management must incorporate proactive management activities that produce benign rather than negative deer impact, either by reducing deer density, increasing forage availability, or integrating both activities.

If increasing forage availability for deer is chosen as an ecosystem management activity, it must be conducted in a manner that does not jeopardize other elements of ecosystem integrity across temporal and spatial scales (e.g., increasing timber harvest or agricultural development must not result in forest fragmentation or proceed at a rate that precludes sustained yields of timber and other forest resources). Consideration should be given to adjusting deer densities, possibly in concert with increasing forage availability, to levels compatible with sustaining ecosystem integrity and to retaining options for producing a variety of desired forest conditions. Practitioners of ecosystem management, where it incorporates activities designed to reduce deer impact, must be prepared to address and counter political and social pressures that will resist such change. Responsible management of deer and forest resources will require that deer impact be investigated and quantified over a range of ecosystem management contexts.

REFERENCES CITED

Alverson, W. W., D. M. Waller, and S. L. Solheim. 1988. Forests too deer: Edge effects in northern Wisconsin. Conservation Biology 2:348–358.

Bjorkbom, J. C., and R. G. Larson. 1977. The Tionesta scenic and research natural areas. U.S. Forest Service General Technical Report NE-31.

Braun, E. L. 1964. Deciduous Forests of Eastern North America. Hafner Publishing Co., New York.

Clepper, H. F. 1931. The deer problem in the forests of Pennsylvania. Pennsylvania Department of Forestry and Waters Bulletin 50, Harrisburg, PA.

deCalesta, D. S. 1989. Even-aged forest management and wildlife populations. Pages 210–224 in Symposium on Effects of Forest Management on Wildlife. (R. H. Yahner and M. Brittingham, eds.) Pennsylvania State University Press, University Park.

deCalesta, D. S. 1992. Impact of deer on species diversity of Allegheny hardwood stands. Proceedings of the Northeastern Weed Science Society Abstracts 46: 135.

deCalesta, D. S. 1994. Impact of white-tailed deer on songbirds within managed forests in Pennsylvania. Journal of Wildlife Management 58:711–718.

Ellingwood, M. R., and S. L. Caturano. 1988. An Evaluation of Deer Management Options. Connecticut Department of Environmental Protection, Wildlife Bureau, Hartford.

Grumbine, R. E. 1994. What is ecosystem management? Conservation Biology 8: 27–38.

Horsley, S. B., and D. A. Marquis. 1983. Interference by weeds and deer with Allegheny hardwood reproduction. Canadian Journal of Forest Research 13: 61–69.

Hough, A. F. 1965. A twenty-year record of understory vegetational change in a virgin Pennsylvania forest. Ecology 46:370–373.

Houston, D. R. 1975. Beech bark disease. Journal of Forestry 73:660–663.

Hunter, M. L. 1990. Wildlife, Forests, and Forestry. Regents–Prentice Hall, Englewood Cliffs, NJ.

Irland, L. C. 1994. Getting from here to there: Implementing ecosystem management on the ground. Journal of Forestry 92:12–17.

Jennings, O. E. 1953. Wildflowers of Western Pennsylvania and the Upper Ohio Basin. University of Pittsburgh Press, Pittsburgh, PA.

Jones, S. B., D. S. deCalesta, and S. B. Chunko. 1993. Whitetails are changing our woodlands. American Forests 99:20–25, 53–54.

Kosack, J. 1991. Hunting is a booming business. Pennsylvania Game News 62: 14–19.

Lutz, H. J. 1930. The vegetation of Heart's Content, a virgin forest in northwestern Pennsylvania. Ecology 11:1–29.

Marquis, D. A. 1975. The Allegheny hardwood forests of Pennsylvania. U.S. Forest Service General Technical Report NE-15.

Marquis, D. A., R. L. Ernst, and S. L. Stout. 1992. Prescribing silvicultural treatments in hardwood stands of the Alleghenies (revised). U.S. Forest Service General Technical Report NE-96.

Marquis, D. A., and T. J. Grisez. 1978. The effect of deer exclosures on the recovery of vegetation in failed clearcuts on the Allegheny Plateau. U.S. Forest Service Research Note NE-270.

McCabe, R. E., and T. R. McCabe. 1984. Of slings and arrows: An historical perspective. Pages 19–72 in White-Tailed Deer: Ecology and Management. (L. K. Halls, ed.) Stackpole Books, Harrisburg, PA.

McShea, W. J., and J. H. Rappole. 1992. White-tailed deer as keystone species within forest habitats of Virginia. Virginia Journal of Science 43:177–186.

McWilliams, W., S. L. Stout, T. Bowersox, and L. McCormick. 1993. Can we regenerate Pennsylvania's hardwood forests? Pages 23–36 in Penn's Woods— Change and Challenge. (J. C. Finley and S. B. Jones, eds.) Proceedings of the Forest Resource Issues Conference, Pennsylvania State University, University Park.

Millers, I., D. S. Shriner, and D. Rizzo. 1989. History of hardwood decline in the eastern United States. U.S. Forest Service General Technical Report NE-126.

Redding, J. A. 1995. History of deer population trends and forest cutting on the Allegheny National Forest. Pages 214–224 in Proceedings of the 10th North-central Hardwoods Conference. U.S. Forest Service Technical Report NE-197.

Salwasser, H. 1994. Ecosystem management: Can it sustain diversity and productivity? Journal of Forestry 92:6–11.

Society of American Foresters. 1993. Task Force Report on Sustaining Long-Term Forest Health and Productivity. Society of American Foresters, Bethesda, MD.

Storm. G. L., R. H. Yahner, D. F. Cottam, and G. M. Vecellio. 1989. Population status, movements, habitat use, and impact of white-tailed deer at Gettysburg National Military Park and Eisenhower National Historic Site, Pennsylvania. U.S. National Park Service Technical Report NPS/MAR/NRTR-89/043.

Thorne, S. G., K. C. Kim, K. C. Steiner, and B. J. McGuinness. 1995. A Heritage for the 21st Century: Conserving Pennsylvania's Native Biological Diversity. Pennsylvania Fish and Boat Commission, Harrisburg.

Tilghman, N. G. 1989. Impacts of white-tailed deer on forest regeneration in northwestern Pennsylvania. Journal of Wildlife Management 53:524–532.

Whitney, G. C. 1984. Fifty years of change in the arboreal vegetation of Heart's Content, an old-growth hemlock–white pine–northern hardwood stand. Ecology 65:403–408.

Witmer, G. W., and D. S. deCalesta. 1992. The need and difficulty of bringing the Pennsylvania deer herd under control. Proceedings of the Eastern Wildlife Damage Control Conference 5:130–137.

17 Deer Populations and the Widespread Failure of Hemlock Regeneration in Northern Forests

WILLIAM S. ALVERSON
AND DONALD M. WALLER

This chapter describes our attempts to determine whether the widespread regenerative failure of eastern hemlock (*Tsuga canadensis* L.) in remnant eastern hemlock and hemlock–hardwood stands in the Upper Great Lakes region can be justly attributed to browsing by white-tailed deer, a native mammal whose populations now commonly occur at two to four times the density of pre-European settlement (e.g., Garrott et al. 1993). These forest types and their resident biota were once widespread and common in the Upper Great Lakes region. Eastern hemlock was a dominant or important canopy component in approximately two-thirds of Wisconsin's northern forest area at the time of European colonization but was reduced by timber harvest and bark extraction to remnant stands covering only 0.5% of the landscape (Curtis 1959; Rogers 1978; Eckstein 1980).

The causes of direct reduction of these forest types are not mysterious but, in contrast, the mechanism of eastern hemlock's regenerative failure remains controversial. Wisconsin Department of Natural Resources and U.S. Forest Service employees have proposed that climatic fluctuations, limited seed dispersal, and lack of appropriate seedbed conditions are better predictors of hemlock regeneration than are deer population densities (summarized in Mladenoff and Stearns 1993), but these hypotheses have not yet been tested.

In a previous paper (Alverson et al. 1988), we evaluated the evidence then available that deer contribute to the widespread lack of regeneration of canopy trees within stands of eastern hemlock and white cedar (*Thuja occidentalis* L.) in northern Wisconsin and the Upper Peninsula of Michigan. In that paper, we cited an abundance of anecdotal information, descriptive data, and historical exclosure studies that indicated that elevated deer populations could greatly alter the composition and structure of several forest types on a local basis. A subsequent pilot field study on Nicolet National Forest and adjacent Menominee tribal lands indicated that regional variation in hemlock regeneration also was strongly correlated with deer abundance (E. J. Judziewicz, S. L. Solheim, D. M. Waller, and W. S. Alverson, unpublished data).

State and federal silviculturalists in our region often suggest that snowshoe hare *(Lepus americanus)* population densities could explain much of the variation in hemlock regeneration, but few data have been available to support or reject this hypothesis. For example, many historical exclosures were fenced to exclude both deer and snowshoe hare (e.g., Alverson et al. 1988: Figure 2), thus confounding their experimental effects. Furthermore, historical exclosures were often erected without replication and subjectively placed within deer yards, maximizing their demonstrative value but minimizing their experimental worth at a regional scale.

In this chapter, we contrast the effects of deer browsing on eastern hemlock seedlings with the effects of browsing by snowshoe hare to test the hypothesis that hare, rather than deer, population levels can best predict hemlock regeneration. We compare descriptive data from demographic plots and experimental data from exclosure plots on a small-scale basis here and on a large-scale basis elsewhere (Waller et al. 1996).

METHODS

Our broad study is based on 190 sites in northern Wisconsin and the Upper Peninsula of Michigan that were selected randomly from lists of eastern hemlock and hemlock-component stands provided by the staffs of county, state, and national forests and Native American reservation lands. At each site, all hemlock juveniles between 2 and 200 cm in height were measured within two randomly selected 7-m × 7-m subquadrats within a randomly placed 14-m × 21-m study quadrat during the summer of 1990. We assessed the recent browsing history of each site by counting the number of browsed and unbrowsed twigs of 10 or more randomly selected sugar maple (*Acer saccharum* L.) seedlings between 30 and 200 cm in height (where these were available).

In the fall of 1990, we initiated an exclosure experiment at a randomly

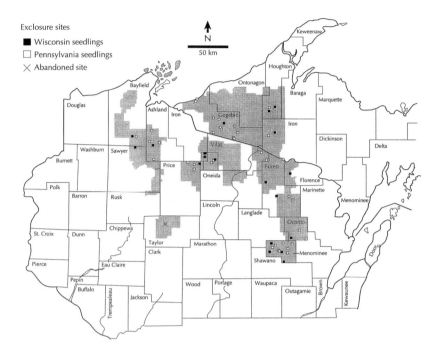

FIGURE 17.1. Map of study sites with mini-exclosures. The sites were located in northern Wisconsin and the Upper Peninsula of Michigan. Shaded areas indicate public forests and Native American lands sampled by the study. The 60 pairs of exclosure plots were planted with either native, wild-collected eastern hemlock seedlings or seedlings transplanted from a Pennsylvania nursery; one exclosure was later vandalized and abandoned.

selected subset of 60 of these study sites (Figure 17.1); one site was subsequently lost to vandalism. At each site, we selected two 9-m² plots as alike as possible with respect to slope, moisture, and canopy and subcanopy cover. We then randomly selected one as the experimental plot and erected a deer-proof cage over it. The other plot was left uncaged as a control. These "mini-exclosure" cages were 2.4 m on a side and 1.3 m tall. Their sides and tops were constructed of rigid cattle panels with 15-cm × 20-cm mesh, thus excluding deer but allowing snowshoe hare and other small herbivores to enter the cages.

We used transplanted eastern hemlock seedlings from two different sources in our experiment. Thirty-nine sites contained large, fertilized, bare-root seedlings from a commercial nursery in Pennsylvania. The other 20 sites received smaller, unfertilized, native Wisconsin seedlings with root balls. The 20 sites with Wisconsin seedlings were chosen randomly from the original list of 60 exclosure sites and represent five ownerships, including three national forests and two Native American reservations (Figure 17.1). The Pennsylvania seedlings were much easier to obtain and transplant in large quantities than were the native Wisconsin seedlings, but we used both types of seedlings to address concerns that the nursery seedlings might be significantly more attractive to deer than wild-collected seedlings, possibly biasing our results. Here we report data on seedling growth and survival for the sites receiving Wisconsin transplants, along with site data (e.g., browse indices and pellet counts) for all 59 nonvandalized sites receiving transplanted hemlocks.

In the spring of 1991, we randomly assigned nine transplanted hemlock seedlings to each of the two exclosure plots at the 59 study sites. We recorded each seedling's height (maximum elevation from substrate) and length (longest distance along stem from base to any branch tip) immediately after transplantation. We then revisited the sites in early spring 1992 and 1993 to record height, length, recent browse, and mortality data. Our experimental design did not require us to distinguish snowshoe hare from deer browse on individual hemlock twigs during censuses, although we routinely did so, because the exclosures were specifically designed not to exclude hare.

At each site, we recorded the number of new deer-pellet groups in eight circular 0.01-acre sample points (which totaled 323.9 m^2 per site; Figure 17.2) during early spring 1991–93. We also noted the number of these circular plots that contained any new hare pellets. Both counts reflect the number of pellets deposited during the winter season between leaf fall (October) and snowmelt (mid-April to mid-May). Although we used methods similar to those employed regionally to estimate deer densities in large management units of 500–1,000 km^2 or more in size (e.g., Thompson 1978), our intent was to provide estimates of the relative intensity of deer visitation to our study sites rather than to estimate absolute numbers of deer in larger areas, a much more problematic task. We used multiple plots per site to minimize sampling errors (Eberhardt and Van Etten 1956; Van Etten and Bennett 1965; Neff 1968; Smith 1968; Ryel 1971; Creed et al. 1984), and meticulous pellet counts for all years were made by a single field worker to minimize observer error.

To assess the reliability of our counts, we marked 207 deer-pellet groups at 34 study sites in the spring of 1991. During site revisitations in 1992, we incorrectly scored old pellet groups (from the previous year) as new pellet groups (from the preceding 6 months) in only 7 of 207 in-

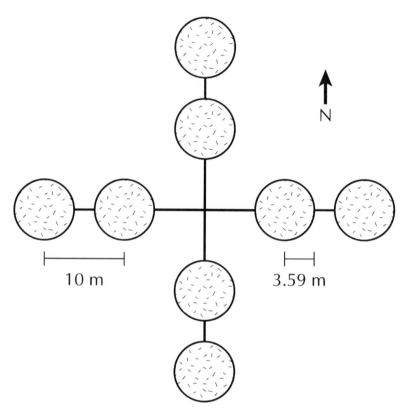

FIGURE 17.2. Layout of sampling points for deer and hare pellets within exclosure sites. The center of this array of eight 0.01-acre points was randomly sited at one of the two ends of the randomly sited study quadrat.

stances (3.4%) with our pellet scoring criteria. In spring 1991, we also removed pellet groups from 136 sample points at these sites for comparison with an equal number of points from which pellets were left unmanipulated. The number of pellet groups scored as new during the 1992 census in all points from which deer-pellet groups had been removed in 1991 was not significantly different from the number of pellet groups scored as new in an equal number of points from which pellets were not removed. Thus, our methods had no significant bias towards misidentification of new pellet groups as old ($t = 0.350$, $P = 0.729$, for respective means of 4.8 and 4.5).

We estimated the relative abundance of showshoe hare at each site during these spring visits in two ways. First, we recorded the number of the eight circular 0.01-acre sample points containing any hare pellets at each site ("hare points"). Second, we counted the total number of hare pellets at least 0.5 m distant from any other hare pellet within each sample point ("independent hare pellets") to differentiate between sites with high and very high population densities of hare.

All analyses were carried out in SYSTAT (Wilkinson 1990; SYSTAT 1992) and InStat (Motulsky et al. 1994).

RESULTS

Occurrence of Hemlock Seedlings

Naturally occurring hemlocks between 4 and 200 cm tall occurred in one or both of the 49-m^2 subquadrats at 62.6% of our 190 study sites; the average was 9.7 juveniles per site (Table 17.1). Seedlings 2–3 cm tall and mostly 1 year old or less (Eckstein 1980) were found within at least one of the subquadrats at 26% of the sites. We did not analyze data for the 2–3-cm size class further because the majority of these individuals were highly ephemeral and differences in abundance between sites reflect, in part, the month of site visitation.

Measures of Deer and Hare Abundance

The number of deer-pellet groups deposited within the eight sample points at individual sites during any winter season ranged from 0 to 66; the 3-

TABLE 17.1
Naturally occurring hemlock seedlings by size class

Size class (height)	Number per 98 m^2		Frequency (fraction of sites)
	Mean	s	
2–3 cm	12.1	65.2	0.26
4–9 cm	3.3	10.0	0.38
10–29 cm	3.0	7.3	0.46
30–200 cm	3.4	10.0	0.40
4–200 cm	9.7	23.2	0.63

Note: Data are from 190 sites in eastern hemlock and hemlock-component stands in northern Wisconsin and the Upper Peninsula of Michigan, 1990.

TABLE 17.2

Relative abundance of deer and snowshoe hare at 59 exclosure sites

	Number of deer-pellet groups in sample points			Number of sample points with hare pellets			Number of independent hare pellets in sample points[a]		
Year	Mean	s	Median	Mean	s	Median	Mean	s	Median
1991	8.6	12.1	5	1.5	2.4	0	4.2	7.9	0
1992	8.7	11.0	4	1.4	2.5	0	5.9	16.5	0
1993	5.9	8.2	2	1.2	2.1	0	3.9	9.8	0

Notes: In total, 323.9 m² within eight sample points were censused at each site in early spring. Values estimate the relative abundance of deer and hare at study sites during the previous winter season.

[a] Total number of hare pellets at least 0.5 m from any other hare pellet within each sample point.

year mean was 7.7 ($s = 9.0$, $n = 59$; Table 17.2). Local deer abundances by this index were significantly correlated between years ($r = 0.571$, $P < 0.0001$, comparison of 1992 with 1991; $r = 0.779$, $P < 0.0001$, 1993 with 1992).

Hare pellets were relatively scarcer in our study area, occurring in 0 to 8 sample points per study site (3-year mean $= 1.4$, $s = 2.2$, $n = 59$; Table 17.2). The number of independent hare pellets deposited within the sample points at individual sites during any winter season ranged from 0 to 111; the 3-year mean was 4.7 ($s = 10.6$; Table 17.2). We report further results based on only data for hare points (the number of sample points with hare pellets) because the two indices of hare abundance were highly correlated ($r = 0.864$, $P < 0.001$, $n = 59$ for 3-year means) and consistent among years (Table 17.3) and because they produced similar results in most comparative analyses.

In contrast, we found no significant association between the number of deer-pellet groups and the number of points with hare pellets per site ($r = -0.052$, $P = 0.694$, $n = 59$; Figure 17.3).

Sugar maple seedlings were present at 102 of the 190 sites used for our broad study (Waller et al. 1996). At these sites, the browse index averaged 0.44 (range $0 - 0.93$), slightly but nonsignificantly greater than the mean for the subset of sites with exclosures and with sufficient sugar maple seedlings to calculate this index (mean $= 0.39$, $n = 38$; $P = 0.373$ for t-test).

Our independent estimates of deer abundance were positively correlated. The browse index, an indicator of browsing at sites prior to 1990,

TABLE 17.3

Pearson correlation values for two indices of local hare abundance

Correlation variable	Hare points			Independent hare pellets		
	1991	1992	1993	1991	1992	1993
Hare points						
1991	1.000	—	—	—	—	—
1992	0.814	1.000	—	—	—	—
1993	0.708	0.773	1.000	—	—	—
Independent hare pellets						
1991	0.936	0.829	0.787	1.000	—	—
1992	0.651	0.761	0.706	0.762	1.000	—
1993	0.621	0.632	0.862	0.720	0.835	1.000

Notes: Hare point values represent the number of 0.01-acre census points per site (eight census points at each of 59 sites) containing new hare pellets in an early spring census. Independent hare pellet values represent the total number of hare pellets at least 0.5 m from any other found in the census points. Each individual comparison is significant at the $P < 0.001$ level.

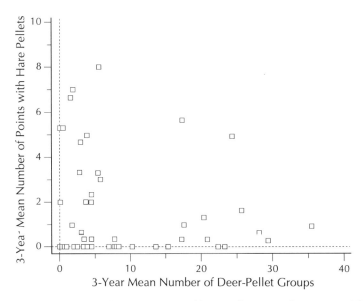

FIGURE 17.3. Association between deer and hare pellets at exclosure sites. Three-year mean number of sample points with hare pellets per site (eight sample points in each of 59 exclosure sites) and the 3-year mean number of deer-pellet groups per site, 1991–93, are compared.

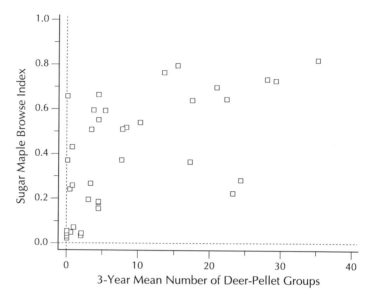

FIGURE 17.4. Association between browse index and deer pellets at exclosure sites. The sugar maple browse index, taken in 1990, was compared with the 3-year average number of deer-pellet groups counted at exclosure sites during early spring, 1991–93 ($n = 38$).

was significantly and positively correlated with the average number of new deer-pellet groups counted during the spring surveys of 1991–93 ($r = 0.602$, $P < 0.001$, $n = 38$; Figure 17.4). In contrast, the browse index varied independently of estimated hare density ($r = -0.027$, $P = 0.873$, $n = 38$ for hare points). Thus, the sugar maple browse index reflects cumulative browsing by deer, not hare.

Correlations of Hemlock Abundance and Height with Deer and Hare Abundance

The average height of eastern hemlock seedlings showed a significant, negative relationship with the browse index at demographic sites at which sugar maple seedlings were sampled ($r = -0.270$, $P = 0.006$, $n = 102$; Figure 17.5). In addition, the variance in average hemlock seedling height was notably reduced at high values of the browse index. The correlation between average heights and the browse index was also negative and of a similar magnitude for the subset of sites with both exclosures and browse index values, but sample size limited the statistical significance ($r = -0.314$, $P = 0.055$, $n = 38$).

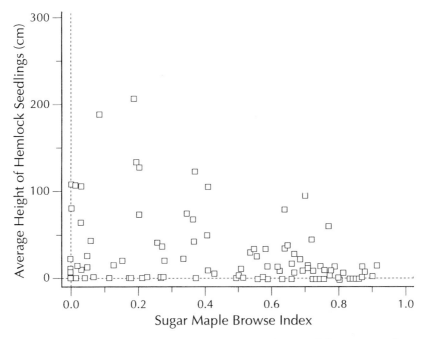

FIGURE 17.5. Average height of eastern hemlock seedlings and the sugar maple browse index. Data are for all demographic sites at which the browse index was scored ($n = 102$).

The abundance and average heights of naturally occurring nontransplanted hemlock seedlings at study sites with exclosures was consistently negatively correlated with the 3-year mean number of deer-pellet groups, but again small sample size limited statistical significance (Table 17.4). In contrast, comparisons of numbers and heights of hemlock seedlings at exclosure sites showed consistently positive correlations with showshoe hare abundance among sites, which reached statistical significance for the 4–200-cm combined size class (Table 17.4). To insure that these relationships were not an incidental artifact of some other factor preventing hemlock regeneration, we reanalyzed these data by removing sites without hemlock seedlings. These reanalyses did not substantially change the patterns of correlation (Table 17.5).

Exclosure Seedlings

Browsing by deer and snowshoe hare significantly increased the mortality rate of hemlock seedlings. Only 9.3% of the 280 unbrowsed, transplanted

TABLE 17.4

Pearson correlation values of the abundance and mean height of naturally occurring hemlock seedlings with 3-year mean measures of deer and snowshoe hare abundance

Abundance of eastern hemlock seedlings by size class	Deer pellets	Hare points
4–9 cm	−0.132	0.290
10–29 cm	−0.171	0.325
30–200 cm	−0.078	0.160
4–200 cm	−0.152[a]	0.314[b]
Average height	−0.236[c]	0.130[d]

Notes: Data are from 59 sites with two subquadrats totaling 98 m² per site for years 1991–93. Tests for the statistical significance of the four summary comparisons are given.

[a] $P = 0.251$.

[b] $P = 0.015$.

[c] $P = 0.071$.

[d] $P = 0.325$.

TABLE 17.5

Pearson correlation values after removal of sites without juvenile hemlocks in either sampled subquadrat

Abundance of eastern hemlock seedlings by size class	Deer pellets	Hare points
4–9 cm (25 sites)	−0.273	0.347
10–29 cm (37 sites)	−0.246	0.334
30–200 cm (34 sites)	0.133	0.067
4–200 cm (48 sites)	−0.162[a]	0.274[b]
Average height (50 sites)	−0.268[c]	0.079[d]

Notes: The number of sample sites with juvenile hemlocks of a given size class are noted in parentheses. Tests for significance of the four summary comparisons are given.

[a] $P = 0.271$.

[b] $P = 0.059$.

[c] $P = 0.06$.

[d] $P = 0.587$.

TABLE 17.6

Growth of browsed versus unbrowsed and caged versus uncaged
transplanted Wisconsin hemlock seedlings

Treatment	Growth in height (cm)			Growth in length (cm)		
	Mean	s	n	Mean	s	n
Unbrowsed	2.18	4.82	247	3.00	5.12	247
Browsed	0.11	6.98	59	0.18	8.53	59
		(P = 0.007)			(P = 0.001)	
Caged	2.13	4.29	150	2.90	4.84	148
Uncaged	0.79	3.39	156	1.29	4.31	156
		(P = 0.003)			(P = 0.002)	

Notes: Over the 2-year period, spring 1991 to spring 1993, uncaged seedlings were exposed to browsing by deer and snowshoe hare but caged seedlings were exposed only to hare. The P-values given are for t-tests of equality of means.

Wisconsin seedlings died between spring 1991 and spring 1993 versus 27% of the 74 browsed seedlings (t-test, $P < 0.001$). Browsing also significantly decreased height and length growth (Table 17.6).

We observed no significant differences in mortality between caged seedlings and uncaged seedlings during the 2-year period ending in spring 1993 (mean mortality caged seedlings = 0.156, $s = 0.202$, $n = 150$; mean mortality uncaged seedlings = 0.131, $s = 0.156$; $n = 156$; $P = 0.226$, t-test).

Despite this similarity in overall survivorship, the additional browse sustained by seedlings surviving in the uncaged plots significantly reduced their height and length growth (Table 17.6). The mean height of seedlings within the exclosures was significantly greater than that of uncaged seedlings after 2 years (Figure 17.6; mean height of seedlings within exclosure = 14.6 cm, outside exclosure = 12.6 cm, $P = 0.017$; respective spring 1991 means, 12.1 and 11.7 cm, $P = 0.517$). Likewise, the mean length of seedlings protected within the exclosures also became significantly greater by spring 1993 (mean length of seedlings within exclosure = 20.2 cm, outside exclosure = 17.3 cm, $P = 0.005$).

Inside the exclosures, growth in neither height nor length of seedlings was significantly related to the average number of deer-pellet groups ($r = 0.418$ and 0.215, respectively) nor to the average number of hare points ($r = -0.318$ and -0.162, respectively). Likewise, outside the exclosures, the average number of deer-pellet groups did not significantly predict

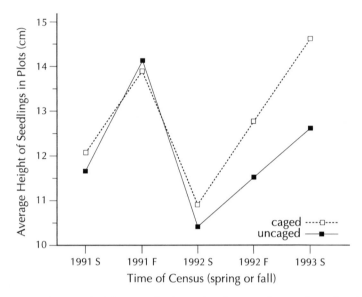

FIGURE 17.6. Average height growth of caged and uncaged transplanted native hemlock seedlings. The reduction in mean height from 1991 to 1992 was caused by dieback and branch repositioning after transplantation.

height or length growth of seedlings ($r = -0.216$ and -0.251, respectively) nor did the average number of hare points ($r = -0.147$ and -0.210, respectively).

To assess the effect of deer browse alone, we compared the difference between the height increment values of the caged and uncaged plots at each site (height excess) against measures of deer abundance. The height excess shows a highly significant correlation with the 3-year mean of deer-pellet groups per site during this 2-year period of seedling growth ($r = 0.756$, $P < 0.0001$). Deer-pellet group counts from the 1992–93 winter season alone predicted the height excess even better ($r = 0.85$; Figure 17.7). Calculations for the difference between the length increment values of caged and uncaged plots at each site (the length excess) indicate a similar relationship. This variable was highly significantly correlated with the 3-year average number of deer-pellet groups ($r = 0.667$, $P < 0.0001$) and with pellet counts from the 1992–93 winter season ($r = 0.648$, $P < 0.0001$).

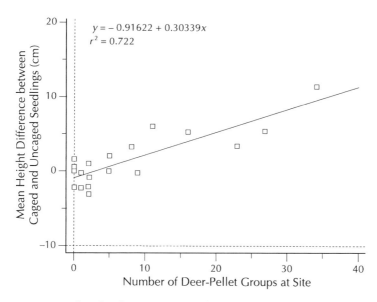

FIGURE 17.7. Seedling height excess versus deer abundance. Height excess, the mean difference in height of seedlings within the exclosure cage and those outside (on a per site basis), was regressed against the number of deer-pellet groups deposited at that site during the 1992–93 winter season.

Overall Effects of Deer and Hare Browsing

On average, browsed seedlings increased in height 2.07 cm (95.0%) less than did unbrowsed seedlings from spring 1991 to spring 1993 (Table 17.6). As a consequence, browsed seedlings were 14.1% shorter, on average, than were unbrowsed seedlings by spring 1993. Of this reduction in height growth, 64.7% can be attributed to deer, as evidenced by the additional growth (mean height excess) of 1.34 cm shown by caged seedlings during this 2-year period.

Likewise, browsed seedlings increased in length 2.82 cm (94%) less, on average, than did unbrowsed seedlings during this same 2-year period. Thus, the average length of browsed seedlings became 14% less than that of unbrowsed seedlings by spring 1993. Of this reduction in length growth, 57.2% can be attributed to deer, as evidenced by the additional growth (mean length excess) of 1.61 cm shown by seedlings protected within the exclosures.

DISCUSSION

This study provides evidence that browsing significantly increases mortality and significantly decreases height and length growth of native eastern hemlock seedlings. The results also suggest that deer have a greater effect on the growth and survival of hemlock seedlings than do snowshoe hare in hemlock stands of the Upper Great Lakes region.

Data from the demographic plots suggest that increased deer abundance reduces the number and size of hemlock seedlings, as evidenced by the consistently negative correlations between our measures of hemlock regeneration and deer abundance. In contrast, we found no support for the hypothesis that snowshoe hare populations significantly reduce hemlock abundance or height within these habitats on a regional basis, though such an effect occurs at some local sites.

The weak correlations between our estimates of deer and hare abundance and hemlock variables probably reflect the relatively small areas and consequent high sampling variation for demographic profiles of hemlock regeneration at study sites. Although 62.6% of these sites contained some hemlock seedlings between 4 and 200 cm tall within the randomly sited 98-m^2 sampling area, such small spatial samples probably underestimated the frequency of hemlock regeneration at larger scales within sites.

As the Wisconsin seedlings transplanted into our study sites continue to grow larger while being differentially exposed to deer over additional winters, we expect the differences in growth and mortality reported here to become more pronounced. Indeed, such larger differences have already been observed in exclosure plots in which larger hemlock seedlings from a Pennsylvania nursery have been planted (W. S. Alverson, personal observation, spring 1995). Data from censuses during the spring of 1997 should allow us to evaluate further how well our indices of deer and hare abundance predict seedling growth. The passage of time will also allow us better to understand mortality, a demographic event that appears to be strongly linked to browsing but more delayed in effect than growth, as well as the biological significance of differences in growth rates between browsed and unbrowsed seedlings.

Ultimately, if we are to build a chain of evidence indicating that deer are responsible for a failure of hemlock regeneration within hemlock and hemlock-component stands in the Upper Great Lakes region, a number of interconnecting links must be established. To discuss these links, we must carefully distinguish between two aspects of hemlock regeneration: reproduction and recruitment. Reproduction is defined here as the input of seeds and small seedlings (<4 cm tall) into forest stands. Recruitment refers instead to the subsequent survival of these young seedlings to sapling and adult size. Successful regeneration of canopy trees clearly requires both adequate reproduction and at least intermittently satisfactory recruitment. That is, both are necessary conditions but neither alone is sufficient.

This study and other published and unpublished studies support three of the evidential links connecting deer and eastern hemlock regeneration. First, we note that hemlock stands in our region frequently produce large seed crops with 25% viability and that there is no evidence that reproduction in any recent decade is limited by availability of seeds (Eckstein 1980). Our studies and observations indicate that seedlings 2–3 cm tall are present within a minimum of 25.6% of our randomly selected 98-m^2 study quadrats and that the local heterogeneity of seedling reproduction results in an even greater frequency of occurrence of small seedlings at larger scales within sites. Thus, it appears doubtful that the number of seeds or small seedlings within these hemlock stands often limits regeneration in the Upper Great Lakes region, as postulated by Mladenoff and Stearns (1993).

Second, our studies also indicate that although the abundance of 2–3-cm-tall hemlock seedlings varies locally in response to many factors, such as snowshoe hare abundance, seedbed conditions, coarse woody debris, and canopy conditions, this variance is less predictive of the abundance of juveniles in larger size classes in remnant hemlock stands than are regionally varying indicators of deer abundance (Waller et al. 1996). Third, these same studies indicate that measures of local deer population density predict growth and survival rates of hemlock seedlings better than do hare abundance or other predictors.

In future studies, we intend to investigate whether browsing by deer directly precludes hemlock seedlings from growing into subadult size classes or if it prevents regeneration indirectly by reducing the growth and survival of hemlock seedlings so that they lose competitive advantages over other woody species (or both). We are also pooling local (study site) data into classes based on ownership, management, and deer population densities (e.g., national forests versus reservation lands; Table 17.7) to investigate how the pattern of missing size classes of juvenile hemlocks characterizing some ownerships, or other classes, will translate into replacement of senescent canopy hemlocks on a regional scale (Waller et al. 1996). Our eventual goal is to determine whether some threshold deer density exists for our region and how long (and often) densities must re-

TABLE 17.7

Population levels of deer and snowshoe hare at exclosure sites by land ownership

Ownership (n sites)	Number of deer-pellet groups		Number of census points with hare pellets	
	Mean	s	Mean	s
Chequamegon National Forest (12 sites)	11.00	9.08	2.75	2.68
Lac du Flambeau Reservation (8 sites)	0.50	0.67	2.63	3.18
Menominee Reservation (13 sites)	3.90	6.24	0.80	1.63
Nicolet National Forest (10 sites)	6.27	7.14	0.60	0.98
Ottawa National Forest (16 sites)	12.85	10.57	0.60	1.23

Notes: Values are 3-year means for eight census points per site, fall 1990 to spring 1993. The Chequamegon National Forest and the Lac du Flambeau Reservation are adjacent, as are the Nicolet National Forest and the Menominee Reservation.

main below this threshold density to allow episodes of successful eastern hemlock reproduction in our region.

ACKNOWLEDGMENTS

Extensive field work for this project was carried out by Mark Leach, Steve Solheim, Emmet Judziewicz, and Kathy Thompson. We thank Kandis Elliot for the illustrations, Tom Brandner for data management, Don Reiter of the Menominee Nation for logistical help and advice, and the staffs of the Chequamegon, Nicolet, and Ottawa national forests and the Menominee and Lac du Flambeau Chippewa tribal councils for their interest in the project and for permission to work on their lands.

REFERENCES CITED

Alverson, W. S. 1988. Forests too deer: Edge effects in northern Wisconsin. Conservation Biology 2:348–358.

Creed, W. A., F. Haberland, B. E. Kohn, and K. R. McCaffery. 1984. Harvest management: The Wisconsin experience. Pages 243–260 in The White-Tailed Deer: Ecology and Management. (L. K. Hall, ed.) Stackpole Books, Harrisburg, PA.

Curtis, J. T. 1959. The Vegetation of Wisconsin. University of Wisconsin Press, Madison.

Eberhardt, L., and R. C. Van Etten. 1956. Evaluation of the pellet group count as a deer census method. Journal of Wildlife Management 20:70–74.

Eckstein, R. G. 1980. Eastern hemlock *(Tsuga canadensis)* in north central Wisconsin. Wisconsin Department of Natural Resources, Research Report 104, Madison.

Garrott, R. A., P. J. White, and C. A. Vanderbilt White. 1993. Overabundance: An issue for conservation biologists? Conservation Biology 7:946–949.

Mladenoff, D. J., and F. Stearns 1993. Eastern hemlock regeneration and deer browsing in the Northern Great Lakes Region: A re-examination and model simulation. Conservation Biology 7:889–900.

Motulsky, H. J., J. R. Pilkington, and P. Stannard. 1994. InStat for Macintosh, Version 2.03. GraphPad Software, San Diego.

Neff, D. J. 1968. The pellet-count technique for big game trend, census, and distribution: A review. Journal of Wildlife Management 32:597–614.

Rogers, R. S. 1978. Forests dominated by hemlock *(Tsuga canadensis):* Distribution as related to site and postsettlement history. Canadian Journal of Botany 56:843–854.

Ryel, L. A. 1971. Evaluation of pellet group surveys for estimating deer populations in Michigan. Michigan Department of Natural Resources, Report 250, Lansing.

Smith, R. H. 1968. A comparison of several sizes of circular plots for estimating deer pellet-group density. Journal of Wildlife Management 32:585–591.

SYSTAT. 1992. SYSTAT Version 5.2. Systat, Inc., Evanston, IL.

Thompson, D. R. 1978. Survey Report: 1978 Deer Management Unit Surveys of Deer and Snowshoe Hare Populations. Wisconsin Department of Natural Resources, Bureau of Research, Madison.

Van Etten, R. C., and C. L. Bennett, Jr. 1965. Some sources of error in using pellet-group counts for censusing deer. Journal of Wildlife Management 29:723–729.

Waller, D. M., W. S. Alverson, and S. L. Solheim. 1996. Local and regional factors influencing the regeneration of eastern hemlock. Pages 73–90 *in* Hemlock Ecology and Management. (G. Mroz, ed.) Michigan Technological University, Houghton.

Wilkinson, L. 1990. SYSTAT: The System for Statistics. Systat, Inc., Evanston, IL.

18 Herbivores and the Ecology of Forest Understory Birds

WILLIAM J. MCSHEA AND
JOHN H. RAPPOLE

Habitat structural complexity has a direct relationship with the number of bird species and individuals living in that habitat (MacArthur and MacArthur 1961; MacArthur et al. 1962). Numerous field tests of this proposition have been made, demonstrating that both vertical (MacArthur and MacArthur 1961; Moss 1978) and horizontal (Karr and Roth 1971; Roth 1976) components of foliage structure affect avian diversity in tropical (Bell 1982) and temperate (Moss 1978) forests. Two principal explanations have been given for these effects: (1) increased structural diversity provides more niches (Lynch and Whigham 1984) and (2) increased structural complexity decreases nest predator efficiency (Bowman and Harris 1980; Martin and Roper 1988).

Structural complexity within forests is viewed principally as a consequence of community age (Kimmins 1987). However, marked differences in structural complexity are found within forests of similar type and age as a result of different histories of understory treatment. Understory can be affected naturally or artificially by herbivores, fire, logging practices, herbicides, and other factors. Within protected forests, active manipulation is often not used, but natural agents can have as profound an effect on avian diversity as logging, herbicide application, or similar activity.

In this chapter, we review the available information on the effects of herbivores on several protected and managed forest communities and assess the possible effect of high densities of herbivores on diversity of bird communities in those forests.

HERBIVORES AND UNDERSTORY COMPOSITION

Large herbivores are an integral part of most natural communities. The most striking examples are in African ecosystems, where large herbivores have significant effects on nutrient cycling and habitat succession (Sinclair and Norton-Griffiths 1979). These present-day effects of large herbivores are dwarfed in comparison to the postulated impact of megaherbivores during the Pleistocene (Owen-Smith 1987). Owen-Smith speculates that the loss of large herbivores at the end of the Pleistocene radically changed the composition of North American forests through loss of these agents of structural change. Even within historical times, forest communities in eastern North America were under the influence of now-extirpated woods bison *(Bison bison)* and elk *(Cervus elaphus)*. How these large herbivores shaped patch structure within forests is unknown.

In most systems, herbivores consume about 10% of the plant productivity (Crawley 1983). Although this 10% may contain valuable reproductive organs (Miller et al. 1992), it is not generally the day-to-day consumption of plants that alters plant communities but the irruption of herbivores, both insects and mammals, that can cause considerable changes (Caughley 1970; Noy-Meir 1981; Crawley 1983). Since Leopold documented deer irruptions within protected areas in the 1940s (Leopold et al. 1947), white-tailed deer populations have been a concern within managed areas (Warren 1991). Recent irruptions of herbivorous insects (e.g., gypsy moth [*Lymantria dispar*] and spruce budworm [*Choristoneura fumerana*]) attest to the power of herbivores to alter forest habitat.

Understory vegetation is composed of herbaceous plants, woody shrubs and small trees that mature within the shade of canopy trees, and woody species that eventually form the canopy but spend many years within the understory layer (Hough 1965; Davidson and Forman 1982). Changes in the amount of light penetrating the overstory foliage usually determines the density and diversity of understory vegetation (Davidson and Forman 1982), and defoliation of canopy trees by herbivorous insects increases herbaceous cover (Houston 1981).

Deer browsing also may greatly reduce the abundance of some understory woody plants. Dense growths of eastern hemlock *(Tsuga canadensis)* and witch hobble *(Viburnum alnifolium)* disappeared during a 20-year study of a mature forest in Pennsylvania (Hough 1965), probably because of increased deer browsing. White cedar *(Thuja occidentalus)* regeneration in Wisconsin is reduced in the presence of even low densities of deer (Alverson et al. 1988). Increased harvest of deer can enhance woody seedling production (Behrend et al. 1970).

Heavy browsing by deer in deciduous forests of the eastern United States shifts the herbaceous layer toward grasses, nonpalatable herbaceous plants, such as bracken fern *(Ptreidium aquilinum)* and garlic mustard *(Alliaria petiolata),* and browse-tolerant plants, such as coralberry *(Symphoricarpos orbiculatus)* or black cherry *(Prunus serotina)* (Tilghman 1989). Miller et al. (1992) list 98 species of threatened or endangered vascular plants that are known to be consumed by deer. It is unknown how significant deer consumption is to the persistence of these species, but Miller et al. (1992) argue that deer densities should be considered in these plant species' management. An examination of the distribution of one of these species, yellow clintonia *(Clintonia borealis),* showed that its occurrence and abundance in Northern Wisconsin is strongly correlated with the abundance of deer (Balgooyen and Waller 1995).

Succession within boreal forests can be manipulated by changes in herbivore population densities. In a simulation of age and species' distributions for mature forests in Michigan, it was found that eastern hemlock forests would be replaced by more open sugar maple *(Acer saccharum)* forests under the present degree of browsing pressure from deer (Frelich and Lorimer 1985). Pastor and Naiman (1992) predicted that browsing intensity by moose *(Alces alces)* would determine whether a climax boreal forest was spruce or aspen. In their simulations, the effect of heavy browsing pressure during early succession persisted for many decades after the browsing was removed. The persistence of browsing impacts decades after removal of deer was evident within a mature forest in southern England (Putman et al. 1989).

The history of a site can affect the composition and density of understory vegetation. Disturbance from forestry practices can still be detected in the composition of herbaceous plants up to 100 years after disturbance in Appalachian deciduous forests (Duffy and Meier 1992). Twenty-two years after release from browsing pressure, colonization of herbaceous and woody plants has been slow within New Forest in southern England (Putman et al. 1989). The authors postulated that the site was under heavy browsing pressure by deer for over 900 years and the exclusion of deer from a small portion of the forest could not compensate for the lack of a diverse seed bank within the site and the low recruitment of seeds from the surrounding heavily browsed forest.

Herbivory by deer or moose has been shown to eliminate highly palatable species such as balsam fir *(Abies balsamea)* (Brandner et al. 1990) or those species associated with winter yards, such as hemlock (Frelich and Lorimer 1985). The most common effect of herbivory by both deer (Tilghman 1989) and moose (Risenhoover and Maass 1986; Brandner et al. 1990) is to retard forest succession. On Isle Royale, Michigan, herbivory by moose did not cause species to disappear from the forest but rather prevented their growth into canopy species (Risenhoover and Maass 1986).

Site quality determines the speed of any recovery from disturbance; higher-quality sites are more productive and thereby recover sooner. High-quality sites suffer less frequent defoliations from herbivorous insects and recover sooner (Houston 1981); gypsy moth outbreaks are less severe within areas with abundant undergrowth and organic litter (Bess et al. 1947).

In eastern U.S. forests, woody plant regeneration is altered by high densities of deer browsing on seedlings (Hough 1965; Tilghman 1989), rubbing antlers on small trees (Hough 1965), and possibly consuming seeds (Pekins and Mautz 1987; McShea and Schwede 1993). Following clear-cut, regeneration has produced monocultures of black cherry or dense stands of bracken fern in areas of high deer densities (Tilghman 1989).

BIRDS AND UNDERSTORY COMPOSITION

Bird communities are sensitive to changes in forest understory. The volume of vegetation is a reliable indicator of the abundance of breeding birds (Mills et al. 1991). The differences in foliage density between layers within a New Guinea forest was used to explain differences in vertical distribution of the bird community (Bell 1982). The density of forest understory vegetation, in addition to total volume, affected the number of bird species and individuals captured during the breeding season (McShea and Rappole 1992). The density of understory vegetation is also negatively correlated with predation rates on artificial ground nests (Leimgruber et al. 1994). Hooper et al. (1973) surveyed 30 forested recreational areas within the southern Appalachians and found bird numbers highly correlated with understory density; however, they did not estimate deer densities at these sites.

The population dynamics of most forest birds can be modeled using vegetation parameters (Urban and Smith 1989). For ovenbirds *(Seiurus aurocapillus)*, territory size increases with decreased forest understory (Smith and Shugart 1987). These authors postulated that the limiting resource within eastern forests is insect availability, and birds are gauging this resource by assessing the understory density. The importance of food limitation also was emphasized by Holmes et al. (1986), who found long-

TABLE 18.1

Number of captured bird species according to nest height and foraging guild

Nest and guild category	All captured species (total = 53)	Migrant species captured (total = 32)
Nest height		
Range includes nests below 2 m	37	20
Mean below 2 m	16	12
Foraging guild		
Hover and glean	5	5
Foliage glean	13	11
Hawking	6	5
Bark glean	8	2
Ground glean	20	9
Probe	1	0
Mean nest height and foraging mode below 2 m	15	10

Notes: Birds were captured during the breeding season (June) at forested sites in northwestern Virginia. Species are listed according to nest height and according to foraging guild (based on standard bird guides; Terres 1980; Erhlich et al. 1988). Species are also identified as neotropical nearctic migrants (Rappole et al. 1995). Species potentially affected most by deer are those that both have a mean nest height below 2 m and predominately forage within 2 m of the ground.

term changes in breeding bird abundance was correlated with the density of insect larvae within a New Hampshire forest.

Within eastern deciduous forests, several species nest or forage within 2 m of the forest floor (Terres 1980; Ehrlich et al. 1988). Of 53 species we have captured at sites within the Shenandoah National Park and George Washington National Forest in northwestern Virginia, 64% are potentially affected by changes in understory because of their foraging or nesting heights (Table 18.1). Twenty-eight percent of these species both nest and forage within 2 m of the forest floor. In addition, canopy birds that prey on insects which mature in understory vegetation may be indirectly affected by changes in understory vegetation.

BIRDS AND DEER DENSITIES

If bird communities are sensitive to understory characteristics that may be strongly influenced by the browsing of deer, there should be evidence that high ungulate populations decrease bird populations within protected forests. Within eastern forests, there is circumstantial evidence that high white-tailed deer densities limit bird populations. A 42% decline in forest understory birds that occurred over a decade at a New York preserve was attributed to high deer densities (Baird 1990). Declines in ovenbird populations within a western Maryland preserve (Boone and Dowell 1986) as well as a lower diversity of birds within a game farm in Pennsylvania (Casey and Hein 1983) were also attributed to high deer densities.

Ten years after a range of deer densities were established within a managed forest in northwestern Pennsylvania, bird communities were different between plots (deCalesta 1994). Although canopy and ground-nesting species were not affected, the species richness and abundance of midlevel canopy birds were reduced at the highest deer densities (27% and 37%, respectively). DeCalesta (1994) found that deer densities above 7.9 deer/km^2 had a significant negative effect on bird populations.

Kentucky warbler *(Oporornis formosus)* abundance and distribution have been tracked for 13 years within a 500-ha portion of protected forest at the Smithsonian's Conservation and Research Center in northwestern Virginia (McShea et al. 1995). Although Kentucky warblers were randomly distributed across five forest types during the 1970s, by the mid-1980s they were confined mostly to a single forest type: bottomland hardwood. Bird distribution remained unchanged in only one section of the forest, a section in which low deer densities were maintained.

With regard to bird communities, it is not known at what temporal scale structural diversity is important. Insect defoliation may increase light to the forest floor and thereby increase understory production (Houston 1981). However, over a several year period, an increase in mean temperature at the forest floor may shift the composition of understory vegetation and insect communities and thereby affect bird species. With herbaceous insect irruptions, the immediate effect is increased insect availability for nesting birds (Holmes et al. 1986), but long-term reductions in vegetation volume may not benefit birds. If the ultimate limitation of migrant birds in temperate forests is insect availability, the proximate measure of that availability may be vegetation volume, and any reductions in total vegetation volume could affect bird communities.

FORESTS TYPES, DEER DENSITY, AND BIRD COMMUNITIES

Managed Forests

The effect of deer on forest understory should be considered within the context of other potential effects. The pasturing of domestic livestock in forests or riparian zones is not favorable for either forest understory development or most migrant bird species (Kauffman and Krueger 1984). The loss of structural diversity along riparian zones as a result of livestock is a major disturbance to migratory birds (Kauffman and Krueger 1984; Taylor and Littlefield 1986). The number of bird species increases in both forests (Dambach 1944) and shrublands (Bock et al. 1984) after removal of livestock. Within a protected forest in North Carolina, the decrease in forest understory was more severe where livestock were pastured than in areas with high deer densities (Bratton 1980).

Within forests managed for timber production, understories have long been managed directly through forestry practices. Structural changes resulting from logging practices may mask effects resulting from changes in deer densities. At least two studies have examined the interaction of logging practices, deer densities, and bird populations (Dessecker and Yahner 1987; DeGraaf et al. 1991). Both studies surveyed sites with different logging and deer population histories and found selective logging practices may enhance bird species diversity whereas high deer densities may depress bird diversity. In deCalesta's (1994) study of bird communities after 10 years at different deer densities, changes in the bird community due to intensive tree harvest within the study plots may have masked the effects of deer on ground- and canopy-nesting birds. A comparison between managed and protected forests in New Hampshire found more species and higher diversity on managed forests (Welsh and Healy 1993). DeCalesta (Chapter 16) suggests that the management of nearby stands can decrease the effect of deer on seedling stocking rates within stands approaching harvest age. Concerns about deer densities may be misplaced in the presence of other, more severe, impacts on understory composition.

Protected Forests

Many forests are protected from timber management and other direct means of understory management. These forests are often closed to direct management of deer through hunting. These protected forests are not unmanaged but rather decisions on deer management, insect control, and edge creation result in indirect management of forest understory. Within protected forests, herbivores, both mammals and insects, will play a large role in the manager's ability to maintain populations of both plants and animals. However, a survey of ungulate management policies in our larger national parks found that 79% of the parks did not survey all their large mammal populations (Robisch and Wright 1995). Most parks lack both population size and trend data for their ungulate populations. In Robisch and Wright's survey, manager concern that high ungulate densities might affect other animals was minimal (1.4 on a scale of 1 to 4; Robisch and Wright 1995).

Within eastern deciduous forests that are protected from human disturbance, most succession occurs at the microhabitat scale of treefalls and blowdowns (Runkle 1982, 1991). These small-scale disturbances create a mosaic of microhabitats that are beneficial for migrant birds (Roth 1976). High densities of deer have been shown to prevent the formation of dense clusters of woody plants following small-scale disturbance (Veblen et al. 1989). The prevention of mosaic patterns within mature protected forests, through deer browsing, may be the proximate mechanism by which high deer densities reduce understory bird populations.

CONCLUSIONS

There is a lack of direct evidence that reducing deer within protected forests would increase bird populations, but evidence from managed forests (deCalesta 1994), and the prevalence of high deer densities and low understory density in areas of low bird numbers (McShea and Rappole 1992; McShea et al. 1995), indicate that deer density should be considered when managing for migratory birds within protected deciduous forests. We agree with Noy-Meier (1981) that herbivore overpopulation occurs when densities reach levels that prevent conservation of rarer species, and actions should be taken at that time. Similar arguments have been made for controlling white-tailed deer populations within our national parks (Warren 1991; although see Underwood and Porter 1991). This is not the same as saying any reduction in plant density or diversity by herbivores must be stopped. Herbivores are a part of forest ecosystems; their abundance, and the abundance of their food, should be expected to fluctuate over time (McCullough, Chapter 6). The difficulty for the manager is determining when herbivore densities have reached the level at which they impinge on conservation efforts for other species. The ranking of species is partially a value judgment, based on policy and aesthetics as much as biology (Underwood and Porter 1991). The use of herbaceous species as indicators of overbrowsing (Balgooyen and Waller 1995) may provide the first warning of when action should be taken, but for most forests we do not know enough to assign indicator status to a specific species.

REFERENCES CITED

Alverson, W. S., D. M. Waller, and S. I. Solheim. 1988. Forests too deer: Edge effects in northern Wisconsin. Conservation Biology 2:348–358.

Baird, T. H. 1990. Breeding Bird Populations. New York State Museum Bulletin 477, State University of New York, Albany.

Balgooyen, C. P., and D. W. Waller. 1995. The use of *Clintonia borealis* and other indicators to gauge impacts of white- tailed deer on plant communities in Northern Wisconsin, USA. Natural Areas Journal 15:308–318.

Behrend, D. F., G. F. Mattfeld, W. C. Tierson, and J. E. Wiley III. 1970. Deer density control for comprehensive forest management. Journal of Forestry 68: 695–700.

Bell, H. L. 1982. A bird community of New Guinean lowland rainforest. 3. Vertical distribution of the avifauna. Emu 82:143–162.

Bess, H. A., S. H. Spurr, and E. W. Littlefield. 1947. Forest site conditions and the gypsy moth. Harvard Forest Bulletin 22.

Bock, C. E., J. H. Bock, W. R. Kenney, and V. M. Hawthorne. 1984. Responses of birds, rodents, and vegetation to livestock exclosure in a semidesert grassland site. Journal of Range Management 37:239–242.

Boone, D. D., and B. A. Dowell. 1986. Catoctin Mountain Park bird study. National Park Service CX-3000-4-0152.

Bowman, G. B., and L. D. Harris. 1980. Effect of habitat heterogeneity on ground nest depredation. Journal of Wildlife Management 44:806–813.

Brandner, T. A., R. O. Peterson, and K. L. Risenhoover. 1990. Balsalm fir on Isle Royale: Effects of moose herbivory and population density. Ecology 71:155–164.

Bratton, S. P. 1980. Impacts of white-tailed deer on the vegetation of Cades Cove, Great Smoky Mountains National Park. Proceedings of the Annual Conference Southeastern Association of Fish and Wildlife Agencies 33 (1979): 305–312.

Casey, D., and D. Hein. 1983. Effects of heavy browsing on a bird community in a deciduous forest. Journal of Wildlife Management 47:829–836.

Caughley, G. 1970. Eruption of ungulate populations, with emphasis on Himalayan Thar in New Zealand. Ecology 51:53–72.

Crawley, M. J. 1983. Herbivory: The Dynamics of Animal–Plant Interactions. Studies in Ecology Volume 10, University of California Press, Berkley.

Dambach, C. A. 1944. A ten-year ecological study of adjoining grazed and ungrazed woodlands in northeastern Ohio. Ecological Monographs 14:69–105.

Davidson, S. E., and R. T. T. Forman. 1982. Herb and shrub dynamics in a mature forest: A thirty-year study. Bulletin Torrey Botanical Club 109:64–73.

DeCalesta, D. S. 1994. Effects of white-tailed deer on songbirds within managed forests in Pennsylvania. Journal of Wildlife Management 58:711–718.

DeGraaf, R. M., W. M. Healy, and R. T. Brooks. 1991. Effects of thinning and deer browsing on breeding birds in New England oak woodlands. Forest Ecology and Management 41:179–191.

Dessecker, D. R., and R. H. Yahner. 1987. Breeding bird communities associated with Pennsylvania northern hardwood clearcut stands. Proceedings Pennsylvania Academy Science 61:170–173.

Duffy, D. C., and A. J. Meier. 1992. Do Appalachian herbaceous understories ever recover from clearcutting? Conservation Biology 6:196–201.

Ehrlich, P. R., D. S. Dobkin, and D. Wheye. 1988. The Birder's Handbook. Simon and Schuster, New York.

Frelich, L. E., and C. G. Lorimer. 1985. Current and predicted long-term effects of deer browsing in hemlock forests in Michigan, USA. Biological Conservation 34:99–120.

Holmes, R. T., T. W. Sherry, and F. W. Sturges. 1986. Bird community dynamics in a temperate deciduous forest: Long-term trends at Hubbard Brook. Ecological Monographs 65:201–220.

Hooper, R. G., H. S. Crawford, and R. F. Harlow. 1973. Bird density and diversity as related to vegetation in forest recreational areas. Journal of Forestry 25:766–769.

Hough, A. F. 1965. A twenty-year record of understory vegetational change in a virgin Pennsylvania forest. Ecology 46:370–373.

Houston, D. R. 1981. Forest stand relationships. Pages 267–293 in The Gypsy Moth: Research toward Integrated Pest Management. (C. C. Doane and M. L. McManus, eds.) U.S. Department of Agriculture Technical Bulletin 1584.

Karr, J. R., and R. R. Roth. 1971. Vegetation structure and avian diversity in several New World areas. American Naturalist 105:423–435.

Kauffman, J. B., and W. C. Krueger. 1984. Livestock impacts on riparian ecosystems and streamside management implications: A review. Journal of Range Management 37:430–438.

Kimmins, J. P. 1987. Forest Ecology. MacMillan Publishing Co., New York.

Leimgruber, P., W. J. McShea, and J. Rappole. 1994. Predation on artificial nests in large forest blocks. Journal of Wildlife Management 58:255–261.

Leopold, A., L. K. Sowls, and D. L. Spencer. 1947. A survey of over-populated deer ranges in the United States. Journal of Wildlife Management 2:162–177.

Lynch, J. F., and D. F. Whigham. 1984. Effect of forest fragmentation on breeding bird communities in Maryland. Biological Conservation 28:287–324.

MacArthur, R. H., and J. W. MacArthur. 1961. On bird species diversity. Ecology 42:594–598.

MacArthur, R. H., J. W. MacArthur, and J. Peer. 1962. On bird species diversity. II. Prediction of bird census from habitat measurements. American Naturalist 96:167–174.

Martin, T. E., and J. J. Roper. 1988. Nest predation and nest-site selection of a western population of the Hermit Thrush. Condor 90:51–57.

McShea, W. J., M. V. McDonald, G. E. Morton, R. Meier, and J. H. Rappole.

1995. Long-term monitoring of Kentucky Warbler habitat selection. Auk 112: 375–381.

McShea, W. J., and J. H. Rappole. 1992. White-tailed deer as keystone species within forested habitats in Virginia. Virginia Journal of Science 43:177–186.

McShea, W. J., and G. Schwede. 1993. Variable acorn crops, and the response of white-tailed deer and other mast consumers. Journal of Mammalogy 74: 999–1006.

Miller, S. G., S. P. Bratton, and J. Hadidan. 1992. Impacts of white-tailed deer on endangered and threatened vascular plants. Natural Areas Journal 12:67–75.

Mills, G. S., J. B. Dunning, Jr., and J. M. Bates. 1991. The relationship between breeding bird density and vegetation volume. Wilson Bulletin 103:468–479.

Moss, D. 1978. Diversity of woodland song-bird populations. Journal of Animal Ecology 47:521–527.

Noy-Meir, I. 1981. Responses of vegetation to the abundance of mammalian herbivores. Pages 233–246 in Problems in Management of Locally Abundant Wild Mammals. (P. A. Jewell and S. Holt, eds.) Academic Press, New York.

Owen-Smith, N. 1987. Pleistocene extinctions: The pivotal role of megaherbivores. Paleobiology 13:351–362.

Pastor, J., and R. J. Naiman. 1992. Selective foraging and ecosystem processes in boreal forests. American Naturalist 139:690–705.

Pekins, P. J., and W. W. Mautz. 1987. Acorn usage by deer: Significance to oak management. Northern Journal of Applied Forestry 4:124–128.

Putman, R. J., P. J. Edwards, J. C. E. Mann, R. S. How, and S. D. Hill. 1989. Vegetation and faunal changes in an area of heavily grazed woodland following relief from grazing. Biological Conservation 47:13–22.

Rappole, J. H., E. S. Morton, T. E. Lovejoy III, and J. L. Ruos. 1995. Nearctic Avian Migrants in the Neotropics. Smithsonian Institution National Zoological Park Conservation and Research Center, Front Royal, VA.

Risenhoover, K. L., and S. A. Maass. 1986. The influence of moose on the composition and structure of Isle Royal forests. Canadian Journal of Forest Research 17:357–364.

Robisch, E., and R. G. Wright. 1995. A survey of ungulate management in selected U.S. national parks. Natural Areas Journal 15:117–123.

Roth, R. R. 1976. Spatial heterogeneity and bird species diversity. Ecology 57: 773–782.

Runkle, J. R. 1982. Patterns of disturbance in some old growth mesic forests of eastern North America. Ecology 63:1533–1546.

Runkle, J. R. 1991. Gap dynamics of old growth eastern forests: Management implications. Natural Areas Journal 11:19–25.

Sinclair, A. R. E., and M. Norton-Griffiths. 1979. Serengeti: Dynamics of an Ecosystem. University of Chicago Press, Chicago.

Smith, T. M., and H. H. Shugart. 1987. Territory size variation in the ovenbird: The role of habitat structure. Ecology 68:695–704.

Taylor, D. M., and C. D. Littlefield. 1986. Willow flycatcher and yellow warbler response to cattle grazing. Population Ecology 40:1169–1173.

Terres, J. K. 1980. The Audubon Society Encyclopedia of North American Birds. Knopf, New York.

Tilghman, N. G. 1989. Impacts of white-tailed deer on forest regeneration in northwestern Pennsylvania. Journal of Wildlife Management 53:524–532.

Underwood, H. B., and W. F. Porter. 1991. Values and science: White-tailed deer management in eastern national parks. Pages 67–73 *in* Transactions of the 56th North American Wildlife and Natural Resources Conference, Wildlife Management Institute, Washington.

Urban, D. L., and T. M. Smith. 1989. Microhabitat pattern and the structure of forest bird communities. American Naturalist 133:811–829.

Veblen, T. T., M. Mermoz, C. Martin, and E. Ramilo. 1989. The effect of exotic deer on forest regeneration and composition in Northern Patagonia. Journal of Applied Ecology 26:711–724.

Warren, R. J. 1991. Ecological justification for controlling deer populations in eastern national parks. Pages 56–66 *in* Transactions of the 56th North American Wildlife and Natural Resources Conference, Wildlife Management Institute, Washington.

Welsh, C. J. E., and W. M. Healy. 1993. Effect of even-aged timber management on bird species diversity and composition in northern hardwoods of New Hampshire. Wildlife Society Bulletin 21:143–1554.

19 Influence of Deer and Other Factors on an Old-Field Plant Community

An Eight-Year Exclosure Study

MICHAEL A. BOWERS

White-tailed deer commonly occur at densities of 5 to 20 deer/km^2 throughout much of the eastern United States and are considered pests in many areas. Deer have been described as "random tip browsers" (Trippensee 1948) and can be extremely generalized in diet. Atwood (1941), in fact, listed 614 species of plants known to be eaten by white-tailed deer. Because of their large body size, high densities, and generalized diet, deer have the potential of affecting successional pathways and local plant species composition, as well as ecosystem processes at both the local and landscape scales. The best-documented cases of such effects come from studies showing that browsing by deer can seriously inhibit the regeneration of a number of commercially important forest trees including hemlock (*Tsuga* spp.), pine (*Pinus* spp.), yew (Taxaceae), and white cedar (*Chamaecyparis* spp.) (Ross et al. 1970; Alverson et al. 1988 for review).

Though deer are generally considered a forest species, it is clear that optimal deer habitat combines dense forests stands for cover with open areas for foraging. Because of their mobility, deer use their landscape in a coarse-grained manner, concentrating foraging activities in areas of high food availability. The effect of deer on vegetation is related to two factors: (1) the intrinsic factors that control vegetation dynamics within communities (Huntly 1991) and (2) the degree to which foraging by deer becomes concentrated at certain sites over the landscape.

Lubchenco (1978) postulated that the effect of herbivory will vary with abiotic conditions, the competitive relationships among forage and nonforage plants, and the intensity of grazing pressure. An important corollary to this is that similar herbivore intensities can produce very different plant responses over a gradient of community types. For example, Armesto and Pickett (1985) suggested that herbivore effects may become more apparent in later successional seres in which species turnover is slow than in earlier successional communities in which turnover is high.

Deer occupy home ranges of 500 ha and make daily forays of 8 km or more (see Alverson et al. 1988). As a result of their mobility and the largely opposing needs of shelter and food, deer have both the potential and motivation to exploit a diversity of plant communities. A number of studies have shown not only do large herbivores respond to plant heterogeneity at the landscape scale but that they are important agents in creating it (see McNaughton 1985; McNaughton et al. 1988; Pastor et al. 1988). Most cases in which deer have been shown to affect vegetation significantly come from studies of mid- to late-successional plant communities in which forest regeneration is the primary focus and prime foraging sites of open areas with high net productivity are localized and limited.

Evaluating the full effect of deer overabundance requires an approach that both stresses within-community responses of vegetation to herbivory as well as considers the importance of landscape structure that may function to increase herbivore intensity in some areas and decrease it in others. More specifically, we need to know (1) what the relative importance of herbivory is compared with other potential important factors working within the plant community (seed dispersal, limiting nutrients, and historical factors) and (2) how the effects of herbivory vary over different communities within and between different landscapes. The first point addresses the relative susceptibility of vegetation to herbivore impact and the second the overall amount of herbivory a plant community might experience.

Here I report the results of a deer exclosure study that is being performed in an early successional plant community that is embedded in what might be called an agroecosystem—it is a landscape with relatively little forest cover (<25%) but with many open fields, pastures and row crops, and high densities of deer. Although hundreds of studies have examined a range of processes important to old-field plant succession in the eastern United States, only recently have effects of vertebrate herbivory been examined (Bowers 1993). My study offers a marked contrast to previous work examining deer effects in mid- to late-successional communities that, for the most part, have also been surrounded by extensive forests. My approach included (1) returning a portion of a field to the colonizing–seed-bank stage of succession so as not to miss early influences of herbivory; (2) constructing replicated series of deer exclosures; and (3) measuring vegetation in the different exclosures over time as a means of evaluating effects that deer have on plant community composition and change. I report the results for the first 8 years following disturbance and attempt to separate effects that are attributable to deer from those involving nutrients, seed dispersal, and historical factors (see De Steven 1991). Finally, I compare my results with those of other studies examining deer effects in different types of plant communities embedded in different types of landscapes.

METHODS

Study Site

This research is being performed in a 20-ha field at the Blandy Experimental Farm (Blandy), a field research station of the University of Virginia located on the west side of the Shenandoah River in Clarke County, Virginia. At an elevation of approximately 190 m, the site has an average annual precipitation of 94 cm and an average growing season of 157 days. Soils are generally deep and well-drained silt loams on gentle slopes (<10%) and originate from colluvial and alluvial sediments derived from limestone, shale, and siltstone.

The landscape surrounding Blandy is best characterized as an agroecosystem: farmlands interspersed with isolated woodlots and hedgerows (Figure 19.1). Forests account for 25% and agricultural land 61% of the 460-km^2 Clarke County area. On the west side of the Shenandoah River, where Blandy is located, the landscape is more open, with forest constituting about 15% and agricultural land about 80% of the total. Most woodlots in the region are isolated and are less than 20 ha.

I estimate the white-tailed deer population at and near Blandy to be relatively high and somewhere in the range of 12 to 20 deer/km^2 (based on casual observations). In 1993, Clarke County had one of the highest deer harvest rates in the state of Virginia, approximately 4 deer/km^2; in forested parts of the county the harvest was much higher, about 12 deer/km^2 (Matt Knox, Virginia Department of Game and Inland Fisheries, personal communication). These harvest figures suggest that my density estimates of deer at Blandy are probably conservative.

The research field has been under agricultural management for many

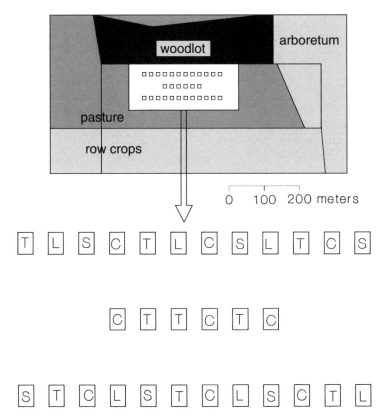

FIGURE 19.1. Surrounding landscape and field design of the experiment. The top figure shows the successional field (no shading), which was on the south side of a 40-ha woodlot and was surrounded by pasture, row crops, and an arboretum. Within the successional field were 30 fenced exclosure and control plots (shown as rectangles) and 9 unfenced controls (not shown). The bottom figure shows the position of total exclosures (T), small-gate exclosures (S), large-gate exclosures (L), and fenced control (C) plots within the successional field.

years and is comparable to old-field situations examined in other studies of succession. From at least 1958 through 1968 the field was managed under a 5-year rotation of 3 years pasture and 2 years crops (corn and barley). From 1969 to 1986, the field was used as a pasture and occasionally mowed for hay. In 1982, the field was the site of a study examining the mechanisms of plant succession relative to seed-bank dynamics and sources of seed input (Everett 1985). It was found that the colonization of disturbed sites was primarily by seeds in the soil (not those in the seed rain) and that the composition of seeds in the soil bank was more diverse than was indicated by the undisturbed plant community.

The research described here was performed in a 3-ha section of the field that was prepared by applying a general herbicide (Roundup at 3 quarts/acre) in April 1986 and, a month later, plowing and disking to a depth of 15 cm. These perturbations totally eliminated the extant pasture vegetation, sending the community back to a very early "colonizing" stage of plant succession. With the exception of a few individuals of common milkweed *(Asclepias syriaca)* and black locust *(Robinia pseudoacacia)* (which sprouted from roots and tubers), plants recolonizing the disturbed area appeared to originate from the seed bank and seed rain.

Experimental Control of Herbivores

Immediately after plowing (May 1986), 30 square 6-m × 6-m fenced herbivore exclosures were constructed in the field. Fences were constructed of 0.64-cm-wire-mesh hardware cloth that extended 0.2 m below and 1.0 m above ground and that was supported by 2-m metal fence posts; 25-cm aluminum flashing was attached to fence tops to discourage climbing by smaller herbivores. A second 2-m-high barbed wire fence was positioned 1 m outside each plot to keep deer from jumping over the interior fence (except for control plots; see below). This double fence design in combination with the relatively small size of exclosures has been totally successful in limiting access to deer.

Exclosures were positioned 15 m apart along three rows that ran parallel to the northeast field boundary, which abutted an 80- to 90-year-old oak–hickory–elm *(Quercus–Carya–Ulmus)* forest (Figure 19.1). Rows were placed at 10, 30, and 50 m distances into the forest—the rows at 10 and 50 m included 12 exclosures each; the row at 30 m had 6 exclosures. Pasture vegetation surrounded the disturbed area on the other three sides.

Treatments were designed to exclude different groups of herbivorous mammals: small-gate exclosures had 5-cm × 5-cm gates (eight per exclosure) at ground level and allowed access to small rodents but excluded larger mammals; large-gate exclosures had 20-cm × 20-cm gates (eight per exclosure) that allowed access to small rodents, woodchucks *(Marmota monax)*, and cottontail rabbits *(Sylvilagus floridanus)*; total exclosures had no gates and effectively excluded all mammals; and control plots had fences on only two sides and allowed access to all herbivores (including deer) but provided a control over which effects of fences per se and grazing could be examined (Bowers 1993).

Three replicates each of the four treatments were randomly assigned to plots in the two rows with 12 plots; three control and three total exclosure treatments were randomly assigned to the middle row with 6 plots. In addition, in 1990 an additional set of three control plots without fences were assigned to each of the three rows (either between fenced plots or at the end of the row). This created an overall design with nine fenced controls, nine unfenced controls, nine total exclosures, and six replicates each of large- and small-gate exclosures. For the purposes of this chapter I combine the five treatments into two groups: those that allowed access to deer (both types of control plots, $n = 18$) versus those that excluded deer (total exclosure and small- and large-gate exclosures, $n = 21$).

Vegetation Measurements

For the first 4 years of the study, percent cover of all plants was measured in 10 permanently located 50-cm × 50-cm quadrats (0.25 m^2) in each of the 30 plots; quadrats were arranged in a stratified block design over the area within plots and at least 0.5 m from exclosure fences. Locations were marked with 5-cm aluminum nails embedded in the soil. Plants were censused in early June and again in late August, 1986–89; the timing of sampling generally matched the phenological peaks of early and late-season plants. To minimize disturbance within exclosures more frequent sampling was avoided. Coverage of living plants was measured ocularly, to species, by use of reference disks of known percent cover. Full censuses of the plots were not conducted between 1990 and 1993. After about 6 years the plant community shifted from lower-growing herbaceous vegetation to larger and taller woody trees and shrubs. The change in the plant community necessitated a change in the sampling methodology. Consequently, starting in 1994, I focused on just the woody plants, and censuses were made by counting the number of woody seedlings and stems by species within 1 m of each fence and in the interior (>1 m from fences) of all exclosure and control plots. Plant identification and taxonomy follows Strausbaugh and Core (1970).

Data Analyses

In this chapter I focus on differences in woody stem abundance and diversity for plots with and without deer access. Data analyses focus on censuses taken in 1994—after 8 years of deer exclusion. I consider both species-level (number of stems by species) and community-level variables. The latter included the sum total of stems of all species combined, plant species richness, and a measure of species diversity, or evenness: $D = 1/$ Σp_i^2, where p_i is the relative number of stems of species i summed over n species. While accessibility of plots to deer is the main treatment factor, I also considered the importance of a number of factors: distance of the plot from the woodlot (in meters), location of stem counts in relation to the fence, and soil moisture as measured in kilopascals with a soil tensiometer (Soilmoisture Equipment Corporation, Santa Barbara, California). Soil moisture was measured in July 1986, 1988, and 1992, and an average value was taken for each plot. I also tested whether features of the colonizing plant community were in any way related to the diversity and abundance of woody plants in 1994. Treating features of the colonizing plant community as explicit variables allowed tests of the importance of relay floristics of herbaceous species to establishment of woody plants (Keever 1950; Egler 1954; Gill and Marks 1991). The colonizing plant community (years 1 through 4) was characterized relative to overall plant cover, year-to-year variability in cover, and species diversity averaged over the first 4 years. Analysis of variance and covariance were used to test for treatment differences. All variables were logarithmically or arcsine (for proportional data) transformed prior to analyses.

I also used logistic regression to provide a more detailed analysis of the various factors that might affect the presence versus absence of particular woody species. This analysis is appropriate because it allows consideration of both categorical (deer access, fence, and row) and continuous (soil moisture and features of the colonizing plant community) variables.

RESULTS

In 1994, after 8 years of succession, 19 woody plant species had colonized the field (Table 19.1); there was an average ($\pm s$) of 1.08 $\pm$ 0.83 woody stems/m^2 over the field. Analysis of variance showed that climbing bittersweet *(Celastrus scandens)*, black locust, and black walnut *(Juglans nigra)* all decreased in abundance and smooth sumac *(Rhus glabra)* increased with distance from the woodlot. Two species showed significant differences between plots with and without deer: honeysuckle *(Lonicera tatarica)* was more abundant where deer were excluded and black walnut was more abundant in plots with deer access.

The density of all woody stems did not vary with distance from the woodlot ($F_{2,36} = 0.08$, $P < 0.80$), near versus away from fences (0.95 $\pm$ 0.68 stems/m^2 versus 1.02 $\pm$ 1.43 stems/m^2), or between deer exclosures and control plots (1.18 $\pm$ 1.03 stems/m^2 versus 1.02 $\pm$ 0.59 stems/m^2;

TABLE 19.1

Number of rooted stems per plot (36 m²) after 8 years of succession

Woody plant species	Near woodlot		Intermediate distance from woodlot		Far from woodlot	
	−	+	−	+	−	+
Climbing bittersweet (Celastrus scandens)	21.5 (22.0)	17.7 (11.7)	15.3 (11.5)	4.2 (3.0)	8.7 (9.3)	8.0 (8.6)
Poison ivy (Rhus radicans)	0.6 (1.1)	6.5 (15.9)	0.0 (−)	20.3 (23.2)	29.0 (49.7)	10.5 (12.3)
Smooth sumac (Rhus glabra)	4.1 (6.9)	0.0 (−)	17.7 (16.7)	17.7 (18.4)	5.1 (10.6)	10.1 (16.0)
Black walnut (Juglans nigra)	2.6 (2.2)	5.7 (3.1)	0.0 (−)	0.5 (0.8)	0.0 (−)	0.2 (0.4)
Honeysuckle (Lonicera tatarica)	3.5 (4.3)	0.0 (−)	0.7 (1.2)	1.0 (2.0)	1.4 (2.0)	0.0 (−)
Black locust (Robinia pseudoxacacia)	2.4 (1.9)	1.0 (0.9)	1.3 (1.5)	0.8 (1.0)	0.1 (0.3)	0.2 (0.4)
White mulberry (Morus alba,)	1.3 (3.0)	0.0 (−)	0.7 (1.2)	0.3 (0.8)	0.2 (0.4)	0.0 (−)
Wild grape (Vitis sp.)	0.2 (0.7)	2.5 (5.6)	0.0 (−)	0.0 (−)	0.0 (−)	0.2 (0.4)
Hackberry (Celtis occidentalis)	1.2 (2.6)	0.0 (−)	0.0 (−)	0.0 (−)	0.2 (0.4)	0.0 (−)
Slippery elm (Ulmus rubra)	0.3 (0.7)	0.0 (−)	0.3 (0.6)	0.0 (−)	0.4 (1.0)	0.0 (−)
Black cherry (Prunus serotina)	0.0 (−)	0.8 (1.6)	0.0 (−)	0.0 (−)	0.2 (0.4)	0.0 (−)
Tree of heaven (Ailanthus altissima)	0.0 (−)	0.3 (0.8)	0.3 (0.6)	0.0 (−)	0.4 (1.3)	0.0 (−)
Coralberry (Symphoricarpos orbiculatus)	0.0 (−)	0.3 (0.8)	0.0 (−)	0.2 (0.4)	0.1 (0.3)	0.2 (0.4)
Privet (Ligustrum vulgare)	0.2 (0.4)	0.0 (−)	0.0 (−)	0.2 (0.4)	0.0 (−)	0.2 (0.4)
Black ash (Fraxinus nigra)	0.0 (−)	0.0 (−)	0.0 (−)	0.5 (1.2)	0.0 (−)	0.0 (−)
Red cedar (Juniperus virginiana)	0.1 (0.3)	0.0 (−)	0.0 (−)	0.0 (−)	0.1 (0.3)	0.0 (−)
Spicebush (Lindera benzoin)	0.0 (−)	0.0 (−)	0.0 (−)	0.0 (−)	0.1 (0.3)	0.0 (−)
Sassafras (Sassafras albidum)	0.1 (0.3)	0.0 (−)	0.0 (−)	0.0 (−)	0.0 (−)	0.0 (−)
Poplar (Populus sp.)	0.0 (−)	0.0 (−)	0.0 (−)	0.0 (−)	0.1 (0.3)	0.0 (−)

Notes: Mean number of stems (standard deviations in parentheses) is given for both deer exclosure (−) and control (+) plots and for distances near, intermediate, and far from the woodlot. The 19 woody plant species are listed in decreasing order of abundance.

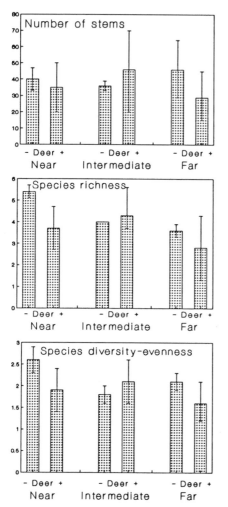

FIGURE 19.2. Community-level effects of treatments. Community-level variables included the number of woody stems, species richness, and species diversity–evenness of woody plants for plots with (+) deer and without (−) deer and for sites near, intermediate, and far from the wood-lot. Standard errors are also indicated.

see Figure 19.2). However, species richness was 128% higher near fences than away from them (3.2 versus 2.5 species/plot; see Table 19.2) and 122% higher where deer were excluded than where they had access to the plants (4.4 versus 3.6 species/plot; $F_{1,38} = 5.2$, $P < 0.02$). The diversity, or evenness, of woody plants showed no field, fence, or deer effect (all tests $P > 0.20$).

Correlation analyses showed that the diversity of woody species in a plot was positively related with the diversity and year-to-year variation in herbaceous plant coverage during the first 4 years of succession (respec-

TABLE 19.2
Community-level variables in relation to exclosure fences and woodlot

Community-level variable and distance from fence	Near woodlot		Intermediate distance from woodlot		Far from woodlot	
	−	+	−	+	−	+
Total stems[a]						
<1 m	1.07 (0.41)	0.67 (0.16)	1.13 (0.28)	1.33 (0.64)	1.38 (1.35)	0.47 (0.08)
≥1 m	1.21 (0.90)	1.58 (0.83)	0.85 (0.28)	1.82 (1.82)	1.18 (2.16)	1.63 (0.70)
Species richness[b]						
<1 m	4.4 (0.5)	2.7 (1.5)	3.3 (0.6)	3.0 (1.7)	3.0 (0.9)	1.7 (0.9)
≥1 m	3.2 (1.7)	3.0 (0.0)	2.7 (0.6)	3.7 (0.6)	1.3 (1.5)	1.7 (1.7)
Species diversity[c]						
<1 m	2.5 (0.5)	1.8 (0.7)	2.0 (0.3)	2.2 (1.1)	2.1 (0.4)	1.6 (0.5)
≥1 m	1.8 (0.8)	2.1 (0.3)	1.6 (0.6)	2.0 (0.8)	1.4 (0.4)	1.1 (0.2)

Notes: Variables were measured within 1 m of and greater than 1 m from fences or sampling area edge for deer exclosure (−) and control (+) plots and at distances near, intermediate, and far from the woodlot. Standard deviations are in parentheses.

[a] Mean number of stems per square meter summed over all species.

[b] Mean number of species per plot.

[c] Number of equally represented species per plot (see text).

tively, $r = 0.49$ and $r = 0.53$, df = 28, $P < 0.01$). There were more woody species in plots that had more variable cover and a higher diversity of herbaceous plants during the first 4 years of succession.

Logistic regression analyses showed that the presence versus absence of woody species was related to six different variables (Table 19.3). The presence of fences and distance from the woodlot were by far the most important of these: climbing bittersweet and honeysuckle were found more often near fences and smooth sumac was found away from fences; black walnut, climbing bittersweet, black locust, and poison ivy were all found closer to the woodlot than away from it. Soil moisture and the mean diversity, mean coverage, and variation in coverage of the herbaceous plant community also appeared to be important to some species. Black walnut was the only species to show a significant effect of deer exclusion; it occurred more frequently where deer were present than where they were excluded.

TABLE 19.3

Correlation coefficients between the presence of woody plant species and potentially important variables

Woody plant species	Soil moisture[a]	Deer exclusion[b]	Proximity to fence[c]	Field position[d]	Colonizing plant community		Species diversity[g]
					Cover		
					Mean[e]	s[f]	
Climbing bittersweet	0.23 (+)	—	0.27 (+)	0.17 (−)	0.11 (+)	—	0.09 (−)
Poison ivy	—	—	—	0.04 (+)	—	—	—
Smooth sumac	0.15 (−)	—	0.26 (−)	—	0.15 (−)	—	0.07 (−)
Black walnut	—	0.15 (−)	—	0.17 (−)	0.15 (−)	0.10 (+)	0.04 (+)
Honeysuckle	—	—	0.29 (+)	—	—	—	—
Black locust	—	—	—	0.24 (−)	—	—	—
White mulberry	—	—	—	—	—	—	—
Hackberry	—	—	—	—	—	—	—

Notes: Correlation coefficients were determined by logistic regression analyses. All coefficients listed are significant at $P \le 0.05$; the sign of the relationship is given in parentheses. Only species that occurred in at least 10% of the plots are included (listed in decreasing frequency of occurrence).

[a] Soil moisture was measured for each plot during July 1986, 1988, and 1992 by means of a soil tensiometer probe. Soil moisture measurements (in negative kilopascals) were averaged over the three sampling periods to yield a mean value for each plot.

[b] Categorical variable corresponding to whether or not deer were excluded.

[c] Categorical variable corresponding to whether the sample was taken near (<1 m) or far (≥1 m) from fences.

[d] Categorical variable indicating position in the field in relation to the woodlots: 1 = near, 2 = intermediate, and 3 = far.

[e] Mean percent cover of plants in plots as determined in 1986–89 censuses.

[f] Standard deviation in cover of plants in plots over the 1986–89 censuses.

[g] Average species diversity of plots in 1986–89 censuses.

DISCUSSION

Within-Community Effects

The results presented here suggest a relatively weak effect of deer on the establishment of woody plants during the first 8 years of plant succession. Specifically, species richness averaged only one species higher where deer were excluded than where they were present. Also, distance from the forest edge, the presence versus absence of fences, soil moisture, and features of the colonizing plant community all accounted for more of the variation in the presence versus absence of individual woody plant species than did the exclusion of deer. Whereas black walnut showed the strongest response to deer exclusion, it occurred more frequently outside than inside deer exclosures—a result that might reflect squirrel accessibility and caching rather than deer effects per se.

A partial explanation for the lack of marked deer effects is related to the dynamical and highly variable nature of early successional plant communities. Armesto and Pickett (1985) suggested that early in succession species turnover may be rapid, and any effect of herbivory may be quickly erased. By contrast, later in succession, when species turnover is slower, herbivory might have larger effects on the plant community. The expectation then is that herbivore effects may be more apparent in later than in earlier successional seres. That many studies have shown that deer influence vegetation in later successional seres, whereas they did not in my study, seems to support this scenario.

In interpreting my results I assume that herbivory by deer was sufficiently intense to represent a potential factor of importance to the vegetation and that my design had sufficient statistical power to detect any effect present. I address these in order. First, the field appeared to be heavily used by deer. Deer were consistently observed in groups of 3 to 30 individuals; some individuals appeared to spend days at a time in the field. In 1989 more than 70% of the 0.25-m^2 censused quadrats and over 80% of some preferred forage species in the field showed evidence of browsing (Bowers 1993). Hence, I conclude that deer were present in high densities, herbivore pressure was moderate to intense, and the potential for strong deer effects was high.

Some herb species showed strong responses to deer exclusion early in the study (Bowers and Sacchi 1991). However, the relationship between short- and longer-term responses of the vegetation to herbivory appeared to be buffered by community-level interactions involving other consumers and plants. For example, Bowers and Sacchi (1991) reported that red clover *(Trifolium pratense)* occurred in deer exclosures 3 years into the study at abundances 150% that in controls. However, a subsequent density-dependent infection of red clover by a rust-forming fungus more strongly affected red clover abundance (especially in deer exclosures) than did herbivory by deer. The result was that after the effects of the fungus were accounted for, red clover abundance was higher where deer were present than where they were excluded. So while the direct effect of herbivory on forage plants was negative, by keeping plant abundances below that at which fungal infections became lethal, the net effect of herbivores was positive for some plant species. Cases like this stress that simple cause-and-effect relationships between herbivore pressure and plant responses may be difficult to infer from abundance data alone.

Second, with 21 exclosures and 19 controls, the design of the experiment had a degree of replication several times that of previous studies using exclosures, the majority of which have been unreplicated (e.g., Ross et al. 1970). Post hoc calculations showed that the power of my design to detect a 50% difference in species- or community-level variables between deer exclosure and control plots ranged from 40 to 70%. Although this level of power can not be considered ideal from a statistical perspective, the fact that I was able to detect a number of other effects suggests that the effect of deer is of relatively minor importance.

The fence effect is clearly related to the dispersal of propagules by birds, who used fence tops for perching and, hence, defecation, thereby contributing to the local seed rain. Other studies have shown the importance of bird-disseminated seeds to patterns of old-field plant succession (Livingston 1972; Smith 1975; McDonnell and Stiles 1983). The three species (climbing bittersweet, honeysuckle, and smooth sumac) that showed a significant fence effect occurred near fences at densities 2 to 24 times that of densities away from the fence. It is clear that the fence effect is partially an artifact of using exclosures to limit accessibility to deer. Nonetheless, data from the unfenced control plots suggest that the dispersal of seeds by birds over the field is perhaps the single most important factor affecting the plant community. Specifically, the gradient in woody plant diversity and the more frequent occurrence of several species near the woodlot than far from it probably also reflected the effect of bird-dispersed seeds (birds tended to forage from the woodlot out into the field). McDonnell and Stiles (1983), in fact, reported that seed recruitment by birds was higher nearer than farther from the edge of a woodlot and higher near artificial perching sites than away—results that are very similar to those reported here.

My results also suggest that the development of vegetation during the first 4 years of succession is at least as important to woody plant establishment as is herbivory by deer. Specifically, I found that the diversity of woody stems was positively related to the year-to-year variation in herbaceous plant coverage and the overall diversity of herbaceous plants and negatively correlated with average plant coverage over the first 4 years of succession. These features of the colonizing plant community were largely independent of herbivore exclusion (Bowers 1993). Gill and Marks (1991) found that the establishment of woody seedlings was much reduced under herbs compared with in the open. They attributed this pattern to more intense competition with herbs and higher levels of herbivory by rodents under cover than in the open—both of which contributed to elevated woody seedling mortality and reduced growth rates. That the diversity of woody plants was higher in plots with lower and more variable herbaceous cover is just what Gill and Marks (1991) predicted.

Herbivory has been treated as representing an important within-community component of disturbance (Denslow 1980; Karr and Freeman 1985). But as Lubchenco (1978) noted, the effects of this disturbance can be variable. In a study of rabbit grazing, Zeevalking and Fresco (1977) found plant species diversity to peak under intermediate levels of herbivory and to decrease under stronger or weaker herbivore pressure. By contrast, Milton (1947) found that grazing by sheep *(Ovis aries)* led to a monotonic decrease in plant species diversity with increasing grazing pressure. These different responses appear to revolve around which plant species are eaten, the intensity with which such species interact with other species in the community, and the rate at which species are replaced. The turnover of species is a key factor determining whether herbivores have an effect or not (Armesto and Pickett 1985). For example, it has been suggested that herbivores can speed up succession by eating earlier successional species, thereby increasing the rate by which later successional species invade (e.g., Whelan and Main 1979; McBrien et al. 1983); herbivores can also slow down succession by eating and suppressing later occurring species, effectively extending the period of dominance of early occurring species (Watt 1981; Brown 1982). The exact form of the response, however, depends on relationships among competitive ability, palatability, and occurrence of species in successional sequences. Thus, effects of herbivory will vary depending on a suite of factors that are both intrinsic and extrinsic to plants composing the plant community (Dirzo 1984; Huntly 1991). In this context, herbivory (and especially herbivory by deer) cannot be viewed as a separate causal factor but rather one of many processes that contribute interactively to successional change (Pickett et al. 1987).

Landscape-Level Effects

One final issue is relating my results, which suggest a weak effect of deer on successional fields, to those studies that show strong deer effects on the regeneration of vegetation in clear-cuts (e.g., Ross et al. 1970; Alverson et al. 1988). Deer have large home ranges (500 ha; Alverson et al. 1988) and therefore have the potential of using a diversity of plant communities. Large herbivores, in fact, often respond to plant heterogeneity at the landscape scale (McNaughton 1985; McNaughton et al. 1988; Pastor et al. 1988). Most cases in which deer have been shown to affect vegetation significantly come from studies of mid- to late-successional plant communities in which forest regeneration is the primary focus, and prime foraging sites of open areas of high net productivity are localized, limited, and surrounded by forests.

Evaluating the full effect of deer overabundance requires an approach that both stresses within-community responses of vegetation to herbivory as well as considers the importance of landscape structure that may function to increase herbivore intensity in some areas and decrease it in others. More specifically, the overall amount of herbivory a plant community might experience could vary with the structure of the landscape. Clear-cuts are typically surrounded by forests within which food availability for deer would typically be low or unavailable. In response, deer undoubtedly concentrate foraging within clear-cuts where net primary productivity and food availability would be high. One result would be strong, localized deer effects on the vegetation. By contrast, my study site was embedded within an agricultural landscape mosaic composed of an abundance of fields but relatively little forest habitat. Even though the density of deer over this landscape approached that of more forested areas, the abundance of field habitat would allow foraging activities to be spread out more equitably over the landscape. Hence, I predict that the per-area use of foraging areas by deer would be lower at my site than in studies focusing on clear-cuts. The point is that the relative effect of deer on vegetation may vary both with the dynamics of vegetational change within habitats and with the arrangement of habitat types over whole landscapes. In both respects, deer effects should have been less in my study than in those focusing on mid-successional plant communities embedded in largely forested landscapes.

ACKNOWLEDGMENTS

I thank J. Yoder for assistance in the field and J. L. Dooley for discussion. Comments by W. McShea, J. F. Rieger, and an anonymous reviewer on an earlier version of the manuscript were very helpful. This project was funded through grants from the Blandy Experimental Farm.

REFERENCES CITED

Alverson, W. S., D. A. Waller, and S. L. Solheim. 1988. Forests too deer: Edge effects in northern Wisconsin. Conservation Biology 2:348–358.

Armesto, J. J., and S. T. A. Pickett. 1985. Experiments on disturbance in old-field plant communities: Impact on species richness and abundance. Ecology 66:230–240.

Atwood, E. L. 1941. White-tailed deer foods of the United States. Journal of Wildlife Management 5:314–342.

Bowers, M. A. 1993. Influence of herbivorous mammals on an old-field plant community: Years 1–4 after disturbance. Oikos 67:129–141.

Bowers, M. A., and C. F. Sacchi. 1991. Fungal mediation of a plant–herbivore interaction in an early successional plant community. Ecology 72:1032–1037.

Brown, V. K. 1982. The phytophagous insect community and its impact on early successional habits. Pages 205–213 in Proceedings Fifth International Symposium on Insect–Plant Relationships. (J. H. Visser and A. K. Minks, eds.) Pudoc, Wageningen, The Netherlands.

Denslow, J. S. 1980. Patterns of plant species diversity during succession under different disturbance regimes. Oecologia 46:18–21.

De Steven, D. 1991. Experiments on mechanisms of tree establishment in old-field succession: Seedling survival and growth. Ecology 72:1076–1088.

Dirzo, R. 1984. Herbivory: A phytocentric overview. Pages 141–165 in Perspectives in Plant Population Ecology. (R. Dirzo and J. Sarukhan, eds.) Sinauer Associates, Sunderland, MA.

Egler, F. E. 1954. Vegetation science concepts. 1. Initial floristic composition—a factor in old-field vegetation development. Vegetatio 4:412–417.

Everett, J. B. 1985. Mechanisms of community establishment in secondary succession. Master's thesis, University of Virginia, Charlottesville.

Gill, D. S., and P. L. Marks. 1991. Tree and shrub seedling colonization of old fields in central New York. Ecological Monographs 61:183–205.

Huntly, N. 1991. Herbivores and the dynamics of communities and ecosystems. Annual Review of Ecology and Systematics 22:477–503.

Karr, J. R., and K. E. Freeman. 1985. Disturbance and vertebrates: An integrative perspective. Pages 153–168 in The Ecology of Natural Disturbance and Patch Dynamics. (S. T. A. Pickett and P. S. White, eds.) Academic Press, New York.

Keever, C. 1950. Causes of succession on old fields of the Piedmont, North Carolina. Ecological Monographs 20:229–250.

Livingston, R. B. 1972. Influence of birds, stones and soil on the establishment of pasture juniper, *Juniperus communis,* and red cedar, *J. virginiana,* in New England pastures. Ecology 53:1141–1147.

Lubchenco, J. 1978. Plant species diversity in a marine intertidal community: Importance of herbivore food preference and algal competitive abilities. American Naturalist 112:23–39.

McBrien, H. R., R. Harmsen, and A. Crowder. 1983. A case of insect grazing affecting plant succession. Ecology 64:1035–1039.

McDonnell, M. J., and E. W. Stiles. 1983. The structural complexity of old field vegetation and the recruitment of bird dispersed plant species. Oecologia 56: 109–116.

McNaughton, S. J. 1985. Ecology of a grazing ecosystem: The Serengeti. Ecological Monographs 55:259–294.

McNaughton, S. J., R. W. Ruess, and S. W. Seagle. 1988. Large mammals and process dynamics in African ecosystems. Bioscience 38:794–800.

Milton, W. E. J. 1947. The composition of natural hill and pasture, under controlled and free grazing, cutting and manuring. Welsh Journal of Agriculture 14:182–195.

Pastor, J., B. R. J. Naiman, B. Dewey, and P. F. McIness. 1988. Moose, microbes and the boreal forest. Bioscience 38:770–777.

Pickett, S. T. A., S. L. Collins, and J. J. Armesto. 1987. Models, mechanisms, and pathways of succession. Botanical Review 53:335–371.

Ross, B. A., J. R. Bray, and W. H. Marshall. 1970. Effects of long-term deer exclusion on a *Pinus resinosa* forest in north-central Minnesota. Ecology 51: 1088–1101.

Smith, A. J. 1975. Invasion and ecesis of bird-disseminated woody plants in a temperate forest sere. Ecology 56:19–34.

Strausbaugh, P. D., and E. L. Core. 1970. Flora of West Virginia. Vols. 1–4. 2nd edition. West Virginia University Press, Morgantown.

Trippensee, R. E. 1948. Wildlife Management: Upland Game and General Principles. McGraw-Hill, New York.

Watt, A. S. 1981. A comparison of grazed and ungrazed grassland in East Anglian Breckland. Journal of Ecology 69:499–508.

Whelan, R. J., and A. R. Main. 1979. Insect grazing and post-fire succession in southwest Australian woodland. Australian Journal of Ecology 4:387–398.

Zeevalking, H. J., and L. F. M. Fresco. 1977. Rabbit grazing and diversity in a dune area. Vegetatio 35:193–196.

20 Role of Refuges in the Dynamics of Outlying Deer Populations

Two Examples from the
Agricultural Midwest

LONNIE P. HANSEN, CHARLES M. NIXON,
AND JEFF BERINGER

Historical trends in white-tailed deer populations of the agricultural Midwest (Kückler 1964) are similar to those reported throughout much of their range (McCabe and McCabe 1984). Deer numbers in the Midwest declined from abundance before the arrival of early European settlers to near extinction in the early 1900s (Pietsch 1954; Robb 1959; Gladfelter 1984). Restoring deer populations usually involved more restrictive hunting regulations, public education, and reintroduction of deer onto newly created refuges from hunting. Often, introduced deer were from outlying states (McDonald and Miller 1993) or private deer farms.

Modern deer hunting in most of the agricultural Midwest began in the 1950s. Habitat loss during the 1970s produced concerns about the viability of deer populations in these landscapes. This prompted recommendations that resource agencies maintain existing refuges and create new ones (Zwank et al. 1979; Gladfelter 1984). Despite the loss of permanent cover to agriculture and urban development, deer populations grew rapidly during the 1980s. This allowed state resource agencies to further liberalize harvests and recreational deer hunting opportunities.

Deer in the agricultural Midwest have adapted to the fragmented habitats created by farming activities by taking advantage of the nutritious and abundant food such activities provide. Carrying capacity in this agricultural setting far exceeds current deer population levels. Deer sampled from areas with densities exceeding 75 deer/km^2 were healthy and showed little evidence of stress often associated with high-density populations in other parts of their range (L. P. Hansen, unpublished data).

Landowner tolerance of deer is the most important issue driving deer management programs in the agricultural Midwest (Stoll and Mountz 1983; Witter et al. 1987; Morgan et al. 1992). Although deer in this region browse on native flora, their effects on forest regeneration and sensitive plant species are somewhat buffered by abundant agricultural crops. As a result, most deer management programs have responded to more sensitive political issues. Currently, deer numbers are managed near a "cultural carrying capacity" based on landowner attitudes. Little research has been done on the effects of deer on flora and fauna in the agricultural Midwest; however, many managers believe deer populations at current levels have minimal effects.

Hunting is usually the primary mortality factor of white-tailed deer in the agricultural Midwest (Gladfelter 1984; Nixon et al. 1991) and is used as a tool for managing deer populations on a regional level. In areas with limited forest cover and high hunter densities, nonrefuge deer populations are annually reduced. Dispersal from high-density sources, usually refuges from hunting, may be necessary to replenish these local populations annually (Nixon et al. 1988, 1991). Conversely, in some areas under less-intensive hunting pressure, deer refuges could deter regional deer population management (Roseberry et al. 1969). Also, refuges supporting large deer populations often suffer from reduced floral and faunal biodiversity as a result of deer browsing (Tilghman 1989).

Our objective was to evaluate the effect of refuges on outlying deer populations within two study sites that represent extremes of farming intensity in the agricultural Midwest. We compared the demography of deer on and off refuge in each area and quantified the contribution of each refuge to outlying deer populations.

METHODS

Study Sites

The study sites were located in east-central Illinois and north-central Missouri. The east-central Illinois study area (ECISA) totaled 3 km² in Piatt County. Sixty-four percent of the site was in row-crop agriculture, and it contained a much higher percentage of forest (36%) than did surrounding landscapes (<3%) because it included a heavily forested 0.6-km² park and 4-H camp (Nixon et al. 1991). The park and camp served as a refuge from hunting. Most of the area outside the refuge consisted of level, intensively farmed landscapes with fragmented forest existing only as narrow bands along streams (Nixon et al. 1991). The north-central Missouri study area (NCMSA) covered 709 km ^{2} in Randolph and Macon counties. Different project objectives prompted selection of a study area much larger than that in Illinois. Topography was gently rolling; the landscape included row-crop agriculture in fertile bottoms (38%), pasture on hillsides and cleared uplands (43%), and scattered forest (18%) (Giessman et al. 1986; Pauley 1991). Surface mining for coal was common before 1993, and mined land in various stages of succession and reclamation dominated parts of the study area. Within NCMSA were two refuges, a 0.7-km ^{2} state park and a 2-km ^{2} privately owned landholding. The two study sites represent the ends of the spectrum of agricultural intensity in the Midwest: the area around ECISA was among the most intensively farmed and that around NCMSA the least intensively farmed (Gladfelter 1984).

Illinois and Missouri progressively liberalized harvest opportunities during our studies to stabilize growing deer populations. More of the landscape around NCMSA was in deer habitat and supported higher deer, hunter, and harvest densities than did the area around ECISA. In 1990, simulated deer densities were 5.3 deer/km ^{2} (42.8 deer/km ^{2} forest), hunter densities were 1.7 hunters/km ^{2} (14.2 hunters/km ^{2} forest), and deer harvest densities were 1.3 deer/km ^{2} (10.3 deer/km ^{2} forest) around NCMSA (Hansen, unpublished data). In 1985, simulated deer densities were 0.4 deer/km ^{2} (16.7 deer/km ^{2} forest), hunter densities were 0.3 hunters/km ^{2} (11.3 hunters/km ^{2} forest), and deer harvest densities were 0.1 deer/km ^{2} (3.8 deer/km ^{2} forest) around ECISA (Hansen, unpublished data).

We had multiple research objectives on each study area that did not include a priori a comparison of refuge effects on two areas of the agricultural Midwest. Funding limitations prevented development of a replicated experiment adequate to make a regional assessment of refuge effects. A posteriori consideration and lack of replication prevented statistical inferences to areas beyond the two study sites (Hurlbert 1984). As a result, our evaluation here is limited to refuge effects on two specific study sites within the agricultural Midwest.

Deer Demographic Measurements

From 1980 through 1986 we captured 115 male and 121 female white-tailed deer on ECISA by means of rocket-powered nets (Hawkins et al. 1968) or a 4.6-m ^{2} drop net (Nixon et al. 1991). From 1988 through 1993 we captured 83 male and 209 female deer on NCMSA by means of rocket nets and modified Clover traps (Clover 1954).

Deer captured on both study sites were manually restrained and placed into one of two age categories—fawn, 1 year or younger, or adult, older than 1 year—based on size and, for males, antler development. We tagged all deer with numbered metal ear tags. Eighty females on ECISA were marked with 7.5-cm-wide plastic collars bearing reflective numbers or letters. Fifty-eight females, some previously marked with plastic collars, received radio collars (Wildlife Materials, Carbondale, Illinois, or Telonics, Incorporated, Mesa, Arizona). We marked all males captured on ECISA with plastic ear tags (Y-Tex Corporation, Cody, Wyoming) that had vinyl strips attached; 38 males received expandable radio collars (Wildlife Materials or Telonics, Incorporated) (Nixon et al. 1991). All females on NCMSA received mortality-sensing radio transmitters (Telonics, Incorporated or Advanced Telemetry Systems, Incorporated, Isanti, Minnesota). Males were marked with only metal ear tags.

We located radio-marked deer three to four times per week on both study areas by means of receivers attached to truck-mounted antennas. Deer that dispersed or migrated were relocated using aircraft.

More females than males were fitted with transmitters, especially on NCMSA, because knowledge of their survival rates was more critical to understanding and predicting population change. Given the low number of radio-collared males and unknown mortality rates due to capture myopathy, especially on NCMSA, survival comparisons here are confined to females.

Annual and seasonal survival rates of radio-collared females on both study areas were determined using the program MICROMORT (Heisey and Fuller 1985). Seasonal survival intervals for yearling and older deer were January–May, June–September, and October–December. We generally first captured fawns when they were 6–9 months, so survival could be directly measured for only the January–May period of their first year.

Sample sizes of deer marked with transmitters on and off the ECISA refuge often were not large enough to make statistical inferences about survival. However, the fate of 93% of all females marked on ECISA was known, and seasonal losses could be enumerated with reasonable accuracy (Nixon et al. 1991).

We determined fecundity of road-killed females from February through May, 1989–93, on NCMSA and in surrounding counties. Data collected for each doe included its age and the number and sex of fetuses (Gilbert 1966). We indirectly measured fawn survival from in utero to

4 months by comparing the mean number of deer recruited with the mean number in utero. Low in utero mortality for white-tailed deer (Teer et al. 1965) suggests that most early mortality occurred between birth and 4 months. We did not measure fecundity of deer on ECISA but did determine the survival of 17 fawns captured and marked when less than 1 week (Nixon et al. 1991).

We categorized seasonal movements of marked deer on both study areas as dispersals or migrations. We defined dispersal as a permanent movement of at least 4 km away from an established home range. Migrations were seasonal movements of at least 4 km between well-defined winter and summer ranges. A comparison of seasonal centers of activity revealed the type of movement (i.e., sedentary, dispersal, or migration) of radio-marked deer. Movement data for marked deer that were not radio collared were based on observations by project staff, reports from the public, and recovery locations of deer killed in collisions with vehicles or during the hunting seasons. Generally for these we did not know when the movement had occurred or if it was a migration or dispersal. These deer were not used in the evaluation of movement types and times but were included when determining contributions of refuges to outlying deer populations. We used chi-square analysis (goodness of fit) to determine sex and age differences in the proportion moving. Unbalanced analysis of variance procedures (SAS Institute 1990) were used to test for differences in distance moved.

We determined fawn recruitment for marked does through repeated observations of does and fawns from August through October during 1981–86 on ECISA and 1989–93 on NCMSA. Many deer on ECISA were easily observable during spotlight counts, routine operations, and periodic drive counts (Nixon et al. 1991). We used similar techniques on NCMSA but made most observations after leaf drop in late October by means of a helicopter fitted with a telemetry antenna. Radio-marked does were located, flushed from cover, and their fawns observed.

The Simulation Model

We used a deterministic model to simulate the dynamics of deer on and off refuge on both study areas and to measure the effect of dispersals from refuges on outlying deer populations. The model added and subtracted deer from an initial population based on observed age-, sex-, and time-specific survival and reproductive rates. The model did not include density-dependent factors because such relationships were not evident at population levels observed on our study areas (Nixon et al. 1991; Hansen, unpublished data).

For the model we used observed values for recruitment and survival of deer on ECISA and NCMSA. We did not have adequate survival data from ear-tagged males on NCMSA because, unless they appeared in the harvest, their fate often was unknown. This was especially true for deer on refuge because hunting was not allowed. Survival input for males on NCMSA was derived from life table analyses (Deevey 1947) of age data collected from males brought to area check stations during the firearms deer season. Although there are problems associated with this type of analysis (Caughley 1966), hunting is the primary mortality factor for male white-tailed deer in the Midwest (Nixon et al. 1991). Mandatory checking of deer taken by hunters ensured that data from most harvested males would be collected. On ECISA, male survival estimates from marked deer were used in the models (Nixon et al. 1991).

We were not able to measure immigration rates onto either study area directly. For the refuge portion of ECISA, we added enough fawns of both sexes and adult females so that the simulated population trends matched those observed during our study (Nixon et al. 1991). It was not possible to measure deer populations annually on NCMSA due to its large size. Therefore, the same proportion of immigrating deer used for ECISA was added to the simulated population of the refuge on NCMSA. To evaluate simulated population trends off refuge without an input of immigrants from an outside source, a net movement of zero was used.

We simulated the contribution of hypothetical 1,000-ha refuges to outlying deer demographics. Simulated outlying deer populations were representative of off-refuge areas associated with ECISA and NCMSA. We used dispersal rates and distribution of dispersal distances observed on each study site to determine the area of influence around each hypothetical refuge. Dispersers were assumed to distribute themselves randomly within four concentric bands with radii that included 25, 50, 75, and 100% of expected dispersal distances (Figure 20.1).

RESULTS

Survival

Our indirect measure of fawn survival between birth and 4 months was 74% on NCMSA. Survival of 17 marked fawns on ECISA was 100%. Survival of fawns from January through May was high on both the ECISA

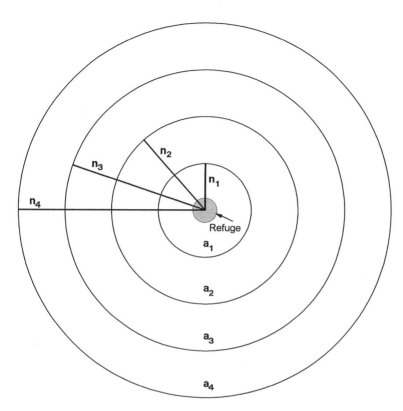

FIGURE 20.1. Area affected by deer dispersing from a hypothetical 1,000-ha central refuge. Radii n_1 through n_4 are based on the observed distribution of dispersal distances, which varied with sex and age of dispersers and the study area with which the refuge was associated. Each concentric band, a_1 through a_4, included the area in which 25% of the dispersers from the refuge would locate.

and NCMSA ($\bar{x} = 0.95$, $s_{\bar{x}} = 0.057$ and $\bar{x} = 0.99$, $s_{\bar{x}} = 0.011$, respectively). We did not compare fawn survival on and off refuge because most fawns were captured on refuge and did not disperse from the refuge until they were about 1 year.

Annual survival of adult females tended to be higher on NCMSA than on ECISA. Survival of adult females approached 100% and did not differ between refuge and off-refuge deer on either study area during the winter–spring or summer periods (Table 20.1). Fall survival was lower on off-refuge portions of both study areas ($P < 0.01$), especially on ECISA. Hunting and deer–vehicle accidents accounted for most mortality on both ECISA (59% and 30%, respectively) and NCMSA (68% and 13%, respectively). Higher losses to collisions with vehicles on ECISA may have

TABLE 20.1

Survival of adult female deer on and off refuges

Study site	Winter–spring		Summer		Fall	
	Number of deer months[a]	Mean survival rate ($s_{\bar{x}}$)	Number of deer months[a]	Mean survival rate ($s_{\bar{x}}$)	Number of deer months[a]	Mean survival rate ($s_{\bar{x}}$)
ECISA[b]						
Refuge	790	0.92 (0.02)	772	0.96 (0.02)	589	0.91 (0.05)
Off refuge	273	0.91 (0.05)	347	0.89 (0.04)	214	0.51 (0.06)
NCMSA[c]						
Refuge	1,165	1.00 (0.00)	839	0.99 (0.01)	575	0.95 (0.02)
Off refuge	1,352	0.99 (0.01)	1,017	0.99 (0.00)	674	0.82 (0.02)

[a] Number of deer months is sum of number of months deer were monitored.

[b] Data from east-central Illinois study area (ECISA) collected 1981–86.

[c] Data from north-central Missouri study area (NCMSA) collected 1989–93.

been the result of a more extensive road system and greater traffic volumes. Two interstate highways passed near ECISA, one less than 1 km from the boundary and the other within 20 km. Also, movement rates and distances moved were greater for marked deer on ECISA than on NCMSA, probably increasing the number of road crossings attempted. Disease, poaching, and unknown causes accounted for the remainder of the mortality on both study areas.

Movements

Most of the deer captured on ECISA were taken on refuge. As a result, we had no measure of emigration rates for fawns originating off refuge. In addition, high mortality of adults off refuge rendered sample sizes too small to determine movement out of these areas. Therefore, analyses of movement data for deer on ECISA were for refuge residents only. On NCMSA, movements of deer away from refuge and off-refuge portions were similar, so the results were combined for further analysis.

A high percentage of fawn males on both study areas and fawn females on ECISA moved away from their natal home ranges (Table 20.2). Relatively more fawn males moved on NCMSA than on ECISA, whereas relatively fewer fawn and adult females moved on NCMSA than on ECISA. Most movements of adult females on NCMSA (88%) and ECISA (67%) were migrations. Most fawn male movements on ECISA (95%)

TABLE 20.2
Movement of marked deer

Sex and age[a]	n	Percent moving	Migrations			Dispersals	
			n	Mean $(s_{\bar{x}})$ distance moved (km)		n	Mean $(s_{\bar{x}})$ distance moved (km)
East-central Illinois study area (ECISA)							
Male							
Fawn	90	60	2	19.5 (4.50)		41	38.6 (4.77)
Adult	25	4	—	—		—	—
Female							
Fawn	67	55	5	28.6 (11.29)		28	40.9 (4.61)
Adult	54	41	12	13.7 (1.50)		6	28.2 (3.68)
North-central Missouri study area (NCMSA)							
Male							
Fawn	69	77	2	5.0 (0)		49	14.3 (1.36)
Adult	14	21	1	5.0 (—)		4	21.0 (13.17)
Female							
Fawn	83	25	10	26.4 (13.28)		13	13.1 (2.03)
Adult	126	13	15	15.6 (2.71)		2	6.0 (2.00)

[a] Fawns are 1 year or younger; adults are older than 1 year.

and NCMSA (96%) and fawn female movements on ECISA (85%) were dispersals. Fawn female movements on NCMSA included 57% dispersals and 43% migrations. Adult male sample sizes on both areas were insufficient to determine movement type.

Most movements occurred in late spring or early summer (85%), and the remainder occurred in the fall (15%). Timing of movement did not differ between study areas. Most fall movements were by adult males.

Fawn male and fawn female dispersal distances did not differ on ECISA ($F_{1,75} = 0.04$, $P = 0.839$) or NCMSA ($F_{1,73} = 1.26$, $P = 0.266$). With sexes combined, fawns on ECISA tended to move longer distances than did fawns on NCMSA. In general, migration distances were shorter than dispersal distances on ECISA. Sample sizes were inadequate to compare migration and dispersal distances on NCMSA, although results for fawn females suggested migration distances exceeded dispersal distances (Table 20.2).

Recruitment

Small sample sizes of off-refuge deer from both study areas prevented analysis of refuge effects on recruitment. Recruitment of fawns into the fall population was higher on ECISA than on NCMSA (Table 20.3). As indicated previously, high fawn survival on ECISA from birth to 4 months accounted for at least part of this difference. Reproductive rates also were apparently higher in east-central Illinois; recruitment by does of all age classes on ECISA was higher than was fecundity of similar-aged does on NCMSA.

Population Growth

Simulated deer populations, based on input data from the ECISA refuge, increased during a 5-year period (Figure 20.2). Conversely, off-refuge populations declined to near zero within 5 years without immigration of deer from an outside source. Despite high recruitment rates on ECISA, the nearly 50% hunting mortality of off-refuge does resulted in annual population declines. In contrast, use of NCMSA input resulted in simulated deer population increases on and off refuge, although increases were smaller off refuge (Figure 20.2).

TABLE 20.3
Recruitment of fawns by marked does

			NCMSA				
	ECISA, marked does, 1981–86		Road-killed does, February–May, 1980–86		Marked does, 1989–93		Proportion surviving from in utero to 4 months[a]
Age of doe	n	Mean no. fawns per doe	n	Mean no. fetuses per doe	n	Mean no. fawns per doe	
1 year or less	59	0.86	116	0.50	29	0.40	0.80
Older than 1 year but less than 2	39	1.82	60	1.68	31	0.98	0.58
Older than 2 years	115	2.10	136	1.86	179	1.29	0.69

[a] Indirect measure of survival: mean number of fawns recruited per marked doe ÷ mean number of fetuses per road-killed doe.

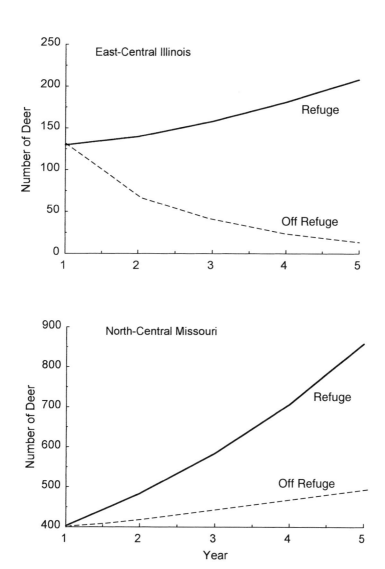

FIGURE 20.2. Simulated deer population growth. Simulations of deer populations were conducted with survival and recruitment rates similar to those on and off refuge on the east-central Illinois (ECISA) and north-central Missouri (NCMSA) study areas. Year-1 deer numbers are arbitrary and do not represent actual densities observed on the study areas.

These simulations suggest that off-refuge deer populations around ECISA would have to be supplemented annually to sustain viable populations. In contrast, off-refuge areas typical of NCMSA would not require immigrants to maintain their populations. In fact, additional deer would only accelerate population growth rates.

We attempted to determine the number of immigrants needed to sustain deer populations on hunted areas typical of east-central Illinois. Deer were added to the simulated spring population in proportion to the sex and age ratios observed in dispersal rates from ECISA. Most of the input consisted of fawn males and females because of their higher dispersal rates. Our simulations indicated that both fawn classes would have to be supplemented by 30% and adult females by 5% to maintain stable deer populations. To sustain a population of 20 deer/km^2 of forest would require an annual input of 0.84 fawn males, 0.88 fawn females, and 0.08 adult females per square kilometer forest. Conversely, off-refuge portions of the NCMSA would require a 22% increase in doe harvest just to stabilize population growth without addition of deer from a refuge.

Contribution of Simulated Refuge

For two hypothetical areas with on- and off-refuge deer demographics similar to ECISA and NCMSA, we considered the contribution of a 1,000-ha refuge to outlying deer populations. Because the fawn age class contributes most dispersers and to simplify the analyses, only fawn dispersers from the refuge were considered. Concentric rings were drawn around each refuge, the area within representing the destination of 25% of the dispersers from the refuge. A 1,000-ha refuge similar to that on ECISA would contribute 39% of the female and male fawns required to maintain stable populations within the first concentric band around the refuge. Decreasing proportions would be contributed in the outer bands (Table 20.4).

Because simulated deer populations off NCMSA refuges were increasing, we determined the additional harvest required to maintain these simulated population trends given supplementation by immigrants from the hypothetical 1,000-ha refuge. Harvests of antlerless deer in the first concentric band would have to be increased by 17% and in the second band by 2%. Insignificant increases in harvest would be necessary in the two outermost bands (Table 20.4)

TABLE 20.4

Simulated contribution to regional deer populations of 1,000-ha refuges

Concentric band and study area	Radius (km)[a]	Area within band (km²)		Percent contribution to deer demographics in outlying bands[b]	
		Total	Forested	Male fawns	Female fawns
Band 1					
ECISA	19	1,083	26	39% (9 deer)	39% (9 deer)
NCMSA	6	63	11	17% (11 deer)	17% (11 deer)
Band 2					
ECISA	32	2,082	50	20% (9 deer)	20% (9 deer)
NCMSA	12	389	70	2% (8 deer)	2% (8 deer)
Band 3					
ECISA	47	3,766	90	12% (9 deer)	12% (9 deer)
NCMSA	17	455	82	<1% (8 deer)	<1% (8 deer)
Band 4					
ECISA	92	19,766	474	2% (9 deer)	2% (9 deer)
NCMSA	26	1,215	219	<1% (10 deer)	<1% (10 deer)

Note: Simulations were based on deer demographics typical of refuges in east-central Illinois study area (ECISA) and north-central Missouri study area (NCMSA).

[a] Radius from center of refuge to outer edge of band. Each band received 25% of dispersals.

[b] For the ECISA simulation, these values represent the percentage (and number) of deer contributed by the 1,000-ha refuge required to maintain a stable population with a density of 20 deer/km² forest. For the NCMSA simulation, the values indicate the increase in antlerless deer harvest that would be required to maintain the outlying deer population at growth rates expected without the input of refuge deer.

DISCUSSION

White-tailed deer in east-central Illinois and north-central Missouri were productive and highly mobile and suffered little mortality outside the hunting seasons. These results are consistent with those reported for survival (Porath 1980; Gladfelter 1984; Huegel et al. 1985; Nixon et al. 1994), reproduction (Nixon 1971; Haugen 1975; Harder 1980; Stoll and Parker 1986), and movement (Zagata 1972; Zwank et al. 1979; Root 1986; Nixon et al. 1991, 1994) in other parts of the agricultural Midwest. Although deer in this region obtain most of their diet from agricultural crops, browsing rates on local flora can be high, especially in high-density populations not controlled by hunting (Hansen, unpublished data).

Given liberal harvest opportunities throughout much of the agricultural Midwest, the success of regional deer population management is dependent on hunter distribution and density. Because of generally small land ownerships in the Midwest, hunting pressure is not evenly distributed on most agricultural landscapes and ranges from unhunted refuges to intensively hunted public lands. Hunting pressure on most private land is somewhere between these extremes. Refuges of various sizes generally occur throughout these landscapes, some on private land where hunting is not allowed or is limited to family or friends. Other refuges occur on public lands mandated as refuge to protect threatened fauna or flora or to simulate natural ecosystems. Still other refuges are created when hunting is not allowed because it conflicts with other activities. Our observations indicate that these refuges may affect deer management in different ways, depending on refuge size and off-refuge harvest rates and landscape characteristics.

Differences in deer mortality rates from hunting on the two study areas could have simply been a function of hunter densities and harvest opportunity. However, hunter densities were higher and opportunities to take antlerless deer were more liberal on NCMSA than on ECISA, yet hunting mortality rates were lower on NCMSA. Apparently, deer were less vulnerable to hunting because of landscape characteristics.

Deer in east-central Illinois occupied fragmented landscapes consisting of small patches (<100 ha) of permanent cover in a matrix of intensive row-crop agriculture. Crop removal, which usually occurred before the firearms hunting seasons, generally confined deer to these small patches of habitat. Under these conditions, deer were highly vulnerable to harvest, and refuges were critical to the maintenance of viable populations.

In landscapes typical of north-central Missouri, permanent cover is prevalent and often occurs in blocks of 1 km^2 or more. Deer appeared less vulnerable to harvest even when hunter densities were high. Refuges here may actually have hindered deer population management by annually providing additional animals through dispersals and migrations.

Mobility of deer is a key element affecting their management in the agricultural Midwest. Stable, matrilineal social hierarchies consisting of an adult doe surrounded by female offspring with overlapping home ranges exist throughout the range of white-tailed deer (Hawkins and Klimstra 1970; Nelson and Mech 1984; Porter et al. 1991; Nixon et al. 1992). In areas outside the agricultural Midwest, few females disperse but dispersal rates of young males are high (Downing et al. 1969; Hawkins et al. 1971; Kammermeyer and Marchington 1976; Nelson and Mech 1984; Mathews and Porter 1993).

Female dispersal rates in the agricultural Midwest often exceed 20% (Sparrowe and Springer 1970; Zagata and Haugen 1973; Gladfelter 1978; Root 1986). Reasons for these higher female dispersal rates are unknown. Nixon et al. (1991) found no relationship between densities of adult females and dispersal rates; however, the range of densities in their study was not great. A density threshold may exist beyond which increasing proportions of young females disperse. The fragmented landscapes typical of east-central Illinois had no transition zone between permanent cover and agricultural fields. Deer used the seasonally abundant cover provided by corn but, after crop harvest, concentrated in permanent cover, often at densities exacerbated by high recruitment rates. Female intolerance of other deer around the time of parturition (Ozoga et al. 1982) and lack of cover at this time may have forced subordinate young females to disperse rather than establish a place within the kin-related social group (Nixon et al. 1992). Highly disjunct habitats and absence of cover in crop fields may have elicited the long dispersal distances observed on ECISA. However, permanent cover is more abundant on NCMSA and throughout much of the range of the white-tailed deer, thus allowing subordinate females to reside in association with their dam and other resident females, resulting in lower dispersal rates.

The importance of refuge to maintaining deer populations has been proposed in other parts of the habitat-limited agricultural Midwest (Zwank et al. 1979; Gladfelter 1984; Nixon et al. 1988), especially in intensively farmed portions of this area. However, results from north-central Missouri suggested that beneficial refuges are not a universal pattern throughout the agricultural Midwest but may be confined to sparsely forested (<5%) areas. Increasing deer populations in most of these sparsely forested areas in recent years, however, suggest that land area currently in refuge is adequate. Hunting pressure is low on many private properties, and the large blocks of permanent cover that survived clearing for farming are often in public ownership: many are unhunted. Current emphasis to reduce deer numbers on refuges in order to decrease crop depredation and protect natural ecosystems creates a dilemma for resource agencies. Agencies should be aware of the effects these efforts may have on outlying deer populations and their management. Refuges in landscapes with more than 5% permanent cover may be hindering resource agency efforts to stabilize regional populations. Annual deer population reductions on these refuges may be a necessary component of any successful deer management program.

ACKNOWLEDGMENTS

We thank all of the paid and unpaid field personnel who participated in this study. We are particularly grateful to Paul Brewer, James Chelsvig, Kevin Dixon, Rick Gann, John Schulz, and Joe Sullivan. This chapter is a contribution (in part) of the Illinois Department of Conservation, U.S. Fish and Wildlife Service, and Illinois Natural History Survey Federal Aid in Wildlife Restoration Project W-87-R, and the Missouri Department of Conservation and U.S. Fish and Wildlife Service Federal Aid in Wildlife Restoration Project W-13-R. The Professional Bowhunters Society and the United Bowhunters of Missouri also provided financial support.

REFERENCES CITED

Caughley, G. 1966. Mortality patterns in mammals. Ecology 47:906–918.

Clover, M. R. 1954. A portable deer trap and catch-net. California Fish and Game 40:367–373.

Deevey, E. S., Jr. 1947. Life tables for natural populations of animals. Quarterly Review of Biology 22:283–314.

Downing, R. L., B. S. McGinnes, R. P. Petcher, and J. L. Sandt. 1969. Seasonal changes in movement of white-tailed deer. Pages 19–24 in White-Tailed Deer in the Southern Forest Habitat. (L. K. Halls, ed.) U.S. Forest Service, Southern Forest Experimental Station, New Orleans, LA.

Giessman, N. F., T. W. Barney, T. L. Haithcoat, J. W. Myers, and R. L. Massengale. 1986. Distribution of forestland in Missouri. Transactions of the Missouri Academy of Science 20:5–14.

Gilbert, F. F. 1966. Aging white-tailed deer by annuli in the cementum of the first incisor. Journal of Wildlife Management 30:200–202.

Gladfelter, H. L. 1978. Movement and home range of deer as determined by radio telemetry. Iowa Conservation Commission, Iowa Wildlife Research Bulletin 23, Des Moines.

Gladfelter, H. L. 1984. Midwest agricultural region. Pages 427–440 in White-Tailed Deer: Ecology and Management. (L. K. Halls, ed.) Stackpole Books, Harrisburg, PA.

Harder, J. D. 1980. Reproduction of white-tailed deer in the North Central United States. Pages 23–35 in White-Tailed Deer Population Management in the North Central States. (R. L. Hine and S. Nehls, eds.) The Graphic Printing Company, Eau Claire, WI.

Haugen, A. O. 1975. Reproductive performance of white-tailed deer in Iowa. Journal of Mammalogy 56:151–159.

Hawkins, R. E., and W. D. Klimstra. 1970. A preliminary study of the social organization of the white-tailed deer. Journal of Wildlife Management 34:407–419.

Hawkins, R. E., W. D. Klimstra, and D. C. Autry. 1971. Dispersal of deer from Crab Orchard National Wildlife Refuge. Journal of Wildlife Management 35: 216–220.

Hawkins, R. E., L. D. Martoglio, and G. G. Montgomery. 1968. Cannon netting deer. Journal of Wildlife Management 32:191–195.

Heisey, D. M., and T. K. Fuller. 1985. Evaluation of survival and cause-specific mortality rates using telemetry data. Journal of Wildlife Management 49: 668–674.

Huegel, C. N., R. B. Dahlgren, and H. L. Gladfelter. 1985. Mortality of white-tailed deer fawns in southcentral Iowa. Journal of Wildlife Management 49: 377–380.

Hurlbert, S. H. 1984. Pseudoreplication and the design of ecological field experiments. Ecological Monographs 54:187–211.

Kammermeyer, K. E., and R. L. Marchinton. 1976. Notes on dispersal of male white-tailed deer. Journal of Mammalogy 57:776–778.

Kückler, A. W. 1964. The Potential Natural Vegetation of the Conterminous United States. American Geographical Society Special Research Publication Number 36, New York.

Mathews, N. E., and W. F. Porter. 1993. Effect of social structure on genetic structure of free-ranging white-tailed deer in the Adirondack Mountains. Journal of Mammalogy 74:33–43.

McCabe, R. E., and T. R. McCabe. 1984. Of slings and arrows: An historical retrospection. Pages 19–72 in White-Tailed Deer: Ecology and Management. (L. K. Halls, ed.) Stackpole Books, Harrisburg, PA.

McDonald, J. S., and K. V. Miller. 1993. A history of white-tailed deer restocking in the United States 1878 to 1992. The Quality Deer Management Association Research Publication 93-1, Greenwood, SC.

Morgan, G. W., C. M. Nixon, J. C. van Es, and J. H. Kube. 1992. Attitudes of Illinois farmers regarding deer and deer hunters, 1990. Illinois Department of Conservation Technical Bulletin 6, Springfield, IL.

Nelson, M. E., and L. D. Mech. 1984. Home range formation and dispersal of deer in northeastern Minnesota. Journal of Mammalogy 65:567–575.

Nixon, C. M. 1971. Productivity of white-tailed deer in Ohio. Ohio Journal of Science 71:217–225.

Nixon, C. M., L. P. Hansen, and P. A. Brewer. 1988. Characteristics of winter habitats used by deer in Illinois. Journal of Wildlife Management 52:552–555.

Nixon, C. M., L. P. Hansen, P. A. Brewer, and J. E. Chelsvig. 1991. Ecology of White-Tailed Deer in an Intensively Farmed Region of Illinois. Wildlife Monographs 118, The Wildlife Society, Bethesda, MD.

Nixon, C. M., L. P. Hansen, P. A. Brewer, and J. E. Chelsvig. 1992. Stability of white-tailed doe parturition ranges on a refuge in east-central Illinois. Canadian Journal of Zoology 70:968–973.

Nixon, C. M., L. P. Hansen, P. A. Brewer, J. E. Chelsvig, J. B. Sullivan, T. L. Esker,

R. Koerkenmeier, D. R. Etter, J. Cline, and J. A. Thomas. 1994. Behavior, dispersal, and survival of male white-tailed deer in Illinois. Illinois Natural History Survey Biological Note 139, Champaign.

Ozoga, J. J., L. J. Verme, and C. S. Bienz. 1982. Parturition behavior and territoriality in white-tailed deer: Impact on neonatal mortality. Journal of Wildlife Management 46:1–11.

Pauley, V. 1991. Missouri Farm Facts 1991. Missouri Agricultural Statistical Service, Columbia.

Pietsch, L. R. 1954. White-tailed deer populations in Illinois. Illinois Natural History Survey Biological Note 34, Champaign.

Porath, W. R. 1980. Fawn mortality estimates in farmland deer range. Pages 55–63 in White-Tailed Deer Population Management in the North Central States. (R. L. Hine and S. Nehls, eds.) The Graphic Printing Company, Eau Claire, WI.

Porter, W. F., N. E. Matthews, H. B. Underwood, R. W. Sage, Jr., and D. F. Behrend. 1991. Social organization in deer: Implications for localized management. Environmental Management 15:809–814.

Robb, D. 1959. Missouri's Deer Herd. Missouri Department of Conservation, Jefferson City.

Root, B. G. 1986. Movements of white-tailed deer in northeast Missouri. Master's thesis, University of Missouri, Columbia.

Roseberry, J. L., D. D. Autry, W. D. Klimstra, and L. A. Mehrhoff, Jr. 1969. A controlled deer hunt on Crab Orchard National Wildlife Refuge. Journal of Wildlife Management 33:791–795.

SAS Institute. 1990. SAS/STAT User's Guide, Version 6 Edition. SAS Institute, Inc., Cary, NC.

Sparrowe, R. D., and P. F. Springer. 1970. Seasonal activity patterns of white-tailed deer in eastern South Dakota. Journal of Wildlife Management 34:420–431.

Stoll, R. J., and G. L. Mountz. 1983. Rural landowner attitudes toward deer and deer populations in Ohio. Ohio Department of Natural Resources, Ohio Fish and Wildlife Report 10, Columbus.

Stoll, R. J., and W. P. Parker. 1986. Reproductive performance and condition of white-tailed deer in Ohio. Ohio Journal of Science 86:164–168.

Teer, J. G., J. W. Thomas, and E. A. Walker. 1965. Ecology and Management of White-Tailed Deer in the Llano Basin of Texas. Wildlife Monographs 15, The Wildlife Society, Bethesda, MD.

Tilghman, N. G. 1989. Impacts of white-tailed deer on forest regeneration in northwestern Pennsylvania. Journal of Wildlife Management 53:524–532.

Witter, D. J., W. R. Porath, S. L. Sheriff, and N. F. Giessman. 1987. Balancing landowner privilege and public recreation in Missouri deer management. Transactions of the North American Wildlife and Natural Resources Conference 52:597–604.

Zagata, M. D. 1972. Range and movement of Iowa deer in relation to Pilot Knob State Park, Iowa. Doctoral dissertation, Iowa State University, Ames.

Zagata, M. D., and A. O. Haugen. 1973. Winter movement and home range of white-tailed deer at Pilot Knob State Park, Iowa. Proceedings of the Iowa Academy of Sciences 79:74–78.

Zwank, P. J., R. D. Sparrowe, W. R. Porath, and O. Torgerson. 1979. Utilization of threatened bottomland habitats by white-tailed deer. Wildlife Society Bulletin 7:226–232.

21

Bottomland Forest Composition and Seedling Diversity

Simulating Succession and Browsing by Overabundant Deer

STEVEN W. SEAGLE AND SUH-YUEN LIANG

When applied to animal populations, the term "overabundance" implies imbalance of a population with one or more aspects of its environment. To understand the effects of overabundance it is necessary to compare species' interactions with their environment under both overabundant and control (i.e., not overabundant) conditions. This task is often difficult because (1) appropriate experiments are not tractable, (2) even if tractable, long-term experiments are needed when dealing with long-lived animals or long-lived organisms that are experiencing the impact, or (3) control conditions to be used in experiments are difficult to define because of inadequate historical records. White-tailed deer are widely recognized, primarily through perceived detrimental effects on vegetation, as over-populated in many areas of the eastern United States (McCabe and McCabe 1984). In response, numerous exclosure or enclosure experiments have been conducted to quantify the effect of deer on vegetation reproduction, growth, and diversity. These experiments have been aided by historical population records that exist because of the popularity of deer as a game species but have been hindered by incomplete understanding of natural vegetation dynamics in many areas and multiple human and environmental impacts on vegetation history. Despite the reactive nature of many of these experiments, clear conclusions about vegetation reproduction at specific experimental sites have often resulted: deer can depress or inhibit new growth in a variety of vegetation types.

Deer browsing effects on forest regeneration and individual tree species have been well documented (Bramble and Goddard 1953; Webb et al.

1956; Curtis and Rushmore 1958; Harlow and Downing 1970; Ross et al. 1970; Anderson and Loucks 1979; Alverson et al. 1988; Stewart and Burrows 1989; Storm et al. 1989; Tilghman 1989; Warren 1991; Anderson and Katz 1993). However, specific effects of browsing on forest tree species is highly dependent on several factors. First, deer can display distinct browsing preferences (Beals et al. 1960; Harlow and Hooper 1972). Second, preferential browsing can be influenced by the "apparency" of preferred species. That is, preferred species may be eaten proportionally less often if rare and dispersed among numerous, less-preferred (but edible) species. We do not invoke a relationship between apparency and chemical defense (Feeny 1976) but view the role of apparency as purely probabilistic. Finally, we suggest that both browse preference and apparency can be strongly affected by deer densities. In particular, overabundant deer can decrease browsed plant populations such that all individual plants are conspicuous to browsers, and overabundant deer can deplete food resources to the extent that all potential food resources are utilized regardless of preference under less abundant conditions. Specific deer population levels at which browsing switches from a selective to an effectively nonselective process will often be site specific and difficult to determine.

The long-term ramifications of deer overabundance for forest-stand dynamics are seldom clear (Frelich and Lorimer 1985). Thus few generalizations are currently possible concerning the effect of deer browsing on rates and directions of forest succession. Mechanistic consideration of the life history attributes of tree species may help develop such generalizations. Forest trees can be conceptualized as having one of four different "roles" with respect to the forest canopy: (1) requires a gap to regenerate and produces a gap upon death (i.e., large size); (2) does not require a gap to regenerate and produces a gap upon death; (3) requires a gap to generate and does not produce a gap upon death; and (4) does not require a gap to regenerate and does not produce a gap upon death (Shugart 1984). This process of canopy gap creation and filling by an individual of the same or different species has been termed "gap dynamics" (Shugart and West 1980) and, barring exogenous disturbance, is the primary mode of secondary forest succession once a mature canopy is achieved. Because of their large size, species of roles 1 and 2 commonly dominate forest biomass, exert much influence over the forest microenvironment through light competition, and affect forest composition by gap effects on species-specific reproduction. Having a greater shade tolerance and large size, role 2 species would be expected to dominate late-successional forests, although the longevity of many role 1 species ($\geq$300 years) can maintain them as high-biomass, low-reproductive stand components for long time periods. Theoretically, selective browsing of seedlings of role 1 species early in stand succession may affect the rate or direction of succession by influencing establishment of role 1 species during high light conditions. However, selective browsing of role 1 species may have relatively little effect if a forest is near the transition from early to late-successional species. Alternatively, heavy selective browsing of role 2 seedlings may have strong effects on the rate and the direction of succession. Thus, browsing selectivity and tree life histories should be key elements in predicting browsing effects on forests.

Long-term ramifications of selective browsing for forest composition have seldom been experimentally determined. Even less common are extrapolations, based on empirical data, that extend for the lifetime of forest overstory trees because of the number of environmental factors that enter into consideration over long time frames. For example, Alverson et al. (1988) suggested that deer browsing is central to decimated eastern hemlock *(Tsuga canadensis)* regeneration in Wisconsin and the surrounding region. The temporal and spatial extrapolations of Alverson et al. (1988) have been questioned (Mladenoff and Stearns 1993) on the basis that alternative hypotheses concerning species life history, ecosystem dynamics, disturbance, land use, and climate have not been adequately evaluated. In fact, Mladenoff and Stearns (1993) found deer browsing to be only a secondary factor in eastern hemlock decline. Without interpretation in long-term contexts, we hypothesize that the impact of deer browsing can be counterintuitive simply because of the inertia inherent in current vegetation composition or successional status. That is, time lags between browsing effects and understory growth to forest dominance must be considered, and tree species' life histories can exert greater control on forest successional trends than can even extreme browsing effects. Our objective in this chapter is to examine the relative effects of deer browsing and tree life history characteristics on long-term vegetation dynamics of a bottomland hardwood forest. Particular emphasis is given to forest composition and diversity.

METHODS

Study Site

The spatial pattern and composition of vegetation on the National Biological Service's Patuxent Wildlife Research Center (Patuxent), Maryland, was characterized by Hotchkiss and Stewart (1947). A major component of Patuxent is bottomland hardwood forest found in the floodplain of the Patuxent River. Mature, and in isolated instances virgin, stands are dominated by American beech *(Fagus grandifolia)*, and younger stands are composed of American beech, yellow poplar *(Liriodendron tulipifera)*, sweetgum *(Liquidambar styraciflua)*, and northern red oak *(Quercus rubra)*. Older stands of American beech forest were found mainly on islands within the river channel, whereas younger mainland stands with large yellow poplar and sweetgum components were second or third growth on farmland abandoned in the early 1900s (Hotchkiss and Stewart 1947). Recent vegetation analyses focused on the bottomland hardwood area (S.-Y. Liang and S. W. Seagle, unpublished data) have confirmed the codominance of yellow poplar, American beech, and sweetgum in the canopy of better-drained mainland sites. Understory species of highest importance include ironwood *(Carpinus caroliniana)* and paw paw *(Asimina triloba)*; the shrub layer is dominated by spicebush *(Lindera benzoin)*.

The main property of Patuxent is not hunted and now supports a deer population that, although exact estimates are lacking, is overabundant judging from vegetation damage. This damage is widespread from upland to bottomland, and a conspicuous browseline is evident throughout the forest. Closer inspection of browse damage in the bottomland hardwood forest (Seagle and Liang, unpublished data) indicates that few seedlings or saplings have not been damaged to some degree by deer browsing. Even American beech, which is generally not a preferred deer browse (Bramble and Goddard 1953; Webb et al. 1956; Curtis and Rushmore 1958), has few small trees in the bottomland forest that lack significant damage. It is unclear what role this browsing will play in stand dynamics and bottomland tree diversity relative to natural successional processes based on tree life histories.

Succession Model

GENERAL ASPECTS   An important tool for projecting forest-stand dynamics and the effects of disturbance on succession are individual-based forest simulation models (Botkin et al. 1972; Shugart and West 1977; Shugart 1984). This genre of models simulates the birth, growth, and death of each individual tree in an area approximating the gap size created by the death of a dominant canopy tree. Thus such models are particularly suited for simulating deer browsing, which ultimately affects individual tree stems.

For this study, we have adapted the individual-based forest model Zelig (Urban 1990) to the Patuxent bottomland forest. The model's biological functions of seedling establishment, height and diameter growth, and death are applied to each individual stem on an annual time step. Individual seedling establishment is based on seed tree availability, seed production of each species, germination site requirements of each species, and tendency of each species to sprout. For our simulations we assumed that all 19 common forest canopy species (Table 21.1) were always available for seed production. Stem growth is decremented from an optimal growth rate by a factor based on light availability and shade tolerance, soil moisture availability, and growing degree-days (Urban 1990). Light availability on a plot is modeled as vertical extinction by a Beer's Law formulation, so that shorter trees or lower levels in the foliage profile of

TABLE 21.1

Browse preference and shade tolerance rankings for the tree species used in bottomland hardwood simulations

Tree species	Browse preference	Shade tolerance
Red maple *(Acer rubrum)*	4	2
Ironwood *(Carpinus caroliniana)*	1	1
Pignut hickory *(Carya glabra)*	3	3
Flowering dogwood *(Cornus florida)*	4	1
Common persimmon *(Diospyros virginiana)*	4	4
American beech *(Fagus grandifolia)*	1	2
Green ash *(Fraxinus pennsylvanica)*	3	3
American holly *(Ilex opaca)*	1	1
Sweetgum *(Liquidambar styraciflua)*	4	3
Yellow poplar *(Liriodendron tulipifera)*	4	4
Black gum *(Nyssa sylvatica)*	4	2
Virginia pine *(Pinus virginiana)*	1	4
Sycamore *(Platanus occidentalis)*	4	4
White oak *(Quercus alba)*	2	3
Swamp white oak *(Quercus bicolor)*	2	3
Overcup oak *(Quercus lyrata)*	2	3
Swamp chestnut oak *(Quercus michauxii)*	2	3
Pin oak *(Quercus palustris)*	2	3
Northern red oak *(Quercus rubra)*	2	3

Notes: Shade tolerance rankings range from 1 to 4, with 1 being most tolerant. Browsing preference ranks were based on unpublished field measurements from the Patuxent bottomland forest and range from 1 to 4, with 4 being most preferred by deer.

an individual tree receive less light. Shade tolerance and soil moisture requirements are species-specific characteristics. Degree-days is also species specific but assumes that a species growth rate is related to its position within physiological tolerances set by the species' geographic range. Death of an individual stem is either probabilistic, such that very slow growing individuals are more susceptible to death, or, in the case of mature individuals, limited by physiological life span.

Physical driving variables of the model are functions of monthly precipitation and temperature (Urban 1990), which were taken from the College Park, Maryland, weather station approximately 19 km from Patuxent. Temperatures are used in calculation of degree-days, which determine growing season length. Soil moisture availability is calculated as a function of potential evapotranspiration (Pastor and Post 1985) and precipitation. When precipitation is less than potential evapotranspiration, soil moisture decreases. Water is available for extraction from the soil by trees until wilting point is reached. Although days when soil moisture is below wilting point are accumulated as drought days and used to decrease tree growth, the combination of precipitation and lowland soils for this bottomland forest resulted in no drought days. Water control along the Patuxent River has alleviated any catastrophic flooding, and spring saturation of soils generally declines before the growing season in the better-drained areas of this forest on which we focus. Thus water stress is not a significant factor in our simulations.

SIMULATION OF BROWSING   To Zelig we have added the effect of deer browsing by introducing another multiplier to decrement growth rate of seedlings and sprouts. Thus, we assume that browsing decreases the growth rate of any individual stem by removal of apical meristems, photosynthetic leaf area, or both. In this fashion browsing does not directly kill individual seedlings but contributes to slow height growth, which increases the probability of dying, especially for shade-intolerant species. We assumed that only stems less than 2 m in height were susceptible to browsing. Species-specific reduction of regeneration rates by seed consumption was simulated during model development and found to have little effect because of low oak abundance due to other environmental factors, prolific sprouting by American beech, and production of seeds not amenable to deer browsing by other forest dominants. Thus seed predation was not considered in the simulations presented here.

Our simulation of deer browsing is predicated on a two-step hierarchy of foraging: the decision whether to browse within a simulated plot followed by the decision on which species to browse within the plot. Plot preference was modeled as

$$BPROB = 1/[1 + e^{(2.67 - BMOD * TDEN)}],$$

where BPROB is the probability that a simulated plot would be browsed, TDEN is the density of seedlings less than 2 m in height on the plot (number/m^2), and BMOD is a constant. Deer population sizes were not simulated explicitly. However, manipulation of BMOD allowed simulation of relative deer densities by assuming that deer are more likely to browse a simulated plot when densities are high. The BPROB was calculated at each model time step and compared with a uniformly distributed random number (in the range 0.0–1.0) to determine whether a plot would be browsed.

Based on published literature and field data from Patuxent, each simulated tree species was given a browsing preference rank of integers 1 to 4 (Table 21.1); a value of 4 indicated highly preferred food species. The browsing factor (BF) by which each individual's growth would be decremented was a function of this rank and that species' relative density within a plot:

$$BF = RELDEN^{(1/PREF)},$$

where RELDEN is the proportion of seedlings (again less than 2 m in height) in a plot belonging to a specific species and PREF is the species-specific browsing rank. When PREF is equal to 1, BF is equal to relative density.

Simulation Scenarios

Initial stand conditions for all of our simulations were identical and dominated by yellow poplar, American beech, and sweetgum to reflect current composition and standing biomass of the study site. Nineteen species (Table 21.1) are found in the forest overstory and all were eligible for regeneration in all model runs. Initial species-specific life history characteristics were drawn from Shugart (1984), Solomon (1986), Burns and Honkala (1990), and Urban (1990). Adjustments to these initial estimates were made based on our observations and measurements at Patuxent, such as prevalence of sprouting. The model experiments presented here represent extrapolations from current conditions, and the simulated future forest may or may not be similar to stand composition measured in the field. Therefore, to verify that the model functions appropriately for our study site, extensive simulations were carried out starting with bare ground (recent release from cultivation) or young early successional species. Because deer populations were lower or nonexistent during the early development of current Patuxent forests, no browsing was allowed for these simulations. Simulated forest composition after 100 years (the approximate time since last cultivation) was then compared with current forest composition. These comparisons verified that the model produces similar forest composition over this time frame, and we thus feel comfortable that extrapolations into the future have a reasonable mechanistic basis, with the obvious caveat that external forces, such as climate, will not change.

Control and experimental model runs were carried out for 600 years. We feel that this time frame is essential because several of the dominant tree species can live 300–350 years. In all experimental scenarios, browsing was implemented at year 100. For comparison of control and experimental model runs, we chose two measures: displacement of experimental forest composition from control forest composition and understory diversity. In calculating these metrics, stems resulting from seeds and sprouts were considered collectively. Stand displacement was measured using chord distance (Ludwig and Reynolds 1988). This resemblance function emphasizes the relative proportions of species and was calculated at each model time step based on species biomasses. Thus time traces of stand displacement were possible. Understory diversity was based on stems less than 2 m in height and was calculated using Hill's N1: $N1 = e^{H'}$, where H' is the Shannon–Weaver measure of diversity. As used here, N1 measures the number of abundant species in the seedling–sapling age class and is thus a very interpretable number (Ludwig and Reynolds 1988). Hill's N1 was also calculated at each model time step to compare diversity through time under different browsing scenarios.

Our control model runs have no deer browsing. For comparison, we have simulated low, moderate, and high levels of browsing (BMOD = 8, 14, and 20, respectively), with browsing preferences as shown in Table 21.1. We also hypothesize that as deer densities become very high browsing selectivity decreases. Thus we present simulations with moderate and high levels of browsing and with all species having a high degree of preference (PREF = 4). Simulation of decreased selectivity in this manner increases browsing of less preferred species. Normally preferred species retain their high preference status. Many model processes are stochastic, so all simulation scenarios represent the mean of 10 simulated plots having identical starting conditions and parameters. A high degree of annual variation was apparent for both stand displacement and diversity. Thus to focus on trends all time traces were smoothed using a lowess algorithm (Anonymous 1993).

RESULTS

Forest Succession

Biomass projections for the control simulation (Figure 21.1) indicate gradual domination of the forest by shade-tolerant species. American beech constituted as much as 55% of forest biomass and was consistently the primary species, followed by red maple *(Acer rubrum)*. American beech and red maple together constituted about 60% of forest biomass for the last 400 years of our simulation. Collectively, oaks *(Quercus* spp.) constituted up to 25% of forest biomass. This genus was represented pri-

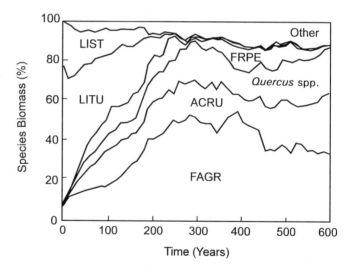

FIGURE 21.1. Control simulation of bottomland forest composition. Time traces are of relative biomasses for dominant bottomland hardwood species experiencing no deer browsing. Species included in the simulation were American beech (FAGR); red maple (ACRU); northern red, white, and swamp white oaks (*Quercus* spp.); green ash (FRPE); yellow popular (LITU); sweetgum (LIST); and ironwood, pignut hickory, flowering dogwood, common persimmon, American holly, black gum, Virginia pine, sycamore, overcup oak, swamp chestnut oak, and pin oak (Other).

marily by northern red oak, with significant components of white oak *(Q. alba)* and swamp white oak *(Q. bicolor)*. Over the last 200 simulated years, American beech remained the dominant single species but declined somewhat as a percentage of biomass while red maple and the oaks increased.

Browsing Effects on Seedling and Sapling Diversity

Temporal fluctuation in seedling and sapling diversity was apparent under control conditions of no browsing (Figure 21.2). Diversity showed a downward trend to a low value of approximately 7, which coincided with greatest dominance by shade-tolerant species. Diversity then exhibited a 50-year recovery to greater than 10 and a final value of 8. An important point of this simulation is that temporal variation in seedling diversity results from species-specific birth and death processes, which are, in turn, dependent on the light and soil conditions created by canopy tree dynamics. The low in diversity resulted from plot domination by large American beech trees (Figure 21.1) that produce many seedlings and sprouts and exclude

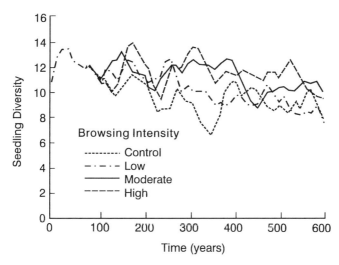

FIGURE 21.2. Seedling and sapling diversity with selective browsing. Seedling and sapling diversity of bottomland hardwood forest was simulated under control conditions of no browsing and low, moderate, and high browsing intensities. Diversity was calculated using Hill's N1 index. Browsing began at year 100 in the browsed scenarios and was selective based on individual species preferences.

seedlings of many less shade-tolerant species. At the death of these canopy dominants, the recovery of seedling diversity results from a mix of tree species seedlings with a broader range of shade tolerances (Table 21.1).

Although also displaying significant temporal variation, both high and moderate browsing scenarios generally resulted in greater understory diversity than did the control simulation (Figure 21.2). This result emerges from diffuse browsing effects based on species-specific combinations of browsing preference and shade tolerance. For example, as late-successional American beech begins to dominate simulated plot biomass, its shade-tolerant sprouts and seedlings numerically dominate the understory because of prolific sprout production and high death rates imposed on less shade-tolerant seedlings by suppressed growth. Browsing increases the seedling death rate of American beech regeneration by slowing seedling growth rate. Decreased survival of American beech seedlings is apparently sufficient to allow establishment of other species, primarily the relatively shade-tolerant red maple, oak species, and green ash *(Fraxinus pennsylvanica)*. Thus, seedling demography in mature browsed stands with an American beech-dominated canopy becomes highly dynamic with annual recruitment of multiple species, high death rates of the less shade-tolerant species (augmented for some species by browsing pressure), and increased death rates of American beech induced by browsing. This high turnover is the mechanism for increased seedling diversity. Low browsing intensity (Figure 21.2), on the other hand, displays only a moderate effect on seedling diversity and actually may lower diversity (see years 375 to 450, Figure 21.2) by having less of an effect on American beech seedlings relative to other species.

If higher deer browsing intensity is analogous to higher deer populations, then deer may browse all tree species more evenly at simulated moderate or high browse intensities. This scenario clearly resulted in increased seedling diversity compared with control conditions (Figure 21.3). The mechanism for increased diversity in this scenario is essentially the same as that for selective browsing, except the browsing effect is accentuated by being spread evenly among species. Shade-tolerant, prolific sprouting, and less-favored browse species, again primarily American beech in mature stands, are more heavily affected than under selective browsing, resulting in increased seedling population turnover and lower dominance in the total seedling pool. This result corroborates our results from the selective browsing simulation and extends our suggestion that heavy browsing in mixed-species forests can interact with species life histories to increase di-

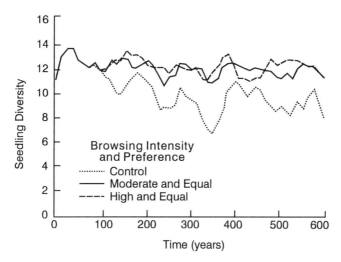

FIGURE 21.3. Seedling and sapling diversity with nonselective browsing. Seedling and sapling diversity for bottomland hardwood forest was simulated under control conditions (no browsing), moderate-intensity nonselective browsing, and high-intensity nonselective browsing. Under nonselective browsing all tree species were assumed to be highly and equally preferred by deer. Diversity was calculated using Hill's N1 index.

versity of the seedling and sapling stratum. This result does not negate the potential for browsing to eliminate preferred species by pushing populations below viable levels or to suppress total understory biomass and stem density.

Browsing Effects on Stand Displacement

The maximum potential value of the chord distance metric is 1.4. This maximum was not expected to occur because browsing cannot completely override species life history characteristics. Nonetheless, displacement of relative stand biomass from control conditions by selective browsing is substantial (Figure 21.4); high-intensity browsing resulted in the fastest departure from control conditions. This rapid departure followed by a decline in displacement is common to all three browsing intensities and results from browsing interaction with tree life histories. The initial displacement is caused by selective browsing of early successional species (yellow poplar and sweetgum). Even under control conditions these early

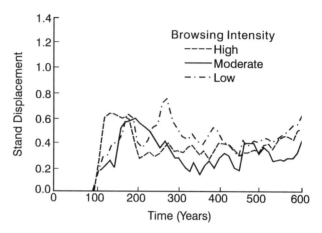

FIGURE 21.4. Displacement of species-specific forest biomass composition under condition of selective browsing. Displacement was simulated for low-, moderate-, and high-intensity selective browsing in comparison with the control condition of no browsing. Stand displacement was calculated using the chord distance resemblance function and has a maximum potential value of 1.4.

successional species are eventually replaced with more shade-tolerant American beech and red maple, and thus the amount of displacement declines over time.

Except for elevated displacement at low browsing intensities between 200 and 400 years, there was generally little difference in stand displacement effects of low-, moderate-, and high-intensity browsing. However, it is informative to consider the cause for the low browsing intensity effect. This degree of displacement over this time period must be associated with a decrease in American beech (Figure 21.1). A review of the biomass dynamics for individual species revealed that this period of high displacement resulted from increased dominance of green ash and red oak at the expense of American beech and, to a lesser degree, red maple. Green ash and red oak are (1) intermediate in browsing preference, so that their growth rates were not severely affected by low browsing intensity, (2) intermediate in shade tolerance (Table 21.1) so that growth into the subcanopy and escape from browsing was possible in a relatively closed stand, and (3) fast enough in growth rate to fill newly created canopy gaps. This shift toward greater dominance of green ash and red oak was transient, as evidenced by the decline in displacement (Figure 21.4) and return toward a forest of greater American beech dominance. Thus, different levels of selective browsing intensity can interact with tree species life history characteristics to promote temporary states of vegetation displacement.

A priori one could hypothesize that nonselective browsing, especially at high intensity, would amplify the effect of tree life histories and further promote shade-tolerant species that dominate the unbrowsed scenario. If this hypothesis were true, then displacement should be lower for nonselective than selective browsing simulations with similar browsing intensities. Our simulations suggest that this hypothesis is incorrect. Nonselective browsing displacement (Figure 21.5) is not lower than selective browsing scenarios (Figure 21.4), and, in fact, peak values of displacement are higher under nonselective browsing. However, relative to moderate browsing, high-intensity nonselective browsing did indeed push displacement values down to increase forest similarity to unbrowsed conditions over part of the simulation (years 300–500). This difference in moderate- and high-intensity browsing occurred because of consistently higher green ash biomass under moderate-intensity browsing and American beech regaining a higher percentage of biomass during years 300–500 under high-intensity browsing. Combined with our results for displacement due to selective browsing, we conclude that (1) browsing does displace relative biomass

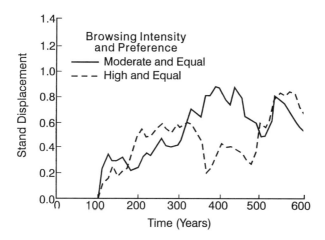

FIGURE 21.5. Displacement of species-specific forest biomass composition under condition of nonselective browsing. Displacement was simulated for moderate-intensity and high-intensity nonselective browsing in comparison with the control condition of no browsing. Nonselective browsing indicates all tree species are highly and equally preferred by deer. Stand displacement is the chord distance metric with a maximum potential value of 1.4.

from control conditions, (2) browsing intensity can influence temporal patterns of displacement by creating conditions under which moderately shade-tolerant and relatively fast-growing species can increase dominance, and (3) temporal patterns of displacement are quite variable and reflect opportunistic growth by species such as green ash versus highly shade-tolerant late-successional species such as American beech.

DISCUSSION

Our simulations represent an initial effort to understand the long-term effects of deer browsing on succession of bottomland forests at Patuxent. The results highlight the complexity of predicting such an outcome because of interactions among (1) the inertia of current vegetation imposed by population age structure, (2) the effects of tree species roles or life histories, (3) the importance of selective browsing, and (4) the potential relationships among deer population size, deer browsing intensity, and browsing selectivity.

Like most forests of the eastern United States, the bottomland of Patuxent has been greatly affected by human land use. The result, in this instance, is a forest in transition from early to later successional species. A forest dominated by American beech should result solely from the inertia of current composition and associated species-specific life history attributes, either with or without any level of deer browsing. This does not mean that deer browsing will not influence specific forest composition. Our measures of displacement make it clear that the degree of American beech dominance may decline under severe browsing, resulting in a more diverse distribution of forest biomass. More important is that such displacements may be prominent but temporally transient. Thus perhaps management of deer impacts on this forest should not be concerned about directional changes in succession but focused on managing deer populations to fine-tune the resemblance of this forest to a desirable objective.

A second management consideration is related to the rate at which forest composition is altered. Our results suggest that the most rapid displacement of relative forest biomasses from control conditions will occur under selective browsing. Paradoxically, our simulations suggest that lower densities of selectively browsing deer can alter forest composition more rapidly than can a high-density, nonselective population, although the long-term effect of the latter on vegetation displacement may be greater. Browsing management priorities may thus be different depending on the planning horizon considered. In addition, we have assumed that browsing selectivity will decline as deer populations become critically overabundant. Because of the different effects of selective and nonselective browsing, an important concern of field studies should be determination of the deer density at which selective browsing ceases. Documentation of browsing selectivity in the context of multiple browse choices is particularly important because strong preference for a single species over a long enough time period could eliminate seed sources and result in local extirpation.

We have not explicitly simulated deer population dynamics. Thus, it is important to consider how our low-, moderate-, and high-intensity browsing categories relate to deer numbers in the field. In our study plots at Patuxent, very few stems within deer reach in our study plots are free of browse damage. We feel this qualifies as high-intensity browsing. In addition, field measurements of browsing severity (Liang and Seagle, unpublished data) strongly indicate that species-selective browsing is occurring. This type of qualitative correlation is useful; however, it would be feasible to link a deer population model to our succession model in order to simulate selective and nonselective browsing as a temporal function of fluctuating deer populations. This increase in reality would also promote more specific management simulations that include both deer population and forest response.

An important goal of managing overabundant species is alleviation of detrimental impacts on other natural resources. Thus managers must determine those measures by which impacts are predicted. In our simulations we have discussed two, seedling and sapling diversity and stand displacement. The ability to make management predictions rests on identifying and quantifying the multiple causes of change and variability within the forest system. Temporal variation of multiple forest attributes, such as seedling diversity, forest composition, and forest biomass, is a consequence of gap-phase succession, tree species life history attributes, multiple-scale disturbances, and biotic interactions. Metrics to be used specifically for browsing management and planning must be distinguishable from such "background noise," have predictive ability, and carry ecological significance. As the temporal variation in our simulations suggests, detecting a clear signal of deer browsing based on seedling diversity is more difficult than using stand displacement. Also, seedling diversity is not as tightly coupled to forest biomass composition in our simulations. Thus, unlike examples of cyclical species replacement (Forcier 1975; Horn 1975; Fox 1977; Woods 1979; Woods and Whittaker 1981), forest seedling and sapling composition is not clearly predictive of relative composition in this forest. Seedling and sapling diversity does reflect forest ability to regenerate under multiple physical conditions resulting from exogenous disturbance and thus carries high ecological significance. In comparison, stand displacement meets all three criteria for usefulness in management planning.

In addition to being an effective metric for management purposes, temporal patterns of stand displacement highlight the interaction between browsing and tree species life history attributes. In particular, it is clear that browsing can give a temporary competitive advantage to species such as green ash, which has a specific suite of life history characteristics that enable it to take advantage of browsing effects. Without long-term forest projections by which to both predict and interpret forest succession, this type of transient response to different levels of deer browsing can be problematic for managers who discover these events in the field but whose management plans do not account for their possibility. In essence, managers must understand that general predictions of forest composition from models such as this one may appear inaccurate at any particular point in time but still will correctly predict the course of succession and the potential for transient events. Such realities of predicting forest dynamics must also be considered in a spatial context. The theory behind multiple stochastic model runs is identical to multiple plot sampling in the field: not all sample plots in a forest have the same composition at any point in time, but a mean of multiple plots should accurately reflect overall forest composition. Application of gap model predictions to a forest of insufficient extent to "average out" spatial variation will increase the likelihood of transient responses appearing to be simply poor predictions.

Temporal variability at small (plot level) spatial scales and larger-scale (whole forest) spatial variability compound the difficulty in predicting the effects of deer overabundance. However, when dealing with long-lived organisms such as trees, temporal predictions of browsing impacts on forest composition are inherently long term. The difficulties of making such predictions were highlighted by Mladenoff and Stearns (1993), who found that alleviation of intense deer browsing may have little direct effect on local and regional eastern hemlock population recovery. Their analysis implicated climate variation, land use, natural disturbance, and natural regeneration cycles as key factors in eastern hemlock decline and decreased potential for population recovery. Similar factors were incorporated in our analysis of the Patuxent bottomland forest. Land-use impacts were explicit through initial starting conditions that reflected time of agricultural abandonment, and dismissal of severe flooding as a potential disturbance was keyed by current flood control practices along the Patuxent River. In contrast, we have not simulated elevated CO_2 or regional changes in temperature and precipitation associated with anthropogenic climate change, all of which may alter species-specific growth rates and competitive interactions. It is clear that deer browsing cannot be isolated as the single direct impact on long-term forest succession. Likewise, indirect effects of browsing cannot be overlooked as a feedback to forest ecosystem processes and succession. Moose *(Alces alces)* browsing (Pastor et al. 1988, 1993) has been demonstrated to influence soil nutrient dynamics significantly by changing boreal forest stand composition and thus the quality and quantity of litter returned to the soil. Even though white-tailed deer browsing affects forest composition, such indirect effects are unlikely in mixed deciduous forest such as the Patuxent bottomland because the variability of litter quality among species is less than in boreal forests and overall soil fertility is much higher. Deer overabundance and resulting imbalances with other forest resources may also partially derive from trophic imbalance. McLaren and Peterson (1994) demonstrated the long-term signal in boreal tree growth resulting from top-down predator (wolf, *Canis lupus*) control of moose browsing. Although such control is not demonstrable for Patuxent and is unlikely for most study sites, documentation of this effect and its interpretation in the context of other ecosystem disturbances underscore the management importance of placing individual tree species characteristics and browsing patterns in the context of time scales that incorporate multiple ecosystem driving variables and trophic levels. Development of general theories of the role that browsing plays in forest ecosystems will depend on interpretation in this context.

ACKNOWLEDGMENTS

Support for this research was provided by the National Biological Service and Patuxent Wildlife Research Center through Cooperative Agreement Number 14-16-0005-92-9014 with the University of Maryland System's Center for Environmental and Estuarine Studies. This publication is Appalachian Environmental Laboratory Contribution Number 2705.

REFERENCES CITED

Alverson, W. S., D. M. Waller, and S. L. Solheim. 1988. Forest too deer: Edge effects in Northern Wisconsin. Conservation Biology 2:348–358.

Anderson, R. C., and A. J. Katz. 1993. Recovery of browse sensitive tree species following release from white-tailed deer *Odocoileus virginianus* Zimmerman browsing pressure. Biological Conservation 63:203–208.

Anderson, R. C., and O. L. Loucks. 1979. Whitetail deer *(Odocoileus virginianus)* influence on structure and composition of *Tsuga canadensis* forests. Journal of Applied Ecology 16:855–861.

Anonymous. 1993. AXUM: Technical Graphics and Data Analysis. 3rd edition. TriMetrix Inc., Seattle, WA.

Beals, E. W., G. Cottam, and R. J. Vogl. 1960. Influence of deer on vegetation of the Apostle Islands, Wisconsin. Journal of Wildlife Management 24:68–80.

Botkin, D. B., J. F. Janak, and J. R. Wallis. 1972. Some ecological consequences of a computer model of forest growth. Journal of Ecology 60:849–872.

Bramble, W. C., and M. K. Goddard. 1953. Seasonal browsing of woody plants by white-tailed deer in the ridge and valley section of central Pennsylvania. Journal of Forestry 51:815–819.

Burns, R. M., and B. H. Honkala, coordinators. 1990. Silvics of North America. U.S. Forest Service, Agriculture Handbook 654, Washington.

Curtis, R. O., and F. M. Rushmore. 1958. Some effects of stand density and deer browsing on reproduction in an Adirondack hardwood stand. Journal of Forestry 56:116–121.

Feeny, P. P. 1976. Plant apparency and chemical defense. Pages 282–310 *in* Biochemical Interactions between Plants and Insects. (J. M. Wallace and R. L. Mansee, eds.) Plenum Press, New York.

Forcier, L. K. 1975. Reproductive strategies and co-occurrence of climax tree species. Science 189:808–810.

Fox, J. F. 1977. Alternation and coexistence of tree species. American Naturalist 111:69–89.

Frelich, L. E., and C. G. Lorimer. 1985. Current and predicted long-term effects of deer browsing on hemlock forests in Michigan, USA. Biological Conservation 34:99–120.

Harlow, R. F., and R. L. Downing. 1970. Deer browsing and hardwood regeneration in the southern Appalachians. Journal of Forestry 68:298–300.

Harlow, R. F., and R. G. Hooper. 1972. Forages eaten by deer in the Southeast. Proceedings of the Annual Conference Southeastern Association of Game and Fish Commissions 25 (1971): 18–46.

Horn, H. S. 1975. Forest succession. Scientific American 232:90–98.

Hotchkiss, N., and R. E. Stewart. 1947. Vegetation of the Patuxent Research Refuge, Maryland. American Midland Naturalist 38:1–75.

Ludwig, J. A., and J. F. Reynolds. 1988. Statistical Ecology. John Wiley and Sons, New York.

McCabe, R. E., and T. R. McCabe. 1984. Of slings and arrows: An historical perspective. Pages 19–72 *in* White-Tailed Deer: Ecology and Management. (L. K. Halls, ed.) Stackpole Books, Harrisburg, PA.

McLaren, B. E., and R. O. Peterson. 1994. Wolves, moose, and tree rings on Isle Royale. Science 266:1555–1558.

Mladenoff, D. J., and F. Stearns. 1993. Eastern hemlock regeneration and deer browsing in the Northern Great Lakes Region: A re-examination and model simulation. Conservation Biology 7:889–900.

Pastor, J., B. Dewey, R. J. Naiman, P. F. McInnes, and Y. Cohen. 1993. Moose browsing and soil fertility in the boreal forests of Isle Royale National Park. Ecology 74:467–480.

Pastor, J., R. J. Naiman, B. Dewey, and P. F. McInnes. 1988. Moose, microbes and the boreal forest. BioScience 38:770–777.

Pastor, J., and W. M. Post. 1985. Development of a linked forest productivity–soil process model. Oak Ridge National Laboratory ORNL/TM-9519, Oak Ridge, TN.

Ross, B. A., J. R. Bray, and W. H. Marshall. 1970. Effects of long-term deer exclusion on a *Pinus resinosa* forest in north-central Minnesota. Ecology 51:1088–1093.

Shugart, H. H. 1984. A Theory of Forest Dynamics. Springer-Verlag, New York.

Shugart, H. H., and D. C. West. 1977. Development of an Appalachian deciduous forest succession model and its application to assessment of the impact of the chestnut blight. Journal of Environmental Management 5:161–179.

Shugart, H. H., and D. C. West. 1980. Forest succession models. BioScience 30:308–313.

Solomon, A. M. 1986. Transient response of forests to CO_2-induced climate change: Simulation modeling experiments in eastern North America. Oecologia 68:567–579.

Stewart, G. H., and L. E. Burrows. 1989. The impact of white-tailed deer *Odocoileus virginianus* on regeneration in the coastal forests of Stewart Island, New Zealand. Biological Conservation 49:275–293.

Storm, G. L., R. H. Yahner, D. F. Cottam, and G. M. Vecellio. 1989. Population status, movements, habitat use, and impact of white-tailed deer at Gettysburg National Military Park and Eisenhower National Historic Site, Pennsylvania. U.S. National Park Service Final Project Report, University Park, PA.

Tilghman, N. G. 1989. Impacts of white-tailed deer on forest regeneration in northwestern Pennsylvania. Journal of Wildlife Management 53:524–532.

Urban, D. L. 1990. A versatile model to simulate forest pattern. University of Virginia, Environmental Sciences Department, Charlottesville.

Warren, R. J. 1991. Ecological justification for controlling deer populations in eastern national parks. Transactions of the 56th North American Wildlife and Natural Resources Conference 56:56–66.

Webb, W. L., R. T. King, and E. F. Patric. 1956. Effect of white-tailed deer on a mature northern hardwood forest. Journal of Forestry 54:391–398.

Woods, K. D. 1979. Reciprocal replacement and the maintenance of codominance in a beech–maple forest. Oikos 33:31–39.

Woods, K. D., and R. H. Whittaker. 1981. Canopy–understory interactions and the internal dynamics of mature hardwood and hemlock–hardwood forests. Pages 305–323 *in* Forest Succession: Concepts and Application. (D. C. West, H. H. Shugart, and D. B. Botkin, eds.) Springer-Verlag, New York.

22 A Spatially Explicit Modeling Environment for Evaluating Deer Management Strategies

KEN L. RISENHOOVER, H. BRIAN
UNDERWOOD, WEN YAN, AND
JERRY L. COOKE

During the past 200 years, land-use changes resulting from colonization and western expansion by Europeans have greatly altered temperate forest communities in the eastern United States (McCabe and McCabe 1984). Changes in harvest regulations, habitat conditions, and forage supply have allowed white-tailed deer to reoccupy most, if not all, of its former nineteenth-century range. Since the turn of this century, white-tailed deer numbers have increased dramatically, especially in urban and suburban areas where populations are protected due to hunting restrictions (Witham and Jones 1987).

Large deer populations are a concern for managers of natural areas, especially in the eastern United States (Warren 1991). Burgeoning deer populations create conflicts with other resource management objectives (Porter 1992), including those mandated by federal legislation (e.g., Endangered Species Act of 1973 [16 U.S.C. 1531–1544], National Environmental Policy Act of 1970 [42 U.S.C. 4321–4337], and Clean Water Act of 1977 [33 U.S.C. 1251–1387]). This situation is further complicated by the opinions of professionals and the public regarding the management of deer in national parks. Attitudes about deer are polarized and range from complete protection to population reduction through culling, hunter harvest, or fertility control. Apparent differences in land-management values, even among federal agencies, are not trivial and will require constant dialogue and a concerted, sincere effort to resolve (Underwood and Porter 1991).

Management guidelines and some alternatives available to the U.S. National Park Service (NPS) are described in *Management Policies* (USDI 1988), but the efficacy of these proposed alternatives is virtually unknown, and their palatability in today's sociopolitical climate is untested. Differences in the pattern and complexity of habitats, the regional demographic characteristics of deer populations, and the size and shape of individual park units, combined with the lack of funding for repeated large-scale experimentation, make it difficult to predict precisely the outcomes of even one management alternative applied at two locations. A better understanding of the responses of deer to resources on the landscape is essential if managers are to be successful in achieving management objectives.

To address the specific deer management concerns of the NPS, we developed the Deer Management Simulator (DMS), an interactive simulation environment for personal computers. Our primary objective in the development of this system was to provide wildlife biologists and natural resource managers with a tool to assist them with decision making regarding strategies for managing overabundant deer populations. The DMS permits users to integrate available Geographic Information Systems (GIS) databases for their management unit with data pertaining to the local deer population in order to gain a better appreciation of how the composition and spatial arrangement of habitats influence the seasonal movements and dispersion of deer across the landscape.

SIMULATION MODELS IN WILDLIFE MANAGEMENT

Simulation modeling provides one means of evaluating the relative importance of animal and habitat factors affecting the success of management alternatives (Starfield and Bleloch 1986; Walters 1986). Models are especially useful for identifying gaps in our knowledge about linkages between system components and the relative importance of model parameters affecting the outcome of a management action (Bunnell 1989). Even simple models often are sufficient to eliminate all but the most parsimonious hypotheses (Caughley 1976). Modeling is a process whereby the biologist or manager is forced to define explicitly *what* is to be done and *how* it is to be accomplished (Porter et al. 1991). In that sense, modeling is the quickest hypothesis generating and testing platform available. Thus, as a precursor to action, modeling can provide great economy of scale by setting the stage for a few well-planned field tests that can be implemented as experimental management (MacNab 1983).

A Spatially Explicit Modeling Approach

Recent technical advances in computer-processing capabilities and the advent of object-oriented programming languages are providing ecologists and natural resource managers with new approaches for investigating wildlife–habitat relationships. A new generation of simulation models combines spatially explicit relational GIS databases with individual-based animal population models. We were particularly interested in developing a tool to facilitate a better understanding of how individuals and populations may respond to modifications in the composition or arrangement of habitat resources on the landscape. Spatially explicit population models already have demonstrated their usefulness in land-use planning (McKelvey et al. 1992), in predicting animal responses to disturbance and habitat modification (Dunning et al. 1992), and in understanding how landscape spatial heterogeneity influences the demographics of metapopulations (Danielson 1991; Pulliam and Danielson 1991). In particular, spatially explicit population models are useful for demonstrating the importance of scale when assessing ecological processes within biotic communities (Addicott et al. 1987; Wiens 1989; Levin 1992).

The Deer Management Simulator

The DMS was developed for use with personal computers and in a DOS environment. This operating system and development environment was chosen to maximize the likelihood that the program would be compatible with computer hardware already available to resource management specialists working at most national park units. The DMS is composed of five modules (Table 22.1) that are integrated within a hierarchical menu system that was developed using Visual Basic (Microsoft Corp. 1992). During the initialization of the DMS system, data structures and specific information about the management area and deer population are provided by the user, interactively, through a series of menus.

LANDSCAPE COMPOSITION AND STRUCTURE   The DMS utilizes GIS map image files (Figure 22.1) containing the specific landscape attributes for the national park management unit as a spatially explicit database for the deer population module and as the background for the simulation module. Thus, users must be prepared to provide a map-based resource matrix and the associated grid coordinates for the management area to be evaluated using the DMS. This map image file can be any existing raster

TABLE 22.1

Primary modules of the Deer Management Simulator (DMS)

Module	Description and function
Landscape	Specify the name and location of landscape map (raster) file and boundary (vector) file; define map GIS coordinates and pixel resolution; delineate seasons; assign relative values to delineated habitat resource types on the landscape for each season
Deer population	Create and characterize the initial deer population for use in the simulation (user-specified input data include population size or density, sex and age composition, age-specific reproductive rates, and nontreatment related mortality rates)
Map utilities	Interactively delineate areas for treatment and census; create barriers to animal movement; modify habitats within specified areas on the landscape map
Data evaluation	Visualize how the seasonal habitat affinities influence animal dispersion over the landscape
Simulation	Design management treatment scenarios; specify how (i.e., intensity and duration) and where the treatment will be applied; specify the number of replicates to be run for each management scenario

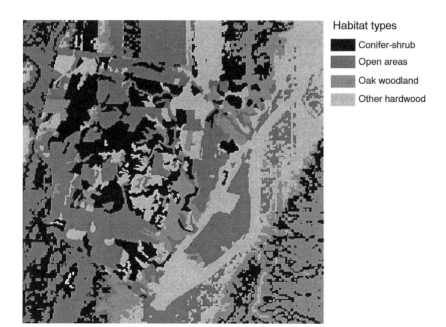

Habitat types
- Conifer-shrub
- Open areas
- Oak woodland
- Other hardwood

FIGURE 22.1. A raster-based GIS map image file (i.e., bare grid map) used as a spatial database by the Deer Management Simulator (DMS).

GIS map database file, or it can be a hypothetical landscape constructed arbitrarily by the user. This flexibility gives the user the opportunity to evaluate how the composition and spatial arrangement of habitat resources influence animal dispersion or to analyze the effects of user-specified treatments on demographic and dispersion patterns of the local deer population. The user also is required to provide a vector-based boundary file that delineates the park management unit on the landscape map. The DMS overlays this boundary file on the landscape image to enhance the user's ability to orient him or herself with map images created during simulations.

The map utilities module (Table 22.1) included with the DMS allows users to alter characteristics of the landscape map and to delineate specific areas for census or treatment (Figure 22.2). Modifications to the landscape map file are accomplished interactively by digitizing any desired changes directly onto the current map image while viewing it on the computer screen. A drawing tool allows the user to digitize lines as barriers and polygons as census or treatment areas based on the landscape map as a spatial reference. Once delineated, these areas can be saved and recalled later for use while evaluating management scenarios in the simulation or data evaluation modules. The drawing tool can also be used to reassign the habitat type within an explicitly defined area, which permits the

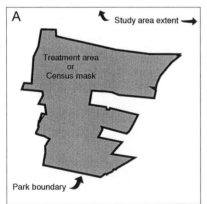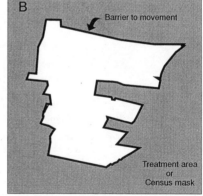

FIGURE 22.2. Treatment or census areas and barriers to animal movements created from within the map utilities module allow the user to control the location where treatments are to occur. Panel A illustrates the creation of an area (shaded) for the treatment of deer occurring inside the park boundary. Panel B illustrates a treatment area outside the park boundary and an installed barrier to prevent the movement of deer into the park.

user to investigate how habitat modifications (e.g., road cut or camp-ground) or disturbances (e.g., windthrow or fire) may affect the local deer population.

THE DEER POPULATION   The centerpiece of the DMS is a spatially explicit deer population model adapted from Cooke (1993). This model interfaces with raster-based GIS map images and databases and simulates individual animal movements in response to landscape features. The user inputs initial demographic properties for the deer population interactively by responding to menu queries in the deer population module. Users have the option of defining the size of the deer population explicitly, or they can specify an average deer density present in their park and have the DMS calculate population size based on area. The user also specifies the population sex and age composition (i.e., fawns, yearlings, and adults) and provides age-specific estimates of reproduction (i.e., pregnancy and fawning rates) and mortality for each class. In the event that site-specific data for these parameters are unavailable, default suggestions are provided based on our review of published studies on white-tailed deer. Values for all deer population characteristics can be reviewed and edited by the user at any time.

Based on the specified properties, the DMS creates a deer population file, which maintains information on the status of each individual in the population and disperses animals over the landscape. Initially, the placement of individual deer on the landscape is random (with the exception of fawns, which remain in close spatial proximity to their mothers until they are 1 year old). However, this initial placement is adjusted prior to any simulation by allowing animals to move and interact with landscape habitat features for one annual cycle (i.e., 365 days). This initialization produces a more realistic dispersion of animals that is dependent on the spatial characteristics of landscape features in the park and their relative values to deer.

In the DMS, the direction and extent of movement by individual deer are calculated on a daily time step and are a function of the quality of habitat resources present in the map pixels encountered by deer during the simulation. Displacement distance and the direction moved are calculated by taking a uniform random number (between 0 and 1) for both the x- and y-axes (i.e., columns and rows of the landscape map image, respectively) and multiplying it by the maximum straight-line distance (in map pixels) a deer can traverse in a 24-hour period. Each deer moves toward its new target location in four phases during each time step of the simulation. As deer move across the landscape, they obtain resources equivalent to the current habitat resource value of each pixel they encounter. During subsequent phases, deer continue moving in the direction of the target location until either (1) their daily resource requirement is met, which terminates further movement, or (2) the target position on the map is reached. Thus, deer encountering habitats containing high-quality resources are displaced less than are deer occupying low-quality habitats.

We chose a behavior-neutral approach to simulating animal movements to minimize assumptions about deer behavior. Behavior-neutral simulation models (Caswell 1976) have several advantages over traditional, data-driven models. First, deer movements and migration tendencies are likely to be site specific, the product of local adaptation in response to environmental conditions. In most cases, detailed information about deer daily or seasonal movements required to model explicitly animal movement and behavior will be unavailable. Second, the implementation of user-defined rules for deer population behavior (e.g., home range size, shape, and overlap and migration tendencies) is more likely to restrict the universe of possible outcomes, thus implicitly rendering the model deterministic. Behavior-neutral models allow population dispersion to emerge in response to individual animal requirements, variation in habitat quality, and other landscape constraints encountered. We embraced this approach because of its potentially broad applicability to a variety of situations.

DATA EVALUATION   After creating a deer population file, delineating important seasons, and assigning seasonal values for each habitat resource type, users can evaluate their initialization of the DMS on deer dispersion, movements, and habitat-use patterns. The consequences of a specific initialization to the deer population can be assessed using the data evaluation module (Table 22.1) before running any simulations. This module allows the user to observe on the computer's screen animal dispersion and movements in response to assigned habitat values as the model steps through the days of the annual cycle. At any point during the simulation, the user can use "hot keys" to obtain details about the number of deer occurring within each habitat resource type and a ratio of use versus availability. If results are inconsistent with expectation, the user may choose to reconsider the basis for assigning these values prior to simulating a management scenario.

Additional options available within the data evaluation module include (1) the ability to census deer within areas delineated in the mapping

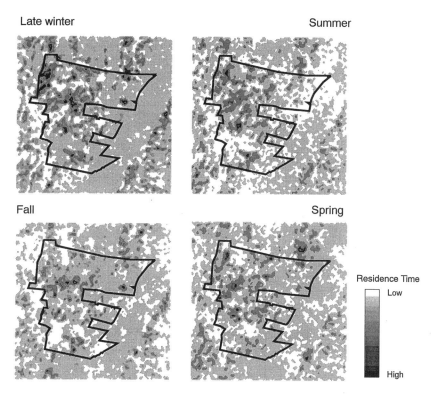

FIGURE 22.3. Deer spatial responses to user-assigned resource values. The data evaluation module permits users to assess how user-assigned seasonal habitat resource values affect spatial patterns of habitat use by deer in their park. The maps presented here are of deer spatial distribution in Saratoga National Historic Park, New York.

utilities module and (2) the ability to observe the accumulation of deer spatial use (i.e., residence time) on the landscape during specific time periods. The resulting deer spatial response maps (Figure 22.3) are especially helpful for identifying areas receiving high or low seasonal or annual use, areas exhibiting unpredictable use by deer, and areas that might be considered movement corridors (i.e., highly predictable use over small spatial extent).

MANAGEMENT SCENARIO SIMULATION   The simulation module of the DMS allows the user to design treatments and to evaluate their efficacy for managing overabundant deer populations in the user's park unit.

Treatments are designed by selecting options in response to menu queries about the type of treatment, the intensity and duration of the treatment, and where it will be applied on the landscape. Available treatment options include (1) animal removals (e.g., transplanting or hunting); (2) animal sterilization; (3) the installation of physical barriers to animal movement (e.g., deer-proof fencing), and (4) a "do nothing" or control option for the purpose of comparison to other treatments. Additional treatment scenarios can be created by combining these options.

For treatments involving animal removals or sterilization, users are asked to specify the rate (percentage of males and females affected) and the time period (starting and ending days) over which the treatment is to be applied. Users specify the location of the treatment on the landscape map by providing the name of a treatment file they have created using the map utilities module. Animals occurring outside the selected treatment are not subjected to the treatment.

Because the DMS is a individual-based simulation model, the deer population response (i.e., sum of individual responses) to any treatment will vary between simulation runs. Just as in nature, stochastic processes affecting the movement of individual deer in the simulation can result in significant differences in deer dispersion between runs despite identical initial population characteristics and treatment conditions. Differences in animal dispersion between runs can produce different exposures to treatments and ultimately result in differential rates of reproduction and survival in the population. Furthermore, differences among runs within a year may be amplified during subsequent years of the simulation. Thus, the DMS was designed to give the user the option of running multiple iterations (i.e., up to 30 replicates per simulated year) of each treatment for periods of up to 10 consecutive years. Multiple iterations allow the user to make probabilistic evaluations of the effects of various management scenarios on the deer population.

The DMS data evaluation and simulation modules generate output in both numerical and graphical forms. Numerical responses (i.e., size and composition) of the deer population to the chosen management scenario are stored in ASCII text files, which can be easily imported into most spreadsheet and statistical programs for graphing or further analysis (Figure 22.4). Spatial responses of the deer population are captured as color spectral map files that make it possible to visualize how treatments have affected the spatial–temporal patterns of deer use over the landscape (Figure 22.5). Spatial response maps are also saved as Idrisi (Eastman 1991) raster image files to facilitate spatial analyses of simulation results. The Idrisi files can be easily converted for use with other GIS software. Both

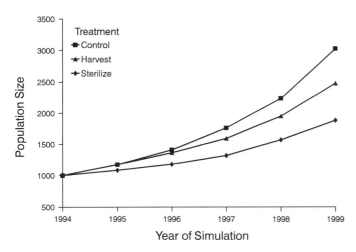

FIGURE 22.4. Numerical responses of deer population to imposed treatments. Output is stored in standard ASCII text files that can be easily imported into other software applications for graphing or analysis.

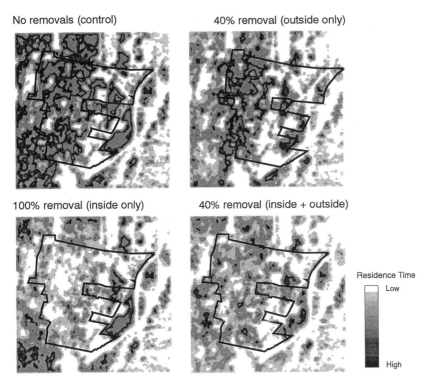

FIGURE 22.5. Deer spatial responses to treatments. The spatial responses of deer to treatments, in this case October–November removals, are recorded in color spectral maps that can be viewed from within the DMS or exported to other software applications for analysis. The maps presented here are of deer spatial distribution in Saratoga National Historic Park, New York.

graphical and numerical output files can be reviewed from within the simulation module of the DMS.

DISCUSSION

The adoption of spatially explicit population models in wildlife management has been relatively slow. This may be due to the fact that most models developed for use in management address very specific questions and often lack the generality needed to be applied broadly without considerable modification. In addition, even very specific models are incapable of accurately predicting the numerical changes in wildlife populations or the dispersion patterns of animals on the landscape (Conroy et al. 1995; Dunning et al. 1995). Given the complexity of most management problems, and the paucity of detailed data, we argue that the greatest utility provided by models like the DMS is their ability to assist resource managers in organizing the available information and integrating it into a spatial context. Projecting potential animal population responses to a set of management alternatives in this context adds more realism to the modeling exercise without sacrificing ease of use and overall utility. For example, such models can be useful for (1) identifying gaps in available data and our understanding of animal–habitat relationships; (2) identifying and evaluating the relative importance of input parameters (i.e., driving variables) on model behavior; and (3) providing justification for difficult or controversial decisions regarding management options.

The DMS is a general, yet powerful, simulation tool designed to assist natural resource specialists in their attempt to manage problems relating to overabundant white-tailed deer populations in national parks. This simulation environment integrates available information on deer population composition, habitat use, and productivity with GIS databases. A methodical application of the model (i.e., replicated runs of scenarios) can assist the user in identifying, in a probabilistic framework, the set of circumstances and conditions necessary for a particular management strategy to succeed. The flexibility of the DMS makes it ideal for conducting a sensitivity analysis of input values and for evaluating assumptions about local deer herd demographics and habitat-use patterns.

As is the case with every dynamic simulation model, the ultimate utility of the DMS will depend upon the user's ability to construct a model that realistically reflects animal responses to temporal changes in habitat conditions. The DMS is a mechanistic model in the sense that the observed deer population response to a user-defined treatment or habitat perturbation is a function of the cumulative responses of the individual deer to their local environment conditions. In developing the DMS, we have avoided imposing assumptions regarding explicit deer behaviors in order to preserve model flexibility. Although the DMS was developed specifically to address white-tailed deer management issues and problems, the structure of the model can be easily adapted to address management questions specific to other ungulates and wildlife species.

SUMMARY

Overabundant white-tailed deer populations can adversely affect features of landscapes being managed for aesthetic or historical values. Under such circumstances active intervention may be required to preserve unique attributes of these areas and to achieve existing management objectives and policies. However, success at managing deer populations is likely to vary among parks depending upon their size, position in the regional landscape, and attractiveness to deer in neighboring areas. Given the potential importance of these variables, it is difficult to predict which treatment option (e.g., harvest, habitat modification, fencing, or sterilization) is most likely to accomplish management objectives (i.e., reduce deer densities). Justification for deer management programs is especially important in national parks because of the increased attention afforded them by the public and special interest groups. We present a simulation environment that combines spatially explicit habitat features from a park's existing GIS with an individual-based deer population model to evaluate the efficacy of competing management strategies. The system imposes user-defined treatments on the deer population, monitors the movements and spatial responses of every individual in the population over a user-specified period, and performs multiple iterations to assess the probability of success or failure in achieving management goals. Deer responses to different treatment scenarios can be viewed as numerical changes in population size and composition over time or as graphical changes in deer spatial dispersion. Additional features of the simulation include identification of potential movement corridors and areas of high seasonal use by deer. Treatments can be designed and applied to entire populations, a specific sex–age class, or specific areas delineated by the user. Results of treatment scenarios can be contrasted by users and can provide strategic input into park management and planning activities.

ACKNOWLEDGMENTS

This project received financial support from the U.S. National Park Service, Texas A&M University, and the State University of New York, College of Environmental Science and Forestry. We especially thank Michael Coffey of the National Park Service for his unwavering support and encouragement throughout this project.

REFERENCES CITED

Addicott, J. F., J. M. Aho, M. F. Antolin, D. K. Padilla, J. S. Richardson, and D. A. Soluk. 1987. Ecological neighborhoods: Scaling environmental patterns. Oikos 49:340–346.

Bunnell, F. L. 1989. Alchemy and uncertainty: What good are models? U.S. Forest Service, Northwest Research Station, General Technical Report PNW-GTR-232.

Caswell, H. 1976. Community structure: A neutral model analysis. Ecological Monographs 46:327–354.

Caughley, G. 1976. Plant–herbivore systems. Pages 94–113 in Theoretical Ecology: Principles and Applications. (R. M. May, ed.) Blackwell Scientific, London.

Conroy, M. J., Y. Cohen, F. C. James, Y. G. Yiannis, and B. A. Maurer. 1995. Parameter estimation, reliability, and model improvement for spatially explicit models of animal populations. Ecological Applications 5:17–19.

Cooke, J. L. 1993. Assessing populations in complex systems. Doctoral dissertation, Texas A&M University, College Station.

Danielson, B. J. 1991. Communities in a landscape: The influence of habitat heterogeneity on the interactions between species. American Naturalist 138:1105–1120.

Dunning, J. B., B. J. Danielson, and H. R. Pulliam. 1992. Ecological processes that affect populations in complex landscapes. Oikos 65:169–175.

Dunning J. B., D. J. Stewart, B. J. Danielson, B. R. Noon, T. L. Root, R. H. Lamberson, and E. E. Stevens. 1995. Spatially explicit population models: Current forms and future uses. Ecological Applications 5:3–11.

Eastman, J. R. 1992. Idrisi Version 4.0 User's Guide. Clark University Graduate School of Geography, Worcester, MA.

Levin, S. A. 1992. The problem of pattern and scale in ecology. Ecology 73:63–87.

MacNab, J. 1983. Wildlife management as scientific experimentation. Wildlife Society Bulletin 11:397–401.

McCabe, R. E., and T. R. McCabe 1984. Of slings and arrows: An historical retrospection. Pages 19–72 in White-Tailed Deer: Ecology and Management. (L. K. Halls, ed.) Stackpole Books Harrisburg, PA.

McKelvey, K., B. R. Noon, and R. H. Laberson. 1992. Conservation planning for species occupying fragmented landscapes: The case of the northern spotted owl. Pages 424–450 *in* Biotic Interactions and Global Change. (P. M. Karieva, J. G. Kingsolver, and R. B. Huey, eds.) Sinauer Associates, Sunderland, MA.

Microsoft Corporation. 1992. Visual Basic Programming System for MS-DOS. Microsoft Corporation, Redmond, WA.

Porter, W. F. 1992. Burgeoning ungulate populations on national parks: Is intervention necessary? Pages 304–312 *in* Wildlife 2001: Populations. (D. R. McCullough and R. H. Barrett, eds.) Elsevier Applied Science, New York.

Porter, W. F., H. B. Underwood, and D. J. Gefell. 1991. Applications of population modelling to management of wild turkeys. Pages 107–118 *in* Sixth National Wild Turkey Symposium, Wild Turkey Federation, Edgefield, SC.

Pulliam H. R., and B. J. Danielson 1991. Sources, sinks, and habitat selection: A landscape perspective on population dynamics. American Naturalist 137: S50–S66.

Starfield, A. M., and A. L. Bleloch. 1986. Building Models for Conservation and Wildlife Management. MacMillan Publishing Co., New York.

Underwood, H. B., and W. F. Porter 1991. Values and science: White-tailed deer management in eastern national parks. Pages 67–73 *in* Transactions of the 56th North American Wildlife and Natural Resource Conference, Wildlife Management Institute, Washington.

USDI (U. S. Department of Interior). 1988. Natural resource management. Pages 5–7 *in* U.S. National Park Service, Management Policies. U.S. Government Printing Office, Washington.

Walters, C. 1986. Adaptive Management of Renewable Resources. MacMillan Publishing Co., New York.

Warren, R. J. 1991. Ecological justification for controlling deer populations in eastern national parks. Pages 56–66 *in* Transactions of the 56th North American Wildlife and Natural Resource Conference, Wildlife Management Institute, Washington.

Wiens, J. A. 1989. Spatial scaling in ecology. Functional Ecology 3:385–397.

Witham, J. H., and J. M. Jones. 1987. Deer–human interactions and research in the Chicago metropolitan area. Pages 155–159 *in* Proceedings of the National Symposium on Urban Wildlife. (L. W. Adams and D. L. Leedy, eds.) National Institute for Urban Wildlife, Columbia, MD.

23

EPILOGUE
Carrying Capacity and the Overabundance of Deer

A Framework for Management

A. R. E. SINCLAIR

Deer are species that respond to an increase in herbaceous and shrubby vegetation. Since human alteration of habitats has promoted early successional stages, deer have benefitted nutritionally and have increased in numbers (Alverson et al. 1988). The conservation problem, therefore, is whether deer affect other species in natural communities as a result of this increase; the management problem is whether deer are a "nuisance" species in human ecosystems. The objectives of this volume, then, are to address two questions (McShea et al., Chapter 1): (1) how does one manage high-density populations of ungulates in protected areas in North America and elsewhere? and (2) how does one manage deer species in North America in all ecosystems?

Deer represent a case study for problem species, examples of which are seen all over the world. Thus, problems occur with kangaroos in Australia (Caughley et al. 1987), elephants and other large ungulates in savanna Africa (Owen-Smith 1983), and rabbits in parts of Europe (Crawley 1990). In North America, one finds problems with geese, gulls, red-winged blackbirds, foxes, raccoons, beavers, skunks, and squirrels, to name just some (Kerbes et al. 1990; Garrott et al. 1993). The questions are the same: are these species out of balance with the community and do they threaten rare species? It is clear from the chapters in this volume and elsewhere that deer in North America are perceived as overabundant, or not, depending on the different perspectives of the observers. My objective in this closing chapter is to synthesize these views within a single framework based on the biological properties of carrying capacity. From this framework one can see that there are two types of problems, those associated with biology and those associated with value judgements. This approach should allow managers to see their own problems with the management of deer in one particular place in the context of a larger array of issues.

Previous volumes (Jewell and Holt 1981; Owen-Smith 1983; Wemmer 1987) have highlighted the preconceptions of many authors in this volume, namely that natural regulation of populations is not possible for a variety of reasons and so active, interventionist management is necessary to counteract overabundance. Intervention has been justified based on criteria developed from human ecosystems (agricultural and residential lands). The interventionist position has been criticized on the grounds that, first, definitions of carrying capacity and overabundance are not clear and, second, management criteria developed for human-disturbed systems (which include small reserves) are inappropriate for natural ecosystems (i.e., large parks and reserves), and vice-versa. In the management of ecosystems (and particularly as it concerns deer), dogma, myth, and untested hypotheses are pervasive. In this volume, the editors have challenged us to examine these myths and develop management actions appropriate for the different systems.

To set up the framework, I first review the meanings of carrying capacity to see how the different definitions are related. I mention briefly some of the evidence presented in this volume relevant to these viewpoints and end by discussing where we should look in future work.

A FRAMEWORK FOR MANAGEMENT

Carrying Capacity: Biological Properties

All problems in wildlife management fall into three categories: (1) too many (overabundance), (2) too few (conservation), and (3) too many harvested (exploitation) (Caughley 1976). These categories, in turn, are unified by one concept, carrying capacity. Unfortunately, this term is rarely defined and so is used in many different ways. Consequently, much unnecessary argument is at cross purposes. The general meanings of carrying capacity and overabundance have already been discussed at length (Caughley 1976, 1979, 1981; McCullough 1979, 1992; Sinclair 1981;

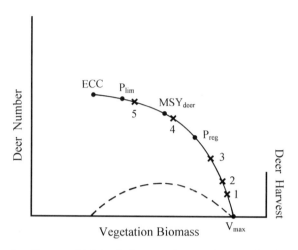

FIGURE 23.1. Isocline at which both deer numbers and vegetation biomass are constant (solid line). A harvest rate (broken line) imposed on deer is necessary to maintain points on the isocline between ecological carrying capacity (ECC) and maximum vegetation (V_{max}). Other points on the isocline are predator limitation of deer (P_{lim}); predator regulation of deer (P_{reg}); maximum sustained yield of deer (MSY_{deer}); rare species carrying capacity (1); timber harvest carrying capacity (2); cultural carrying capacity (3); parasite load carrying capacity (4); and hunter opportunity carrying capacity (5). Terms explained in the text.

Macnab 1983, 1985), and I have used these to construct Figure 23.1, which should be thought of as a hypothetical phase diagram of deer numbers and vegetation biomass.

Any definition of carrying capacity must imply a long-term stability of herbivore numbers, vegetation biomass, and community species composition; that is, biodiversity should be stable. The timescale for this stability is rarely discussed in the literature, but I suggest that a reasonable value for "long term" would be the average longevity of the habitat in question. This avoids the need to suggest absolute values, and so one can apply the term carrying capacity to different systems with different timescales.

In Figure 23.1 the solid line represents a series of points at which deer numbers can hold vegetation biomass constant (an isocline). Some natural biological equilibria can be identified along this isocline (the solid points). One is the trivial point of maximum vegetation, V_{max}, at which there are no deer. Another is the equilibrium of maximum deer numbers determined by intraspecific competition for food under long-term natural conditions. This is the ecological carrying capacity (ECC), as represented by K in the logistic equation. All other points between ECC and V_{max} require that deer are harvested by predators or humans, the harvest rate being indicated by the broken line.

Predators can limit prey numbers anywhere between a point near ECC and some minimum number required to maintain the predator population, depending on the biological features of prey and predator. Theoretical predator–prey interactions are complex and nonlinear and are discussed elsewhere (Ricklefs 1979; Sinclair 1989; Messier 1994; Pech et al. 1995). However, for present purposes one can hypothesize that a predator of deer could, with the same predation rate, or off take, regulate deer numbers at a low level through density-dependent predation or limit them at a high level through nondensity-dependent predation. These points, chosen arbitrarily on the harvest curve, can be identified on the isocline as P_{reg} and P_{lim}, respectively. In reality, one or the other or both points could occur.

If a harvest was to be imposed on the deer population with the intention of maximizing the yield, then the biological properties of the population would determine where the maximum sustained yield (MSY) point lies. This point, at the peak of the harvest curve (Figure 23.1), can then be identified on the isocline as MSY_{deer}. This is not to say that MSY is achievable in practice. Indeed, most managers recognize the intrinsic dangers in harvesting at this level (Walters 1986).

Carrying Capacity: Arbitrary Values

Most definitions of carrying capacity are arbitrary rather than biological. Various contributors to this volume have identified a number of other management objectives, and all of these are arbitrary in the sense that they can, unlike biological properties, be located anywhere along the isocline in Figure 23.1, depending solely upon the priorities of the managers. For present purposes the exact location of points for the various management objectives is unimportant. My intention is to show that a wide range of points exist, and in Figure 23.1 their location has been chosen, with some hand waving, by general consensus of this volume's authors. These are the points indicated by X.

Knox (Chapter 3) recorded the increase in white-tailed deer numbers in Virginia since the 1940s and the parallel increase in damage to crops and vehicle collisions. He suggested that deer numbers should be reduced and maintained at some lower density at which damage to crops was perceived by landholders to be insignificant. This level, labeled by deCalesta

(Chapter 16) as "cultural carrying capacity," is considered to have low deer numbers and is located close to V_{max}.

Even moderate deer densities (over 4 deer/km^2) reduce tree regeneration (Alverson et al. 1988; Alverson and Waller, Chapter 17; deCalesta, Chapter 16) and, in turn, lower the timber harvest. Thus, timber companies would like the "timber carrying capacity" to be closer to V_{max} also. There is, however, another group of exploiters of the ecosystem, the deer hunters, who have an opposite view. At first sight they would require maximum off take, which would suggest a carrying capacity at MSY_{deer}. However, hunters perceive the health of a deer population by the numbers alive (see McCabe and McCabe, Chapter 2)—the more the better—so that ECC would be appropriate. This presents a conundrum, since both MSY_{deer} and ECC cannot occur simultaneously. Thus, I have chosen the "hunter opportunity carrying capacity" as somewhere between the two.

Conservationists, concerned about the viability of rare species, have suggested that high deer numbers either degrade habitat (McShea and Rappole, Chapter 18) or threaten rare plant species (Alverson and Waller, Chapter 17). McShea and Rappole demonstrated that white-tailed deer may reduce the number of breeding songbird species in hardwood forests. Their perception was that even very low densities of deer were detrimental to conservation objectives; therefore, the "rare species carrying capacity" must be placed very close to V_{max}.

Veterinarians and parasitologists, whose training is with domestic stock normally kept near MSY and, therefore, in good nutritional condition, tend to see wild animals that die from heavy parasite loads as overabundant (Davidson and Doster, Chapter 11). Such populations are at ECC, but the perception is that they should be much lower. The consensus for "parasite load carrying capacity" was somewhere below MSY_{deer}, although of course it could be anywhere on the isocline because animals carry parasites whatever their density.

Carrying Capacity: Potential Changes

Leopold (1943) produced a diagram (Figure 23.2) indicating that carrying capacity could decline as herbivore numbers increased (see Davidson and Doster, Chapter 11; McCullough, Chapter 6). It is not entirely clear what this carrying capacity represents. One possibility is that it refers to vegetation biomass: it is at maximum where there are no herbivores. If this is the case, Leopold's carrying capacity merely refers to V_{max}, and of course vegetation biomass declines with increasing herbivore numbers until ECC

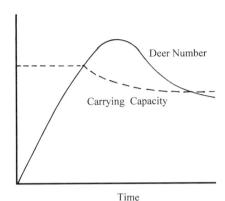

Deer Number

Carrying Capacity

Time

FIGURE 23.2. The relationship between carrying capacity and deer numbers over time, interpreted from Leopold (1943).

is reached. However, the context of the article suggests that Leopold may be referring to some long-term decline in ECC itself. The assumption is that deer would increase above carrying capacity, crash, and thus cause a decline in the carrying capacity itself. There follows a second increase in herbivore numbers above the now lower carrying capacity, causing a further reduction, and so on. If this carrying capacity stabilized, it would represent the long-term ECC as defined earlier. The isocline in Figure 23.1 represents long-term stability conditions, so that ECC as shown represents this value. In Figure 23.3 the long-term isocline is indicated by the stability point ECC_{long}, and the short-term isocline with higher deer numbers for the same vegetation biomass is indicated by the stability point ECC_{short}. The latter point would represent an unexploited habitat where deer had been absent for a long time, such as occurred in eastern North America in the last half of the nineteenth century. If I interpret Leopold's diagram (Figure 23.2) correctly, the short-term isocline will merge gradually with the long-term isocline. If the deer–plant system did not stabilize in the long term, then it would go extinct. This trend would be represented by the isocline sinking onto the x-axis, and the only stability point would be V_{max} again.

It is possible that ECC could also change during vegetation succession, most likely moving from high to low deer numbers for the same vegetation biomass as plant species change from herbaceous to shrubs to trees. Alternatively, there could be two states, as suggested by Schmitz and Sinclair (Chapter 13), and the ecosystem could jump between the two. This could occur, for example, if deer built up in numbers during early succession and so held the vegetation in an herbaceous state. This state, labeled ECC_{reg}, is one in which herbivores determine the structure of the plant

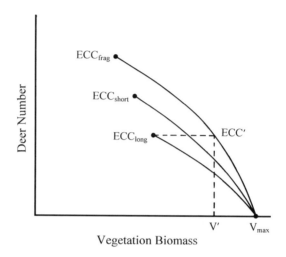

FIGURE 23.3. Deer–vegetation isoclines. Isoclines are given for an ecological carrying capacity (ECC) with long-term stability (ECC$_{long}$), short-term stability (ECC$_{short}$), following deer invasion of unexploited habitats, and stability in fragmented habitat (ECC$_{frag}$). In fragmented habitats, a reduction in deer numbers from ECC$_{frag}$ to those equivalent to ECC$_{long}$ (ECC') will result in vegetation biomass increasing to V'.

community. However, if deer numbers were reduced until succession had proceeded to a woody vegetation community, then much of the vegetation would be out of reach, and a different isocline and stable point (ECC$_{lim}$) would be reached. At ECC$_{lim}$, herbivores, although having some browsing impact, do not determine the structure and species composition of the plant community.

EVIDENCE FOR THE DIFFERENT INTERPRETATIONS OF CARRYING CAPACITY

Food Supply

One must presuppose that before the arrival of humans in North America, deer, hardwood forests, and the understory flora coexisted. One might consider that prehistoric conditions are now irrelevant because there are no undisturbed habitats left. However, prehuman conditions are a useful logical starting point, and certainly such habitats in representative areas are an objective of "restoration" ecology. Even in the period prior to European arrivals, deer were moderately abundant (McCabe and McCabe, Chapter 2). Evidence that they can exist at the level of their food supply (ECC) comes from the George Reserve experiments for white-tailed deer (McCullough, Chapter 6) and the measures of density dependence in mule deer *(Odocoileus hemionus)* (White and Bartmann, Chapter 8). Furthermore, there does not appear to be a decline in ECC either (McCullough, Chapter 6; Palmer et al., Chapter 10; Underwood and Porter, Chapter 12), and this is consistent with other studies of ungulates (Houston 1982; Clutton-Brock et al. 1991; Singer and Norland 1994; Sinclair 1995). However, I should add the caveat that all these studies are short when compared to the timescale of habitat longevity. I doubt that there are any data to demonstrate whether or not long-term stability occurs; it may, but we have to wait and see.

In the early 1900s white-tailed deer were hunted almost to extinction in the eastern hardwood forests (Healy, Chapter 15), and at this time one would have seen V_{max}, an artifact of the commercial hunting. In the subsequent 40 years, deer populations rebounded and vegetation would have declined from V_{max} to ECC. Both the total plant biomass and the species composition would have changed during this period, and such changes may have influenced Leopold (1943) in producing his figure (Figure 23.2). There is abundant evidence that herbivores have such effects (e.g., Coppock et al. 1983; Miles 1987; Brown and Heske 1990; Huntly 1991).

Predators

During prehistoric times, indigenous peoples were hunting deer, and this would have held deer populations at some level below ECC. Hunting by indigenous peoples has been advanced to suggest that food plants never experienced browsing at the levels of ECC and so were not adapted to such browsing. Sport hunting, it has been argued, should replace prehistoric hunting as a biological necessity. The problem with this rationale is that the period of time over which hunting by indigenous peoples occurred (10–20 thousand years) is far too short to have affected the evolutionary coexistence between deer and their food supply. A second argument to justify sport hunting suggests that deer never reached ECC because their predators kept numbers at lower levels (see Caughley 1970 for review). The argument is that because predators have been removed in many areas, hunters must take the place of the predators. Biologically, the only situation in which deer browsing may not affect their food plants is when predators regulate deer. At present there is a dearth of information concerning predator regulation of deer, which suggests that regulation may not be a frequent occurrence. I expect it does occur in some areas but that limitation is more the norm; that is, there is an interaction of food and predation in regulating deer. Therefore, the absence of predators does not necessarily imply an unregulated system requiring the intervention of hunters.

The third argument in favor of hunting proposes that woodland species composition has been changing over most of this century, coinciding with increasing deer numbers. This implies a lack of balance in the system, and hunting is required to reimpose the balance. However, so called "ancient forests" in New England and elsewhere are now known to have been constantly disturbed (Edwards 1986; Mitchell 1988; Foster 1992; Foster et al. 1992; Foster and Zebryk 1993; Bush and Colinvaux 1994; Davis et al. 1994; Willis 1994). Thus, present changes in woodland composition cannot be used as evidence for present day imbalances in deer numbers because such vegetation changes can be produced by other factors related to climate (e.g., precipitation and fire). Logically, therefore, the case for sport hunting cannot be based on biological grounds. The level of hunting must be based on value judgements such as pleasure, tradition, and economics, and it is constrained only by the biological level of MSY_{deer}.

Although some form of ECC determined by food supply has been demonstrated for deer, there is also evidence that predators can limit deer numbers (Keith 1974; White and Bartmann, Chapter 8). Thus, although the evidence for predator regulation holding deer at low density is still missing, one can at least say that P_{lim} occurs.

Parasites

It is now reasonably well established that parasites and diseases act synergistically with undernutrition to regulate ungulate populations at ECC (Sinclair 1977), Davidson and Doster's (Chapter 11) abundant evidence that deer die with heavy parasite loads when at high density is consistent with the interpretation that the cited deer populations were at ECC. The suggestion that deer should not be allowed to die from such causes is, therefore, not a biological argument but an aesthetic one.

The Multistate Hypothesis

Several studies in this volume have examined the effect of deer on plant succession and shrub layer biomass. Two studies showed little effect of deer on succession and seedling species diversity (Bowers, Chapter 19; Healy, Chapter 15). In contrast, many studies show severe depletion of seedlings and shrub biomass (Alverson and Waller, Chapter 17; de-Calesta, Chapter 16; McShea and Rappole, Chapter 18) or depletion of dominant seedlings (Healy, Chapter 15; Seagle and Liang, Chapter 21). Schmitz and Sinclair (Chapter 13) also provide support that deer could produce multistates in vegetation biomass. This is an aspect that requires further investigation, particularly because it is related to Underwood and Porter's (Chapter 12) hypothesis that woodland fragmentation has resulted in overabundance.

The Fragmentation–Nutrition Hypothesis

Overabundance can be defined quite simply as more animals than the particular carrying capacity the observer chooses to consider can accommodate. For some carrying capacities, the evidence suggests deer are not overabundant: they do not exceed ECC, there is no decline in ECC at least in the short term, nor do deer carry more parasites than expected at ECC. Because deer are native to North America (unlike many introductions in New Zealand and Australia, for example), they are part of the ecosystem, and so V_{max} is an unreasonable carrying capacity for which to strive. On the other hand, in agricultural and residential ecosystems, deer are overabundant according to the needs of society.

However, the most important issue arising from this volume is whether there are more deer than the original prehistoric plant community evolved to tolerate. This could occur if the deer–vegetation isocline was artificially raised so that there were more deer for the same vegetation biomass (Figure 23.3). Such a change would come about if deer were provided with abnormally high nutrition. Do we have this situation? There is increasing evidence that fragmentation of forests into small patches surrounded by highly nutritious croplands provides the conditions for a new carrying capacity (Alverson et al. 1988; Palmer et al., Chapter 10; Underwood and Porter, Chapter 12), labeled ECC_{frag} in Figure 23.3. I have called this the "fragmentation–nutrition hypothesis." In fragmented habitats one would see high levels of browsing on herbaceous and shrubby vegetation (Alverson et al. 1988; Hanson et al., Chapter 20; Palmer et al., Chapter 10). In addition, this nutritionally enriched environment should produce instability and fluctuating populations of deer and vegetation (Rosenzweig 1971; Taylor 1984). If this is the case, then human activities have created an artificial situation in which deer are now overabundant from the standpoint of the original hardwood forests. Deer numbers would then have to be reduced from the high numbers in artificially fragmented habitats, ECC_{frag}, to the point equivalent to ECC_{long}, or ECC' on the ECC_{frag} isocline (Figure 23.3). This reduction would allow vegetation biomass to increase, and plant and animal survival and diversity would also increase.

THE NEED FOR ADAPTIVE MANAGEMENT

Although there is much evidence in favor of what I have outlined above, the ideas remain largely hypothetical, and there is some contrary evidence (Mladenoff and Stearns 1993). Consequently the ideas must be tested experimentally. Such experiments are usually so large that they should employ the approach of adaptive management (Holling 1978; Walters 1986; Walters and Holling 1990). This approach uses management itself as the experimental manipulation, but the essential requirement is that the manipulation is varied over as wide a range as possible. A variation of this approach is to use natural disturbances, particularly local extinctions and recoveries, as a way to understand the ecological influences of the herbivore (Estes et al. 1989). For example, to test the multiple-state hypothesis (Schmitz and Sinclair, Chapter 13), deer densities would be managed so that they vary from no removal to extremely severe removal over short and long time periods. Realistically, sociopolitical pressures will constrain some measures and push the system toward fewer deer than the biology would suggest. If the fragmentation–nutrition hypothesis is to be tested, then the effects of mammals on the survival of rare plants, birds, and so on, need to be examined in a wide range of fragment sizes (e.g., Robinson et al. 1992), up to areas of 250 km² or more. (This size appears to be necessary to mimic the original contiguous forest; W. Alverson and D. Waller, University of Wisconsin, personal communication). Without such an adaptive management approach, the issue of overabundance cannot be resolved, and the problem will remain subject to debate.

CONCLUSION

This volume addresses an important general problem in conservation: how does one manage an abundant large mammal in protected areas where they could be threatening the survival of rare species? The authors in this volume appear to present conflicting data and conclusions. However, by viewing the results in an appropriate herbivore–vegetation framework, the different approaches can be reconciled. First, it is important to distinguish between scientific issues and value judgements so that biological reasons are not used to justify aesthetic values. Second, it is necessary to define the terms. It is then possible to identify the important hypotheses explaining the apparent overabundance of deer. One of the important hypotheses that has come out of this debate is the fragmentation–nutrition hypothesis, which proposes that once-contiguous hardwood habitats have now been fragmented and surrounded by highly nutritious cropland. This fragmentation has produced an abundance of deer higher than the community of native plants and animals evolved to tolerate. As a result, both alternative community states and local species extinctions could occur. This hypothesis now needs testing through adaptive management. This is the conservation objective, however. There are many other valid objectives to satisfy, including those of hunters, farmers, timber companies, suburban householders, and animal welfare groups. Because all objectives cannot be accommodated simultaneously, they must be partitioned in space. A regionwide council that addresses all these objectives together would perhaps be the appropriate method of coordination.

ACKNOWLEDGMENTS

I thank Bill McShea and the Smithsonian Institution for inviting me to contribute to this volume and Os Schmitz, Bill Alverson, Dan Edge, and an anonymous reviewer for constructive comments on earlier versions of this chapter.

REFERENCES CITED

Alverson, W. S., D. M. Waller, and S. L. Solheim. 1988. Forests too deer: Edge effects in Northern Wisconsin. Conservation Biology 2:348–358.

Brown, J. H., and E. J. Heske. 1990. Control of a desert-grassland transition by a keystone rodent guild. Science 250:1705–1707.

Bush, M. B., and P. A. Colinvaux. 1994. Tropical forest disturbance: Paleoecological records from Darien, Panama. Ecology 75:1761–1768.

Caughley, G. 1970. Eruption of ungulate populations, with emphasis on Himalayan thar in New Zealand. Ecology 51:53–72.

Caughley, G. 1976. Wildlife management and the dynamics of ungulate populations. Pages 183–246 in Applied Biology. (T. H. Coaker, ed.) Academic Press, New York.

Caughley, G. 1979. What is this thing called carrying capacity? Pages 2–8 *in* North American Elk: Ecology, Behavior and Management. (M. S. Boyce and L. D. Hayden-Wing, eds.) University of Wyoming, Laramie.

Caughley, G. 1981. Overpopulation. Pages 7–19 *in* Problems in Management of Locally Abundant Wild Mammals. (P. A. Jewell and S. Holt, eds.) Academic Press, New York.

Caughley, G., N. Shepherd, and J. Short, eds. 1987. Kangaroos, Their Ecology and Management in the Sheep Rangelands of Australia. Cambridge University Press, Cambridge, United Kingdom.

Clutton-Brock, T. H., O. F. Price, S. D. Albon, and P. A. Jewell. 1991. Persistent instability and population regulation in Soay sheep. Journal of Animal Ecology 60:593–608.

Coppock, D. L., J. K. Detling, J. E. Ellis, and M. I. Dyer. 1983. Plant–herbivore interactions in a North American mixed-grass prairie. Oecologia 56:1–9.

Crawley, M. J. 1990. Rabbit grazing, plant competition and seedling recruitment in acid grassland. Journal of Applied Ecology 27:803–820.

Davis, M. B., S. Sugita, R. R. Calcote, J. B. Ferrari, and L. E. Frelich. 1994. Historical development of alternate communities in a hemlock–hardwood forest in northern Michigan, USA. Pages 19–39 *in* Large-Scale Ecology and Conservation Biology. (P. J. Edwards, R. M. May, and N. R. Webb, eds.) Blackwell Scientific, Oxford, United Kingdom.

Edwards, M. E. 1986. Disturbance histories of four Snowdonian woodlands and their relation to Atlantic bryophyte distributions. Biological Conservation 37:301–320.

Estes, J. A., D. O. Duggins, and G. B. Rathbun. 1989. The ecology of extinctions in kelp forest communities. Conservation Biology 3:252–264.

Foster, D. R. 1992. Land-use history (1730–1990) and vegetation dynamics in central New England, USA. Journal of Ecology 80:753–772.

Foster, D., and T. M. Zebyk. 1993. Long-term vegetation dynamics and disturbance history in a *Tsuga*-dominated forest in New England. Ecology 74:982–998.

Foster, D., T. Zebryk, P. Schoonmaker, P.-A. Lezberg. 1992. Post-settlement history of human land-use and vegetation dynamics of a *Tsuga canadensis* (hemlock) woodlot in central New England. Journal of Ecology 80:773–786.

Garrott, R. A., P. J. White, and C. A. V. White. 1993. Overabundance: An issue for conservation biologists? Conservation Biology 7:946–949.

Holling, C. S. 1978. Adaptive Environmental Assessment and Management. John Wiley and Sons, London.

Houston, D. B. 1982. The Northern Yellowstone Elk: Ecology and Management. Macmillan Publishing Co., New York.

Huntly, N. 1991. Herbivores and the dynamics of communities and ecosystems. Annual Review Ecology and Systematics 22:477–503.

Jewell, P. A., and S. Holt, eds. 1981. Problems in Management of Locally Abundant Wild Mammals. Academic Press, New York.

Keith, L. B. 1974. Some features of population dynamics in mammals. International Congress of Game Biologists, Stockholm 11:17–58.

Kerbes, R. H., P. M. Kotanen, and R. L. Jefferies. 1990. Destruction of wetland habitats by lesser snow geese: A keystone species on the west coast of Hudson bay. Journal of Applied Ecology 27:242–258.

Leopold, A. 1943. Deer irruptions. Transactions of the Wisconsin Academy of Science, Arts and Letters 35:351–366.

Macnab, J. 1983. Wildlife management as scientific experimentation. Wildlife Society Bulletin 11:397–401.

Macnab, J. 1985. Carrying capacity and related slippery shibboleths. Wildlife Society Bulletin 13:403–410.

McCullough, D. R. 1979. The George Reserve Deer Herd. Michigan University Press, Ann Arbor.

McCullough, D. R. 1992. Concepts of herbivore population dynamics. Pages 967–984 *in* Wildlife 2001: Populations. (D. R. McCullough and R. H. Barrett, eds.) Elsevier Applied Science, New York.

Messier, F. 1994. Ungulate population models with predation: A case study with the North American moose. Ecology 75:478–488.

Miles, J. 1987. Vegetation succession: Past and present perceptions. Pages 1–30 *in* Colonization, Succession and Stability. (A. J. Gray, M. J. Crawley, and P. J. Edwards, eds.) Blackwell Scientific, Oxford, United Kingdom.

Mitchell, F. J. G. 1988. The vegetational history of the Killarney oakwoods, SW Ireland: Evidence from fine spatial resolution pollen analysis. Journal of Ecology 76:415–436.

Mladenoff, D. J., and F. Stearns. 1993. Eastern hemlock regeneration and deer browsing in the northern Great Lakes region: A re-examination and model simulation. Conservation Biology 7:889–900.

Owen-Smith, R. N., ed. 1983. Management of large mammals in African conservation areas. Haum, Pretoria, South Africa.

Pech, R. P., A. R. E. Sinclair, and A. E. Newsome. 1995. Predation models for primary and secondary prey species. Wildlife Research 22:55–64.

Ricklefs, R. E. 1979. Ecology. 2nd edition. Chiron Press, New York.

Robinson, G. R., R. D. Holt, M. S. Gaines, S. P. Hamburg, M. L. Johnson, H. S. Fitch, and E. A. Martinko, 1992. Diverse and contrasting effects of habitat fragmentation. Science 257:524–526.

Rosenzweig, M. L. 1971. Paradox of enrichment: Destabilization of exploitation systems in ecological time. Science 171:385–387.

Sinclair, A. R. E. 1977. The African Buffalo. University of Chicago Press, Chicago.

Sinclair, A. R. E. 1981. Environmental carrying capacity and the evidence for overabundance. Pages 247–257 *in* Problems in Management of Locally Abundant Wild Mammals. (P. A. Jewell and S. Holt, eds.) Academic Press, New York.

Sinclair, A. R. E. 1989. Population regulation in animals. Pages 197–241 *in* Ecological Concepts. (J. M. Cherrett, ed.) Blackwell Scientific, Oxford, United Kingdom.

Sinclair, A. R. E. 1995. Serengeti past and present. Pages 3–30 *in* Serengeti II: Dynamics, Management and Conservation of an Ecosystem. (A. R. E. Sinclair and P. Arcese, eds.) University of Chicago Press, Chicago.

Singer, F. J., and J. E. Norland. 1994. Niche relationships within a guild of ungulate species in Yellowstone National Park, Wyoming, following release from artificial controls. Canadian Journal of Zoology 72:1383–1394.

Taylor, R. J. 1984. Predation. Chapman and Hall, New York.

Walters, C. J. 1986. Adaptive Management of Renewable Resources. Macmillan Publishing Co., New York.

Walters, C. J., and C. S. Holling. 1990. Large-scale management experiments and learning by doing. Ecology 71:2060–2068.

Wemmer, C., ed. 1987. Biology and Management of Cervidae. Smithsonian Institution Press, Washington.

Willis, K. J. 1994. How old is ancient woodland? Trends in Ecology and Evolution 8:427–428.

Index

Page-number citations followed by t refer to tables, and those followed by *f* refer to figures.